D1558330

FILE DESIGN AND PROGRAMMING

FILE DESIGN AND PROGRAMMING

W. Wesley Peterson and Art Lew
University of Hawaii at Manoa

John Wiley & Sons, New York • Chichester • Brisbane • Toronto • Singapore

Library of Congress Cataloging-in-Publication Data

Peterson, W. Wesley (William Wesley), 1924–
  File design and programming.

  Bibliography: p.
  Includes index.
  1. File organization (Computer science)
2. Electronic digital computers—Programming.
I. Lew, Art. II. Title.

QA76.9.F5P47 1986   005.74   85-22666
ISBN 0-471-82311-2

Printed in the United States of America

10 9 8 7 6 5 4 3 2 1

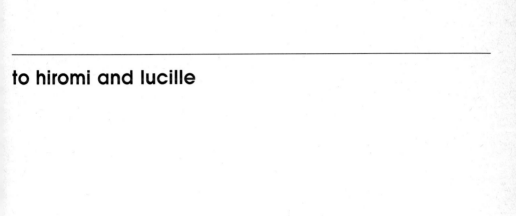

to hiromi and lucille

Preface

Files are second in importance in computer science to algorithms and techniques for their implementation as programs. In all systems that handle large amounts of information, files play an essential role. A computer without a file system is hardly more important than a large calculator. Thus, it is essential for computer scientists and systems analysts and designers to have a good fundamental understanding of files. In this book we provide this basic information on files, including methods for their analysis and design, and algorithms and programming language facilities for their processing.

At the University of Hawaii, we have offered a required one-semester course on files for the past eight years. This book is based on course notes that evolved over these years. The course is roughly equivalent to the course CS 5 *Information to File Processing* in the ACM Curriculum 78, and the book is most suitable for that course. At the University of Hawaii, we cover the entire book, except for Appendices F and G and some of the finer details, in one semester. Our students have at least sequential I-O programming experience with Pascal, COBOL, and FORTRAN, but very limited knowledge of data structure analysis and design when they take the course. Students with a good introduction to data structures but no experience with PL/I, COBOL, or FORTRAN should be about as well off. We find that a writing knowledge of one language provides a sufficient reading knowledge of others, especially when the programs perform the same tasks, to warrant the presentation of file algorithms in several different languages. This kind of presentation also makes this book accessible to those having a variety of backgrounds. Those interested in only a single language will find that the additional information reinforces and clarifies the most important concepts, especially the relationships between languages and operating systems.

We have restricted ourselves to programming languages that are defined by national standards and that include random-access file handling techniques. These languages are representative of most others, and there seems to be no need to include material that is dependent on a particular language implementation. Ada, C, and Pascal are clearly very important languages, but they do not have file I-O capabilities included in standardized definitions that are comprehensive enough to justify including them. In Pascal, for example, file I-O is not specified by programming language statements but, instead, by calls to implementation-dependent procedures.

In this book, we usually describe the *logic* of algorithms in Pascal form, but use COBOL, PL/I, and FORTRAN (in Chapter 8 and the Appendices) to provide actual programming examples that can be used by the reader with little if any modification in whatever computer system is available. We believe it is essential that the reader try running one or more of these actual programs and experiment by perturbing them in various ways. It also would be instructive for readers to translate these programs to nonstandard implementations and various other languages. Where this book is used as a textbook, these would make good programming assignments.

We also place considerable emphasis in this book on calculating timing and space requirements for files. These are not necessary for writing file processing programs, and for many applications the time and space requirements are obviously small and need not be calculated before a system is developed. This is certainly true of students' programming exercises. However, it is clearly important for a computer scientist or systems analyst to be able to predict the performance of a large system and to do a good deal of analysis and design before any appreciable investment is made in producing it. Therefore, a large portion of this book consists of quantitative examples illustrating the kinds of calculations that can be made with a minimum amount of mathematics. (No calculus is needed.)

Part 1 of this book is devoted to file analysis and design techniques. Part 2 and much of the Appendices are devoted to file processing algorithms and programming language facilities to implement these algorithms. The two parts of the book are fairly independent and can be covered in either order with a minimum amount of cross-referencing. This might be appropriate for two single-quarter courses, or for independent study. However, to teach both parts in a one-semester course requires covering the material concurrently so that students can start working on simple programming exercises while studying the analysis and design concepts, and then gradually increase the complexities of their programs while learning more and more of the principles.

We gratefully acknowledge the support of the Department of Information and Computer Sciences at the University of Hawaii, without which this book would not have been possible. Our production of the first draft of this book was supported in part by the National Bureau of Standards. The nice unified treatment of file maintenance in Chapter 7 is based on an unpublished report by Diana Foley. Anne Niethammer contributed a number of suggestions. We received a good deal of support from our secretary Ethel Shintaku and her student helpers. Finally, we have both learned a great deal from our students. We owe sincere thanks to all of these people.

W. Wesley Peterson
Art Lew

Contents

File Analysis and Design

1

Introduction

1.1. FILES IN COMPUTER SYSTEMS

A typical computer is made up of a processor, a main memory, input and output devices, and a file system. File systems play such an important role in computer systems that it is essential for computer scientists to understand them thoroughly.

The processor does the actual calculation using data and instructions stored in the main memory. The input and output devices allow communication with the rest of the world—they include the terminal keyboard, display, and printers. The file system stores information just as the memory does. Technically, they are distinguished by the fact that the processor uses information in the memory directly, but information in the file system must be brought into the memory before it can be processed. Practically, there are two other differences in typical systems, although systems exist that do not conform.

(a) The file system almost always has a much larger capacity than the memory. Almost invariably, very fast and therefore fairly expensive devices are used for the main memory, while cheaper, somewhat slower devices are used for the file system. For example, integrated-circuit memory devices usually are used for main storage. When this book was written, the cost of such storage was roughly $\frac{1}{10}$ to $\frac{1}{3}$ cent per byte, and the access time was in the neighborhood of $\frac{1}{10}$ microsecond. "Winchester" type disk storage units commonly are used for file storage. When this book was written, their cost was on the order of $\frac{1}{200}$ cent per byte, and the access time was in the neighborhood of $\frac{1}{20}$ sec. (By the time you read this, both will probably be faster and cheaper, but the comparison will be similar.)

(b) The main memory is usually "volatile," that is, when the computer is turned off, the information in the main memory is lost. (Many computers have at least a small amount of "read-only memory" or ROM, which is not volatile, as a part of their main memory.) On the other hand, in general the file system is not volatile—when the computer is turned off and then on, the information in the file system is unaffected. Thus, the main memory is used typically as a kind of scratchpad, while "permanent" storage of programs and data is the principal function of the file system. It is also common for files to be created on one computer system and used on another. Furthermore, file systems are commonly used to store information temporarily, as when a program must process more information than can be stored in the memory. A few computer systems have a part of their file system made up of very fast volatile memory, used for temporary files that need not be saved when the computer is turned off.

Computers exist that do not have file systems. Examples are special-purpose computers that control appliances such as microwave ovens, video-tape recorders, and automobile ignition systems. Computers designed especially for video games also do not have file systems. Instead, their programs and fixed data are stored in read-only memory. The common video-game computers that play different games accomplish this by having some read-only memory in replaceable cartridges. Such computers do not have nearly the versatility of computers with file systems.

It is the file system that makes the general-purpose computer possible. The file system can store a variety of programs, and the user can add programs freely. It also stores data. It is the file system that makes it possible for a single computer to do an unlimited number of different tasks using different programs and data.

Clearly, computer scientists, programmers, and systems analysts must understand files. They must know how to use files and how to write programs that use them. They also must know how to analyze and design systems that use files. This is an essential aspect of *systems analysis and design*, the primary job of the systems analyst. But all programmers do some systems analysis; some do a great deal. All computer scientists do systems analysis as well.

Suppose, for example, that a nationwide chain car-rental agency is considering an on-line reservation system. The capacity and desired response time would be specified. Before the company spends millions of dollars on hardware and software, it will want to know how much they will cost—in particular, how much and what kind of hardware will be needed. The systems analyst must choose a suitable file structure—perhaps after evaluating several alternatives in detail—and then determine the required capacity. The analyst also must be able to predict timing and thus assure that the response-time specifications will be met. Analysts must be able to do this analysis and design without buying a lot of hardware and doing a lot of programming and experimenting, because their report must be done quickly and at reasonable cost.

Computer scientists are faced with essentially the same problems—every computer scientist must expect to do some systems analysis and design. For example, if a computer scientist has a revolutionary idea for a new database system or a new type of knowledge base for an expert system, then he or she almost certainly will have to do some file design and must analyze the resulting system. Timing and hardware requirements and, hence, costs must be determined before an investment of a large amount of time in software development and a large sum of money in equipment is made.

This book explains the basic concepts of systems analysis and design of file systems, including file structures, the most common file algorithms, calculation of file capacity and timing, and an introduction to file programming. In the remainder of this chapter, we present file storage devices and their place in computer systems, the nature of files, and finally an overview of this book.

1.2. INFORMATION STORAGE DEVICES IN THE COMPUTER SYSTEM

Devices for storage of information are available in a wide range of speeds and costs. In general, the faster the access time, the higher the cost per bit, the greater the size and weight per bit, and the larger the amount of energy required per bit. Nearly all computers have a combination of two or more storage devices of different speeds in order to achieve economically both fast processing and large storage capacity. In fact, one might take the view that the subject of file processing deals with techniques for making the best use of a computer system that has several types of storage devices of different speeds.

Physically, modern computers usually have all these devices communicate through a *data bus*, as shown in Figure 1.1(a). Thus, ways exist to communicate between the processor and any storage device, or directly between two storage devices. (In practice, circuit boards plug into *edge connectors* on which the corresponding positions are all connected together. When all the circuit boards are inserted into the system, the communication paths are established.) In practical systems, however, not all possible communication paths are actually used. There are two main types of less general arrangements:

Type I. The processor may access both devices directly, as shown in Figure 1.1(b).

Type II. The processor may access only the faster storage—data from the slower storage must be moved to the faster storage before it can be used by the processor, as shown in Figure 1.1(c).

The Type I arrangement is used, especially in very small computers, because it requires simpler hardware and therefore is cheaper. The Type

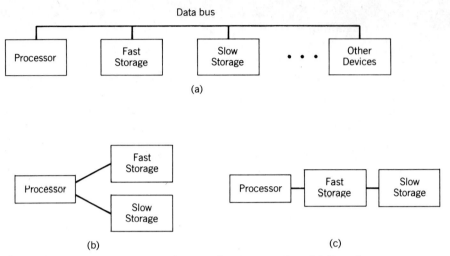

Figure 1.1 Common Computer-Storage Interconnection. (*a*) Data bus;
(*b*) Type I; (*c*) Type II.

II arrangement, which uses an I-O processor to communicate between
the two storage devices, is more common because it is faster and easier
to use. There may be more than two kinds of storage and almost any
combination of interfaces. It is even common to have the slow devices
connected to a medium-speed device that, in turn, connects to the fast
storage. The Type II arrangement also models the situation where external I-O devices are connected directly to memory rather than the main
processor. More detailed discussion of the interface between a processor
and storage devices is given in Chapter 4, Appendix G, and books on
computer architecture.

There are two techniques, cache memory and virtual storage, that under proper conditions accomplish efficient use of both fast and slow storage devices in a manner transparent to the user. These techniques use
the configuration shown in Figure 1.1(c). Although they are not thought
of as file systems, they are related. Further information and some references to more detailed accounts are included in Appendix F.

1.3. BASIC FILE CONCEPTS

The word "file" originally meant a thread. Later, wires or strings were
used to hold papers, and the word file was used to mean such a device.
The Oxford Dictionary (James A. H. Murray, Ed., *A New English Dictionary, Vol. 4, F and G*, Oxford at the Clarendon Press, 1901) gives the
following relevant definitions for the word file:

3. A string or wire, on which papers and documents are strung for preservation and reference. In recent use extended to various other appliances for holding papers so that they can be easily referred to.

4. A collection of papers placed on a file or merely arranged in order of date or subject for ready reference.

Modern dictionaries give remarkably similar definitions, in spite of the passage of over 80 years. Definition 3 dates back to about the year 1525, and definition 4 dates back to about 1626.

For these definitions to apply to modern information systems, they must be generalized; at least "papers" should be replaced by "data" or "information," which no longer need be stored on paper and, in fact, usually is not. Paraphrasing the above definitions, we may define a file as something that stores information for preservation or reference, or alternatively as a collection of information placed in a file for ready reference. Both definitions are used, although the first is the more common meaning in computer science. Thus, we speak of creating a file and writing some information into it, which implies that the file is the object that contains the information. We also speak of sorting a file, which means sorting the information in the file.

A typical manual file system consists of a file cabinet. Files consist of folders with labels. We create a file by labeling a folder and inserting it in the file cabinet in a place convenient for reference. The file may be listed in a *catalog* or *directory* to facilitate locating it. We can insert, remove, or revise papers in it. We also can delete a file, which frees space that can be used for other files. In computer file systems, the disk and tape systems play the role of the file cabinet. A file usually is created by setting aside some space for it and listing it in the catalog or directory. It is common to maintain an overall *system* catalog to facilitate locating the correct disk unit and for each disk unit to contain a catalog of the files it contains.

Because the process of reading information from a terminal or sending information to a device such as a video terminal or printer is very similar to the process of reading information from a file or writing information to a file, data sent to a printer, a card punch, or a terminal and data read from a deck of cards or a terminal are sometimes considered files—we will call these *communication files*. This book deals primarily with *storage files*.

Just as manual files consist of pieces of paper, files in computer systems also are made up of pieces called *records*. There are two reasons for this:

1. For reasons related to the hardware, there is a convenient amount or range of amounts of information that can be read at one time, just as there is a convenient size or range of sizes of pieces of paper.

2. There is often a natural division of the information in the file. For example, in the student records file at a university, a natural unit is all the information relating to one student.

Both of these units are often referred to as records, which causes confusion. To distinguish the two, the first is often called a *physical record* and the second a *logical record*. Another choice is to call the first a *block* and the second a *record*. Because this latter choice seems to be less confusing, we generally follow this style in this book. In a manual file, a piece of paper is a physical record or block, and a logical record might consist of less than a full sheet of paper, a full sheet, or a number of sheets of paper (perhaps stapled together). Similarly, we will find in computer files that there may be one logical record in a block—a particularly simple arrangement—or several logical records in a block, or a single logical record may require more than one block.

The I-O processor also has its analogy in the manual file system. Suppose that a person—let us refer to him as a secretary—is processing records in a manual file system. The secretary finds that he is spending a significant part of his time on the processing itself, and also a significant part of his time on fetching records from the file system and replacing them. He may be able to do the job faster if he has an assistant—a file clerk—who fetches records and replaces them in the file while the secretary is processing records. The secretary is analogous to the main processor in a computer and the file clerk is analogous to the I-O processor.

In order to save much time, the secretary must be able to tell the file clerk which record(s) he will want after processing the current record(s). Then the file clerk can replace any finished records in the file and fetch the next ones while the secretary is working on the current record(s). This is quite straightforward in the case where all records are processed sequentially—while the secretary is processing record n, the file clerk replaces the just-finished record, record n-1, in the file and fetches record $n + 1$. Using the I-O processor in this manner is known in computer science as *buffering*.

1.4. OVERVIEW OF THIS BOOK

Chapter 2 presents the use of magnetic tape. Data are ordinarily stored on tape in blocks with some spacing between blocks. The capacity and the timing of the devices depend on the sizes of the blocks used. The concept of blocking is introduced, and calculations of capacity and timing are treated in some detail. This chapter serves two purposes. First, magnetic tape is important as a storage medium, because it is fast and the most economical machine-readable medium. It is even competitive with paper; it is a little more expensive initially, but it is reusable and more economical to store. We expect tape to be used for some time, at least for "back-up" copies of files and for permanent storage of large quantities of data.

Another reason for studying magnetic tape is that it is conceptually simpler than magnetic disk storage and serves as a stepping-stone toward the more complicated disk unit space and timing calculations. In particular, the concept of blocking is much easier to understand and appreciate in tape systems, although it is also extremely important with disk systems. The same is true of buffering, which we will study in Chapter 4.

Chapter 3 includes timing and capacity calculations for magnetic disk units. Most disk units have a moveable read-write head, and the total time required for an input or output operation is a combination of the times to move the head, the wait for the desired data to rotate to the head, and the actual read or write time. Detailed discussion of timing calculations is included both for sequentially accessed and randomly accessed file systems with and without blocking. Magnetic disks are the most important auxiliary storage devices, an essential part of all but the very smallest and simplest computer systems.

Chapter 4 is concerned with I-O processors, and especially with the effect that the interaction of the main processor with I-O devices has on the overall time required to do a task. The concept of buffering is introduced and its use both with magnetic tapes and the more complicated magnetic-disk file systems is explained.

Chapter 5 gives a brief review of data-structure concepts as they relate to files. Various physical arrangements of data appropriate for common logical data structures are discussed. The use of pointers in files is explained. A description of the file structures used in the main types of database systems is included.

Chapter 6 is concerned primarily with the two most common and practical types of random-access files—indexed and hashed files. The chapter includes examples of detailed timing calculations for these types of files. Also included are discussions of file record structures, data compression, and file system allocation.

There are a few tasks that occur so commonly with files that they account for a large fraction of computer usage. These are discussed in Chapter 7. The first is sorting—we give a survey of file sorting and reference comprehensive books on the subject. The other problem is file maintenance, which encompasses the bulk of computer data processing. File maintenance tasks include data editing, file updating, and report writing. We discuss good algorithms for these tasks.

Chapter 8, the final chapter, discusses file programming, starting with a general discussion of the language features that are generally provided and ending with a brief description of the features in the most commonly used languages. The individual statements are explained, and their use is illustrated in examples that show the details of file handling necessary to complete the programs discussed in Chapter 7.

Appendices include complete program listings of the program examples discussed in Chapters 7 and 8, a brief discussion of "job control language" or "command language" concepts, a brief discussion of data coding in computers, an introduction to cache memory and virtual storage concepts, and some details of the implementation of a typical I-O processor.

NOTES

Introductions to files appear in numerous general books on computer software systems, such as [A1]–[A3]. Books dealing specifically with files include [A4]–[A7]. The file management facilities of operating systems are described in greater detail in [J3], [J5], and [J7]. Files are of special concern in data processing and information retrieval; for example, see [A8]–[A13]. Descriptions of memory devices appear in [B1]–[B7] and [K6]. In this book, we deal mainly with tapes and disks.

EXERCISES

1-1. (a) Compare the access times for semiconductor memory, magnetic tapes, and disks.

(b) Why has the fastest device not made the slowest obsolete?

1-2. What term is used to characterize a storage device on which information is lost when its power is turned off? Name a storage device that has this property and another that does not.

1-3. Draw a figure like Figure 1.1 for any actual computer system showing how storage devices and communication devices are interfaced.

1-4. Extend the "manual file system" example to model an actual office more realistically.

Magnetic Tape

2.1. INTRODUCTION

Most computer tape systems use ½ in. wide plastic tape coated with an iron compound that can be magnetized. Basically, the tape is the same as that used for audio-tape recorders, but it is stronger and has a better quality coating especially free of small defects. Data are recorded as varying magnetized patterns in *tracks* along the tape, very much as in audio-tape recorders. The ½ in. computer tape usually uses nine tracks, although some of the older seven-track systems are still in use. All tracks are recorded or read simultaneously. During recording, one binary digit, 1 or 0, is recorded on each track simultaneously. The set of binary digits recorded together is called a *character* or *byte*. The data are recorded in *blocks* of characters with interblock gaps between blocks. Tape drives cannot stop and start in the middle of a block where data are densely recorded. Gaps are provided so that the drive can stop and restart after reading or writing a convenient-sized block of data. The data format on a tape looks something like Figure 2.1.

Data block

Figure 2.1 Data Arrangement on Tape.

One track is normally used for checking. The binary digit in that track is a check digit chosen to make the number of ones in the recorded character odd or, in some cases, even. When the tape is read, a check is made whether the number of ones in each character is odd or even. If there is an error in one track, this "parity" check will detect that fact. In tapes, errors result most frequently from a small defect in the magnetic coating or a piece of dust or dirt on the tape. Such a defect or piece of dust is likely to affect successive characters within a track because the data are densely recorded within the track (usually hundreds or thousands of characters per inch), but it is unlikely to affect more than one track because the tracks are well separated (one character per ½ in.). Because it is unlikely that at any one point there will be more than one track in error, the parity method provides good error protection. In addition, generally one or more check characters are recorded at the end of a block or even within the block to provide further protection against errors, and in some cases, the ability to correct occasional errors.

Since one track is devoted to checking, each character or byte on a nine-track system contains eight binary digits of information. On a seven-track system, each character contains six binary digits.

2.2. TAPE CAPACITY

Table 2.1 shows the characteristics of important standard tapes. Most of these were originally standards for IBM tape units. For competitive reasons, other companies have found it advantageous to be able to read IBM tapes on their computers; thus, these standards have become widely adopted. The American National Standards Institute (ANSI) has adopted

Table 2.1   Specifications for Some Common Formats for ½ in. Computer Tape

Number of Tracks	Characters per Inch	Gap Width, Nominal (min–max)	Block Size (Characters or Bytes)	Remarks
7	200	0.75 in.	—	Widely-used, IBM-compatible
7	556	0.75 in.	—	Widely-used, IBM-compatible
9	200	0.6 in. (0.5 in.–25 ft.)	18–2048	ANSI Standard [C1]
9	800	0.6 in. (0.5 in.–25 ft.)	18–2048	ANSI Standard [C2]
9	1600	0.6 in. (0.5 in.–25 ft.)	18–2048	ANSI Standard [C3]
9	6250	0.3 in. (0.28 in–15 ft.)	18–2048	ANSI Standard [C4]

standards for nine-track tapes with recording densities of 800, 1600, and 6250 characters per inch (*cpi*). They also adopted a standard for the rather uncommon 200 cpi nine-track tape. A list of other standards appears in [C6]. Standard tapes provide a very convenient and reliable way of passing information from one computer to another, even though the computers may be very different.

Tape is available in standard reels containing 2400, 1200, 600, 400, or 300 ft. The price depends on the manufacturer and the quantity. When this book was written, a 2400 ft. reel of tape cost about $14, and a 600 ft. reel cost about $8. A 600 ft. reel of tape is shown in Figure 2.2.

Example 2.1

Assume that we want to copy all the information from a certain disk pack for back-up. Assume that the disk pack has 4000 tracks with 6000 eight-bit characters (or bytes) on each track. If we copy it onto a nine-track 800 cpi tape and if we record each disk track as a separate tape block, then each block consists of $6000/800 = 7.5$ in. of recorded data plus a 0.6 in. gap (Table 2.1) for a total of 8.1 in. Because there are 4000 tracks on the disk, there will be 4000 blocks on the tape and a total of $4000 \times 8.1 = 32{,}400$ in., or 2700 ft., which requires one 2400 ft. reel plus an additional 300 ft.

Let us consider the same problem and assume a density of 6250 cpi. A block consists of $6000/6250 = 0.96$ in. plus a gap of 0.3 in. for a total of 1.26 in. Then 4000 blocks require 4000×1.26 in. $= 5040$ in. $= 420$ ft., which will fit comfortably on a single 600 ft. reel.

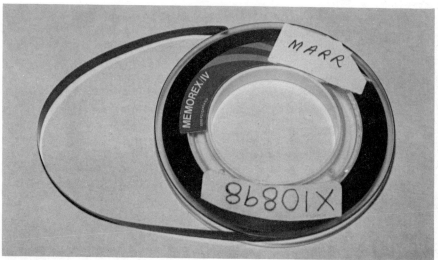

Figure 2.2 A 600 Ft. Reel of Tape.

Many hardware systems allow longer block sizes than are given in Table 2.1. The ANSI limits should probably be adhered to for information interchange between different kinds of systems.

2.3. BLOCKING

Files generally are divided into parts called records; processing at any one time may involve single or several records. For example, the personnel file of a corporation might have one record for each employee, containing all information pertaining to that employee. The number of characters in a record varies greatly with the application. For example, an inventory file might have records consisting of a part number and a quantity—perhaps as little as 10 characters—although other information such as name, price, and reorder quantity also may be included. At the other extreme, a university student's record might include a name, local address and phone, home address and phone, a list of all courses taken and grades, as well as miscellaneous other information. This might total well over 1000 characters. A library catalog file record might include a book name, authors, publisher, date, and a 250-word abstract for a total of about 2000 characters. Telephone directory entries could probably be handled in 80-character records. The simplest tape format would be to use one block on the tape for one record. The next example will show that this may not be the best choice.

Example 2.2

Assume a file of 100,000 80-character records is to be placed on 1600 cpi nine-track tape. Assume one record becomes one block. Then each block consists of $80/1600 = 0.05$ in. of recorded data plus a gap of 0.6 in., or a total of 0.65 in.. Altogether we need $0.65 \times 100,000 = 65,000$ in. or 5417 ft., which requires about $2\frac{1}{4}$ 2400 ft. reels of tape.

If we examine this last calculation, we note that for each record there is 0.05 in. of data followed by a 0.6 in. gap. Thus, the tape is more than 92% gap and less than 8% data! It is possible to increase "efficiency" by using a larger percentage of the tape for data.

$$\frac{\text{(tape used for data)}}{\text{(tape used for gaps)}} = \frac{\text{(data block size)}}{\text{(gap size)}}$$

Therefore, we must use a larger block size.

Example 2.2 (continued)

Suppose we want the tape to contain 90% data and 10% gaps. Then the block size must be nine times the gap size. Again, assuming 1600 cpi nine-track tape, the gap size is 0.6 in., so the block would have to be 9 × 0.6 = 5.4 in. long. Such a block would contain 8640 characters. That happens to be 80 × 108. If we put data from 108 records in each block, the blocks will be the required length. The file then requires 100,000/108 = 926 blocks. (The last one is not quite a full block.) Because the 5.4 in. block and the 0.6 in. gap together make 6 in., this requires 926 × 6 = 5556 in. or 463 ft. of tape, or one 600 ft. reel, compared to the previous 2¼ 2400 ft. reels, a considerable improvement. As we will see, much time can be saved too.

This technique of combining several records into a block is called *blocking*. If there is only one record per block, the file is said to be *unblocked*. The number of records per block is called the *blocking factor*.

Blocking is done by computer programs, not hardware. The read procedure must read a block into a memory area set aside for that purpose. Then each time the application program requests a record, the read procedure must pass a record to that program, reading a new block each time a block is used completely. Similarly, when the application program requests that a record be written, the write procedure must place it in a block-sized memory area set aside for assembling blocks and, whenever a complete block is ready, write it onto the I-O unit. Read and write procedures that do blocking are usually provided with the operating system, and the application programmer generally needs at most to specify parameters such as the desired record and block sizes.

There is a cost to using a large block size and the systems analyst or programmer must decide the compromise between any savings and the cost. A tape unit cannot stop in the middle of a block. When it starts to read a block, it must read the whole block. This means that the computer must be prepared to accept a whole block, so an area of memory equal in size to a block must be set aside as a read area. Conversely, on writing, because the block must be written without stopping, it is necessary to place a whole block of data in a write area before starting to write. For very large blocks, very large memory areas are required for reading and writing.

Let us define efficiency e to be the percentage of the tape actually storing data. Thus,

$$e = \frac{\text{block length}}{\text{block length} + \text{gap length}}$$

$$e = \frac{\dfrac{n}{d}}{\left(\dfrac{n}{d}\right) + g} \qquad (2.1)$$

where n is the number of characters per block, d the recording density in characters per inch, and g the gap length in inches. Solving Equation (2.1) for n we find the minimum block length required to achieve efficiency at least e is

$$n - \frac{edg}{(1 - e)} \qquad (2.2)$$

From these formulas we find that when the block size is small, increasing the block size a small amount increases the efficiency greatly, but the larger the block size the smaller the relative gain. For the 800 cpi nine-track tape, for example, block size 54 gives 10% efficiency and 480 gives 50% efficiency. To get 90% efficiency requires a block of 4320 characters, 95% requires 9120, and 99% requires 47,520. That last 4% requires a lot of additional memory! It should also be noted that ANSI standards specify both a maximum and minimum block size.

The most economical compromise between block size and efficiency of tape use depends on (1) the amount of data, (2) the amount of memory available, and (3) its cost. We will see that the larger block also saves time. If the amount of data is large, the savings in time and tape may be very significant. On the other hand, if the amount of data is small, the time for reading and the cost of the tape also will be small.

It is interesting to compare the costs of tape and punched cards. The cost of tape per character of data depends on the density and the block size. Let us consider one example, using figures from the previous example.

Example 2.3

Assume records of 80 characters (equal to a card) and 108 records per block. Assume 1600 cpi nine-track tape. Then one block is $80 \times 108 = 8640$ characters and $8640/1600 = 5.4$ in.. With the 0.6 in. gap, a total of 6 in. is required per block. Thus, a 2400 ft. reel of tape can hold 4800 blocks for a total of 518,400 records. Cards are packaged in boxes of 2000, five boxes to the carton. One tape stores as much information as 52 cartons of cards. At current prices of roughly $2.50/1000 cards, the cards would cost $1300 compared to $14 for the tape. A 6250 cpi tape with fairly large blocks would be significantly more economical. Even the lowest density with one 80-character record per block will give significant savings in cost and space compared to cards.

2.4. TAPE TIMING

The machine used to read tape is called a *tape drive*. A typical tape drive is shown in Figure 2.3. The most important characteristics of a tape drive are the tape speed and the start time. Time required for rewinding a reel of tape also may be important. Commonly, tape speeds range from 37.5 to 200 inches per second (*ips*). Some units rewind at the same speed, while others have high-speed rewind capability.

To calculate running times for programs using tape, one must know the time required from the instant a read or write command is given until the required block has been read (or written) completely. (We are not concerned with the time it takes the tape to stop after it finishes actual reading, because the computer can proceed without waiting for the tape to stop.) This time consists of two parts—the interval between the command and the start of the reading, and the actual read time for the block. Given the tape speed, we can calculate the actual time to read a block of data. In the previous example, we had blocks of 5.4 in. of data. If the tape speed is 200 ips, the time to read a block is 5.4/200 = 0.027 sec.

With respect to the interval between the read command and the start of actual reading, there are two extreme cases: the command may be given while the tape is stopped in the gap or it may be given immediately after a previous command is completed while the tape is still moving at full speed. Let us call the time required if the command is given imme-

Figure 2.3 An IBM 3350 Tape Drive.

diately after a previous command T_g and the time to start from a dead stop T_s. If a read command is given immediately after the completion of a previous command, the tape will continue at full speed across the gap. Thus, T_g is the time it takes to cross the gap at full speed. For example, a tape with density 1600 cpi has a 0.6 in. gap. At a speed of 200 ips, crossing the gap will require $0.6/200 = 0.003$ sec. Timing is the same for writing.

The start-up time T_s it takes from a command given when the tape is stopped until actual reading or writing of data begins is usually specified by the manufacturer. T_s typically differs from T_g by no more than about 50%. For example, the IBM 3420 Model 7 is a 200 ips drive. The specified T_s is 0.002 sec. The Burroughs B9495 Model 5 has the same specifications. For these machines, T_g is equal to 0.003 sec, assuming 1600 cpi density, or 0.0015 sec, assuming 6250 cpi density. Note that if the drive stops in the center of the gap and it accelerates in such a way that its average velocity while crossing the half of the gap that lies ahead is one-half of its full velocity, then T_s would exactly equal T_g. One would expect that the drive would stop with the head near the center and that the average velocity as the tape accelerates cannot differ greatly from half the full velocity; therefore, it is not surprising that T_s does not differ greatly from T_g.

In the intermediate cases, the situation is not quite so clear. On some machines, if the command is given after the tape drive has started to stop the tape, acceleration will start immediately. In such a case the time between the command and the actual reading or writing would be between T_s and T_g. On other drives, once the process of stopping has been initiated, it must be completed. Stopping takes about the same amount of time as starting. In this case the maximum time would be about twice T_s if the command is given just after the stop process was initiated. For a command given later than this, the time would consist of the remaining time to come to a dead stop plus T_s and thus would be between T_s and $2 \times T_s$.

Note that if the gaps are shorter than the blocks, as required to use the tape efficiently, then the time to read the gaps will be shorter than the time to read the blocks. If one always assumes that the access time (from the read or write command to the beginning of data transfer) is equal to T_g, the time to move across the gap at full speed, although the error in access time might be as great as 50%, the error in total time will be much less.

Example 2.4

In the preceding example, the data block was 5.4 in., the gap 0.6 in. If we assume a speed of 200 ips, then if the read or write command is

given immediately after the end of the previous block, the time is
0.6/200 = 0.003 sec for the gap, 5.4/200 = 0.027 sec for the data
block, or a total of 6/200 = 0.030 sec. If we assume starting from a dead
stop on an IBM 3420, the start time is 0.002 sec, the read or write time
is the same as before (0.027 sec), and the total is 0.029 sec, about 3
percent shorter. If the tape on an IBM 3420 has started to decelerate
when the command is given, it immediately starts to accelerate again
so that the times for commands given while the tape is decelerating
will be between 0.029 and 0.030 sec.

Thus, if read or write commands do actually come almost immediately
after the end of the previous block, then the total of all the times from
giving a command until its completion for reads or writes for a whole
program is simply equal to the time it would take to read the tape used
moving at full speed. To this we may have to add the total of any processing delay, that is, the time between the end of a read or write operation
and the next read or write command.

Since blocking reduces the total amount of tape needed, it also will
reduce the total tape read or write time. Let us reconsider the first example of blocking and examine timing.

Example 2.5

In Example 2.2, we assumed 100,000 80-character records recorded at
1600 cpi on a nine-track tape. Unblocked, they required 65,000 in. of
tape (2¼ 2400 ft. reels). At 75 ips, reading or writing requires 65,000/75
= 867 sec, or about 14.5 min. With 108 records per block, only 5556
in. of tape would be needed, and the read-write time becomes 5556/75
= 74.1 sec or 1.24 min, a substantial saving.

Further examples of timing with tapes and an explanation of buffering
are included in Chapter 4, where the interface between I-O units and
the processor is discussed.

2.5. OTHER TAPE CONCEPTS

Tape units all have a way to rewind tape. The speed may be anywhere
from the same as the forward speed to five or six times as fast. It commonly takes on the order of a minute to rewind a 2400 ft. tape.

Some tape units and computers have the capability of reading backwards. When a block is read backwards, it is placed in the main memory starting from the end so it appears normal in the memory. This can save rewind time in cases where a tape is written and then must be read. This feature usually is used to advantage in tape sorting. It generally is not available in higher-level languages.

Capability for backspacing one block at a time usually also is provided in hardware. One may backspace over the last block and reread or rewrite it. If you backspace and rewrite the last block, the rewritten block cannot be expected to be precisely in the same place as the original. Doing this a few times should cause no problem, but doing it many times will cause the last block to drift so that it may fall too close or too far from the previous block. It is safe to backspace two blocks, read one, and then write each time, because the last block always will be positioned relative to the next-to-last block, which would not drift. Because of this awkward problem, most high-level languages do not provide for backspacing.

The standard tape unit does not allow rewriting a record without rewriting all records that follow. The problems are (1) positioning, and (2) "noise" written on the tape at the point where the writing stops. This hardware limitation is commonly reflected in programming language restrictions.

It should be clear from the preceding discussion that data written on magnetic tape can be read conveniently and quickly if the records are read in the order they appear on the tape, which is the same order in which they were written, but to read the records in any other sequence is at best awkward and slow. Thus, random reading of tape data is almost never done, especially because random reading can be done efficiently on disks and other devices.

On standard tapes, small reflective spots of aluminum foil are fastened to the tape near the beginning and near the end. The spot at the beginning is used to locate the first record. The one at the end enables the machine to sense the end of the tape before the tape runs off the reel.

There is a special *end-of-file* mark written as a record on standard tapes. It is recognized by the hardware, which then gives an end-of-file signal to the computer. Conceptually, a file is a group of records where the grouping is done for the user's convenience. There may be few or many records in a file. There may be several files on one reel of tape, or one file may require several reels of tape. Normally, an end-of-file mark would be placed at the end of each file and an end-of-volume mark at the end of all data on each reel of tape.

It is very important to protect tape against accidental erasure and to assure that the computer operator mounts the correct tape for the job at hand. The *file-protect ring* is a hardware protection feature. There is a ring-shaped slot in the back of each tape reel into which a plastic ring may be inserted. The tape unit will not write on a tape unless a ring is

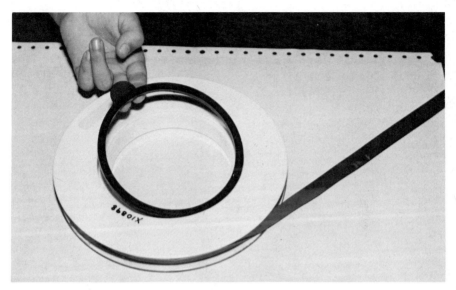

Figure 2.4 A Reel of Tape Showing the File Protect Ring.

placed in the slot. Any tape that provides input data can be protected by having the ring removed. This is shown in Figure 2.4.

Tape labels are a software protection feature. Tape labels are records normally written and processed by the operating system. One reel of tape is considered to be one volume. A labeled tape will have a label record identifying the volume at the beginning of the tape and another at the end of the tape. There will also be a label record at the beginning and end of each file that identifies the file. The programmer specifies the tape volume name and file name as parameters passed to the operating system. The system will terminate a job if the labels on the tape do not match those provided by the programmer. There is an ANSI Standard for tape labels[C5], but some manufacturers adopted their own label formats instead. Typically, a tape label has the information listed in Table 2.2.

Tapes are susceptible to errors. An error may occur because of a small defect in the magnetic coating, in which case the information is not on the tape and cannot be read. Another cause of error is dust or dirt deposited on the tape after writing, in which case the data can be read if the tape is cleaned. The use of high-quality certified tapes minimizes the first type of error, and the second type can be minimized by taking great care to keep the tapes clean. To help control the first type of error, many modern tape units are equipped with separate write and read heads, and blocks can be read and checked simultaneously with writing. If a block is not valid, then the tape is backspaced and rewritten. If this is not successful after several attempts, then several inches of tape are erased

Table 2.2 Main Fields of a Tape Header Label

---

1. Keyword identifying this as a header label. (Trailer labels are also used at the end of each file and tape, marking the end and containing count fields for checking purposes.)

2. File name. (This is the physical file name, as described in Section 8.3)

3. Reel number (to permit multi-reel files).

4. Date written.

5. Retention period.

6. Generation or version number (to permit updating of files while retaining earlier versions).

---

and an attempt is made in the new position. If the write is still unsuccessful after repositioning, the procedure is repeated, a number of times if necessary, before the computer gives up and informs the operator that the tape is defective. (Although the nominal interblock gap is 0.6 in. on a standard 1600 cpi tape, for example, the ANSI standards specify that the machine should accept any size between ½ in. and 25 ft.!)

If the data are unreadable on reading, the tape can be backspaced and the read retried several times. If the problem is due to dirt or dust, then retrying is likely to dislodge it. Some units are equipped with a brush or blade for cleaning the tape while reading. Tape error recovery procedures are normally implemented as a part of the operating system software.

There do exist nonstandard tape units. The concepts and principles are the same, but the details may differ greatly. Nonstandard tapes are most common on microcomputer systems where economy may be all-important. A number of manufacturers are making units that use standard audio cassettes, although they generally use higher quality tape. One "standard" records 187 bytes per sec, although units several times faster are available. Conventional audio-cassette tape recorders with tape speeds of 1⅞ ips are also commonly interfaced to microcomputer systems for data recording.

One example of a tape system with unique features is *formatted* tape. Formatted tapes are used on a number of small computers. One such system, originated by Digital Equipment Corporation and called Linc tape, uses ¾ in. tape on 3½ in. reels that hold 260 feet of tape, recorded at 350 cpi, with a gap of 0.36 in. between blocks. Its unique features are: (1) a permanently recorded "timing" track and a permanently recorded "mark" track that fixes the position of each block, and (2) identifying information for each block including a block number. Since each block is recorded in a predetermined place on the tape, it is possible to rewrite a block in the middle of the tape without rewriting the following blocks.

NOTES

The basic principles of recording digital information on magnetic surfaces are described in [E4]. The design of tape drives also is discussed in [E4]. ANSI standards for tapes are given in [C1–C4]. The standard for labels is given in [C5]. General discussions of tapes appear in [C6] and [C7]. The use of very large systems of tapes for "mass storage" is described in [C8]. A discussion of cassette tape timing is given in [C9].

EXERCISES

2-1. Suppose a surface imperfection makes a bit on a tape unreadable. Which is more likely also to be unreadable: another bit in the same byte, or another bit in an adjacent byte? Explain!

2-2. In Section 2.2, tape densities of 200 to 6250 characters or bytes per inch are mentioned. In other books, densities of 200 to 6250 bits per inch are mentioned. Explain this discrepancy. (Which is wrong, if either, and why?)

2-3. Note from Table 2.1 that gaps may be up to 25 ft. in length. Why would a gap this long be desirable?

2-4. What limitation on tape efficiency (i.e., ratio of data to data plus gap) is imposed by ANSI standards?

2-5. If a magnetic tape unit records at 320,000 bytes/sec, and has a tape speed of 200 ips, and a gap size of ½ in., how many inches of tape are required to record 2000 blocks of 320 bytes each?

2-6. (a) If 400-byte records with 10 records per block are stored on a nine-track 1600 cpi tape, what is the length required to store 10,000 records?

(b) How long would it take to completely read this file sequentially, assuming a tape speed of 75 ips and negligible processing?

2-7. There is a file of 500 records of 1500 characters each to be stored on tape. Assume standard 6250 cpi tape and a 200 ips drive with a start time of 2 msec. Assume a blocking factor of 5.

(a) How many feet of tape are required?

(b) How long will it take to read the file from beginning to end if the processing time is negligible?

2-8. Let us assume that the State of Hawaii wants to keep a record of 1000 characters on each of its roughly 1,000,000 residents. Assume 6250 cpi standard tape and a blocking factor of 10.

(a) How much tape is required?

(b) How long would it take to read through all these data, for example, to search for all persons whose records contain a certain piece of data? Assume a 200 ips tape drive and that processing and printing times are negligible.

2-9. Estimate how much tape would be required to store all of Webster's Unabridged Dictionary on magnetic tape and how long it would take to read through it sequentially from beginning to end. Assume 6250 cpi tape, 90% efficiency, and a 200 ips tape drive.

Rotating Storage

3.1. INTRODUCTION

A magnetic drum storage unit contains one or more cylinder-shaped drums. The outside cylindrical surface is coated with the same type of magnetic material that is used for magnetic tape, and information is recorded using similar techniques. A magnetic drum is shown schematically in Figure 3.1(a). The drum continuously rotates and a magnetic recording read-write head in a stationary position very close to the magnetic surface either records information on the surface or reads previously written information at the direction of a processor. The information is recorded in a circular band on the surface called a *track*. There may be several hundred tracks on one surface. There may be one permanently fixed head for each track or only a single head that can move from one track to another. It is cheaper to have one moveable head to read many tracks, but moving the head takes time. On a fixed-head system, switching from

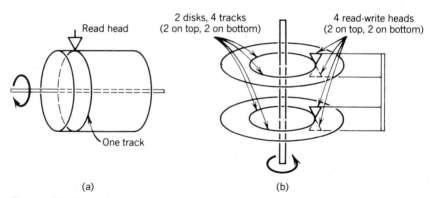

Figure 3.1 Schematics of Rotating Storage. (*a*) Magnetic drum; (*b*) Magnetic disk unit.

track to track is done electronically and requires a negligible amount of time.

A magnetic disk storage unit differs from a drum storage unit in that the magnetized surface used to store the information is the flat surface of a rotating disk. A schematic illustration of a magnetic disk unit is shown in Figure 3.1(b). A disk unit may have only one disk or a "pack" of, say, 10 or more disks. Both surfaces of a disk may be used if there is a head on each side. Figure 3.1(b) shows a pack of two disks with one head on each of the four surfaces. On some units, a disk pack may be removed, stored, and remounted, as is common with tapes. Then we must distinguish the storage medium (the disk) from the device in which it is placed (the drive).

Information is recorded in concentric rings, again called *tracks*, on each disk surface on which there are read-write heads. (The heads need not actually touch the surface.) There may be one read-write head per track or one or more heads that can move from one track to another between reads or writes. Figure 3.2 shows a bank of IBM 3350 disk drives, and Figure 3.3 shows a disk pack of the type used in the IBM 2316 drive.

In the past 10 years, *floppy disk* (or diskette) units have come into wide use, especially with small computers. The disk is flexible (unlike the earlier rigid ones), packaged in a protective plastic envelope, and is easily inserted and removed from the disk drive. The 8 in. disks were introduced

Figure 3.2 A Bank of IBM 3350 Disk Drives.

Figure 3.3 A Disk Pack for the IBM 2316.

first, then 5¼ in. disks, and quite recently 3½ in. disks. Disks cost about $3 and store from about 70,000 to 1,000,000 characters or bytes, depending on the size, recording density and whether or not both sides of the disk are used. Figure 3.4 shows an 8 in., a 5¼ in., and a 3½ in. floppy disk. Some floppy disk units (for smaller microcomputers) are designed so that when they are not actively in use they stop rotating. These systems are like tape units in that there can a significant start-up time. However, in most larger systems, the disks rotate continuously.

Recently, small *fixed-disk* (or *hard-disk*) drives have been developed. These units use basically the same rigid disk technology as the IBM 3350, but are much smaller. Currently, 5¼ in. diameter disks are most common, and a pack contains one or at most a few disks. Typical capacities are 5 to 150 million bytes, and the physical size is roughly the same as the floppy disk drives. Figure 3.5 shows an IBM PC XT microcomputer system that contains a 5¼ in. floppy disk drive and a 5¼ in. fixed-disk drive, side by side.

Laser disk units using the same technology as the new video and audio laser disks, have appeared on the market. These units resemble magnetic disk units both physically and logically. Data are recorded on disks in tracks, and there is typically a single read-write head per surface that moves mechanically to the desired track. Laser disks differ from magnetic disks in that they are either read-only or are write-once and after that read-only. They also have a larger capacity—currently a billion bytes on a single 12 in. disk surface.

Figure 3.4 An 8, 5¼, and 3½ in. Floppy Disk.

Figure 3.5 A Microcomputer with a Floppy Disk Drive and a Fixed-Disk Drive.

Charge-coupled-devices (CCD) and magnetic bubble memories (MBM) store data in a long shift register that acts very much like a magnetic drum or disk [B5]. Only one point, called the *window*, in the shift register is accessible at any one time, and the register must be rotated before the desired data can be accessed. In this respect, shift registers are similar to disks and drums. These devices differ from drums and disks in that they can be started and stopped at electronic speeds. The magnetic bubble memory, like drums and disks, is nonvolatile—the information remains in the device, even when power is removed from the system. The CCD memory is volatile; the signals gradually weaken even when power is applied, and they must be passed by the window of the shift register within a specified interval and refreshed, and thus essentially must rotate continuously. In practice, both CCD and MBM are rotated continuously and thus are logically equivalent to fixed-head disks or drums, one shift register corresponding to one track. (As technology develops, some advantage may be taken of the fact that the rotational speed can be changed almost instantaneously[B6].)

Some data on rotating storage units are listed in Table 3.1. Technology is changing so fast that these data must be considered only indicative of trends; current data must be obtained if one wants any realistic estimates.

Table 3.1 Characteristics of Typical Rotating Storage

Machine	Cylinders per Unit	Tracks per Cylinder	Bytes per Track	Rotational Speed (rpm)	Average Seek Time
IBM 2305-2 (head per track)	1	768	14,858	6000	0 msec
IBM 3330-1	404	19	13,165	3600	30 msec
IBM 3380	885	15	47,476	3600	16 msec
Burroughs B9484	406	20	10,800	2400	30 msec
HP 3933	1321	13	23,552	2700	24 msec
DEC RP07	630	32	25,600	3633	23 msec
HP 7925	823	9	16,384	2700	25 msec
Miniscribe 4020 (5.25 in. hard disk)	480	4	8,192	3600	120 msec
Maxtor XT1140 (5.25 in. hard disk)	918	15	8,192	3600	30 msec
Shugart SA850 (8 in. floppy disk)	77	2	6,656	360	91 msec
TEAC FD-55F (5.25 in. floppy disk)	80	2	4,096	300	94 msec

Note 1 The bytes per track figure is typical and varies with the exact format used—see Section 3.2 and Table 3.3.

Note 2 The "average seek time" given is the figure specified by the manufacturer. See Section 3.4 *et seq.* for more detail.

3.2. DISK CAPACITY

Data are recorded on a track in *sectors*. Most commonly the track number and sector number are recorded as a header on the track, and the disk unit identifies the sectors and chooses the correct sector to read by the information in the header rather than the physical location of the sector. (Disks recorded with this kind of format are sometimes referred to as *soft-sectored*, while those in which the locations of the sectors is fixed by the hardware are called *hard-sectored*.) Table 3.2 shows the complete format of a sector for a typical soft-sectored disk.

A sector is usually used as a block. In some units, the sector size and the number of sectors per track are fixed. In other units, the programmer may choose sector size and the number of sectors per track within limits. In the latter case, each block generally has overhead in addition to the data: a gap and/or special data such as block identification, status, format, and size. The exact format depends on the design of the unit and may not be simple. The manufacturer will provide either a formula or a table indicating capacities for various block sizes. Table 3.3 gives some data for fixed-format disks. The situation for variable-format drives is more complex, as we will see below.

For the IBM 2305, 3330, and 3380, there is considerable freedom in choosing the number of sectors or blocks per track. For the IBM 2305-2,

Table 3.2 Sector Format for a 8 in. Single-Density Floppy Disk

Number of Bytes	Hex Value of Byte Written
55	FF
6	00
1	FC (Index Mark)
26	FF

Repeat the following 26 times, once for each sector.

Number of Bytes	Hex Value of Byte Written
6	00
1	FE (ID Address Mark)
1	Track Number
1	00
1	Sector Number
1	00
2	Cyclic Redundancy Check Bytes
11	FF
6	00
1	FB (Data Address Mark)
128	Data
2	Cyclic Redundancy Check Bytes
27	FF

Then write FF until the index mark (the hole in the disk) is reached.

Table 3.3 Examples of Track Capacity Data for Fixed Format Devices

Device	Sectors per Track	Bytes per sector
Burroughs B9484-4	60	180
DEC RP07	50	512
	43	(256 18-bit words)
HP 3933	92	256
HP 7925	64	256
Miniscribe 4020	56	128
or Maxtor XT1140	32	256
	17	512
	9	1024
Shugart SA850 (8 in. floppy disk)		
Single Density	26	128
	15	256
	8	512
Double Density	26	256
	15	512
	8	1024
TEAC FD-55F (5.25 in. floppy disk)		
Double Density	16	256

the track capacity is 14,858 bytes, but that includes an overhead of 198 bytes per block if the data blocks do not have separately recorded keys, or 289 bytes per sector of overhead if the blocks do have separately recorded keys. Note that when blocks are recorded with separate keys, there is additional overhead (e.g., for a gap separating the key from the data). For the IBM 3330, the track capacity is 13,165, but this includes an overhead of 135 bytes per block if there are no separately recorded keys, or 191 bytes per block if there are separately recorded keys. The IBM 3380 is a little more complicated. All data are recorded in 32-byte increments and the track capacity is 1499 32-byte increments. Each block requires enough 32-byte increments for the data plus 492 bytes of overhead. If there are separately recorded keys, additional increments are needed to accommodate the key plus 236 additional bytes of overhead. The following examples illustrate how to use these data.

Example 3.1

On the IBM 3330, each block takes 135 bytes for overhead and the track capacity is 13,165. If we assume that each block has 1000 bytes of data and no keys, then each block requires 1135 bytes including overhead. We can record $13,165/1135 = 11$ blocks on one track. (Note that with fixed-size blocks, some space in each track may be wasted.) If there is only one block per track, it may be as large as $13,165 - 135$

= 13,030 bytes. If there are four equal blocks, there is space for 13,165/4 = 3291 bytes per block including overhead or 3291 − 135 = 3156 bytes of data in each block.

On the IBM 3380, if we assume no separate keys and that each block has 1000 bytes of data, then with the 492 bytes of overhead each block requires 1492/32 = 47 32-byte increments. (Note that this is rounded up to the next integer.) Since the track capacity is 1499 32-byte increments, on a single track we can put 1499/47 = 31 blocks, each containing 1000 bytes of data. If there is only one block per track (and no keys), then the maximum block size is 1499 × 32 − 492 = 47,476 bytes. If we record four blocks per track, then each block may have 1499/4 = 374 32-byte increments. Each block may contain 32 × 374 = 11,968 bytes including overhead or 11,968 − 492 = 11,476 bytes of data.

Blocking is advantageous when using rotating storage as well as tapes, as we illustrate in the following example.

Example 3.2

Suppose we have 80-byte records. It is natural to use one record per block. If we do using the 3330 disk unit, then each block is 80 + 135 = 215 bytes in size including overhead. A total of 13,165/215 = 61 records can be stored in each track.

In this case, each block has 80 bytes of data and 135 bytes of overhead—over 60% overhead. By blocking several data records into one block, we can reduce this ratio. If we put 10 records in each block, the block becomes 800 + 135 = 935 bytes long and we can put 13,165/935 = 14 blocks or 140 records in each track—more than double. Frequently, block sizes of 1, ½, ⅓, or ¼ of a track are used. IBM 3330 track capacities for various blocks sizes are compared in Table 3.4, assuming 80 bytes per record.

Table 3.4 Track Capacity for Various Block Sizes

Records per Block	Blocks per Track	Records per Track
1	61	61
10	14	140
39	4	156
53	3	159
80	2	160
162	1	162

As in the case of tapes, we will see that saving space generally implies saving time. The disadvantage of blocking is much the same as with tapes—it is not possible to read part of a block, and therefore one must provide a storage area to read into or to write from that is the size of the block. Blocks also may be used in a file where the records are accessed in random order. In this case, although less space is occupied by the file, a whole block must be read even though only one record is desired.

It is also common for the block size to be fixed, and in this case, the fixed-size recorded block is usually called a *sector*. Some typical data on fixed-format disks is given in Table 3.3. Some disks can be used with one disk format in one system, but with a different format in another system. It is common for the 8 in. floppy disk systems to accept the single-density 128-byte sector disks, which are a de facto standard and widely used for distribution of programs and data, and also to accept at least one double-density format.

When the format of tracks is fixed, one may use larger blocks by considering a block to consist of several sectors. Then the *blocking factor* (number of records per block) may still affect efficiency.

Example 3.3

On the Burroughs B9484-4, each track is divided into 60 sectors, each with a maximum capacity of 180 bytes. Let us consider the possibility of using several sectors together as a block. Let us also assume 80-byte records again. With one record per block, we can put one block per sector and store 60 records per track. With two records per block, we can still put one block in each sector and store 120 records in a track. The calculations are summarized in Table 3.5.

Table 3.5 Effect of Blocking on a Fixed Format Disk Unit

Records per Block	Sectors per Block	Blocks per Track	Records per Track
1	1	60	60
2	1	60	120
3	2	30	90
4	2	30	120
5	3	20	100
6	3	20	120
7	4	15	105
8	4	15	120
9	4	15	135

In the last case, the block size is an exact multiple of the sector size ($9 \times 80 = 720 = 4 \times 180$) and maximum efficiency is achieved. The minimum block size (in bytes) for maximum efficiency is the least common multiple of the record size and the sector size.

3.3. HEAD-PER-TRACK DISK AND DRUM TIMING

In general, the time required to read a block on a disk or drum storage unit consists of three parts:

1. Seek time, which is the time required to position the read heads over the required track.

2. Latency, which is the time required for the disk to rotate to the position where the beginning of the desired block arrives at the read-write head.

3. The actual read or write time, that is, the time required to transfer the data between main storage and the device.

If every track has its own read-write head, then the seek time is zero and the situation is somewhat simplified. We will consider this case first.

If you know the exact position of the disk when the read or write statement is given, you can calculate the latency time. For example, suppose that the disk rotates at 2400 revolutions per minute (rpm) and the beginning of the record is ¼ revolution from the read-write head. Then the time for each revolution is $60/2400 = 0.025$ sec, and the time to rotate ¼ revolution is 0.00625 sec or 6.25 msec.

Commonly you have no knowledge of the position of the disk. The latency may be anything between zero and a full revolution with all possibilities equally likely. With this assumption, on the average the data will be ½ revolution from the head and the average latency time is, for the unit assumed above, 12.5 msec. Manuals for disk units usually give 1/2 revolution as the average latency time. In many cases, as subsequent examples will illustrate, the position of the disk at the time the read or write command is given is not random, and accurate estimates of latency time can be obtained only by taking this into account.

There are two methods of calculating a close approximation to the actual read time. If you know the data rate as specified by the manufacturer, you can divide the number of bytes in a block by the data rate. Alternatively, if you know what fraction of a track the block occupies, you can multiply this by the time for one revolution. The first figure will be a little low—it does not account for the overhead information recorded with each block or sector. The latter will be a little high—it includes the gap at the end of a block and the processor may not have to wait for the gap. To get more accurate figures would require very detailed information about the data format on the disk unit. In practice, counting revolutions is easier and more accurate in general, and has the advantage of giving a slightly conservative estimate.

Example 3.4

On the IBM 2305-2, the time per revolution of the disk is 10 msec. One-fourth revolution requires 2.5 msec. The quoted data transfer rate is 1.5 megabytes/sec. (One million bytes is called a megabyte.) The maximum block size for four blocks per track (using the data from Section 3.2) is $(14{,}858 - 4 \times 198)/4 = 3516$ bytes. The calculated read or write time is 3516 bytes divided by 1.5×10^6 bytes/sec $=$ 2.344 msec or about 6% less than the time for 1/4 revolution. The actual time is somewhere between. Note, however, that if you want to read all the blocks on 100 tracks, then except for the small gap at the end of the last block, the disk must complete 100 revolutions.

In practice, there are many circumstances in which the exact position of the disk is known at the time the read command is given. The simplest case is when reading a number of tracks in succession as quickly as possible. For the first track, you do not know the position of the disk, but for all others, at the end of reading one track the disk is in exactly the right position to start reading the next. Because switching from one head to another is electronic, if there is one head per track, switching to another track can be done in negligible time.

Example 3.5

Suppose you are using the IBM 2305-2 disk unit and you want to read a table of size 100,000 bytes into the memory. If you use one block per track, (from the data in Section 3.2) we find that the block size is $14{,}858 - 198 = 14{,}660$ so you need seven blocks. (The last block will be only 12,040 bytes.) On the average, the latency time for the first track will be ½ revolution, but after that, the seven tracks can be read on seven successive revolutions. At 10 msec per revolution, this will require about 75 msec including latency time. (Actually the last block being less than maximum size will require a little less time, roughly $(12{,}040/14{,}660) \times 10 = 8.2$ msec instead of 10 msec.)

If we choose a block size of 1000, we need 100 blocks. Then the number of blocks per track is $14{,}858/(1000 + 198) = 12$, so 8⅓ tracks are needed. The time, including the 1/2 revolution average initial latency time is $(0.5 + 8.33) \times 10$ msec. $= 88.3$ msec. It is slower because with a smaller block size there are more blocks, more overhead, and the total number of tracks is larger.

Further examples of sequential reading and writing, including accounting for processing time and buffering, are presented in Chapter 4,
where the interface between I-O units and the processor is discussed.

A large file of information often is kept on a rotating storage and
accessed in random order either (1) to inquire about contents or (2) to
update information. Examples are inventory control systems, reservations systems, and look-up in large tables stored on disk or drum. Update
usually involves reading a block, modifying part of it, and then rewriting
it, whereas inquiry involves only reading. In general, the requests may
be for access anywhere in the file and come randomly in time.

In many cases, the best estimate of latency time is ½ revolution. However, if requests are queued and as soon as one is processed the next is
started, then the average latency time does not average ½ revolution.
Also, for the update case, the latency time for rewriting is exactly pre-
dictable. This can be seen most easily from an example.

Example 3.6

Suppose there are three blocks per track in a system that requires 15
msec per revolution. If we have no knowledge of the disk position when
the read command is given and can assume it random, we must
assume average latency time of ½ revolution or 7.5 msec. However, if a
request has just been serviced, then we know the disk is positioned
exactly at the end of a block and hence at the beginning of another.
The latency time is either exactly 0, exactly ⅓ revolution (5 msec), or
exactly ⅔ revolution (10 msec), and all three cases are equally likely.
Therefore, the average access time is (0 + 5 + 10)/3 = 5 msec. In the
case of an update, after reading, processing is done and the block
must be rewritten. The block cannot be rewritten until it comes to the
head again, which will require exactly 2/3 revolution (10 msec). If
processing has finished by this time, the record will be rewritten then.

In general, if the head is at the beginning of a sector when the latency
starts, then the average latency time to a randomly chosen next sector
is given by the following formula:

$$\left(\frac{r}{m}\right)\left(\frac{0 + 1 + 2 + 3 \cdots + m - 1}{m}\right) = r\left(\frac{m - 1}{2m}\right) = \frac{r}{2} - \frac{r}{2m} \quad (3.1)$$

where r = time per revolution and m = number of blocks per track.
That is, the latency is ½ revolution less ½ the read time per sector. Note
that if the latency starts anywhere except at the beginning of a sector
(for example, as a result of waiting for seek or processing), then the time
to move to the beginning of the next sector must be added to the figure
given in Eq. (3.1).

If we want the time to do an inquiry or update, we must add read time r/m for an inquiry (assuming that processing time is negligible). For an update, assuming that after reading, any processing is finished before the disk rotates back to the record being updated, exactly one revolution must be added. Thus

$$\text{Average inquiry time} = \frac{r(m-1)}{2m} + \frac{r}{m} = \frac{r(m+1)}{2m} \qquad (3.2)$$

$$\text{Average update time} = \frac{r(m+1)}{2m} + r = \frac{r(3m+1)}{2m} \qquad (3.3)$$

These equations apply when one update or inquiry immediately follows another. (Note also that these equations apply only when there is no seek time and you can neglect processing.)

Example 3.6 (continued)

For our example, $r = 15$ msec and $m = 3$. The equations give an inquiry time of 10 msec and an update time of 25 msec. If we assume $\frac{2}{3}$ inquiries, $\frac{1}{3}$ updates, then the average time per transaction would be $\frac{2}{3} \times 10 + \frac{1}{3} \times 25 = 15$ msec. This indicates that no more than $60/0.015 = 4000$ transactions per min can be handled. In fact, if transactions come randomly, there are sometimes more than average and sometimes less, and during those periods when they exceed the average, the queue will grow very large. In practice, probably something like 75% of the above upper limit or about 3000 inquiries per min can actually be handled.

Example 3.7

There is a way of using knowledge of disk position more effectively on head-per-track disk systems. Let us assume the same example as above. Let us keep three queues (m queues, in general), one for each block position in a track, and queue all requests to read or write a block in the first position in its track in the first queue, all requests for a block in the second position in its track in the second queue, and all requests for a block in the third position in its track in the third queue. Now we service a request from queue 1, then one from queue 2, then one from queue 3, then from 1 again, etc., skipping over empty queues. If a block is read or written by a request from queue 1, then when that read or write is finished, the head is in exactly the right position to read or write a block from queue 2 with no delay. Latency time will occur only when one of the queues is empty. Thus, one read or write can be handled from each queue on each revolution.

Note that an inquiry requires only a read, while an update requires a read and a write.

For this example, the number of reads or writes that can be handled is $60/0.015 = 4000$ per min in each queue, because there are 4000 revolutions per min. Thus, the total is $4000 \times 3 = 12{,}000$. However, each update requires a read and a write. Suppose we have i transactions per min, of which ⅔ are inquiries and ⅓ are updates. Then the total number of reads and writes is

$$\left(\frac{2i}{3}\right) \times 1 + \left(\frac{i}{3}\right) \times 2 = \left(\frac{4i}{3}\right) = 12{,}000$$

Solving this equation gives $i = 9000$ transactions per min, a substantial increase. (Again, in practice, to keep the queues manageably short, one would need to limit the average number of requests to perhaps 75% of this level or roughly 6750 requests per min.)

In the example it was assumed that one block can be processed while another is being read or written. Overlapping reading and/or writing with processing is possible in most computers. This is called *buffering*, and is discussed in detail in Chapter 4. Most computers have buffering routines included in the operating system for sequential files, but not for random-access files. With some programming languages, it is possible to program buffering like that described in the previous example. One also should keep in mind that here we have assumed that the seek time is zero; the situation changes significantly when seek time is introduced.

In the previous discussion, the word "blocks" was used, implying that there might be more than one record per block. We have seen that blocking is often advantageous for sequential reading and writing. Even if a file is used for random access, blocking can mean less overhead per record and hence greater capacity per track. On the other hand, in a random-access situation, one would have to read a whole block but would probably reference only one record in the block. Generally this will waste time. If the unit has moveable heads, the fact that more records are put on each track means that the head will not have to move so far—in this case there is a possibility that overall the system may be faster blocked than unblocked. Thus, blocking may be advantageous and should be considered.

On some disk units, for example, the IBM 3330, there is a provision for sensing the rotational position. This can be used to save I/O time. For example, if you have two blocks to read or write, you can check the position of the disk and determine which will come to the read-write heads first and give that request first. Assuming they do not come at the same time, if the requests are given in the right order, both reads or writes can be started within one revolution, whereas if they are given in the wrong order, more than one revolution will be required. Note, however, the ability to sense rotational position was not assumed and was not needed in the preceding examples.

3.4. MOVEABLE HEAD DEVICES

The most common arrangement uses a pack of one or more disks rotating together, as shown in Figure 3.1(b) and Figure 3.3. There is one head per usable disk surface. All heads are mounted rigidly on an arm, which is driven by a motor radially toward or away from the center of the disk. The heads are aligned so that when one lines up with the kth track on its surface, all line up with the kth tracks on their respective surfaces. These tracks are exactly above or below each other, so that they lie on a cylinder and the set of kth tracks is called the kth *cylinder*. Seeking moves the heads from one cylinder to another.

For example, the Burroughs B-9484-4 disk unit uses disk packs having 20 usable surfaces with 400 tracks on each surface. (Actually there are, in addition, six spare tracks.) Thus, there are 400 cylinders with 20 tracks per cylinder. Each pack can be mounted or dismounted like tapes, but not as easily. A *subsystem* may have as many as 16 packs. Each track on the Burroughs B-9484-4 has 60 sectors of 180 bytes each; thus, each track may store as many as 10,800 bytes. The total capacity of a pack is $10,800 \times 400 \times 20 = 86,400,000$ bytes, and of a subsystem 1,382,400,000 bytes.

The time to read or write is made up of three parts: (1) the time to move the head, called seek time, (2) the latency time, and (3) the actual read-write time. (Most disk drives rotate continuously. On some small computers, the drive motor may shut off automatically after a period of inactivity. In such a system, the disk start-up time must be added to the read or write time when needed.) Except for the fact that moving the head may affect latency time and the ability to predict it, calculation of latency time and read time is the same whether the disk is the fixed-head type or moveable-head type, and so the general principles presented in the previous sections apply. First we will consider seek time alone. At the end of this chapter we will consider several examples of calculating time completely, including seek, latency, and read-write time.

If it is not necessary to move the head, that is, when reading or writing another block in the same cylinder, the seek time is zero. Otherwise, the time is a function of how far the heads move. We will denote by $t(n)$ the time required to move the heads a distance of n cylinders. Then $t(1)$ is the time required to move to an adjacent cylinder. There are two kinds of head-positioning motors in common use. One kind is a stepping motor, which moves one step for each electrical impulse it receives. For some stepping motors, notably those in most floppy disk drives, the time per step is constant. After the head is moved, you must wait for the head to come to a complete stop. This is called the *settling time*. For stepping motors with constant step rate, seek time is given by a simple equation:

$$t(n) = bn + s \qquad (3.4)$$

where $t(n)$ is the time to move to the nth cylinder away from the initial position, b is the time to step from one cylinder to the next, and s is the settling time. The Shugart SA850 drives use a stepping motor; for them, the time per step is $b = 3$ msec and the settling time is $s = 15$ msec.

The other kind of seeking motor is called a *voice coil* motor because it resembles and uses the same principle as a loudspeaker voice coil. The seek time for such a system resembles the solid curve of Figure 3.6. The voice-coil motors provide the fastest access, but stepping-motor systems are simpler. Disk drives on large computers almost invariably use the voice-coil motors. The smaller fixed-disks may use a voice-coil or stepping motor for seeking, but in the latter case, they generally provide for taking the steps faster for longer seeks, resulting in a curve similar to Figure 3.6.

For the purpose of analysis we are going to derive some equations based on Eq. 3.4. The results apply accurately to stepping-motor driven systems with a constant step rate. We also will derive formulas that could be used for accurate seek-time calculations in the general case. In the examples, we will assume that Eq. 3.4 applies approximately to the voice-coil units. In that case, the value of s is the height of the approximating line at zero cylinders crossed. Then b can be determined by the height of the line at the maximum distance. For example, the dashed line on the graph approximates the curve and that line corresponds to $s = 15$

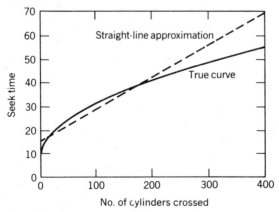

Figure 3.6 Typical Seek-Time Curve.

and $b = 0.135$. The approximation is not very good. Calculations made using a table of values of $t(n)$ give accurate numeric answers, but will not be pursued here (except to derive general equations) because they do not provide more insight than we get from using our simple equations.

3.5. SEEK TIME FOR SUCCESSIVE ACCESSES IN SAME FILE

Assume we have a data file consisting of w successive cylinders on a disk unit and suppose that after one block is read or written the next is chosen completely randomly. First let us ask two questions: (1) What is the probability that the next access is on the same cylinder, and (2) if it is not, what is the probability of each possible move? If there are w cylinders and all are equally likely, then a fraction $1/w$ of the time the next block will be in the same cylinder, while $(w - 1)/w$ of the time there will be a jump to a different cylinder.

Getting the probabilities for the possible numbers of cylinders crossed is more difficult. Let us suppose all are possible and in fact are equally likely. The possible moves for $w = 4$ are as follows:

Distance = 1	Distance = 2	Distance = 3
1 to 2	1 to 3	1 to 4
2 to 3	2 to 4	
3 to 4		

(Moves in the opposite direction also are possible, equally likely, and of the same average distance.) Thus, the probability of a move of distance 1 is $\frac{3}{6} = \frac{1}{2}$, the probability of a move of distance 2 is $\frac{2}{6} = \frac{1}{3}$, and the probability of a move of distance 3 is $\frac{1}{6}$. The sum of the distances moved is $3 \times 1 + 2 \times 2 + 1 \times 3 = 10$. There are six cases. The average distance moved is $\frac{10}{6} = 1.667$.

For the general case, denote by $p(n)$ the probability of moving a distance n. There are $w-1$ ways to move one cylinder, $w-2$ ways to move two cylinders, ... , one way to move $w-1$ cylinders. The total number of possible moves is

$$m = 1 + 2 + \cdots + w - 1 = \frac{w(w - 1)}{2} \tag{3.5}$$

Thus, the probabilities are

$$p(n) = \frac{w - n}{m} = \frac{2(w - n)}{w(w - 1)} \qquad \text{for } 1 \leqslant n \leqslant w - 1 \tag{3.6}$$

and the average time can be calculated as

$$t_{ave} = t(1)p(1) + t(2)p(2) + \cdots + t(w - 1)p(w - 1) \tag{3.7}$$

This formula could be programmed easily on a computer if a table of values for $t(n)$ were known. Such a table could be read from the graph supplied by the manufacturer, or if no table or graph were supplied, could be found by writing a program to measure these values experimentally. Since such a calculation does not give much insight, we will proceed to calculate a formula based on a linear function for $t(n)$, Eq. 3.4.

The sum of the distances for all these moves is

$$
\begin{aligned}
d &= 1(w-1) + 2(w-2) + \cdots + (w-1)1 \\
  &= 1w + 2w + \cdots + (w-1)w \\
  &\quad - 1^2 - 2^2 - \cdots - (w-1)^2 \\
  &= w[1 + 2 + \cdots + (w-1)] \\
  &\quad - [1^2 + 2^2 + \cdots + (w-1)^2] \\
  &= \frac{w^2(w-1)}{2} - \frac{w(w-1)(2w-1)}{6}
\end{aligned}
$$

$$
d = \frac{w(w-1)(w+1)}{6} \tag{3.8}
$$

The sums $1 + 2 + \cdots + (w-1)$ and $1^2 + 2^2 + \cdots + (w-1)^2$ can be found or verified by methods given in most books on algebra. Then the average distance is

$$
\begin{aligned}
d_{ave} &= \frac{(\text{sum of distances for all moves})}{(\text{number of moves})} \\
        &= \frac{d}{m} = \frac{(w+1)}{3}
\end{aligned} \tag{3.9}
$$

which gives 1.667 for $w = 4$, as we found previously. (One might expect the answer to be about one-half the width rather than about one-third of the width—the reason it is less is that there are more possible short moves than long moves.)

Now suppose the time required to move the head across n cylinders is, as given by Eq. 3.4,

$$
t = s + bn
$$

Also, again assume completely random moves. Since the assumed equation for t is linear, the average t can be obtained by substituting the average value of n for n. Then the average seek time will equal

$$
\begin{aligned}
t_{ave} = {} &(\text{probability of move to same cylinder}) \times 0 \\
          &+ \text{probability of move to different cylinder} \\
          &\times \text{average seek time for jump to a different cylinder}
\end{aligned}
$$

$$
t_{ave} = \frac{(w-1)}{w}\left(s + \frac{b(w+1)}{3}\right) \tag{3.10}
$$

$$
t_{ave} = s + \frac{bw}{3} \quad \text{approximately if } w \text{ is large} \tag{3.11}
$$

Example 3.8

Assume seek time is given by the straight line in Figure 3.6 and all w = 400 cylinders are equally likely. For that straight line, s = 15 and b = 0.135. Eq. 3.4 gives the seek time 15.135 msec for n = 1 cylinder and 69 msec for the maximum n = 400 cylinders. Eq. 3.10 gives the average as 32.96 and approximate Eq. 3.11 gives 33 msec. If a file requires only one-fourth of the pack, w = 100, Eq. 3.10 gives 19.35 msec as the average seek time, while Eq. 3.11 gives 19.5 msec. Of course, the straight line in Figure 3.6 is not a very good approximation to the curve, and so these answers cannot be expected to be very accurate for the machine whose seek times are represented by the curve.

Example 3.9

The Shugart SA850 floppy disk drive uses an 8 in. two-sided disk. It is driven by a stepping motor and requires b = 3 msec to step from one cylinder to the next and s = 15 msec settling time after seeking. There are 77 cylinders. The seek time to move n = 1 cylinder is, by Eq. 3.4, 18 msec. The maximum seek time, the time to move 76 cylinders, is 243 msec. The average, by Eq. 3.10, is

$$ t_{ave} = \frac{76}{77} \times \left(15 + \frac{3 \times 78}{3} \right) $$
$$ = 91.79 \text{ msec} $$

Eq. 3.11 gives 92 msec. If the file uses only 10 cylinders, then the average access time becomes, by Eq. 3.10,

$$ t_{ave} = \frac{9}{10} \times \left(15 + \frac{3 \times 11}{3} \right) = 23.4 \text{ msec} $$

Eq. 3.11 gives 25 msec—the n in this case is small enough so that the approximate Eq. 3.11 is not very accurate.

When a manufacturer quotes "average seek time," the calculation is normally based on the assumption of completely random accesses in the entire disk pack, and the calculation made using Eq. 3.7. For example, for the Burroughs B-9484-4 disk unit, the manufacturer quotes the seek times for moving one cylinder as minimum 10 msec, maximum 55 msec, and average 30 msec. IBM quotes the same figures for their 3330-1. Both units have 400 cylinders. From this fact and the maximum and minimum seek times, it is possible to determine that if the equation $t = s + bn$ applied, then s = 9.887 and b = 0.113. (However, we will continue to use s = 15 and b = 0.135 in later examples.) Eq. 3.11 for average access time then gives 24.9 msec, about 17% low.

The reason for this discrepancy is that the true curve of seek time versus distance moved has greater seek times than the straight-line approximation for the more likely shorter distances, as shown in Figure 3.6. In fact, a more exact calculation using the true curve in Figure 3.6 with Eq. 3.7 gives an average of about 33 msec seek time—the minimum is 10 and the maximum 55. Using an approximating straight line that is a good approximation over the distances that actually occur, that is, if the file has only 50 cylinders, a straight line approximating the curve from 0 to 50 cylinders as well as possible, would give improved results with Eqs. 3.10 and 3.11. Note that since the curve is not linear, it would not be correct to conclude that the average seek time is the time required to cross the average number of cylinders.

3.6. SEEK TIME FOR ACCESS FROM ONE FILE TO ANOTHER

Let us assume file 1 has width w_1 cylinders and file 2 has width w_2 cylinders, and they are separated by d cylinders on the disk pack, as in Figure 3.7. Assuming all cylinders in file 1 are equally likely for the starting position and all cylinders on file 2 are equally likely as the destination, we want to calculate the probability $p(n)$ of having to move a distance of exactly n cylinders. Clearly, $p(n)$ will be the same whether we are moving from file 1 to file 2 or vice versa. Therefore, there is no loss of generality in assuming that file 1 is smaller than file 2, which we do in the following derivations.

First we will calculate $r(n)$, the number of distinct pairs of records, one in file 1 and one in file 2, that are separated by distance n cylinders.

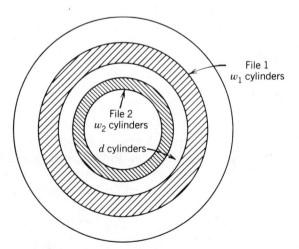

Figure 3.7 Seek From One File to Another.

Note that $r(n)$ is zero if $n < d$—the inside cylinders in file 1 and file 2 are not that far apart. Similarly, $r(n)$ is zero if $n > w_1 + d + w_2$—no cylinder in file 1 and cylinder in file 2 are that far apart. There is exactly one cylinder in file 1 and one in file 2 that are a distance $d + 1$ apart, namely, the ones nearest to each other. There are two pairs that are a distance $d + 2$, the one nearest file 2 in file 1 and the second one from the edge in file 2, and the one nearest the edge in file 2 and the second one from the edge in file 1. Similarly, there are three pairs at distance $d + 3$, four pairs at distance $d + 4$, and so on, up to w_1 pairs at distance $d + w_1$. At the other extreme, there is one pair at distance $w_1 + d + w_2 - 1$, the two cylinders that are farthest apart. There are two pairs at distance $w_1 + d + w_2 - 2$, namely, the farthest one in file 1 with the next to farthest one in file 2, and the farthest one in file 2 with the next to farthest one in file 1. Similarly, there are three pairs with distance $w_1 + d + w_2 - 3$, four pairs at distance $w_1 + d + w_2 - 4$, and so on, up to w_1 pairs at distance $w_1 + d + w_2 - w_1 = d + w_2$. Finally, for any value of n between $w_1 + d$ and $d + w_2$, for each cylinder in file 1, there is exactly one cylinder in file 2 at distance n, so $r(n)$ is equal to w_1. This may be summarized as follows:

$$
\begin{aligned}
r(n) &= 0 & &\text{if } n \leq d \\
r(n) &= n - d & &\text{if } d \leq n \leq w_1 + d \\
r(n) &= w_1 & &\text{if } w_1 + d \leq n \leq d + w_2 \\
r(n) &= w_1 + d + w_2 - n & &\text{if } d + w_2 \leq n \leq w_1 + d + w_2 \\
r(n) &= 0 & &\text{if } w_1 + d + w_2 \leq n
\end{aligned}
\tag{3.12}
$$

where w_1 is the width in cylinders of the smaller file, w_2 is the width of the larger file, and d is the number of cylinders between them. A graph of $r(n)$ is shown in Figure 3.8. It is a symmetric trapezoid of height w_1.

The total number of pairs, which is the sum of all the values of $r(n)$, must be equal to $w_1 w_2$, because there are w_1 choices of the starting point and w_2 choices for the destination. (Note that this is exactly the area of the trapezoid for $r(n)$ in Figure 3.8.) Since we are assuming all cases equally likely, the probability $p(n)$ is

$$
p(n) = \frac{r(n)}{w_1 w_2}
\tag{3.13}
$$

Thus, the graph for $p(n)$ is also a trapezoid of the same form as the graph for $r(n)$, except that the maximum height is $1/w_2$ (and, hence, the area of the trapezoid is 1).

Now if a table of values of $t(n)$, the time required for a seek of distance n cylinders, is available, the average time required can be calculated as

$$
\begin{aligned}
t_{ave} = {}& t(d + 1)p(d + 1) + t(d + 2)p(d + 2) + \cdots \\
& + t(w_1 + d + w_2 - 1)p(w_1 + d + w_2 - 1)
\end{aligned}
\tag{3.14}
$$

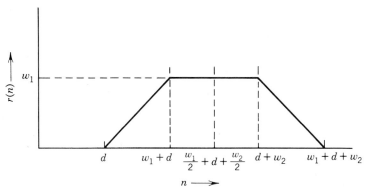

Figure 3.8 Graph of r(n).

This could easily be programmed on a computer and accurate calculations of seek time for this case could be made. Again we will not pursue this here, but will go on to derive an equation that applies in the case where the function $t(n)$ is linear.

Because the trapezoid in Figure 3.8 is symmetric, the average value of n must be the center of the trapezoid, which is

$$n_{ave} = \frac{w_1}{2} + d + \frac{w_2}{2} \qquad (3.15)$$

and because Eq. 3.4, which we now assume holds, is linear, we can obtain the average time for a seek by substituting the average distance into that formula:

$$t_{ave} = s + b\left(\frac{w_1}{2} + d + \frac{w_2}{2}\right) \qquad (3.16)$$

Clearly, the same formulas apply to a move from file 2 to file 1.

Let us consider one variation of this. Suppose there are two files, file A of width w_a and file B of width w_b, with file B split into two equal parts of width $w_b/2$ each, placed immediately before and immediately after file A as in Figure 3.9. Eq. 3.15 above can be applied to get the average seek time for a move from file A to the first half of file B, using $w_1 = w_a$, $w_2 = w_b/2$, and $d = 0$,

$$n = \frac{w_a}{2} + \frac{w_b}{4} \qquad (3.17)$$

$$t = s + b\left(\frac{w_a}{2} + \frac{w_b}{4}\right) \qquad (3.18)$$

The same result applies to a move from file A to the other half of file B, so the average for any move from file A to file B is given by these equa-

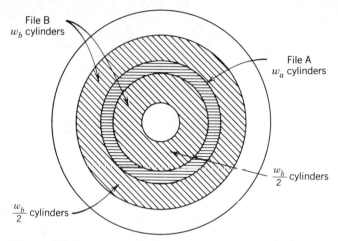

Figure 3.9 Seek When One File is in the Middle of the Other.

tions. Furthermore, they also apply to a move from file B to file A. Comparing Eqs. 3.16 and 3.18 shows that the latter gives a shorter average search. Eq. 3.18 also shows that the seek time will be minimized by putting the smaller file in the middle.

If file B requires an odd number of cylinders, then it must be divided so that one part contains one more cylinder than the other. A detailed analysis shows that the seek time will be very slightly greater than that given by Eq. 3.18, so that formula can be used for all practical purposes. This is illustrated in Example 3.11.

It is quite common to keep an index on a disk unit to tell exactly where to locate a particular record. The above formulas suggest that placing the index in the middle of the main file may decrease average access time. This is commonly done. Example 3.12 shows that this is not always the optimum choice, however.

Example 3.10

Let us assume, to get a specific numeric answer, $s = 15$, $b = 0.135$, and a file of 50 cylinders with an index of one cylinder. If the index is adjacent to the file, the seek time is given by Eq. 3.16.

$$t = 15 + 0.135 \times \left(\frac{1}{2} + \frac{50}{2} \right) = 18.4 \text{ msec}$$

This applies to each access to the index and each access to the data, assuming they occur alternately, so the combination of reading from the index and then getting the data requires 36.8 msec.

If the index is placed in the middle, then Eq. 3.18 applies:

$$t = 15 + 0.135 \times \left(\frac{1}{2} + \frac{50}{4}\right) = 16.8 \text{ msec}$$

or 33.6 for the combination of index read and data read, about a 9% saving.

Example 3.11

Assume the Shugart 850 floppy disk drive again. For this drive, $s = 15$ msec and $b = 3$ msec. Assume a file uses cylinders 0 and 1 for an index and cylinders 2 through 76 for the main file. Finding a data item requires reading one index block and then one block in the file. Assuming this is done repeatedly, Eq. 3.16 applies to each seek with $w_1 = 2$, $w_2 = 75$, and $d = 0$. This gives as average seek time from index to file or vice versa, $t = 15 + 3 \times (1 + 0 + 37.5) = 130.5$ msec, so a complete access requires $130.5 + 130.5 = 261$ msec.

We cannot place the index in the exact middle, so let us place it in cylinders 37 and 38, with 37 cylinders (0–36) on the outside and 38 cylinders (39–76) on the inside of the index. The derivation assumed exactly the same number of cylinders on each side. Let us do an exact calculation first. We can apply Eq. 3.16 to each side. Assume we start in the index, go to the outside part of the file, and return back to the index. Eq. 3.16 applies in each case, with $w_1 = 2$, $w_2 = 37$, and $d = 0$, and gives an average of 73.5 msec for each seek or 147 msec for the two reads. Similarly, if we start in the index, move to the inner half of the file, and then return to the index, Eq. 3.16 applies with $w_1 = 2$, $w_2 = 38$, and $d = 0$, giving 75 msec. for each seek and 150 msec for the two reads. Assuming all file blocks are equally likely, the probability of an access to the outside part of the file is 37/75 and to the inside part is 38/75. The average then is

$$\left(\frac{37}{75}\right) \times 147 + \left(\frac{38}{75}\right) \times 150 = 148.52 \text{ msec}$$

Simply applying Eq. 3.18 with $w_a = 2$ and $w_b = 75$ gives 74.25 for each access or 148.5 for the combination, which is very accurate even though the two halves of the file are not precisely equal.

Example 3.12

Let us assume there are three files on a disk pack—File S has 25 cylinders, File T has 50 cylinders, and File U has 100 cylinders. File U has a one-cylinder index. Repeatedly, an access is made to File T, then to File U (via the index), and then two accesses to File S. On each access, all parts of the file are assumed equally likely.

The first problem is to arrange the data on the disk in order to minimize time. In this case, the optimum place for the index is clearly beside file U—not in the center—on the side nearest file T so the head can stop at the index on the way from T to U. One file must be in the middle and it is best to put the smallest there. The middle file has to be crossed once, no matter which one is in the middle, and except for that, the total number of cylinders passed over on the average is the same. That this is the best choice can be verified by a detailed analysis involving complicated derivations, or by making numeric calculations for each viable choice.

With this choice made, the calculation is straightforward. On the first access, the head comes from file S to file T, and because S is in the middle, they are adjacent. Eq. 3.16 applies with $w_1 = 25$, $w_2 = 50$, and $d = 0$. Assuming $s = 15$ and $b = 0.135$ as before, the seek time for this step is 20.1 msec. The next step is from T across to the index for U, for which Eq. 3.16 applies with $w_1 = 50$, $d = 25$, and $w_2 = 1$, giving a seek time of 21.8 msec. The next step is from the index into file U, for which we again use Eq. 3.16, with $w_1 = 1$, $d = 0$, and $w_2 = 100$, giving 21.8 msec again. Next the head moves from U to S, for which Eq. 3.16 applies with $w_1 = 100$, $d = 1$ (for the index), and $w_2 = 25$, giving average seek time 23.6 msec. Finally, for the move from one record in file S to another, Eq. 3.10 or the approximate Eq. 3.11 applies with $w = 25$. Using Eq. 3.11, we get an average of 16.1 msec. The total average seek time for the cycle of five accesses to the disk is

$$(20.1 + 21.8 + 21.8 + 23.6 + 16.1) = 103.4 \text{ msec}$$

To this, one would have to add latency time and read time for each access. One could in this case do no better than to assume ½ revolution of latency time for each access.

3.7. COMPLETE ACCESS TIME CALCULATIONS

The time to read a block from a file consists of three parts: (1) seek time, (2) latency time, and (3) actual read time. The seek time can be calculated using the methods described in the preceding sections. The latency time is affected by the seek time—latency starts when seek ends. If you know exactly when the seeking ends, you can sometimes make accurate predictions of latency. This is the case when a file is read sequentially, as shown in Example 3.13. Another example is shown in Example 3.15.

Generally, however, there are many possible values that the seek time may take, and you have only an estimate of the average seek time. This is the situation in Example 3.14. In this case, if the range of actual seek times is at least on the order of the time to read a sector, then ½ revolution is a good estimate of average latency time. This can be seen as follows. The latency can be thought of as made up of two parts: (a) the time it takes to first reach the beginning of a sector, and (b) the additional time it takes to get from there to the desired sector. If the seek time is randomly distributed and at least as long as the average time to read a sector, then the time to first reach the beginning of a sector may be any value between zero and the time to read a sector, which on the average is about one-half the time to read a sector; this equals $r/2m$, where r is the time per revolution and m is the number of sectors in a track. The additional time to reach the desired sector from the beginning of a randomly chosen sector is given by Eq. 3.1 as $r/2 - r/2m$. Adding these two times gives $r/2$, or ½ revolution.

In this section, the complete calculation will be done for several illustrative simple cases. In the next two examples, we will assume an IBM 3330-1, which has 19 tracks per cylinder, a rotational speed of 3600 revolutions per min, which corresponds to 16.7 msec per revolution, and we will assume that seek time is given by $t = s + bn$ (Eq. 3.4) with $s = 15$ and $b = 0.135$ as before, except that we will assume that a move to an adjacent cylinder requires 10 msec, according to the specifications for the machine.

Example 3.13

Let us consider reading a file of 1,000,000 80-byte records from an IBM 3330 disk file. Let us assume the block size is ¼ of a track. Recalling Example 3.1, we find that ¼ track can store a maximum of 3156 bytes, so we choose to put 39 records or 3120 bytes per block. Then we need $1,000,000/39 = 25,642$ blocks. (The last block will only be partly full—in fact, it will contain only one record.) This requires 6410.5 tracks and, because there are 19 tracks per cylinder, 337 complete cylinders plus 7.5 tracks in the 338th cylinder are required.

Initially, the head must be moved to the first cylinder—let us assume that the head might have been anywhere on the disk and use the estimate 30 msec, which is the average seek time for the IBM 3330. Next is latency time—let us estimate ½ revolution or 8.3 msec. Then reading can proceed through an entire cylinder with no seek or latency time, because after each block the next block is in the correct position to be read. At the end of a cylinder, the head must move to the next cylinder—this requires 10 msec. Then the disk must rotate to the beginning of the next track. In 10 msec it rotates over half a revolution, and it must exactly finish that revolution. Thus, the total delay between cylinders, consisting of seek and latency time, is exactly one revolution. In addition to the initial 38.3 msec, 6410.5 revolutions are needed for reading and 337 revolutions for transitions from cylinder to cylinder, a total of 6747.5 revolutions or 6747.5/3600 = 1.87 min. The initial seek and latency times turn out to be negligible.

Example 3.14

Next, let us consider random accesses to a file for an inquiry-update system. Let us assume that a file has four blocks per track and occupies 100 cylinders and that each access is preceded by two accesses to a one-cylinder index in the middle of the file. For the first step—from the file to the index—Eq. 3.18 applies with $w_a = 1$ and $w_b = 100$, giving an average seek time of 18.4 msec. To this we add an average latency time of ½ revolution or 8.3 msec and a read time of ¼ revolution or 4.2 msec to give a total of 30.9 msec. The second access into the index is in the same cylinder, so seek time is zero. Latency time may be exactly zero, ¼, ½, or ¾ revolution. Assume those equally likely and use the average, ⅜ revolution or 6.2 msec. With the ¼ revolution read time, the total is 10.4 msec. The access from the index to the file requires the same 30.9 msec. The combination of three accesses requires a total 30.9 + 10.4 + 30.9 = 72.2 msec.

For an update transaction, the computer must update and rewrite the record after reading. Since the rewrite is on the same track, the seek time is zero. The disk would have to rotate back to the beginning of the record, during which time the computations would, in most situations, be completed. Then the write would be completed precisely one revolution after the read was completed. Thus the average time for an update transaction in the above example would be exactly one revolution more than the inquiry time or 72.2 + 16.7 = 88.9 msec.

With a mix of ⅔ inquiries and ⅓ updates, the number of transactions per min would satisfy

$$72.2 \times \frac{2i}{3} + 88.9 \times \frac{i}{3} = 60,000 \text{ msec}$$

from which we find a capability for handling an average of $i = 771$ transactions per min. If (as might occur in a system for airline reservations) inquiries came randomly at this rate, queues would become excessively long—rates up to perhaps 75% of this probably would be satisfactorily handled.

If you have more specific knowledge of seek times, a more accurate estimate of overall time can be made because closer estimates of latency time are possible.

Example 3.15

Let us first determine, for the Shugart SA850 floppy disk drive, how far one can seek in one revolution. Because this disk drive has a rotational speed of 360 revolutions per min, the time per revolution is 167 msec. For this unit, $b = 3$ msec/cylinder and $s = 15$ msec. Solving

$$167 = s + bn$$

for n gives $n = (167 - s)/b = 50.6$. Thus, a seek of 50 cylinders would be completed in less than one revolution. Let us assume a file of 20 cylinders (or 40 tracks, because one cylinder consists of two tracks, one on each side of the disk) and assume that each time we read, we read a complete track. We know that for successive reads in the same cylinder, the seek time and latency time are zero and the read takes exactly one revolution. If there is a seek to another cylinder, then we know that the combined seek and latency time take exactly one revolution. Assuming randomly selected tracks on successive reads, the probability is $1/20$ that a read will be in the same cylinder as the previous one, and $19/20$ that it is in a different cylinder, which gives an average of

$$\left(\frac{1}{20}\right) \times 1 + \left(\frac{19}{20}\right) \times 2 = 1.95 \text{ revolutions}$$

or $1.95 \times 167 = 325$ msec per access.

The above assumes that you may by chance choose to read the same track twice in succession. If the program checks whether the track needed is in memory, this unnecessary read may be eliminated. The probability then becomes $1/40$ that no read is needed, $1/40$ that a read but no seek is needed, and $19/20$ that a seek and a read are needed, and the average becomes

$$\left(\frac{1}{40}\right) \times 0 + \left(\frac{1}{40}\right) \times 1 + \left(\frac{19}{20}\right) \times 2 = 1.925 \text{ revolutions}$$

or $1.925 \times 167 = 321$ msec per access.

NOTES

Manufacturer descriptions of direct-access storage devices are given in [D1] and [D2]. Disk and drum units also are described in [D3]. Other surveys of rotating storage devices appear in [D4] and [D5]. There are ANSI standards for diskettes [D6] and large disk packs.

Examples of space calculations appear in many of the books on files cited in Chapter 1, such as [A9]. Other examples of timing calculations appear in [D7] and [D8]. Seek time curves appeared over two decades ago, for example, in [D9]. The timing calculations in this chapter assume that only one user has access to a given disk unit at a time. In a multi-user environment, scheduling of requests in other than first-come-first-serve order may significantly improve system performance. Example 3.7 is an illustration of a "shortest-access-time-first" policy. File scheduling algorithms are surveyed in [J1] and analyzed in [J6].

EXERCISES

3-1. Assume a file consisting of 200-byte records is to be stored on an IBM 3330 disk sequentially. (Also assume no spanning.)

(a) How many records will fit on a track

(i) for a blocking factor of 1?

(ii) for a blocking factor of 32?

(iii) for a blocking factor of 66?

(iv) with four blocks per track?

(v) with one block per track?

(b) For what blocking factor would the most records fit per 3330 track? For what blocking factor would the least records fit per 3330 track?

3-2. Consider a file consisting of 240-byte records with embedded keys, stored on a 3330 disk, formatted with 14-byte keys.

(a) If the records are not blocked, what is the maximum number of records that can fit on one track?

(b) If the records are blocked, what is the maximum number of records that can fit in one track, and for what blocking factor is this maximum achievable?

3-3. Consider a file consisting of 80-byte records, stored on an IBM 3330 disk, formatted without keys.

(a) If the records are blocked, what is the maximum number of records that can fit on one track, and for what blocking factor is this maximum achievable?

(b) At most 160 records will fit on one track for blocking factors of both 80 and 160. How many records will fit on a track for blocking factors of 81 and 159?

3-4. For the IBM 3330, what is the maximum size a block can be such that 40 blocks will fit on a track with each block having an eight-byte key? (These eight bytes do not count as part of the block size.)

3-5. (a) If we wanted third-track blocking (i.e., three blocks per track) for 100-byte records on a 3330 disk, what is the block size (in bytes) and what is the blocking factor?

(b) If we wanted third-track blocking for 100 byte records on a 2305-II disk, how many records fit per track?

(c) If we want third-track blocking for 100-byte records on an IBM 3380 disk drive, how many records fit per track?

3-6. The following questions relate to the IBM 3330 disk unit.

(a) Using the parameters given in Section 3.2, estimate the data transfer rate (i.e., the number of bytes per second that can be read or written) for the 3330, during the actual read excluding seek and latency.

(b) In the manufacturer's manuals, the data transfer rate is quoted as 806,000 cps. This figure is greater than the correct answer to (a) because the number 13,165 does not include the space taken on each track by "system" overhead. Estimate the amount of system overhead space per track.

3-7. Assuming records are not spanned, what is the longest time it can take to read a record using a 3330 disk? (Make worst-case assumptions.)

3-8. Assume that on an IBM 3380 disk drive, we have two files, File A and File B, each consisting of 30 full cylinders, that are adjacent to each other on the disk.

(a) What is the average seek time to a randomly chosen cylinder in File A from a randomly chosen cylinder in the same file, File A?

(b) What is the average seek time to a randomly chosen cylinder in File A from a randomly chosen cylinder in File B?

For the rest of the problems, let us assume a "double-sided double-track double-density" 5¼ in. floppy disk drive. These drives have the following characteristics: (These data are taken from the manual for a TEAC Model FD-55F half-height drive.)

Number of cylinders	80
Number of tracks per cylinder	2
Number of sectors per track	16
Number of bytes per sector	256
Rotational speed	300 rpm
Seek time	3 msec per cylinder
Settling time	15 msec

The head is driven by a stepping motor and Eq. 3.4 is accurate. Tracks 0 and 1 make up the first cylinder, tracks 2 and 3 the second cylinder, etc.

3-9. Assuming the read head is already on the correct cylinder, how long will it take to read all the sectors in the track in the following sequence: 1, 7, 4, 12, 14, 5, 10, 11, 13, 2, 3, 6, 8, 9, 15, 16.

3-10. Let us assume a file of 300 blocks of 1024 bytes each, stored in adjacent cylinders.

(a) How much time will it take to read the file from beginning to end, neglecting all processing time?

(b) How much time will it take to read the file, block by block, backwards, that is, to read block 300, then block 299, then block 298, etc., back to block 1? (You can calculate the latency time exactly, but not using any formula in the text.)

(c) Assume that an inquiry consists of reading a randomly chosen block in this file, and an update consists of an inquiry followed by rewriting the block read. Neglecting processing time and assuming that the only use of this disk is for inquiries and updates for this file, what is the average time per inquiry and what is the average time per update?

3-11. Let us assume an on-line system that uses two files, file A and file B. Assume that file A consists of 10 tracks—tracks 2 through 11, and file B occupies 30 tracks—tracks 12 through 41. Assume that an inquiry requires reading one sector in file A and then one sector in file B, and an update requires the same two reads plus rewriting the sector in file B.

(a) How many bytes are there in each file?

(b) What is the average time required for an inquiry, and what is the average time required for an update?

Processor-Storage Interface and Buffering

4.1. INTRODUCTION

The central processor and main memory are the heart of a computer. The slower auxiliary storage devices—usually tape and disk units—are generally thought of as peripheral devices, even though they are an integral part of the computer system. Moving data from an auxiliary device to the processor or main memory is called *input*; moving data from the processor or main memory to an auxiliary device is called *output*. Bringing data from a terminal or card reader to the processor or main memory is also called input and sending data from the main memory or processor to a terminal or printer is output. Input-output (I-O) operations, whether they are true external input and output as with a terminal or they refer to a kind of auxiliary storage, are handled by basically the same techniques.

It is possible for a computer to be simultaneously writing, processing, and reading. For example, it may be writing the record that was just processed, processing a second record, and reading the next record to be processed. This chapter explains briefly how this is accomplished and the effect on the timing of I-O operations.

In this chapter, we will explain how the processor, main memory, and I-O devices are connected and interact. A verbal explanation is given for each case. For the reader who is unsatisfied with this level of explanation, simplified machine language programs are included and explained in Appendix G.

4.2. TYPICAL COMPUTER ORGANIZATION

A typical computer consists of a *bus* which connects various other units. The units include a main processor, one or more memory units, and one or more *I-O units*. The bus is simply a collection of wires or lines carrying all the signals each unit sends to every other unit. There are data lines, address lines, and some control lines. The control lines include signals that indicate (in coded form) when the processor is doing a memory read, a memory write, an I-O read, or an I-O write.

One of the control lines brings a signal to the processor that causes the processor to wait—a zero signal on the wait line causes the processor to stop at the end of the machine cycle in progress; when the wait line goes back to its normal value of one, the processor continues where it left off. When the processor stops in response to the wait signal, it puts an acknowledgment signal out on another control line to indicate that it is waiting. These signals facilitate having two or more processors share a single memory. There is also an interrupt line. When the interrupt line goes from its normal 1 to 0, the processor finishes its current instruction, interrupts what it is doing, saves some information, and jumps to a fixed location. These signals normally are all connected to the bus as *bus signals* available to all other units connected to the bus.

A memory unit connected to the bus serves a range of addresses. Circuits in the memory unit continuously examine the bus signals. When the memory unit finds an address on the bus that references its memory and control signals indicate a memory read, the memory unit reads the indicated data from its memory and places the data on the bus data lines. If the address is within range and the other signals indicate a memory write, the memory unit writes the data from the bus into the indicated cell in its memory.

4.3. DIRECT I-O

It was pointed out in Chapter 1 that an input or output device may interface directly with the processor [as in Figure 1.1(b)] or the main memory [as in Figure 1.1(c)]. We will discuss the former, simpler case first. The simplest type of interface with the processor is a machine instruction that moves one unit of data—one bit, one byte, or one word—from an I-O device into a register in the processor on input or from a register in the processor to an I-O device on output. For example, small computers commonly have an instruction that reads one byte from a terminal into a register in the processor. Reading a block of data requires a loop that includes a read instruction and a store instruction for each byte.

Typically, there is an input instruction that gets status information from the I-O device. The status information tells whether there is input information ready to read for an input device or the I-O unit is ready to accept data for an output device. Various other status information may include indications of various kinds of errors, or whether a printer is out of paper, a tape drive is at end of file, or a disk is inserted in a floppy disk drive.

The programmer is responsible for timing—usually the I-O control circuits have a one-byte storage buffer; therefore, a read instruction must be given after each byte is received but before the next byte is received. The simplest way to do this is by the following algorithm for input:

```
repeat
     read status
     until data is available;
read data from I-O device;
```

or for output:

```
repeat
     read status
     until I-O device is ready;
write data to I-O device;
```

With this very simple approach to I-O, the processor does nothing but continually check the status of the I-O device while it is waiting for the I-O device to either write or read data. It does not address the problem of simultaneously reading, writing, and processing, but it is often used, especially in microcomputers, because it is the simplest and cheapest way to implement I-O.

There are two ways of enabling the computer to do other processing while it is waiting for the I-O device. One way uses *polling* and the other uses interrupts. As an example of polling, let us assume that we want to do some processing while we are waiting for input from one or more I-O devices. For polling to work we must know that if we check the status and the device is not ready, then it is not necessary to check the status again immediately but it is permissible to do something else for a time t and then check the status again. For example, suppose the input device is a terminal running at 120 characters or bytes per second (1200 baud). Most systems require that a byte be read any time after it is received, but before the next one is received. This means that if the I-O device is not ready now, we will not be too late if we wait a time of $\frac{1}{120}$ sec (8.3 msec) before checking status again. Then the following algorithm will work:

```
repeat
     read status of I-O device 1
          if ready, do the I-O operation
     read status of I-O device 2
          if ready, do the I-O operation
               .
               .
               .
     read status of I-O device n
          if ready, do the I-O operation

     do some processing

     until processing is finished
```

The maximum time for one iteration of the loop must be small enough so that each device is checked often enough to prevent I-O errors. This is a very simple algorithm that is effective in many fairly simple situations. Useful computing is done while I-O device(s) such as a terminal are being used to enter data into or write data from the computer. In this sense, reading and computing are being done simultaneously.

The second method uses an interrupt system. For example, assuming the I-O device is a terminal, whenever the terminal has a byte ready for the processor to read, the I-O device puts a signal on the interrupt line, which causes an interrupt. The program is written so that every time the interrupt occurs, the processor jumps to a special input procedure that gives the read command, moves the data to main memory at a designated "data address," and then returns control to where it was when the interrupt occurred. On output, the program gives an output instruction to send one byte from main memory to the terminal. The interrupt occurs when the terminal is ready to accept the next byte.

With this system it is possible to have "simultaneous read, write, and compute." To illustrate what we mean, let us assume a 120 byte per second terminal as an input device. Typical minicomputer instructions require on the order of a microsecond. Each time a byte is sent to the processor, an interrupt signal causes control to jump to the input procedure, which typically saves the contents of some of the processor registers, reads the one byte into the processor, perhaps checks for error conditions, moves the one byte to main memory at the designated data address, modifies the data address to be ready for the next byte, restores the saved values into the registers, and jumps back to the main program at the point where the interrupt occurred. The total may come to 20 or 30 instructions, which takes roughly 20 or 30 microseconds. Bytes are transmitted at most 120 per second or one each 8333 microseconds, but only 20 or 30 or so microseconds of the processor's effort must be spent in the read procedure. Therefore, during most (over 99%) of the time that the terminal is busy transmitting, the processor can do other things.

Most minicomputers and microprocessors have provisions for an interrupt system and commonly use this type of I-O. It is even used on some of the larger computers to handle I-O to slow devices such as terminals.

4.4. I-O PROCESSORS

It is possible for more than one processor to share the same main memory (or for that matter, any storage device). One way to implement this with two processors is to provide a way for the high-priority processor to signal "hold" to the other when it wants the bus. The other processor will finish its current cycle, release the bus, and then acknowledge the request. At that point, the high-priority processor starts using the bus. When it is finished with the bus, it removes the hold signal and the other processor proceeds. Alternatively, the memory may have a signal that indicates whether it is busy or not. Any time a processor wants to access the memory it must first check whether the memory is busy, and if so it must wait until the memory is again ready to be used. If two or more processors request access at the same time, access is given to the one with highest priority and the busy signal is given to the others.

In the configuration shown in Figure 1.1(b), the auxiliary memory (or any I-O device) is not connected directly to the main memory. The interface is actually another processor, the *I-O processor* that accesses the main memory, but is often designed only to read a block of data from an input device into main memory and/or write a block of data from main memory to an output device. The names *DMA* (direct memory access) and *channel* also are commonly used for the I-O processor. There may be one or more I-O processors in a system, and one I-O processor may be connected to one or more I-O devices. In the latter case, the I-O processor may operate in the selector or burst mode (where a single fast device has the exclusive use of the I-O processor at any one time) or in the multiplexor mode (where several slower devices *time-share* the I-O processor).

The highest priority is given to the processor for which timing is most critical. For an I-O processor and a main processor, the I-O processor generally has deadlines to meet but the main processor does not. Thus, the I-O processor is given higher priority.

Communication between the main processor and the I-O processor typically proceeds as follows:

1. The starting location (or data address) and size of the data block or *buffer* in main memory and perhaps the number of the I-O device (device address) are typically placed by the main processor program in preassigned locations in main memory to be used by the I-O processor.

2. The main processor sends a "start" signal to the I-O processor, and the I-O processor sends a "finished" signal to the main processor at the appropriate times.

Typically, there is a *start I-O* machine instruction in the main processor which sends the start signal to the I-O processor. The I-O processor recognizes this instruction as a signal to start. The *finished* signal from the I-O processor typically is placed on the main processor interrupt line and causes an interrupt in the main processor. To perform an I-O operation, the programmer places the information required by the I-O processor in memory and issues the "start I-O" instruction. Then the program may do other things or just wait. When the I-O operation is finished, an interrupt occurs. The programmer has the choice of handling the interrupt when it occurs or of *masking* it and checking periodically to see whether it has occurred (with a *read I-O status* machine instruction, for example).

Although the I-O processor is often a special-purpose computer, the job can be and often is done by general-purpose computers. For example, IBM markets *I-O channels* which are special-purpose machines, but some customers use smaller general-purpose machines to do the same job. The Intel 8086 is used sometimes as an I-O processor, but Intel also makes another microprocessor chip, the 8089, especially designed as an I-O processor.

Figure 4.1 attempts to put this section in perspective by showing in more detail what we mean by Figure 1.1(c). What was labeled simply "slow storage" in Figure 1.1(c) refers to the combination of an I-O processor that accesses main memory and the disk, drum, or tape storage device that it controls. Both the main processor and the I-O processor actually communicate with the fast main memory via the bus. No data are sent directly from the main processor to the I-O processor or vice versa—the actual data coming from the slow storage devices are put in main memory by the I-O processor, and data going to the storage devices is taken from the main memory by the I-O processor. Communication directly between the main processor and the I-O processor is limited to instructions and status; these signals typically are carried by control-signal lines on the bus.

If a system serves only one user at a time, as do most microcomputer systems, the machine instructions that cause I-O operations are available

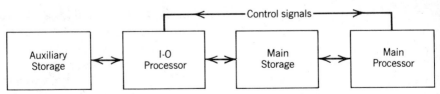

Figure 4.1 Processor-I-O Interface Showing I-O Processor.

to the user writing in assembly language. Standard system I-O procedures that can be called using ordinary procedure calls or assembly language macros usually are also available. In multiprogrammed systems, where several programs use the computer simultaneously, the operating system must make sure that only one program uses one I-O device at one time, so that I-O operations from different programs do not interfere with each other. This I-O management is an integral part of the system I-O procedures. In this case, the ordinary assembly language programmer is prohibited from using the actual machine instructions and instead must use the system I-O procedures that typically include ones to start an I-O operation and to recognize (wait for or test for) an interrupt.

For a general description of I-O processor architecture, see [E1]. Machine language manuals provided by computer manufacturers should be consulted for programming details. Textbooks providing such details include [E10-E13]. As one example, we discuss IBM channel programming in the next section. Appendix G provides another example, showing very simplified assembly language programs for a hypothetical I-O processor using an Intel 8085 as the main processor. Section 4.6 discusses how an I-O processor can be used to do I-O and processing simultaneously.

4.5. IBM 370 CHANNEL PROGRAMMING

The IBM 370 series of machines (as well as some of its predecessors and successors) have four machine-language I-O instructions: *SIO, HIO, TIO,* and *TCH*. In these instructions, the address portion specifies a device number, as well as the channel (I-O processor) by which the device is to be accessed.

SIO (start I-O) initiates an input or output on the designated device.

TIO (test I-O) and TCH (test channel) test the status of the designated device or channel, respectively.

HIO (halt I-O) terminates an input or output operation, if it has not already terminated.

The SIO instruction sends a signal to the I-O processor (or channel) requesting that it read or write data or initiate other device-dependent "control" operations. Some examples of control operations are listed in Table 4.1. The SIO instruction does not specify file parameters (e.g., number of bytes to be read or written, main memory address of data to be read or written, track and sector number for direct-address devices, or even whether data are to be read or written). These parameters are specified in an I-O processor program, called a *channel program*, and made up of a list of channel command words (CCWs) in the main memory. Each CCW contains a command type (get, put, or the control operation) and the associated parameters. Prior to executing the SIO instruction,

Table 4.1 Examples of IBM 370 Channel Commands

Device	Command Type
Card Reader	Read
	Control (Select stacker)
	Control (Feed w/o reading)
Line Printer	Write, No space
	Write, Space after printing
	Control (Double space)
	Control (Skip to top of page)
Magnetic Tape	Read
	Write
	Control (Rewind)
	Control (Write tape mark)
	Control (Set density)
Disk	Read
	Write
	Control (Seek)
	Control (Search)

the channel program must be placed in the main memory and its starting address must be loaded into a special register called the CAW. The main-processor SIO instruction causes the I-O processor to start, and then the I-O processor executes the CCWs sequentially until the command EOCP (end of channel program) is encountered. (Actually EOCP is not a separate command, but is instead a flag set in the last CCW of a channel program that marks the end of the list of commands.)

The following is an example of a channel program (shown symbolically):

```
READ  A,50
READ  B,30
EOCP
```

This reads from the device identified in the SIO instruction that initiated this program. It reads two blocks, the first consisting of 50 bytes read into main memory starting at data address A, and the second consisting of 30 bytes read into main memory starting at data address B. It is possible to flag the first read command to cause the program to "chain" the data

```
READ(C)  A,50
READ     B,30
EOCP
```

so that it will read a single 30-byte block, transferring the first 50-byte field to A and the next 30 bytes to B.

Following the execution of the SIO instruction, a *condition code* flag is set to indicate whether the channel program was successfully started. If the channel does not start successfully, it immediately stores information on what went wrong in a special register called the channel status word (CSW). If the channel starts successfully, the TIO instruction may be used at any later time to determine whether the channel program has terminated. When the channel program terminates, information about any exceptional conditions that arose (e.g., incorrect length of block or end-of-file) is stored in the CSW. There are also channel commands that permit conditional branches within a channel program; this permits the I-O processor and the main processor to operate more independently.

In Section 2.3, we noted that a read-tape command reads data until a gap is reached. The tape cannot stop in the middle of a block, and additional commands are required to read additional blocks. If the block read is not exactly the same length as specified in the channel command, the device signals an error. If less data is requested than exists in the block, the excess is lost. If more data is requested, then the buffer is simply not filled completely. (This is analogous to the situation for card input.) One consequence of this hardware characteristic is that when reading blocks of variable (and hence unknown) length, some maximum length must be requested in the channel command. If the block actually read has less than the maximum amount of data, then the device signals an error condition that may be ignored. If the block has more than the requested amount of data, then the excess is lost and an error message to the effect that there is a block larger than the specified maximum size should be reported by the program.

4.6. SIMPLE INPUT BUFFERING

Very commonly a computer program repeatedly reads one or more records, does some processing, and then writes one or more records. Simultaneous reading, computing, and writing then can be implemented as follows: simultaneously with the processing of one step by the main processor, the output records for the previous step are written and the input records for the next step are read by I-O processors. This technique, which is explained in more detail in the following paragraphs, is called *buffering*. It can be used also with processing and reading only or processing and writing only. It is ordinarily used with sequential files, but also can be used effectively with random access systems, if it is possible to predict before doing the processing for one step what record will be needed in the next step. Prediction is possible, for example, if the transactions for an on-line system are queued. Buffering for sequential files is usually provided as one operating system service. For random access files, it is not usually provided with the operating system—it can be programmed if the programming language includes concurrent processing facilities.

Let us consider a simple case with input and processing. Let us assume a file of 10,000 records on tape and that the computer repeatedly reads a record and does some processing. Let us assume that the system uses an I-O processor to do the reading. The main program written by the user might look something like this:

```
open input file;
repeat
      read input file (into work area);
      process record;
      until end-of-file;
```

In the unbuffered case, the **open** statement would call (or more accurately would be translated by the compiler into a call to) a system procedure to "open" the file, that is, to find the file and set up the necessary information needed to read the file. The **read** statement would call a system procedure that would do the actual reading. Without buffering, this read routine would do the following (although it would be written in an assembly language or some system programming language):

```
set the data address used by the I-O processor
      to point to the work area;
start the I-O processor;
wait until the I-O processor completes its read;
return to main program.
```

With this arrangement, the main processor must wait during the entire time the I-O processor is running, and the total elapsed time is equal to the time required to read plus the time required to process.

Now let us consider how to program simple buffering as described previously. The program written by the user is exactly the same as in the unbuffered case, but the system procedures for opening the file and reading must be modified. There also must be a procedure—we will call it **reader**—that reads data into a *buffer*, a main memory area which is set apart from the input record work area. This procedure must do the following in this very simple case:

```
reader procedure:
      set buffer flag false (indicating record not ready);
      place parameters (data address, byte count, etc.) in
            memory in predetermined place;
      if no more data in file, set end-of-file flag true
      else give start I-O commmand (to start I-O processor).
```

The data address is that of the buffer. The buffer flag is set to false to indicate that the data record has not yet been read. The instructions that set the buffer flag to true when the I-O processor finishes and cause the main-processor interrupt also might be considered part of the **reader** procedure:

```
interrupt procedure: {executed when I-O processor
         causes interrupt}
     set buffer flag true {indicating record ready}.
```

In addition, the **open** procedure must do the following:

```
open procedure:
     locate file {using directory} and initialize tables;
     set end-of-file flag false;
     call reader procedure {to read first record}.
```

Finally, the **read** procedure, called when the main program **read** statement is executed, now does the following:

```
read procedure:
     while buffer flag is false, wait;
     move data from buffer to work area;
     call reader procedure {to read next record}.
```

Note that calling the **read** procedure does not cause the desired record to be read. That record has already been read or is being read. The **read** procedure merely moves it to the place in main memory where it will be used. It also initiates reading the next record that will be needed.

In a practical system, the **reader** procedure would be much more complicated. It might handle several input devices and more than one I-O processor. The buffering system might be more complicated, and the **reader** procedure probably would queue requests for input and keep track of which buffers are full and which empty. Also, in a practical system, the **read** procedure would handle unblocking of records. That is, if records are blocked, it would move one record at a time from the buffer to the program's input record work area; when the buffer becomes empty, it would call the **reader** procedure to read the next block.

There are three possible conditions that may occur at the beginning of the execution of the **read** procedure:

(a) the I-O processor may have finished at precisely the moment when it is checked by the main processor, or

(b) the I-O processor may have finished and be waiting, or

(c) the I-O processor may not be finished, in which case the main processor must wait.

Cases (b) and (c) are illustrated in Figure 4.2. The cross-hatched areas represent waiting. Which case occurs depends on whether it takes more time to read a record or to process a record. In general, the main processor must wait for the first record before processing it. After that, if processing

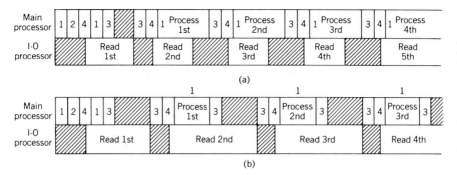

Key: 1, main program; 2, open procedure; 3, read procedure; 4, reader

Figure 4.2 Complete Timing Diagram for Input Buffering. (*a*) I-O processor must wait for main processor; (*b*) Main processor must wait for I-O processor.

a record takes long enough, the I-O processor will finish before the main processor checks its status; on the other hand, if processing takes a short enough time, the main processor will finish first and have to wait for the I-O processor. Even in the latter case, a short wait is shown for the I-O processor—this is the time interval between the time when the main processor checks the status of the buffer and time when it starts the I-O processor again; it includes the time required to move the data from the buffer to the input record work area.

Generally, the processor times required by the **open**, **read**, and **reader** procedures are small. If we assume that these times are negligible, then the timing diagrams simplify to become those shown in Figure 4.3. For clarity we will use these simplified diagrams in the following analyses. The fastest tape units have a start time of a few milliseconds; with the fastest disk units, an I-O operation ordinarily would require a similar

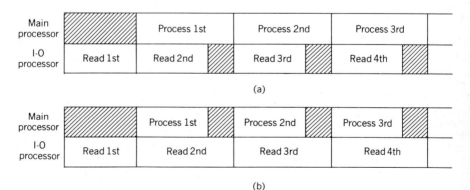

Figure 4.3 Simplified Timing Diagram for Input Buffering. (*a*) I-O processor must wait for main processor; (*b*) Main processor must wait for I-O processor.

amount of time, whereas the **read** procedure normally should not require more than a few hundred instructions and therefore only a fraction of a millisecond. The exception is that moving data from the buffer to the work area may require time that is a substantial fraction of the time required to read from very fast disk or tape units. This is discussed at the end of this chapter. Even then the following analyses will be quite accurate if the times required by the **read** and **reader** procedures are included as part of the *processing time* for each record.

Now let us again assume an unblocked file of 10,000 records (on tape) and that the time to read one record is 0.020 sec. Let us assume that each record requires 0.020 sec of computer processing, and that the computer repeatedly reads a record and then processes it. Without buffering, the time required to do the job would be $10,000 \times (0.020 + 0.020) = 400$ sec, or 6 min 40 sec. The timing is shown diagrammatically in Figure 4.4(a).

With input buffering, while the computer is processing one record, it reads the next record. Before the computing starts on a given record, it must be entirely in the memory, because it is not possible to process a record while reading it. Therefore, the first record is read into the buffer, copied from there into the work area, and processed. While the first record is being processed, the second record is read into the buffer. When processing of the first record is finished, the second record is copied from the buffer into the work area and processed, and simultaneously the third record is read into the buffer. With this scheme, 0.02 sec is required to read the first record plus 9999×0.02 sec to process records 1 to 9999 while simultaneously reading records 2 to 10,000, respectively, plus 0.02 sec to process the last record. The total is only 200.02 sec. The timing is shown diagrammatically in Figure 4.4(b).

With the same assumptions about the tape, that is, a read time of 0.020 seconds per record, if the processing time is 0.002 sec, the total time is $10,000 \times 0.02 = 200$ sec to read all the records, plus 0.002 sec to process the last record, because after the processing is finished on one record, the processor would have to wait until the next record is completely in the memory and ready to process. See Figure 4.4(c).

On the other hand, if the processing time is, say, 0.03 seconds per record, then reading always is completed first and the tape unit must wait for the processing to finish before reading the next record. The time becomes 0.02 sec to read the first record, plus $10,000 \times 0.03$ sec to process all the records for a total of 300.02 sec. This case is shown in Figure 4.4(d). In general, except for the first read and last processing, the time per record is the greater of the read time and the processing time. The percentage improvement with buffering is greatest (50%) if the read time and processing time are equal. If either one is negligible compared to the other, buffering gives negligible improvement in overall time.

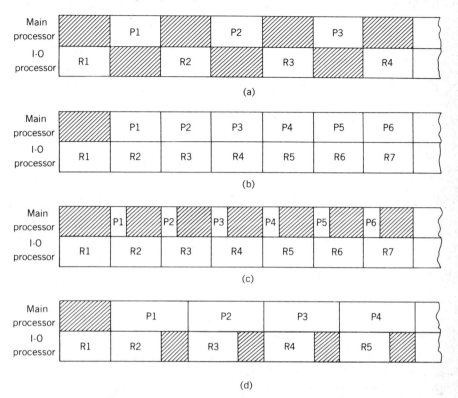

Figure 4.4 Input Buffering Timing Examples. (*a*) No buffering, read time = processing time = 20 msec; (*b*) Read time = processing time = 20msec; (*c*) Read time = 20 msec, processing time = 2 msec; (*d*) Read time = 20 msec; processing time = 30 msec.

4.7. SIMPLE OUTPUT BUFFERING AND MULTIPLE BUFFERING

Buffering can be used with writing equally well. Without buffering, after a record is ready to write, the processor must wait until the record is physically written before continuing processing because the main memory work area occupied by that record must not be changed. With simple output buffering, the record is copied to a buffer and written from there. That leaves the work area free, and processing can continue simultaneously. The programming is similar to that for input.

```
main program:
    open output file;
    repeat
        process record;
        write output file (from work area);
```

```
        until processing is finished;
    close output file.
```

open procedure:
```
    locate file {using directory} and initialize tables;
    set buffer flag true.
```

write procedure {*called when write statement*
    is executed}:
```
    while buffer flag is false, wait;
    move data from work area to buffer;
    call writer procedure.
```

interrupt procedure: {*executed when I-O processor*
    causes interrupt, upon completion of write operation};
```
    set buffer flag true {indicating buffer empty and
        ready for more data}.
```

writer procedure:
```
    set buffer flag false {indicating buffer is in use};
    place parameters {data address, byte count, etc.} in
        memory in predetermined place;
    give start I-O commmand {to start I-O processor}.
```

The **close** procedure must wait if necessary for the last record to be written and then append an end-of-file record to the output file. The timing relations are shown in Figure 4.5.

There are a number of variations to the very simple buffering described so far. In some cases the computer will read several, say, n, records, process them together, then read n records again, and so on. Alternatively, it may process and put out n records (e.g., n printed lines), process again, then put out n records, and so on. In this case, buffering as described above will not be of much help. However, if we have n buffers, each of which can hold a record (in addition to space in the main memory work area for the n records being processed), then while processing the first n records we can read the next n records into the buffers. Similarly on writing, while we are writing the first n records we can continue processing to produce the next n records. Such a system is called *multiple buffering*. (The simple buffering case where $n = 1$ is also called *single buffering*.)

Examples of timing charts for multiple buffering with $n = 2$ buffers (also called "double" buffering) are shown in Figure 4.6. Figure 4.6(a) corresponds to a main program like this:

```
open input file;
repeat
    read first record;
    read second record;
    process records;
    until end-of-file;
```

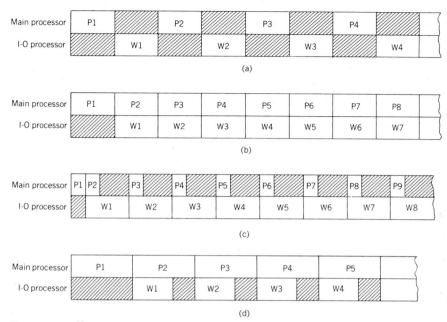

Figure 4.5 Timing for Simple Output Buffering. (*a*) No buffering, processing time = write time = 20 msec; (*b*) Write time = processing time = 20 msec; (*c*) Write time = 20 msec, processing time = 2 msec; (*d*) Write time = 20 msec; processing time = 30 msec.

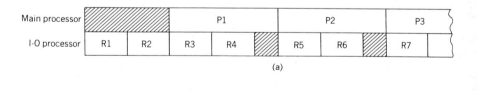

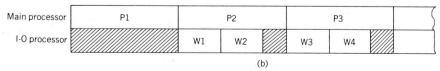

Figure 4.6 Timing for Double Buffering. (*a*) Double buffering with read—Each processing requires two records; read time = 20 msec; processing time = 50 msec; (*b*) Double buffering with write—Each processing produces two records; processing time = 50 msec; write time = 20 msec.

When the file is opened, the first two records in the file would be read into the two buffers. When the first **read** statement occurs, the first record would be moved to the work area, after which reading the third record into the first buffer would be requested and initiated. When the second **read** statement is executed, the record in the second buffer would be moved into the work area, after which reading the next record into the buffer would be requested. Thus, while the two records in the work area are being processed, the next two records may be read into the two buffers. Then the procedure would repeat.

Figure 4.6(b) corresponds to double buffering with output, for which the main program might look like this:

```
open output file;
repeat
     process records;
     write a record;
     write a record;
     until processing is finished;
close output file.
```

When the file is opened, the two buffers would be made available. When the first **write** statement is executed, the record would be moved to the first buffer and writing would be requested and initiated. When the second **write** statement in the main program is executed, the second record would be moved to the second buffer and a request to write it would be made. Then processing can continue while these two records are being written and the procedure would repeat.

Up to this point we have assumed only one input or output device. If there are two I-O devices, then one must consider whether or not they share the same I-O processor. (If there are more than two, then there are more possibilities but the principles are the same.) Generally, only one fast I-O device like tape or disk can use one I-O processor at one time, and this affects the running time for a program.

For example, suppose a program repeatedly reads, processes, and then writes. Suppose reading and writing each take 0.020 sec and processing takes 0.030 sec. If the input and output are on a single I-O processor, then reading and writing cannot occur simultaneously, and for each record, 0.040 sec of I-O processor time and 0.030 sec of computational processing are required. I-O will be overlapped with computational processing because of buffering; the actual elapsed time per record is 0.040 sec. If input and output are on separate I-O processors, then input, output, and processing all can be done simultaneously, and the input and output both will be overlapped with processing so that only 0.030 sec per record are required. The timing relationships are illustrated in Figure 4.7. (The precise order of reading and writing in the single I-O processor case

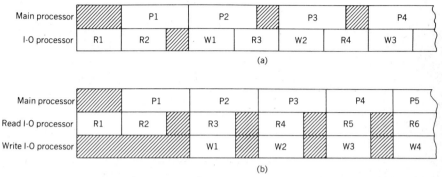

Figure 4.7 Buffering both Input and Output. (*a*) One I-O processor for both read and write; (*b*) Separate I-O processors for read and write.

depends on the order in which requests for I-O are given and queued. For example, Figure 4.7(a) assumes that, after the processing of record n is finished, the request to write record n precedes the request to read record $n + 2$.)

Up to this point we have assumed that the buffer is distinct from the work area used by the program. On input, the information is read into the read buffer, moved from the read buffer to the input work area, and then processed. On output, after processing, the information is moved from the output work area used by the program to the buffer and it is written from there. This is called the *move mode* of buffering. Moving every record between the buffer and the area where it is used requires processor time; the amount required is a very significant fraction of the total time in some cases.

This moving of records can be avoided by a buffering method called *locate mode*. On input, the program uses the same memory area into which the records are read. The simplest case of locate-mode buffering requires two buffers but no separate input work area. The first record is read into the first buffer and processed there. While it is being processed, the second record is read into the second buffer. While the second record is processed in the second buffer, the third record is read into the first buffer, which is now free, etc. Output buffering can be done similarly. Since the program uses the record in the buffer area, but not always in the same place, the program must "locate" the record and reference it using some kind of pointer, hence the term *locate mode*. Versions of it are also known as the *exchange mode* of buffering or *buffer switching*.

Locate mode buffering can be implemented most simply by allocating to each file its own set of buffers, and keeping pointers to the buffer to be processed next and the buffer to be read into or written from next. In this case, the buffers are usually considered a part of the program workspace; the program must pass the location of the buffer to be used to the read or write procedure. This is the usual case with COBOL.

A more general form of buffering can be implemented by having a common pool of buffers for all files and programs, and dynamically allocating buffers in any fashion as needed, for example, as an input buffer for one file, an output buffer for another file, a processing area for one program, or a processing area for another program. In this case, the *buffer pool* is usually considered a part of the operating system. On input, the system read procedure must provide the program with the location of the buffer into which the data has been read. On an output operation, the program must get the location of the buffer from the system before assembling the data to be written, for example, by calling a procedure whose purpose is to assign a buffer for output. The IBM implementation of PL/I handles locate-mode buffering this way.

There is an interesting side-effect that may occur with locate-mode buffering on output. Certain information such as alphanumeric labels on printed output may remain the same for successive records. With move-mode buffering, it suffices to insert this information into the output work record once, since there is only one work record. With locate-mode buffering, inserting it for the first record puts it in the first buffer, but not the second. One must insert the information at least as many successive times as there are buffers; in the case of dynamic allocation of buffers, the information must be inserted every time! This also accounts for some unexpected output if buffers are not cleared before reuse.

For more detailed accounts of buffering techniques, see [J5] and [F5].

4.8. BLOCKING AND BUFFERING WITH TAPES

It is possible to do both blocking and buffering. Each buffer area in the memory must be large enough for reading or writing a whole block. Move-mode input buffering with blocking requires one or more buffers into which blocks are read and a single input work area into which single records are copied for processing. Similarly, move-mode output buffering would have a single output work area where each record is assembled, and one or more buffers into which assembled records are copied, to be written as a block when a buffer is full. With locate-mode buffering and blocking, two or more buffers (but no work area for record processing) are needed.

The fact that blocks of several records are read or written results in partial buffering—it is not necessary to read each time a single record is needed. It is frequently worth considering actual timing details in a given application.

The result of using blocking and buffering together is essentially the same as without blocking. Except for the details at the beginning and end of the file, I-O time and processing time are overlapped, and the total time required is, except for end effects, either the I-O time or the processing time, whichever is greater. It is worthwhile understanding the details of what occurs. The following example illustrates these details and how to analyze them.

Example 4.1

Let us assume a program that repeatedly reads, processes, and writes records. Let us assume that both the input file and output file are blocked three records per block. Let us assume that there are two buffers each for the input file and the output file. We will consider the details of what occurs with one or two I-O processors, and move-mode and locate-mode buffering.

The program will look something like this:

```
open input file and output file;
repeat
   read input file;
   process input record, making output record;
   write output record
   until end-of-file;
close input file and output file.
```

The **read** statement in the program requests one record. Of course, the operating system read procedure does not read single records. When the **read** statement is executed, it obtains a record from a block usually already read and available for processing.

Let us consider the details for the case of a single I-O processor with move-mode buffering. First let us consider the sequence in which requests occur. At the time the file is opened, requests to read blocks 1 and 2 will be made to fill the two input buffers. As soon as block 1 is read, processing can start. The first execution of the read statement in the program causes one record to be moved to the work area. The first write causes the first output record to be moved to the first output buffer. The next read causes the second record to be moved from the first input buffer to the work area. The second write causes the second output record to be moved to the first output buffer. The third read causes the third input record to be moved to the work area, and because that empties the first input buffer, a request is issued to fill it again, that is, to read block 3. The third write causes the third output record to be moved to the first output buffer. The output buffer is then full, and a request is issued to write that buffer to the output file.

Then this pattern repeats. Thus, the requests occur in the following order:

REQUEST:	MADE WHEN:
read block 1;	open statement is executed
read block 2;	open statement is executed
read block 3;	last record in block 1 is moved to work area
write block 1;	last record in input block 1 is finished processing and output record is moved to output buffer, filling it
read block 4;	last record in block 2 is moved to work area
write block 2;	second output block fills
etc.	

In order to make a timing diagram, we have to know a few additional facts. Let us assume that the I-O processor services I-O requests in the order in which they are received, that is, with simple queuing of requests. We also observe that the main processor may have to wait because (1) a record cannot be moved to the input work area and processed until the block containing that record has been read into a buffer, and (2) a record cannot be moved to the output buffer if no output buffer space is available. A timing diagram for these conditions is shown in Figure 4.8(a). In the diagram, we have assumed that the time to read a block is twice the time to process one record or two-thirds the time to process a block. Processing record 1 cannot start until block 1 has been read. The next time that waiting occurs is after processing record 13—the output should go into block 5, which should be assembled in the first buffer, but that buffer is not available because it still contains records 7, 8, and 9, that is, block 3, which is currently being written. (The other buffer already has records 10, 11, and 12, that is, block 4, in it.) Thereafter, this pattern repeats, with the main processor doing three records and waiting while the I-O processor reads one block and writes another.

Now let us assume one I-O processor again, but with locate-mode buffering. The difference will be that the record is processed in place in the buffer; therefore, the system must regard the buffer as in use until a record is requested that is in a different block. Thus, buffer 1 containing block 1 is in use until record 4, which is in block 2 and buffer 2, is requested by the program. Buffer 2 containing block 2 is in use while records 4, 5, and 6 are being processed and the system must regard it as in use until the program requests record 7. Thus, the sequence of I-O requests is:

REQUEST:	MADE WHEN:
read block 1;	open statement is executed
read block 2;	open statement is executed

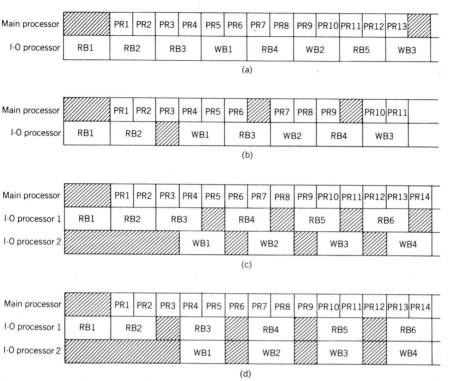

Figure 4.8 Timing with Blocking and Buffering. (*a*) One I-O processor, move mode buffering; (*b*) One I-O processor, locate mode buffering; (*c*) Two I-O processors, move mode buffering; (*d*) Two I-O processors, locate mode buffering.

write block 1;   last record in first block is finished processing, and the output records fill buffer

read block 3;   read statement occurs for first record in second block (so we know previous record is no longer needed)

write block 2;   last record in second block is finished processing

read block 4;   read statement occurs for first record in third block

etc.

The timing diagram is shown in Figure 4.8(b). After reading block 2, the I-O processor must wait because the I-O request for block 3 does not occur until the program requests record 4 thereby freeing the first buffer for reuse. Prior to this, the first three output records go into the output buffer and a request is made to write it, so block 1 is written before block 3 is read. It turns out that when a request is made for record 7, block 3, which contains it, is not yet completely read and hence not available. Therefore the processor must wait. After that the pattern of processing three records and waiting while simultaneously writing and reading a block repeats until the last block is read. There is some minor variation at the end similar to the beginning. In this example, additional processor waiting is required using the locate mode because the move mode utilizes an additonal storage area (the work record) that in effect serves as an extra buffer. The locate mode with three buffers would result in no processor waiting at all.

If there are two I-O processors, the diagrams are simpler. The diagram for move-mode buffering is shown in Figure 4.8(c) and for locate mode buffering in Figure 4.8(d). Note that for move-mode buffering, the read request can occur when the last record in a block is "read" by the main program, while in the locate-mode case, the read request occurs when the first main-program "read" in the next block occurs—otherwise, these diagrams are the same. In both cases, the processor never waits (except for the first block).

Sometimes the question is asked, which is more effective, blocking or buffering? The answer is that they are not comparable. Blocking increases the efficiency of input or output and decreases the time required. Buffering allows processing and input and/or output to occur simultaneously. The effects must be evaluated in each application. In general, however, the following observations hold:

1. If I-O time is small compared to processing time, neither blocking nor buffering will have more than a small or negligible effect on the total time to run the program.

2. If the processing time is small or negligible compared to I-O time, then buffering will have no more than a small or negligible effect. Blocking, by decreasing I-O time, may have a large effect in this case.

3. If processing time is comparable to I-O time, then there exists at least the possibility of overlapping I-O time with processing time by buffering, which may decrease the total time by as much as 50%. If a complete overlap is achieved by buffering, no further decrease is possible and, in particular, blocking will not help.

4. If I-O time exceeds processing time, then blocking, to decrease I-O time, and buffering, to overlap processing and I-O, may both contribute in an important way.

5. Even if blocking does not decrease running time, it may be desirable because it decreases the amount of file storage required. On the other hand, both blocking and buffering require extra main memory.

4.9. BLOCKING AND BUFFERING WITH DISKS

Now let us consider some further examples of timing with disk units. First let us consider an example without buffering.

Example 4.2

Suppose we have a file of 3000 blocks of 1000 characters each written on an IBM 2305. From Example 3.5 we determined that there will be 12 blocks per track, so the file will require 250 tracks. Let us assume we read a block, do 0.5 msec of processing, then read the next block, process again, etc. How long will it take? To wait for the first block requires on the average ½ revolution or 5 msec, and to read it requires $\frac{1}{12}$ revolution. After processing the first block, the second block has passed the read head by 0.5 msec or $\frac{1}{20}$ revolution, and a latency time of $\frac{19}{20}$ revolution or 9.5 msec is required to bring the disk back to the beginning of the next record. This is shown in Figure 4.9. (In the figure, R1 means "read block 1" and P1 "process block 1.")

For the first block we require an average of 5 msec latency time, 0.833 msec to read, and 0.5 msec to process. Each succeeding block will require exactly 9.5 msec latency time, 0.833 msec to read, and 0.5 msec to process. The total will be

$$5 + 0.833 + 2999 \times (9.5 + 0.833 + 0.5) + 0.5 = 32{,}494.5 \text{ msec}$$

or about 32.5 sec.

Another way to look at this is after the initial latency and read, each additional read will finish $1\frac{1}{12}$ revolutions later. At the end, 0.5 msec processing is still needed. This gives

$$5 + 0.833 + 2999 \times 10.833 + 0.5 = 32{,}494.5 \text{ msec}$$

which is the same as before.

Suppose instead, we process blocks 1, 3, 5,..., 2999, then 2, 4, 6,..., 3000. First, there will be the unpredictable latency time averaging 5 msec. After the first block is read, the processing is done and will finish while block 2 is passing the read head. Block 3 will be ready to read $\frac{1}{12}$ revolution after block 1 finished reading. Processing plus latency time will be $\frac{1}{12}$ revolution between blocks (except between block 2999 and block 2, where it is $\frac{1}{6}$ revolution). It is not difficult to see that six blocks are read on each revolution. From the beginning of the reading of the first block to the end of reading the last is precisely 500 revolutions. Before that, there is the 5 msec average latency time and after that 0.5 msec to process the last block, a total of 5005.5 msec, slightly more than 5 sec, or more than six times faster.

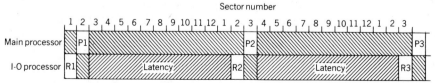

Figure 4.9 Disk I-O with Processing Time.

Microcomputers commonly use no buffering, sacrificing speed to save memory space and complexity. It is also common to arrange data on the file so that in normal processing every nth block or sector is used, where n is an integer chosen to minimize average latency. This is referred to as *sector interleaving* with *offset n*.

Each sector on a disk has a header that includes an identification field that usually contains the cylinder number, the track number within the cylinder, and the sector number. On input or output, as soon as a seek is completed, the system reads data from the track, searching for a header that has the desired sector number. (The cylinder and track numbers are used only for checking.) The sectors may or may not be arranged physically in sequence by their sector numbers. In either case, we will refer to the sector number written in the header as the physical sector number. Then there are two ways of accomplishing sector interleaving.

The sectors may be arranged physically on the disk in sequence by their *physical sector number*, that is, so that successive physical sectors are adjacent to each other. Then a *logical sector number* may be associated with each physical sector number in such a way that successive logical sectors are spaced n sectors apart physically on the disk. For a track with ten sectors and offset $n = 3$, the following arrangement would be used:

Case (a)

Physical position	1	2	3	4	5	6	7	8	9	10
Physical sector number	1	2	3	4	5	6	7	8	9	10
Logical sector number	1	4	7	10	3	6	9	2	5	8

Alternatively, the sectors may be arranged on the disk in such a way that sectors with successive physical sector numbers occur spaced n sectors apart physically. Then the physical sector number can be used as the logical sector number. For a track with ten sectors and offset $n = 3$, this could be achieved with the following arrangement:

Case (b)

Physical position	1	2	3	4	5	6	7	8	9	10
Physical sector number	1	8	5	2	9	6	3	10	7	4
Logical sector number	1	8	5	2	9	6	3	10	7	4

These arrangements work out perfectly if the number of sectors per track is relatively prime to the offset. Note that even the spacing between the last record read on one track and the first one on the next is three. When the number of sectors per track and the offset have common factors, this arrangement can be approximated. For example, if the number of sectors per track is 10 and the offset is 4, the following arrangements could be used:

Case (a)

Physical position	1	2	3	4	5	6	7	8	9	10
Logical sector number	1	2	3	4	5	6	7	8	9	10
Physical sector number	1	5	9	3	7	2	6	10	4	8

Case (b)

Physical position	1	2	3	4	5	6	7	8	9	10
Physical sector number	1	6	4	9	2	7	5	10	3	8

In the second case, the spacing between records on successive reads is $n = 4$, except between the fifth and sixth records read, where the spacing is 5, and between the last record on one track and the first on the next, where the spacing is 3.

Now let us consider buffering. The basic concepts apply to disks as well as to tape. If the read or write time exceeds processing time, all processing except the last block can be overlapped with I-O just as with tape. However, reading or writing cannot be started at just any time but depends on the rotational position of the disk, which complicates the situation where processing time exceeds the I-O time.

Example 4.3

Suppose that we are using the IBM 2305, with a total of 1000 blocks written 5 blocks per track so that reading one block takes 2 msec. Suppose that the processing time is less than or equal to the read time. If the first block is processed while the second is being read, the second processed while the third is being read, etc., the whole job requires (1) the 5 msec initial average latency, (2) 200 revolutions to read through the 200 tracks of file, and (3) 0.5 msec to process the last block, a total of 2005.5 msec or slightly over 2 sec. The situation is very similar to blocking with tape.

Now suppose that processing time per block is 3 msec per block, which exceeds the read time. For the corresponding problem with tapes, all reading is overlapped with processing, and after reading the first block, exactly 3 msec total would be required for each block. With the disk, it is not that simple. Assume simple move-mode buffering with a single buffer (or, equivalently, locate-mode buffering with two buffers). The first block is read into the buffer (and moved into the work area for processing). While it is being processed, the second block is read. Until processing finishes on the first block, no buffer is available and the third block cannot be read on this revolution. There is a latency time delay until the third block comes around on the second revolution. This is shown in Figure 4.10. Except for the initial 5 msec latency and the last two blocks, each pair of blocks requires 1.4 revolutions. We must add to that the time to read record

80 File Analysis and Design

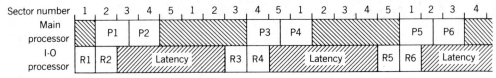

Figure 4.10 Simple Buffering with Disk.

999 and to process records 999 and 1000. (The reading of record 1000 will overlap the processing of record 999.) So the total is

$$5 + \frac{998}{2} \times 1.4 \times 10 + 2 + 2 \times 3 - 6999 \text{ msec}$$

or almost 7 sec, although the processing time is only 1000×3 msec = 3 sec.

Now let us consider what occurs for move-mode buffering with double buffers (or locate-mode buffering with three buffers). The timing is shown in Figure 4.11. Note that block 1 finishes processing before block 4 comes to the read head, which frees a buffer for block 4. Similarly, block 2 finishes processing just in time to allow reading block 5 on the first revolution, but block 3 does not finish in time to allow reading block 6—that must wait one revolution. The pattern repeats—five blocks are read on one revolution, then one revolution passes with no reading, and so on. The total time is the initial average 5 msec latency followed by $(995/5) \times 2$ revolutions of alternate reading and waiting, followed by 2 msec to read block 996 and 5×3 msec to process the last five blocks:

$$5 + \frac{995}{5} \times 2 \times 10 + 2 + 5 \times 3 = 4002 \text{ msec}$$

We note that, in the example, processor waiting can be reduced if additional buffers are used. There will be no processor waiting at all in the limiting case where there are as many buffers as blocks in the file, but this is unrealistic. Let us determine the minimum number of buffers n required to avoid processor waiting in the general case in which processing time per block exceeds read time per block (not counting seeks or latency).

Assuming move-mode buffering, there are n buffers in addition to the

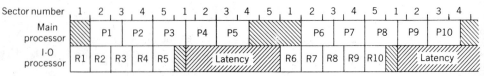

Figure 4.11 Double Buffering with Disk.

work area where a block is stored while it is being processed. (This means that $n+1$ block-size areas must be available.) Because processing is slower than reading, buffers will fill faster than they are used. Eventually the time will come when all the buffers are full and reading will be delayed after reading, say, the kth block. The next block cannot be read until (1) a buffer becomes available, and (2) the desired block comes back to the read head. There are two cases:

(a) If processing all the records in the buffers takes less time than one revolution plus the time to read the next block, then the processor will have to wait until after this read is finished.

(b) If processing all the records in the buffers takes longer than one revolution plus the time to read the next record, then the processor will not have to wait for reading.

We note that if processing time is too large—say, greater than one revolution—then more than one buffer will not be needed and, furthermore, reading the next block may be delayed for several revolutions; we will assume that processing time is less than the time for a revolution.

To see the exact requirements quantitatively, study the timing chart in Figure 4.12. A wait for a revolution is shown starting at point C, immediately after reading block k. Processing block k-n cannot be finished yet, because otherwise there would have been an available buffer, making waiting unnecessary. On the other hand, processing the previous block must have finished before point B, where reading block k started, because otherwise there would have been no buffer available for block k. The time from point C to point E is one revolution plus the time to read one record. Let us denote by e the time between point C and point D. Then the time between point C and point F, where block k finishes processing, is equal to the sum of e and the time to process n blocks. If point F occurs after point E, then the processor would not have to wait. On the other hand, if point F occurs before point E, then the processor will have to wait from point F to point E, which we can calculate by subtracting the time from point C to point F from the time from C to E.

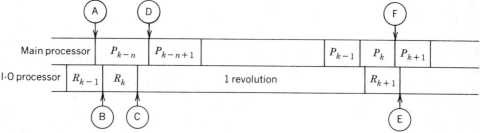

Figure 4.12 General Timing for Disk Buffering.

To obtain a formula, let us let

n = number of (move-mode) buffers
p = time to process one block
m = number of equal sized blocks per track
r = time per revolution

The time to read a block is r/m, which we have assumed is less than p. The time from C to E is $r + r/m$. The time from C to F is $e + np$. Therefore, the processor waiting time is

$$t_{wait} = r + \frac{r}{m} - np - e \quad \text{or} \quad 0$$

whichever is greater.

All the quantities in this formula are known except e. Even so, this gives a fairly close estimate of t_{wait}, because e is generally quite small. In fact, we know that point A precedes or coincides with B, and C precedes D, and from this and the fact that the time from A to D is p and the time from B to C is r/m, we can see that

$$0 < e \leq \left(p - \frac{r}{m} \right)$$

Using the lower bound for e we can derive an upper bound for t_{wait}, and using the upper bound for e, we can derive a lower bound for t_{wait}:

$$r + \frac{r}{m} - pn - \left(p - \frac{r}{m} \right) \leq t_{wait} < r + \frac{r}{m} - pn, \quad \text{or}$$

$$\left(\frac{r}{m} \right)(m + 2) - p(n + 1) \leq t_{wait} < \left(\frac{r}{m} \right)(m + 1) - pn \qquad (4.1)$$

and in addition, of course, $t_{wait} \geq 0$, so that if Eq. 4.1 indicates a negative value, the actual t_{wait} is zero. With this equation, we can derive the conditions that n must satisfy. If the right-hand side of Eq. 4.1 is zero or less, then processor waiting can be avoided; thus, a sufficient condition is

$$\left(\frac{r}{m} \right)(m + 1) - pn \leq 0 \quad \text{or} \quad n \geq \frac{r(m + 1)}{mp} \qquad (4.2)$$

On the other hand, if the left-side of Eq. 4.1 is greater than zero, then at least some processor waiting cannot be avoided; thus, a necessary condition is that

$$\left(\frac{r}{m} \right)(m + 2) - p(n + 1) \leq 0 \quad \text{or} \quad n \geq \left(\frac{r}{mp} \right)(m + 2) - 1 \qquad (4.3)$$

The right-hand sides of these two inequalities (4.2) and (4.3) differ by less than one, and in many cases, taking into account that n must be an integer, they determine completely the minimum value of n needed to eliminate processor waiting.

Example 4.3 (continued)

For this example, $p = 3$ msec, $r = 10$ msec, and $m = 5$ blocks per track. The value of $(m + 1)r/pm$ is 4, and so $n = 4$ suffices. The value of $(m + 2)r/pm - 1$ is $3\frac{2}{3}$; because n must exceed this, we know that $n = 3$ buffers will not suffice. These facts can be verified easily by making timing charts for these specific cases similar to Figure 4.11.

4.10. OTHER TOPICS

We have assumed in the preceding sections that I-O operations can be done simultaneously with processing. That is not completely true. Both must share the main storage. Generally, the processor utilizes the main storage continuously or very nearly continuously. When input or output is being done and a storage transfer is required, the channel uses the storage, generally for one storage cycle, and the processor waits. This is called *cycle stealing*. Generally, the processor time lost is small, but it may not be negligible. For example, a typical large computer may transfer 16 characters in a storage cycle of one microsecond. One 6250 cpi tape running at 200 ips transfers 1,250,000 characters per second while it is actually reading a block. On the average, it will need a storage cycle $1,250,000/16 = 78,125$ times per second. This amounts to 7.8% of the 1,000,000 storage cycles per second, and the processor will be slowed down 7.8% during reading or writing.

On the other hand, a 1600 cpi tape on a 75 ips machine transfers only 120,000 characters per second and requires a storage cycle only $120,000/16 = 7500$ times a second. Such a tape requires only 0.75% of the storage cycles and slows the processor only 0.75% during actual reading. If there are several I-O devices attached to several channels, then each slows down the main processor.

If any situation where the data rate is so great that cycle stealing requires a nonnegligible amount of time, then moving records from a buffer to a separate work area also will require a nonnegligible amount of time. In fact, moving data requires both a main storage read and a write. Thus, it will require at least twice as much time as cycle stealing for reading or writing. In this case, locate-mode buffering has a distinct advantage over move-mode buffering.

Up to this point, it has been tacitly assumed that if processing on a particular program must wait for an input or output operation, then the processor is idle and the time wasted. Modern large computer systems generally do multiprogramming. This means that there is more than one program in the memory at one time; while one is waiting for input or output, processing can proceed on another. Is there any point, then, in considering blocking and/or buffering? Blocking, of course, actually increases the efficiency of the input or output operations as well as saves space and will be beneficial generally. Buffering merely overlaps processing with input and output and thereby decreases the amount of time wasted by an idle processor. Multiprogramming also decreases idle processor time. If multiprogramming in a given situation eliminated all processor waiting time, then there is nothing to be gained by buffering. However, buffering can make it easier to eliminate processor waiting, as the following discussion will show.

Suppose we have several programs to run simultaneously. Each does repeatedly a 0.010 sec read operation, 0.005 sec of processing, and a 0.010 sec write. With no buffering, the processing would be running not more than 20% of the time on each program, and at least five such programs would have to be run simultaneously to use the processor 100% of the time. (In practice, the times probably would not mesh perfectly, and there would still be times when no program could make use of the processor.) Memory space for five programs would be needed, but with careful scheduling this could be done with four I-O processors.

If we buffer and use separate I-O processors for input and output, reading, writing, and processing could be overlapped. Each record would require a total of 0.010 sec, of which 50% is processing time. There exists the possibility, although again one could not expect to achieve it fully, of using 100% of the processor time with only two programs in memory. Four I-O processors are needed. Even though each program would require extra memory for buffers, the total memory required would be significantly less. Thus, one may conclude that buffering may be beneficial even in a multiprogramming environment, although it is difficult to evaluate precisely how beneficial.

For sequential file processing, the algorithm for buffering is quite straightforward. For read buffering, when the program starts, input data should be read into the first buffer and reading should continue as long as there are available buffers. If reading must be stopped because no buffers are available, it should be started again as soon as a buffer becomes free. On writing, as soon as a buffer becomes full and ready to write, writing should start and continue as long as any buffer is ready to write, stopping only when no buffer is full and ready to write.

Buffering and blocking for sequential file processing, being so well defined, are normally built into the I-O procedures provided with the operating system of a computer. The programmer may be required to furnish or have the option of furnishing the information passed to the I-O procedures, such as the record size, the block size, the number of buffers, the type of buffering (move-mode or locate-mode), and other details. At the assembly language level, the programmer can program buffering and blocking or elect to use the system I-O procedures. The blocking and buffering provided in the system I-O procedures also is available to the programmer who uses a higher-level language such as FORTRAN or COBOL. In fact, some reasonable buffering is generally provided by default if not specified by the programmer. Although blocking is simple in higher-level languages, buffering requires access to the read or write interrupts, which are not provided in most higher-level languages. Concurrent Pascal, Ada, C with UNIX, versions of PL/I including multitasking, and some systems implementation languages provide ways to initiate concurrent processes and can be used to implement buffering.

Example 3.7 showed an example of how buffering can be used with random access files. This underlying concept is the same as for buffering with sequential files, that is, processing continues on one record while another is being read. This is possible in any situation where you know while processing one record which record will be needed next. This occurs, for example, when there is a queue of requests. However, buffering programs for random access are not generally available in operating systems. Programmers must write such buffering procedures themselves, usually in assembly language or any language that handles concurrent processes.

NOTES

General discussions of computer architecture appear in [E1] and [E8]. Other books that describe I-O systems include [E3]–[E6]. Microcomputers are discussed in [E9]. IBM channel programming is briefly described in [E10] and [E11]. I-O programming examples for other computers appear in [E12] and [E13].

Buffering is covered in operating systems literature, such as [J2], [J4], and [J5]. Timing calculations for buffered I-O appear in [E11]. A statistical (queueing theoretic) treatment is given in [J6]. Processes that "produce" data for buffers can be executed concurrently with processes that "consume" the data. The programming of such buffering processes using coroutines is described in [F5]. Related synchronization problems are described in [K11]. An example of file updating using PL/I's multitasking facilities appears in [J3]. Other concurrent programming examples in Pascal and Ada appear in [K12].

EXERCISES

4-1. What would be the effect of executing the following magnetic tape channel program?

```
WRITE(C)     LOC,50
WRITE        LOC+50,50
```

4-2. A program must retrieve two consecutive data blocks from a magnetic drum storage device with a fixed recording element for each track. Consider the following two approaches:

(i) A channel program with two chained READ commands is used.

(ii) A channel program with a single READ is executed twice with enough of a delay between the two to necessitate an intervening revolution.

Assume the first (or only) SIO is executed when the recording element is ½ revolution from the beginning of the first desired block. Assume the rotational period of the drum is R msec and there are 10 fixed-length blocks per track.

(a) Determine the elapsed time for reading the two blocks using approach (i).

(b) Determine the elapsed time for reading the two blocks using approach (ii).

(c) For the two approaches, compare the channel programs and their respective calling CPU programs assuming the two data blocks will be *moved* to separate working storage areas. Be specific enough to show the actual channel commands, SIOs, and data move instructions.

4-3. Consider a simple program that reads, processes, reads, processes, etc. Assume this program loops N times, and that the read and processing times for each record equal 1 msec. (Ignore device characteristics.)

(a) Draw a timing chart for locate-mode buffering, assuming three system buffers.

(b) Draw a timing chart for move-mode buffering, assuming two system buffers and assuming move times are negligible.

(c) Draw a timing chart for move-mode buffering, assuming two system buffers and assuming move times equal ½ msec per record.

(d) For the three cases above, determine the completion time (i.e., the time between the start of the first read and the end of the last processing).

(e) Assuming a blocking factor of two so that the time required to read a block equals 2 msec, recalculate the completion time for case (a).

4-4. (a) Draw a timing chart illustrating the move mode of output buffering assuming two system output buffers and that the time required to write a record is twice its compute time, but the time required to move a record is half its compute time (hence is not negligible). (Be sure to indicate which buffer is being accessed in each compute or write block.)

(b) Draw a timing chart illustrating the locate mode of output buffering assuming *three* system output buffers and that the time required to compute a record is ¾ of its write time (and the time required to set pointers and flags is negligible).

4-5. (a) Draw a timing chart illustrating the move mode of input buffering assuming *three* system input buffers and that the CPU time required to process a record is 2½ times its read time (and that move times are negligible). (Be sure to indicate which buffer is being accessed in each read or compute block.)

(b) Draw a timing chart illustrating the locate mode of input buffering assuming four system input buffers, and that the CPU time required to process a record is 2½ times its read time (and the time required to set pointers and flags is negligible).

4-6. Determine how the locate mode of buffering is handled in computer systems available to you.

4-7. Assume a file of 2500 records on 6250 cpi tape with 1000 characters per record and 25 records per block. Assume a 200 ips tape drive with a start time of 2 msec. Assume that the program is written to read one record, do 1.5 msec of processing, and then write a record of the same format on another tape. How long will this take

(a) if no buffering is used?

(b) if buffering is used and there are two I-O processors, one for input, the other for output?

(c) if there is only one I-O processor, which must be shared by the input tape drive and the output tape drive, only one drive being able to use the I-O processor at one time?

4-8. Assume three blocks per track on an

IBM 3380 disk drive and a file that consists of 20 full cylinders. Assume that a program reads all the blocks in sequence with simple buffering. How long will it take to read and process the whole file

(a) if there is 5 msec of processing for each block?

(b) if there is 6 msec of processing for each block?

4-9. Assume a disk drive that runs at 3600 rpm and assume five blocks per track. Assume that the file exactly fills one cylinder. Assume that you read one randomly chosen block, do 10 msec of processing, then read another randomly chosen block, then do 10 msec of processing again, and so on.

(a) How long will this take with no buffering?

(b) How long will this take with simple buffering? (Assume that before you start processing one block, you know which one you need next, and you have programmed the computer to have the I-O processor reading the next block you will need while you are actually processing the current block. However, assume that the next block might be any block in the file, all blocks being considered equally likely. Note that 10 msec is exactly the time required for three blocks to pass by the read-write head.)

4-10. Assume a disk drive that runs at 3600 rpm and assume five blocks per track. Assume that the program repeatedly reads the next sequential block and then processes for 10 msec. How many buffers will you need to completely avoid waiting by the processor (except possibly when changing cylinders) after the first read? (Use the Eqs. 4.2 and 4.3. Draw a timing diagram to check your answer.)

4-11. Suppose the CPU time required to process a block is twice the data transfer time required to read it from a drum file.

(a) How many buffers are required to assure that processing never waits for rotational delay, according to Eqs. 4.2 and 4.3?

(Your answer should depend on the number of blocks per track.)

(b) If the number of blocks per track is odd, you should find that Eqs. 4.2 and 4.3 at the end of Section 4.9 give the same answer, but for an even number of blocks per track, the answers differ by one. By drawing a timing diagram, determine the actual number of buffers needed.

4-12. A CPU and a channel operate "independently" in the sense that the former can execute a CPU program while the latter executes a channel program. Execution of a CPU program is slowed when an unrelated channel program executes concurrently. Why?

4-13. *If you have a single-user computer such as a personal computer available:* Determine from the documentation for your computer as much as you can about the disk file system. Then devise experiments to determine additional facts about the system. You may want to use calls to the "BIOS" (the basic I-O subroutines) in some experiments and to the "DOS" (the disk operating system) in others. Note that the disk I-O may or may not be buffered, and even if it is not, the documentation may use the word "buffer" to refer to an area into which a block is read. Note also that, especially with small computers, you usually cannot neglect the processor time required by the file I-O subroutines, such as for blocking and deblocking.

(a) What is the rotational speed of the disk drive?

(b) What size sectors are used, and how many per track?

(c) Is buffering used, and if so, how many buffers?

(d) Are the sectors offset, and if so, by how much?

(e) How much processing time per block is used by the I-O subroutines?

(f) Make a graph of seek time vs. number of cylinders crossed.

File Structures

5.1. DATA STRUCTURES

This chapter introduces the basic concepts of data structures from the viewpoint of files. These concepts provide a framework for the discussion of database file structures and file design. There are a number of good books that give a complete course on data structures, for example, [F1,F5,F8—F11].

A data structure is a collection of data items (usually numbers or character strings) that are somehow related to each other. The most general relationship we need consider can be described by a *directed graph*. The data items are the *nodes* of the graph. *Branches* join certain nodes to certain other nodes, showing the relationship between data items. If a branch goes from node A to node B, then we say A is an immediate predecessor of B and B is an immediate successor of A. Node A is called a predecessor of node B and B is a successor of A if there is a set of nodes $A = N(0), N(1), N(2),..., N(n) = B$ such that $N(i + 1)$ is an immediate successor of $N(i)$ for $i = 0, 1, 2,..., n-1$.

Example 5.1

Figure 5.1 shows a data structure in which the nodes are cities and the branches (arrows) show possible airline flights during a certain period. In this example, Atlanta is an immediate predecessor of New York and New York is an immediate successor of Atlanta. New York has no successors. Los Angeles is both an immediate predecessor and immediate successor of San Francisco. New York is a successor of San Francisco because you can go from San Francisco to Denver to Atlanta to New York. San Francisco is not a successor of Chicago, however.

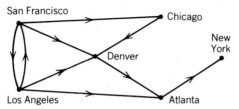

Figure 5.1 An Example of a Directed Graph.

This chapter discusses a number of special kinds of graph structures, and indicates some of their uses and how they may be implemented in computer systems.

5.2. ARRAYS, RELATIONS, AND TABLES

Arrays can be considered graphs, for example, as shown in Figure 5.2. (Perhaps arrows should be shown in both directions.) They can be implemented by the techniques discussed later for general graphs, but generally they are stored in the obvious way. Computer memory—either main storage or disk or tapes—consists of cells that have a natural order and can be considered to be numbered from 0 to some upper limit. This number is called the *address* of the cell. A one-dimensional array, or list, is usually stored in the memory in its natural sequence. A two dimensional array, also called a table or matrix, is usually stored row-by-row—

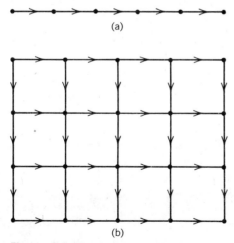

Figure 5.2 An Array as a Directed Graph. (*a*) A one-dimensional array; (*b*) a two-dimensional array.

the first row first, then the second, etc. If you know where the first element of an array is, you can calculate the location of any element. For a one-dimensional array A, let us assume that each array element uses c cells, and the first element $A(1)$ starts at cell address a. Then $A(2)$ is displaced c cells from $A(1)$ and must be at $a + c$, $A(3)$ is displaced $2c$ cells from $A(1)$ and must therefore be at $a + 2c$, and, in general, $A(i)$ is displaced $(i-1) \times c$ cells from $A(1)$, and so must be at $a + (i-1) \times c$.

For a two-dimensional array A, let us assume that each element uses c cells and there are r elements in each row, s elements in each column, and $A(i,j)$ represents the element that is in row i and column j. Assume $A(1,1)$ is at cell address a. Then, stored row-by-row, element $A(i,j)$ is preceded by $(i-1)$ complete rows and $j-1$ elements of row i, so it must be displaced $((i-1) \times r + j-1) \times c$ from $A(1,1)$, and it is at $a + ((i-1) \times r + j-1) \times c$. This can be generalized in the obvious way for arrays of higher dimensions.

It often happens that the number of cells required for each element of a one-dimensional array is not constant. For example, it is common for one cell to store one character, and we may have an array whose elements are English words or sentences. There are two choices. The maximum required space can be reserved for each element and unused spaces filled with the code for a space. Then the displacement formulas can be used to locate any item easily. Alternatively, the items can be stored in sequence separated by a special mark such as a comma or carriage-return character. This latter method uses less storage in general, but there is no easy way to locate a specific element. In choosing which method to use, one must weigh the relative importance of saving storage and fast access. This problem of "variable length records" is discussed further in Section 6.10.

Arrays are not commonly used as file structures, except as a means to implement relations. The concept of a *relation* occurs in relational database theory. A relation and a table are essentially the same. Both consist of a number of rows and columns. Each column contains data items from a given set, possibly different sets for different columns. (This is what distinguishes relations from matrices.) For example, one column may be names, another phone numbers, and another department numbers. Then the data in a row are presumably related, for example, the person whose name is given has the phone number and is in the department indicated in the same row. An example is shown in Figure 5.3, along with a possible graphical representation. One column of the relation is usually considered the primary key. There may be duplicate entries in any or all columns of a relation, but completely duplicate rows are not allowed. Theoretically, the sequence in which rows are arranged in a relation has no significance. In practice, this is usually not the case;

Name	Phone number	Department
Jones	345-6789	2
Smith	987-6543	7
Lee	237-4681	11

(a)

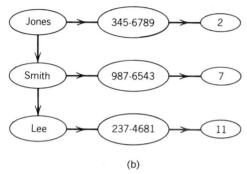

(b)

Figure 5.3 An Example of a Relation. (*a*) A simple relation; (*b*) A possible graphical representation.

at least the rows will be arranged to expedite access. They might be arranged in sequence (e.g., alphabetically) by primary key, for example.

Relations or tables may be stored in auxiliary storage. Each row usually is stored as a record, and the entire relation becomes a file. In fact, one may think of a file of fixed-format records as a relation. Relations stored in main memory usually are represented either (1) using separate one-dimensional arrays for each column, or (2) as a two-dimensional array stored row-by-row in successive memory locations. The second alternative is probably more natural because it stores each set of related items physically close to each other in memory; it corresponds to the usual way relations are stored on disk or tape. With the FORTRAN and BASIC languages, there is no easy way to store relations in memory row-by-row as a two-dimensional array unless all the columns are the same kind of data. Hence, the first alternative also is common. Either method is accommodated in most modern programming languages, including COBOL, PL/I, PASCAL, SNOBOL, and APL. Note that as long as the rows of a relation all have the same length, the location of a particular element of a relation in memory (either main memory or auxiliary storage) can be calculated easily using displacement formulas.

5.3. LINKED DATA STRUCTURES

Any data structure that can be represented as a directed graph can be implemented as a linked data structure. A linked data structure uses pointers. A pointer is a data item that gives the location of another data item. For data in memory, for example, it is common to use the memory address as a pointer. For data in an array in memory, the subscript value can be used as a pointer. For data on a disk unit, one may use the cylinder number, track number, and sector number within the track. Alternatively, one may use a file name and record number within the file. One may also use a record key as a pointer to a record, if there is a way to locate the record, given the key.

A directed graph may be represented in the computer by storing all the nodes, and then storing with each node a pointer to each of its immediate successor nodes. The nodes usually are stored as a table in any order. For example, the data structure shown graphically in Figure 5.1 might appear in a computer memory as follows:

LOCATION	CITY	POINTERS		
1	New York	NULL	NULL	NULL
2	Chicago	8	NULL	NULL
3	Atlanta	1	NULL	NULL
4				
5	San Francisco	2	8	6
6	Los Angeles	3	5	8
7				
8	Denver	3	NULL	NULL

It is common to provide space for the maximum number of pointers with each node and to put a special value called NULL that cannot be a pointer in unused locations. This keeps the node record length constant and facilitates calculating the location of these records. In this example, because zero is impossible as a pointer value, it can be used to represent NULL.

The *base* of a linked data structure is a data item that is sufficient for locating the linked data structure in memory. Usually a pointer to some special place in the structure is used as the base. If there are no nodes in the data structure, then the base may be NULL. When a linked data structure is used as a file structure, usually each node is stored as a record and the entire structure is a file.

5.4. LINKED LISTS

Although simple lists usually are implemented as one-dimensional arrays or relations stored sequentially in memory, as discussed in Section 5.2, lists also are commonly implemented with pointers corresponding to the graph structure in Figure 5.2(a). A linear linked list is a linked data structure with only one pointer field per node, where each node points to its immediate successor in the list. The last node in the linear linked list (called the tail) has a null pointer. The base of a linear linked list is a pointer to the first node (called the head); if the linear linked list is empty (i.e., contains no nodes), then the base is a null pointer. Figure 5.4(a) illustrates a linear linked list; its head is at address 112 and its tail is at address 130. Here the null pointer has been given the value -1.

A linked list requires more storage than a list simply stored sequentially in memory, because space is needed for a pointer for each data item. Generally, accessing each item also will require more time. It is not possible to calculate the location of the Nth item in a linked list, as can be done for sequentially stored lists. (See Section 5.2.) Even so, in certain circumstances, the linked list has advantages. Inserting and deleting items is easier with this kind of implementation; any number of items can be inserted into the middle of a linked data structure by adjusting pointers but without moving any existing data. Inserting an item in a sequentially-stored list requires moving all following items down to make space for the new item; deleting an item requires moving all items up to fill the vacated space. Inserting an item X between nodes A and B in a linked list requires the following:

1. Store the item X in the area used for the linked list.
2. Change the pointer in A to point to X instead of B.
3. Set the pointer in X to point to B.

Similarly, to delete an item B between nodes A and C in a linked list requires the following:

1. Erase the data in B, or mark it unused.
2. Change the pointer in A to point to C.

Note that no data items need be moved, except perhaps the one being inserted. Figure 5.4(b) shows the linked list of Figure 5.4(a) with an item Mi inserted and Ch deleted.

As another example of a situation where the linked list is advantageous, consider the case where there are, say, at most 1000 items altogether on five lists, but any number of items might be on any list. If the

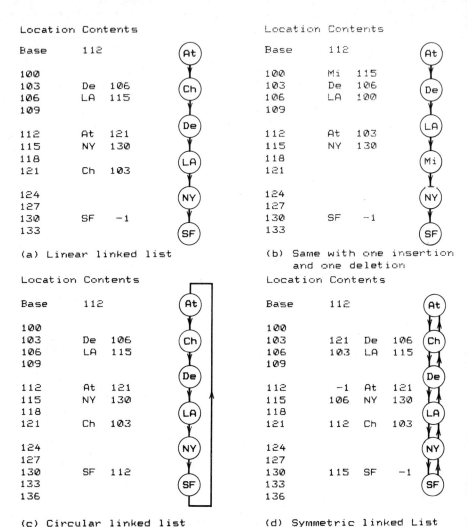

Figure 5.4 Examples of Linked Lists.

lists are stored sequentially, space must be provided for 1000 items for each list, so the total storage requirement is for 5000 items. With linked lists, space is needed only for only 1000 data items plus 1000 pointers. In general, the linked list would require less memory. (It is possible to reduce the storage requirement for sequentially stored lists by storing two lists in a single array, one starting from the beginning and the other backwards starting from the end of the array. Then an array of length 1000 could store two lists. Because the total length of the two lists could not exceed 1000, they could not overlap. However, even this arrangement would require more space than with the linked list.)

A circular list is like a linear linked list except that the pointer in the tail, instead of being null, points to the head. This allows access to each node in the list, starting at any one of them, not just at the list head. Figure 5.4(c) shows a circular list.

A symmetric list is like a linear linked list except that each node has an additional pointer to its immediate predecessor in the list. This also allows access to each node in the list, starting at any one of them, but more important it allows faster access to immediately preceding nodes. On the other hand, storage space for a second pointer in each node is necessary. Figure 5.4(d) shows an example of a symmetric list.

It often happens that access is required only at the head and/or the tail of a list. A *stack* is a list where an item may be inserted only at one end, called the *top*, of the list (this is called *pushing* an item onto the stack) and where only the top item may be accessed and removed (this is called *popping* an item from the stack). A *queue* is a list where insertions are only permitted at one end and deletions at the other. Stacks and queues can be implemented conveniently as linked lists.

Linked lists often are used as random-access file structures, where each node on the list is a record. A variation of a linked list commonly used on disk units stores a file as a linked list where each node is a block of records. Each block contains one pointer to the next block and possibly one to the preceding block.

5.5. TREES

A *tree* is a linked data structure generally having more than one pointer field per node, and satisfying the additional properties:

(a) One and only one node, called the *root*, is not a successor of (i.e., is not pointed to by) any other node.

(b) Each node other than the root is the immediate successor of exactly one other node.

(c) The root is a predecessor (not necessarily immediate) of each other node.

Note that no restriction has been made on the number of immediate successors a node may have: if there is a maximum limit t, the tree is called t-ary. A node without any successors is called a *leaf* of the tree, and the other nodes are said to be *internal*. A linear linked list may be regarded as a 1-ary tree. A 2-ary tree, the most common kind, is called a binary tree. The root of a tree is used as the base of the tree.

Figure 5.5(a) illustrates a binary tree whose root is at address 106. A convenient graphical representation is shown in Figure 5.5(b). Note that tree graphs usually are drawn with the root at the top.

```
Location   Contents

Base       106

100
103           -1  De   -1
106          121  LA  130
109

112           -1  At   -1
115           -1  NY   -1
118
121          112  Ch  103

124
127
130          115  SF   -1
133
```

(a) Representation in memory   (b) Graphical representation

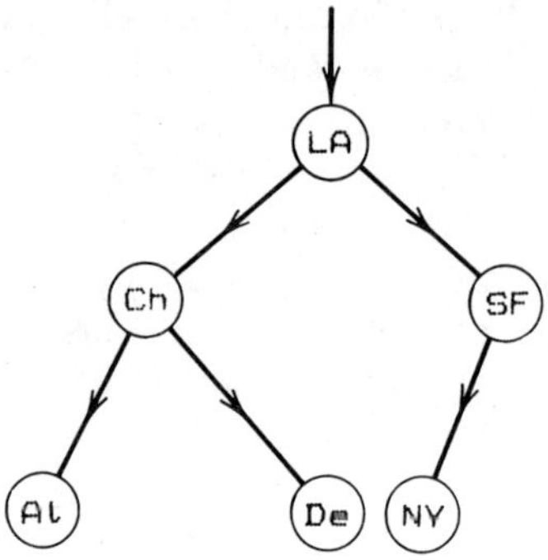

Figure 5.5 An Example of a Tree.

Trees are used in situations where the data naturally has a "hierarchical" structure. Such structure is common. Most organizations have a tree structure with, for example, the president as the root, several vice presidents under the president, perhaps several divisions under each vice president, and several departments under each division, etc. Algebraic expressions can be represented as trees, with variables and constants as leaves, and a node for each operation with pointers to its operands, which are subtrees. The flow of control in a computer program which contains **if** statements but no loops has a treelike structure; similarly, any decision procedure that contains no loops corresponds to a tree structure. Classification is usually hierarchical and, hence, structured as a tree—each category corresponds to a node that points to a number of nodes that are its subcategories.

File directories commonly are organized as trees. A hierarchical tree is a (nonbinary) tree whose subtrees correspond to partitions of the file records. In particular, a *trie* is a tree in which the keys in each subtree (partition) have a common prefix.

Example 5.2

Assume that a system has file names that may be qualified, that is, names consist of one or more identifiers separated by punctuation marks, for example, A.B.C. The part preceding any punctuation mark is a qualifier for the part that follows it. Presumably, files with the same qualifier are somehow related. A catalog for such a system could be organized as follows: If an identifier is a qualifier, the catalog

entry points to a list of all things that it qualifies. Otherwise, the
catalog entry points to the start of the file. Here is a list of file names:

```
AL.COMP                    WWP.PROJA.PROGB.OLD
AL.EDIT                    WWP.PROJA.PROGB.NEW
BILLING                    WWP.PROJB.PHASE1
WWP.PROJA.PROGA            WWP.PROJB.PHASE2
                           WWP.PROJC
```

   The natural data structure for such a catalog is a trie, with each
qualifier used as the name of a node. In a file system, each node might
be a record containing the names of and pointers to the next level
nodes. (If there are so many names that more than one record is
needed for a node, continuation records may be chained to the first.)
For the previous file names, the catalog might be stored as shown
in Figure 5.6. The pointers to record numbers greater than 6 are
supposed to be pointers to the start of the files, for example, file
WWP.PROJA.PROGA starts at record number 41.

   It frequently occurs that all the nodes of a tree must be processed in
some special order. There are several orders that occur often. The following algorithms define the three most commonly used orders of traversal:

(1) **Preorder**
```
     If the tree is null, do nothing.
     Otherwise,
          Process the root.
          Then process the subtree of each successor
               of the root, left to right,
               in preorder sequence.
```

(2) **Postorder**
```
     If the tree is null, do nothing.
     Otherwise,
          Process the subtree of each successor
               of the root, left to right,
               in postorder sequence.
          Then process the root.
```

(3) **Inorder (for a binary tree)**
```
     If the tree is null, do nothing.
     Otherwise,
          Process the subtree of the left successor
               in inorder sequence.
          Process the root.
          Process the subtree of the right successor
               in inorder sequence.
```

Node Name	Record No.	Contents					
Root Node	0	AL	1	BILLING	15	WWP	2
AL	1	COMP	23	EDIT	29		
WWP	2	PROJA	3	PROJB	4	PROJC	35
PROJA	3	PROGA	41	PROGB	5		
PROJB	4	PHASE1	47	PHASE2	56		
PROGD	5	OLD	61	NEW	68		

Figure 5.6 An Example of a Tree.

These definitions are recursive and can be programmed as recursive procedures just as simply as they appear. Greater care should be exercised to program them using iteration.

To process the nodes of the tree in Figure 5.5 in inorder sequence, for example, the algorithm specifies that first you process the left subtree, that is, the subtree whose root is Ch, in inorder sequence. To do that, first you process its left subtree, that is, the one whose root is At. To do that, you must process the left subtree of At, but this being null, you do nothing. Then you process At. Then its right subtree, which is null. Now go back and process Ch, and then its right subtree. Processing its right subtree requires processing De. Then the complete left subtree of LA has been processed, and you process LA. After that you process the right subtree of LA, which turns out to require processing NY and then SF. (The right pointer on SF is null.) Thus, the inorder sequence is At, Ch, De, LA, NY, SF. The preorder sequence of nodes for the tree in Figure 5.5 is LA, Ch, At, De, SF, NY. The postorder sequence is AT, De, Ch, NY, SF, LA.

5.6. TREE SEARCHING AND SORTING

There is another important application of the tree concept in file systems. A file can be organized as a tree in such a way as to facilitate both sequential and random access, and so that insertion and deletion of records also is convenient. This involves using a sorted tree.

An example of a file organized as a sorted tree is shown in Figure 5.7. Each node has a key (and usually some data or a pointer to some data) and two pointers, which together usually are stored as a record. In the figure, null pointers are represented by the letter N. All the records that are successors of a given record by the left pointer have smaller keys than the given record; all records that are successors by the right pointer have greater keys.

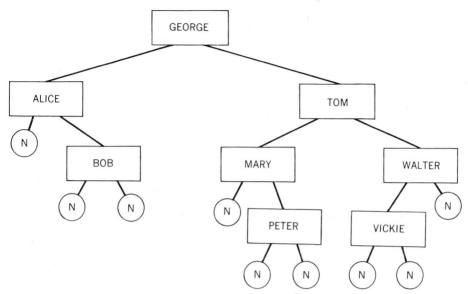

Figure 5.7 A Tree-Sorted File.

To search for a record having a given key, you start at the root of the tree and compare the given key to the key at the node being examined. If the given key equals the node key, the record is found. If it is smaller, then you go to the node that the left pointer points to; if it is greater, you use the right pointer. If you find a null pointer before you find the desired record, the record is not in the file. For example, to locate PETER in the file in Figure 5.7, you compare PETER to GEORGE, and PETER being greater, you go right to TOM. PETER is smaller, so you go left to MARY. PETER is greater than MARY, so you go right and find PETER.

Inserting a record with a given key is very simple—you simply search for the record, and if it is not already there, the search terminates at a null pointer. This null pointer is changed to point to a new node into which the given record is placed. Both pointers of the new node are made null. A sorted tree can be created by starting with an empty tree and inserting the records of a file one by one.

Deletion of records from a sorted tree is slightly more complicated. If a record has two null pointers, then you delete it by simply making the pointer that points to it null. If it has one null pointer and, hence, only one nonnull subtree, then you can delete it by simply changing the pointer that points to it to point to its subtree. If a record, say, R, has two nonnull pointers, then deleting it is more difficult. One method is to find the next sequential record after R, say, S. It turns out that S will have a null left pointer: note that to find that next record, you follow down the left side of the right subtree of R until you find a null left pointer, and that record must be the next one after R. Then you remove S from where it was and replace R by S. In the example shown in Figure 5.7, suppose we want to delete GEORGE. The next sequential record after GEORGE is MARY, so we delete the node that contains MARY by making the left pointer in TOM simply point to PETER, and replace GEORGE by MARY.

The records in this kind of file can be read sequentially by key by traversing the tree in inorder sequence. Thus, it is possible to sort a file by inserting the records into a sorted tree and then reading them out in inorder sequence. Note that it is easy to find the next record after a given record or the preceding record by first finding the record in question and then going one step forward or backward in the inorder transversal.

There are a number of variations possible [H1, pp. 422–480]. In particular, searching is fastest if the tree is "balanced," and there are algorithms for inserting or rearranging a tree to balance it. Tree searching as described here is quite suitable for use within the main memory of a computer. It could be used also with disk storage. One variation that is very well suited for disk storage applications is called a B-tree, and is discussed in the next section.

5.7. B-TREES

A B-tree is one possible generalization of the binary sorted tree. A B-tree is defined as a tree that satisfies the following conditions:

1. Each node has a maximum of $m-1$ records and m pointers. (The case $m = 2$ gives a binary tree.)

2. Some nodes have no pointers (or all null pointers)—they are called leaf nodes. All other nodes have one more nonnull pointer than records. The root node has at least one record unless the tree is empty. All other nodes have at least $[(m-1)/2]$ records, where $[n]$ denotes the integer part of n, or n rounded down to the nearest integer.

3. All leaf nodes are at the same level, that is, at the same distance from the root.

4. Let us call the records in a node R_0, R_1,..., R_{n-1}, where n is not greater than $m-1$, and let us call the pointers P_0, P_1,..., P_n. For each i between 0 and $n-1$, all records in the subtree that P_i points to are less than R_i and for each i between 1 and n, all records in the subtree that P_i points to are greater than R_{i-1}.

B-trees are well suited for disk files, because (1) there are simple algorithms for searching, sequential access, insertion, and deletion, (2) searching is quite fast because the tree is quite well balanced, and (3) regarding a node as a block of data on the disk, the condition that every node (except the root) has at least $[(m-1)/2]$ records means that every block except the root must be at least half full if m is odd and nearly half full if m is even. Therefore, it is guaranteed that the storage is used fairly efficiently.

We insert and delete records in a B-tree in such a way that the result remains a B-tree. Then we can start with an empty tree and apply the following insertion algorithm repeatedly to build a B-tree.

If the tree is empty, create a node with all null pointers and put the record in it. This is the root node of the B-tree, and at the same time it is a leaf node. If the tree is not empty, then do a tree search and find the leaf node into which this record ought to be inserted. If that node has fewer than $m-1$ records in it, insert the record in that node. If that node has $m-1$ records, you divide it.

To divide a node while inserting a record, first you put the $m-1$ records from the old node together with the new record being inserted in sequence, find the middle record (as closely as possible), put those records below the middle record in the old node, and put those records above it in a new node. If the node being divided is the root node, you create a new root node and put the middle record and pointers to the other two nodes in it. If the node being divided is not the root node, you insert the middle record and pointers to these two nodes into the immediate predecessor of the original node. When you insert that middle record into the immediate predecessor node, if there are fewer than $m-1$ records in the immediate predecessor node, you simply insert the record (and pointers). If the immediate predecessor node was full, you divide it.

To delete record R_i, first you locate it. If it is not in a leaf node, you replace it with the first record in the node to which P_{i+1} points. If it is a leaf node, you delete it; if the number of records remaining in the node is at least $[(m-1)/2]$, you are finished. If the number of nodes becomes smaller than that, you combine this node with an adjacent one that has the same predecessor, putting (as closely as possible) half the records in each and adjusting the pointer and associated record in the predecessor node. If the adjacent leaf node also is at the minimum size, then you combine these two nodes into one, including with them the record in the predecessor node. Then you remove that record and pointer from the predecessor node. Similarly, if the number of records in that node becomes less than $[(m-1)/2]$, you move a record and pointer from an adjacent node at that level to that node or combine that node with an adjacent node, making the necessary adjustments at the next lower level. If the number of records in the root node becomes zero, then it is deleted and the one node that it points to becomes the new root node.

It should be clear that inserting or deleting a record into a B-tree using these algorithms results in a tree that is still a B-tree. Note that with the algorithm described previously for binary trees, the node that is originally the root node is always the root node and the tree grows by creating new leaf nodes. For B-trees, however, a node created as a leaf node is always a leaf node, and when the tree grows in depth, it grows by creation of a new root node.

Example 5.3

Figure 5.8(a) shows a two-level B-tree with $m = 5$. Suppose we insert FRED into that tree. By searching we find that FRED should go into the node that contains ED, HAL, IRMA, and JANE. That node is full, so it must be divided. HAL is the middle record. ED and FRED go into one node, IRMA and JANE into the other, and HAL must be inserted

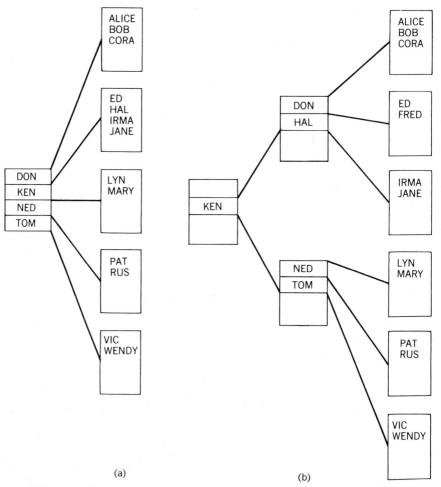

(a)   (b)

Figure 5.8 An Example of a B-tree. (*a*) Before inserting FRED; (*b*) After inserting FRED.

into the predecessor node, which happens to be the root node (the one that contains DON, KEN, NED, and TOM). Because it is full, it also must be divided. Inserting HAL, we find that KEN is the middle record, DON and HAL go in one node, and NED and TOM into the other. We must create a new root node and put KEN into it. The resulting tree is shown in Figure 5.8(b).

Now let us delete FRED from the B-tree in Figure 5.8(b). First we locate FRED and remove it from the leaf node. Then, since that leaf node is left with fewer than $[(5-1)/2] = 2$ records, we examine an adjacent node. If we choose the preceding one, then we could move CORA where DON is and move DON into the node with ED, make the necessary adjustments on the pointers, and thus satisfy all requirements for a B-tree.

If we choose instead to examine the next node, the one containing IRMA and JANE, then we find that that node contains the minimum number of records, so we cannot move one out. Then we combine the two nodes, deleting one pointer from the predecessor node and moving the record, HAL in this case, from the predecessor node to the newly combined node. The new node contains ED, HAL, IRMA, and JANE. The predecessor node has only DON remaining in it, which is less than the specified minimum number of records. Therefore, we examine the next adjacent node at the same level, that is, the one containing NED and TOM. We cannot move a record out of it, so we combine these two nodes, removing a pointer from their predecessor and moving the corresponding record from the predecessor to the combined node. This combined node now contains DON, KEN, NED, and TOM. The predecessor, the root node, which previously contained only KEN and two pointers, now contains no records and only one pointer. Therefore, we eliminate it, and the node that it points to, namely, the node with DON, KEN, NED, and TOM, becomes the new root node. This leaves exactly the graph of Figure 5.8(a).

The definition of the B-tree guarantees that every node except the root will be at least half full if m is odd, and nearly half full if m is even. If records are inserted in random sequence, one would expect the actual record counts to have approximately a uniform distribution, and the average number of records per node would be about 75% of the capacity. On the other hand, if records are inserted in sequence by key using the above insertion algorithm, then records would always be inserted in the rightmost leaf node or its predecessors. Therefore, after a node is split, records would not be inserted in the left one of the two nodes produced; it would remain with the minimum number of records. Therefore, most nodes would have the minimum number of records, and the nodes would be, on the average, near 50% full. If a file is created initially from a sorted file of records, it would be worthwhile to have a separate utility program to create the file putting a specified number of records in each node.

It is fairly easy to read records from a B-tree in sequential order by key. This requires a direct generalization of the algorithm for inorder processing:

B-tree inorder processing algorithm:
>   If the tree is empty, do nothing.
>   Otherwise, assuming there are n records and
> $n+1$ pointers,
>   For i = 0 to $n-1$
>   Process the B-tree that P_i
>   points to.
>   Process record R_i;
>   Process the B-tree that pointer P_n
>   points to;

There are a number of variations of B-trees that have been proposed. For example, one may postpone splitting nodes until a node and an adjacent node are both full. Then the two nodes are split, making three nodes. This guarantees that every node is about two-thirds full. Knuth calls such a tree a B*-tree[F5]. Obviously this could be generalized to make trees in which the nodes are fuller, but insertions and deletions more difficult.

Another more important generalization is the B$^+$-tree. For this structure, all the records are stored in leaf nodes. Thus, there are two kinds of nodes, leaf nodes with a capacity of r records, and nonleaf nodes with a capacity of m pointers and $m-1$ keys. The B$^+$-tree is defined to be a tree that has the following additional properties:

1. All leaf nodes have at least $r/2$ records, that is, are at least half full, unless the leaf node is also the root node.

2. All nonleaf nodes except the root node have at least $m/2$ pointers and always one less key than pointers.

3. The records in a leaf node are in sequence by key. Let us call the keys in a nonleaf node $K_0, K_1,..., K_{n-1}$, where n is not greater than $m-1$, and let us call the pointers $P_0, P_1, P_2,..., P_n$ (the rest of the m pointers are null if there are fewer than $m-1$ keys). Then if $0 \leqslant i \leqslant n-1$, all the records in the subtree that P_i points to have keys less than or equal to K_i, and if i is between 1 and n, then all the records in the subtree that P_i points to are greater than K_{i-1}.

The key K_i may be chosen to be the last key that appears in a record in the subtree that P_i points to, or any value that is at least that large and still less than the key of the next record. It serves essentially as a separator between the records of the subtree to which P_i points and those of the subtree to which P_{i+1} points.

Records are inserted as follows. First you locate the leaf node that should contain the record. If it is not full, you simply insert the record in an open space. If it is full, you take those records together with the one to be inserted and put the first half (as closely as possible) into the old node and the last half into a new node. Then you insert a pointer to the last record in the new node and the last key in the old node following the pointer to the old node in the predecessor node. Insertion into the predecessor node is done in essentially the same way as for the leaf node. If insertion into the root node is required and the root node is full, then it is split and a new root node is created that points to the two nodes produced from splitting the old root node.

Similarly, a record is deleted by locating it in the leaf node and simply deleting it. If, as a result, the node becomes less than half full, an adjacent node is examined; if it contains more than the minimum number of records, a record is moved from it to the node in question, and the key in the predecessor node is changed to reflect that change. If that adjacent node also contains the minimum number of records, then the two nodes are combined and the corresponding key and pointer are deleted from the predecessor node in an analogous manner. If a key and pointer are deleted from the root node and it is left with one pointer and no key, then the root node is eliminated and its one successor becomes the new root node.

One way to process all the records of a B^+-tree sequentially is to visit all the nodes in either preorder or postorder sequence, processing the records whenever a leaf node is met. In a practical system, however, usually an additional pointer is included in each leaf node pointing to the next one in sequence, making them into a linked list, and keeping a pointer to the first leaf node. Then sequential processing simply requires accessing the leaf nodes in sequence.

The B^+-tree is simpler conceptually than the B-tree—the leaf nodes contain the records and the nonleaf nodes form a multilevel index in the usual sense. Note that if the leaf nodes are tracks, then the nonleaf nodes indicate the highest keys in each track. The insertion and deletion algorithms are simpler and require somewhat less record moving. There is a distinct advantage in reading the file sequentially. For these reasons, B^+ trees usually are used in practical implementations of indexed sequential file systems.

Example 5.4

Figure 5.9(a) shows a two-level B^+-tree that has three records in every leaf node and five pointers in every internal node. Records are shown with a name and phone number to distinguish them from keys, which consist of the name alone. Suppose we insert a record for DON. It

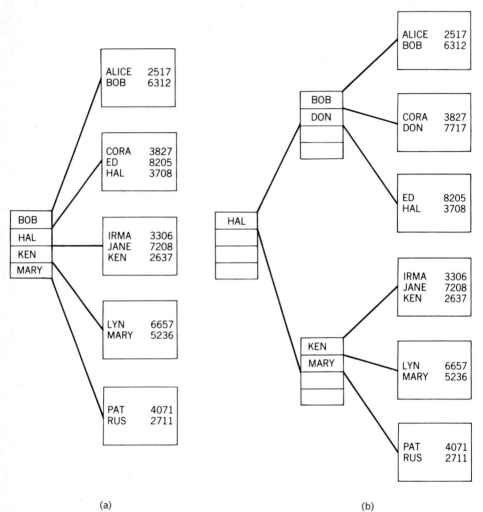

(a)   (b)

Figure 5.9 An Example of a B$^+$-tree. (a) Before inserting DON; (b) After inserting DON.

should go into the second leaf node, but that node is full. Therefore, we split it, putting CORA and DON in the old node and ED and HAL into a new one. Now it is necessary to insert a pointer to the new node and a key, DON, into the predecessor, but that node is also full. Therefore, we split it, putting pointers to the first three leaf nodes in the old node and pointers to the last three into a new node, with appropriate keys. Because this was the root node, we create a new root node and put pointers in it pointing to the old root node and the node just created with an appropriate key, HAL, separating them. The result is shown in Figure 5.9(b).

Now let us delete DON. We find the record in the leaf node and simply delete it. However, this leaves the leaf node less than half full. Therefore, let us consider taking one record from the next leaf node and putting it into the leaf node with CORA. This will not work because the next leaf node, that with ED and HAL in it, has the minimum number of records permitted. Therefore, we combine these two nodes, producing a node with CORA, ED, and HAL in it. Then the node that had ED and HAL in it is eliminated, and the pointer to it and the key DON must be deleted from the predecessor. This leaves the predecessor less than half full and the adjacent node, the one with KEN and MARY in it, also is at the minimum. Therefore, these two nodes must be combined. This necessitates deleting a pointer from their predecessor, the root node, leaving it with only one pointer. It is then eliminated and the node to which it pointed becomes the new root node. The result is exactly the tree in Figure 5.9(a).

5.8. MULTILISTS AND RINGS

It is common for the data records of a file to have multiple keys. For example, in a telephone directory file, names, addresses, and telephone numbers can serve as three different keys. We may wish to access a record by any one of these keys. Such a file has multiple logical orderings, but can have only one physical sequential ordering according to a *primary* key (say, by name). To process the file sequentially by *secondary* keys (i.e., in address or telephone number order) requires either indexes (hence, considerable redundancy) or pointer fields in each record so that the records can be organized as linear linked lists in the other logical orders. A file that has multiple logical sequences is called a *multilist*. It is not necessary for each record to be in each list.

If an index is used for a secondary key, then each of its entries consists of a secondary key and a pointer to the appropriate record or a list of pointers to all appropriate records. (Efficient methods for organizing and searching indexes are discussed in Chapter 6.) There may be multiple indexes, one for each secondary key.

Often, secondary keys are not unique, and it is desirable to chain together in no particular order all records having a common secondary key value or *attribute*. A multilist, having one list per attribute, is used frequently.

Insertions and deletions into multilist files are fairly simple to perform if additional backward pointers are maintained so that the lists are symmetric. Sequential processing of a multilist on a secondary key order is ordinarily slow because frequent jumps causing seeking are necessary. If sequential processing is important, the most-used key should be chosen as the primary key and the file stored so that the physical ordering corresponds to the order by primary key.

In some cases, the records associated with a secondary key have no significant logical ordering, for example, when records having a common attribute are chained together. Chaining these records in their physical order would make their sequential processing more efficient. If records are frequently inserted and deleted, however, such an ordering will be hard to maintain.

It is often advantageous for the linear linked lists of a multilist to be circular, so that the heads of each list to which any record belongs can be found. A file organized this way is called a *ring*. In a ring, when a record is accessed because it has a particular attribute, it is easy to find all records sharing a second attribute. Suppose a telephone directory is organized as a ring, with all persons living on the same street chained together. To find the neighbors of a given individual, the record for that person would be accessed by the primary key (name) and a secondary key chain would locate each neighbor.

Example 5.5

In the file shown in Figure 5.10, the employee number (ID) is the primary key and the other data include the employee's name, location, and job classification. If we wish to access this file by name, an index of the record(s) for each name may be made, as shown in Figure 5.11. If we wish to list all employees at a given location or with a given job classification, the other indexes shown in Figure 5.11 may be used. The result is a multilist with tabular secondary indexes.

Alternatively, in a linked multilist, there may be a pointer in each record pointing to the next record in alphabetic sequence by name. There also may be a pointer pointing to the next record with the same location and to the next record with the same job classification, as

Record No.	ID	Name	Loc.	Job
0	2484	Jones	C	ET
1	2627	Chang	C	SP
2	2712	Baker	C	SP
3	2883	Davis	A	EE
4	2939	Hall	B	EE
5	4151	Adams	A	AP
6	4227	Fox	A	ET
7	6225	Carter	B	SP
8	7127	Castro	C	AP
9	9227	Jordan	A	AP

Figure 5.10 A Multilist.

Name	Record No
ADAMS	5
BAKER	2
CARTER	7
CASTRO	8
CHANG	1
DAVIS	3
FOX	6
HALL	4
JONES	0
JORDAN	9

Loc.	Record Nos.
A	3, 5, 6, 9
B	4, 7
C	0, 1, 2, 8

Job	Record Nos.
AP	5, 8, 9
EE	3, 4
ET	0, 6
SP	1, 2, 7

Figure 5.11 Tabular Indexes for the Multilist of Figure 5.10.

shown in Figure 5.12. Note that the last record of each list points back to the first record and, hence, the result is a ring structure.

With the information in Figure 5.12, one can easily process in sequence by name or list all employees in a given location or job classification. To facilitate random access by name, one could make an index of every kth entry for some k, thus limiting searching to the index and at most k records. For example, for $k = 3$, for the above file we have

NAME	RECORD NO.
ADAMS	5
CASTRO	8
FOX	6
JORDAN	9

To find DAVIS, for example, we note that it lies between CASTRO and FOX. We access the file CASTRO, record number 8, and note that the next record in sequence by name is record number 1. That is not the desired record, but the next after it is 3, which is the desired record.

As an example of a typical inquiry, we might wish to find employees at location C whose job classification is SP. To do so, we start at record 0 (the first record of Location C), note its job attribute is ET, try

Record No.	ID	Name	Ptr	Loc	Ptr	Job	Ptr
0	2484	Jones	9	C	1	ET	6
1	2627	Chang	3	C	2	SP	2
2	2712	Baker	7	C	8	SP	7
3	2883	Davis	6	A	5	EE	4
4	2939	Hall	0	B	7	EE	3
5	4151	Adams	2	A	6	AP	8
6	4227	Fox	4	A	9	ET	0
7	6225	Carter	8	B	4	SP	1
8	7127	Castro	1	C	0	AP	9
9	9227	Jordan	5	A	3	AP	5

First Record Alphabetically by Name = 5

First Record for LOC A = 3
                 LOC B = 4
                 LOC C = 0
                 JOB AP = 5
                 JOB EE = 3
                 JOB ET = 0
                 JOB SP = 1

Figure 5.12 A Multilist Constructed with Linked Lists.

the next record on the Location C chain, namely, record 1, note its job attribute is SP as desired, thus finding CHANG. Continuing on the Location C chain, we would inspect records 2 and 8 and find BAKER and no others.

5.9. INVERTED FILES AND CELLULAR MULTILISTS

It is common in linked multilist files having one list per attribute to keep the attribute in the list-head or a separate table (or index) rather than in the data records. The index would contain all possible attribute (key) values and pointers to one or more records having each attribute (if any): these records would be the heads of the linked lists of records having the given attribute. We then say that the file is *partially inverted*. If the index contains pointers to each record having a given attribute and these records are no longer chained together, we say that the file is *fully inverted* with respect to the attribute.

Random access by secondary key is fast in a fully inverted file. Sequential processing by a secondary key or attribute may be made in physical record order if the index is so sorted, thereby enabling more efficient access than is possible with a multilist. Insertions and deletions can be handled efficiently by organizing the index as an indexed-sequential file or a hashed file, as described in Chapter 6. A partially inverted file in which the index contains for each attribute pointers to one record on each *cell* (i.e., a block or track or cylinder) and where these designated records serve as the heads of lists of other records contained in their respective cells and having the same attribute, is called a *cellular multilist*. This type of file permits blocking when the cells are blocks or tracks and eliminates unnecessary seeks when the cells are cylinders.

A more significant advantage of inverted files is that the identities of all records having a given attribute can be found without having to access the records themselves (or to follow a chain of records). This is of great importance if we wish to find a record having some specified combination of attributes. We need only compare the lists of records associated with each attribute.

A disadvantage of inverted files is the difficulty in deleting a record having a given attribute. The indexes for all but the primary key attributes must be searched for the occurrence of this record, unless pointers back to the indexes or at least attribute values are kept in the main file.

Example 5.6

The data in the previous examples are shown in Figure 5.13 in a file fully inverted on all three secondary keys. In addition, pointers to the indexes are included in the main file. For example, for record number 3, the name is the fifth entry in the name index, the location is the zeroth entry in the location index, and the job classification is the first entry in the job index. These additional pointers make it possible, given the record number, to find the name, location, and job classification. They also very much simplify the job of deleting a record, because they indicate which index entries must be deleted.

With this organization one can find the original record(s) given the name, location, or job classification. Suppose one is looking for an AP at location C. Then since 5, 8, 9 are AP's and 0, 1, 2, 8 are at location C, we know that the only candidate in both lists is 8. Looking at the main file, we find the employee's ID number, 7127. The employee's name is number 3 in the name index, CASTRO.

Note that although in these simple examples the indexes are simple sequential lists, in a large file system, especially if insertions and deletions occur, each index probably would be organized either as an indexed sequential file or a hashed file, as described in Chapter 6.

5.10. DATABASE SYSTEM DATA STRUCTURES

This and the following several sections introduce the reader to the data structures used in database systems and illustrate how the concepts of files and data structures described in this chapter relate to database

Main File:

Record No.	ID	Name	Loc	Job
0	2484	8	2	2
1	2627	4	2	3
2	2712	1	2	3
3	2883	5	0	1
4	2939	7	1	1
5	4151	0	0	0
6	4227	6	0	2
7	6225	2	1	3
8	7127	3	2	0
9	9227	9	0	0

Index by name:

Entry No	Name	Record No in main file
0	ADAMS	5
1	BAKER	2
2	CARTER	7
3	CASTRO	8
4	CHANG	1
5	DAVIS	3
6	FOX	6
7	HALL	4
8	JONES	0
9	JORDAN	9

Index by Location:

Entry No.	Location	Record Nos. in main file
0	A	3, 5, 6, 9
1	B	4, 7
2	C	0, 1, 2, 8

Index by Job Classification:

Entry No.	Job	Record Nos. in main file
0	AP	5, 8, 9
1	EE	3, 4
2	ET	0, 6
3	SP	1, 2, 7

Figure 5.13 An Inverted Multilist.

system data structures. Several excellent books on database systems are given in the bibliography. In particular, Date's book gives an excellent introduction to the field, and the presentation here is based to a large extent on it.

Date[G7] gives the following definition for a database:

A database is a collection of stored operational data used by the application systems of some particular enterprise.

A database system may handle one or more unrelated databases. In practice, one database generally consists of a number of related files, and provision is made for including in the database information about the relationships between data within a file and between data in different files. In fact, the need for coordination of files was one of the important motivations for developing database systems. Previously all too often several isolated systems with isolated files were developed; then a need would arise for a program requiring data in more than one of these files, and very great difficulties were caused by the lack of coordination.

All information about the relationships between data may take either of two forms. It may appear as ordinary data or as pointers. For example, consider the relationship that one employee is another employee's manager. This fact could be entered into the database by including the manager's name or ID number in the employee's record, or alternatively, a pointer to the manager's record could be included in the employee's record. These are relationships within a single file. As an example relating two files, suppose we have one file of employee records and another file with a record for each department. The fact that an employee is in a department could be included in the employee's file either by including the department name or number in the employee's record or by including in the employee's record a pointer to the appropriate record in the department file. Similarly, each department record might include a list of all its employees, or alternatively, the employee records might contain pointers linking all employees in a department into a list, and then the department record might include a pointer to the head of that list.

In general, including actual data items makes files structurally simpler and easier to understand. Pointers, on the other hand, tend to be more concise. In many cases, accesses using pointers avoid the use of indexes and therefore are faster. Furthermore, there tends to be less redundancy in the data, which makes it easier to maintain a consistent database. For example, if a name is changed and appears in many places, then it would be easy to overlook one place. If, on the other hand, it appears in only one place and many places contain pointers to it, then it need be changed in only one place.

In studying a real database system, it is important to make a clear distinction between the "conceptual model" and the actual implementation. The conceptual model is a representation of all the data in the database that is used by the programmer and database user. It is described in the users' manual and instructions about how to use the system are explained in terms of the conceptual model. Therefore, it is essential that the database system function as if it were implemented in a manner identical to the conceptual model. However, it is not essential that a system actually be implemented in this way, as long as it is indeed equivalent.

The characteristics that one wants to optimize in the conceptual model are somewhat different from those that should be optimized in the actual implementation. The conceptual model should be as simple and clear to the human user as possible. The actual implementation should be fast and efficient, and these take precedence over simplicity. Thus, it is reasonable to expect the conceptual model and the actual implementation to differ. One might expect less use of pointers in the conceptual model than in the actual implementation, because pointers tend to make the database appear more complicated but often can be used to advantage to gain speed or save memory space.

Database systems usually are categorized according to their data structure. The categories usually chosen are called *hierarchical, network,* and *relational,* although many database systems do not fit precisely into one of these categories. The most important example of a hierarchical database system is IMS (Information Management System), which was developed by IBM, was one of the earliest systems, and is still very widely used. We will use it as an example.

The most important example of a network database system is the DBTG (Data Base Task Group) system. Clearly it is an attractive idea to standardize the structure and language of database systems, and the DBTG system is the result of a standardization project. It was developed by a subcommittee of the same committee that developed specifications for COBOL and was adopted by ANSI. It has been implemented for a number of computers. We will use it as an example of a network database.

Meanwhile, the concept of a relational database arose and was studied extensively. The relational database has a simple, clear, and uniform structure, and therefore is mathematically tractable. There is a good body of theory that makes our understanding of relational databases better than that for the other kinds. Also, its simplicity makes it attractive for users. Most recent database systems are relational or closely related types.

5.11. HIERARCHICAL DATABASE STRUCTURE

The hierarchical database structure is based on a tree structure. Every data item except the roots of trees has a parent in the structure and may be the parent for other data items. To illustrate this idea, let us consider an example of a database for a university with a record for each department. Each department has students and professors. Each student has an advisor and a list of courses. These relationships can be represented diagrammatically as a tree, as shown in Figure 5.14.

The actual data structure is more complicated than Figure 5.14. Actually, there is one tree for each department. For each department, there

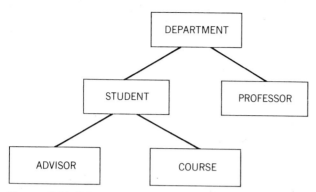

Figure 5.14 Schematic of Hierarchical Database Example.

are a number of students and a number of professors. Furthermore, each student has an advisor and a number of courses. Each tree is called a hierarchical record, and each part of the tree is called a segment. Thus, the database consists of a number of records more or less like that shown in Figure 5.15. In terms of graphs, the database consists of a number of isolated trees each with a structure something like the tree shown in Figure 5.15.

There is a well-defined order for the data in an IMS database. All the records are ordered by a primary key that is in the root segment. Within each record, the data items are arranged in the order of preorder transversal of the tree. For example, for the university database, first would be the root segment, DEPT, and then going down and left, STUDENT, and following each student, again down and left, ADVISOR, and then right COURSE. The PROF segments would follow all the STUDENT subtrees.

There are a number of versions of IMS, which differ most significantly in their methods of accessing records. Versions are available that access the hierarchical records sequentially, or as an indexed sequential file, or as a hashed file, in each case using a key from the root segment of each record. Indexed sequential and hashed file accessing is discussed in detail in Chapter 6.

IMS also provides for secondary indexes. Each index has a name that must be specified by the programmer when access using that index is desired.

IMS normally is used with a programming language, usually COBOL, FORTRAN, or PL/I. IMS is called as a subroutine; the parameters communicate to IMS what command should be done. A typical accessing command has this form:

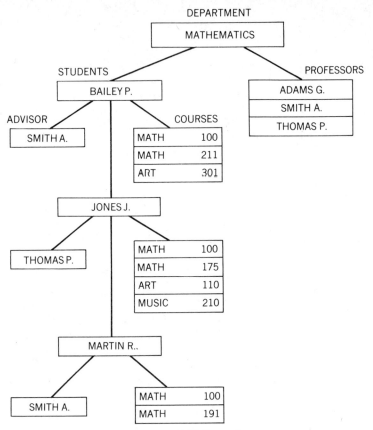

Figure 5.15 An Example of an IMS Record.

```
GN DEPT (NAME = "MATH")
   STUDENT
   ADVISOR (NAME = "SMITH A.")
```

Here GN stands for "get next" and the command means to get the nex
student segment (in hierarchical sequence) satisfying the conditions tha
the NAME field in the DEPT segment is MATH and the NAME field i
the ADVISOR segment is SMITH A. The following accessing command
are available:

GU	Get Unique
GN	Get Next
GNP	Get Next Within Parent Group
GHU, GHN, GHNP	Get and hold
IN	Insert
DE	Delete
MO	Modify

GU gets the unique entry, or if the entry is not unique, the first entry satisfying the specified conditions. GNP terminates when there are no more segments satisfying the specified conditions within the same parent group as the previous access. IN, DE, and MO must be preceded by a "get and hold" type of command, which will determine which segment to delete, modify, or where to insert. If access using a secondary index is desired, it must be specified explicitly. For example, assume that there is a secondary index on professors' names and the name of the index is PPP. To get the record of a professor named J. Jones via this index, the statement would be

```
GU PROF (PPP = "JONES J.")
```

Although in hierarchical systems it is certainly possible to have significant differences between the conceptual model and the actual implementation, this is not the case with IMS. This is probably because IMS is a very early system and, at the time of its design, database systems, and in particular the concept of distinct conceptual model and actual implementation, were not well understood.

5.12. NETWORK DATABASE STRUCTURE

We will discuss the DBTG database proposal as an example of a network-type database. The DBTG database consists of *records* and *DBTG sets*. The records have their usual meaning. Each record contains zero or more data items in a format that could be defined by a COBOL structure, for example. There will in general be several types of records. Thus, one may consider the records in the database to consist of one or more files.

The DBTG proposal provides a method for the programmer to specify pointers from any record to any other record that is not in the same file. When you want to get the next record along some path, it is necessary to specify which pointer to use. Thus, the pointers are organized into structures called DBTG sets.

A DBTG set involves two different files, an *owner file* and a *member file*. An *occurrence* of a DBTG set consists of one record (called the owner) from the owner file, and a list of zero or more records from the member file. A DBTG set consists of a collection of these occurrences with different owners. Duplicates are not allowed on the list, and each record is allowed in at most one occurrence of any one DBTG set. Each DBTG set has a name, and the programmer must use this name to designate which pointer to use when moving from one record to another. This is the conceptual model. It can be thought of as being implemented by having a pointer from the owner record to the first member record, a pointer from each member to the next, and finally, a pointer from the last member back to the owner record, forming a ring. Of course, it may not actually be implemented exactly this way, but it will certainly appear to the programmer as if it is, at least with respect to the results of an operation.

As a simple example, let us consider again a file of department records and a file of student records. Then the relationship that each student belongs to one department can be expressed using a DBTG set that has as its owner the department record and as its members all the students in that department. We might call that set DEPT-STUDENT. As a graph, this might look like Figure 5.17, where two departments are shown with a few students in each. This relationship is sometimes represented schematically as shown in Figure 5.16.

Now let us consider the full example of the previous section. There might be four files: DEPT, STUDENT, PROF, and COURSE. Presumably every advisor is a professor, so there is no need for a separate file for the

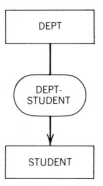

Figure 5.16 Schematic of a DBTG Set.

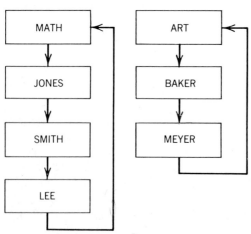

Figure 5.17 Example of a DBTG Set.

advisor. We will have a DBTG set DEPT-STUDENT to show which students are in each department, a DBTG set DEPT-PROF to show which professors are in each department, and a DBTG set ADVISOR to show which students are advised by each professor.

There is a requirement that no record occur more than once in a set. Therefore, we cannot simply make a file of courses and show which courses were taken by each student as a set with a STUDENT record as owner and COURSE records as members, because COURSE records would have to occur as members for more than one STUDENT. This can be handled by having a file ENROLL of course enrollments. One record in this file would represent one student's taking one course. Then two DBTG sets could be made, one with a STUDENT as owner and a number of ENROLL records as members, and another with a COURSE record as owner and a number of ENROLL records as members. To show simply which courses each student took, the ENROLL records would not need to contain any data items (other than the pointers needed for the DBTG sets). However, they probably would actually contain data such as the grade and the date. Omitting the COURSE file and the COURSE-ENROLL DBTG set so that the database contains very closely the same information as was used in the IMS example, these relationships are shown schematically in Figure 5.18. An example of a graphical representation of some data in this structure is shown in Figure 5.19.

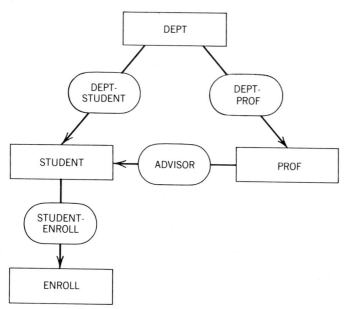

Figure 5.18 Schematic of a Simple DBTG Database.

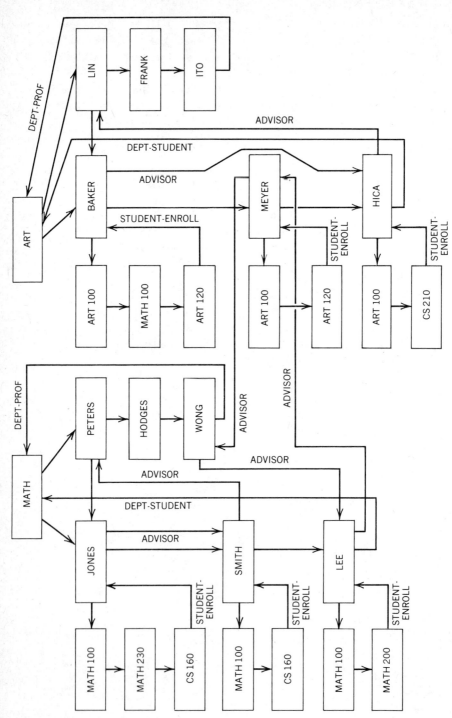

Figure 5.19 Example of a Simple DBTG Database.

Note that the database shown in Figure 5.18 is not hierarchical—neither the schematic representation in Figure 5.18 nor the graphical representation in Figure 5.19 is a tree. STUDENT and PROF are connected, but neither is above the other. The requirement that each node of a tree has no more than one predecessor is not satisfied at the STUDENT node. It is also possible for one DBTG set to relate two records with one as owner and the other as a member, and for another DBTG set simultaneously to relate the same two records in the opposite way. For example, in addition to the DBTG set ADVISOR, in which a professor is owner and students are members, one might have a DBTG set COMMITTEE with a student as owner and the professors comprising that student's thesis committee as members.

In some cases, we want to show a relationship between records of the same file. However, a set is supposed to have its owner and its members in different files. This can be handled with the DBTG system by introducing a new file of *links*. For example, in a personnel file, we might want to show the immediate supervisor of each person. We would make a new file that has one member for each person who serves as a supervisor for someone, and a DBTG set that has the supervisor's record as parent and the corresponding link record as its only member. Then we make another DBTG set that has this link record as owner and each person that this supervisor supervises as a member.

In some cases, it is desirable to link all the records in a file into a single list in some order (such as alphabetically). This can be done using DBTG sets as described above by defining a new file with a single record containing no information to use as the owner. This seems awkward if there is no other use for that file. Therefore, the DBTG database definition allows for *singular sets* that have no owner. (In practice, the SYSTEM is declared to be the owner.)

Each record has a *database key* that is unique, and given this database key, the system can find the record, presumably quickly. This might be implemented as a combination of the disk unit number, track number, and record number within the track, for example.

Now let us consider accessing a DTBG database. The concept of *currency* is essential in understanding the type of statements used. The system keeps track of the last record accessed in each file, and this is referred to as the current occurrence of that file, for example, the current DEPT occurrence or the current PROF occurrence. It also remembers the last occurrence of any record, owner or member, associated with each DBTG set. This record is referred to as the current occurrence of that DBTG set. For example, the current PROF-STUDENT occurrence might be a STUDENT record or a PROF record. It also keeps track of the very last record accessed, no matter which file.

The key statement in accessing the database is the FIND statement.

It has a number of forms. If the database key of the desired record is known, that is, saved from an access to the same record earlier in the same run, then the record can be accessed simply:

```
FIND PROF DB-KEY IS PROF-KEY.
```

where PROF-KEY is a data item in working storage where the database key was saved. If the key of the desired record is known, then the record can be found:

```
MOVE "JONES J" TO NAME IN PROF
FIND ANY PROF.
```

or in case duplicate keys are allowed and the next record with the same key is desired,

```
FIND DUPLICATE PROF.
```

Provision is made for finding records by hashing. Otherwise, it is not clear from the conceptual model how access is achieved. Each of these FIND's establishes the record found as the current occurrence of that record.

Next, there are several forms of FIND that use DBTG sets. To find the first student on the list of math students, we could use the following statements:

```
MOVE "MATH" TO NAME IN DEPT
FIND ANY DEPT
FIND FIRST STUDENT WITHIN DEPT-STUDENT.
```

The first two statements establish MATH as the current DEPT, and then the last statement finds the first STUDENT record on the list in the DEPT-STUDENT DBTG set. To find the next STUDENT on the list,

```
FIND NEXT STUDENT WITHIN DEPT-STUDENT.
```

and this could be used in a loop to scan the whole list of STUDENT records. To find who is a particular student's advisor, we could use the following statements:

```
MOVE "SMITH R" TO NAME IN STUDENT
FIND ANY STUDENT
FIND OWNER WITHIN ADVISOR.
```

It also is possible to scan the list of a DBTG set looking for a member in which certain fields match. For example, to find a student who was born in 1963 and advised by Professor Smith, assuming YEAR is a field in the STUDENT record denoting his year of birth, the following could be used:

```
MOVE "SMITH" TO NAME IN PROF
FIND ANY PROF
MOVE 1963 TO YEAR IN STUDENT
FIND DUPLICATE WITHIN PROF-STUDENT
   USING YEAR IN STUDENT.
```

The FIND statement does not bring a record into working storage. That task is done by the GET statement:

```
MOVE "SMITH J" TO NAME IN STUDENT
FIND ANY STUDENT
GET STUDENT.
```

To update a record, you get it as above, change the data in it as desired, and then use the statement MODIFY:

```
MODIFY STUDENT.
```

To insert a new record, you move the desired data into the record structure and then give the command STORE:

```
STORE STUDENT.
```

To delete a record, first you GET it and then you give the command ERASE:

```
ERASE STUDENT, or
ERASE STUDENT ALL.
```

The first form will erase the record, if it is not the owner of a nonempty DBTG set, and delete its occurrence as a member in any DBTG sets it may be in. The second will delete the record even if it is an owner, and delete all members of any DBTG set that this record owns, and any records owned by records that will be deleted.

To insert a new member into a DBTG set, first you establish the desired owner and member as current by FINDing them and then you give the command CONNECT. For example, to include a new student in a department,

```
MOVE "LEE H" TO NAME IN STUDENT
FIND ANY STUDENT
MOVE "MATH" TO NAME IN DEPT
FIND ANY DEPT
CONNECT STUDENT TO DEPT-STUDENT.
```

Removing a member from a DBTG set is done in an analogous manner.

The conceptual model of a DBTG database system does not make clear how access to a record given the key is to be done. The actual implementation might use sequential searching, an indexed sequential system, or hashing. For accesses using DBTG sets, one would expect the implementation to follow the conceptual model quite closely, although certainly variations are possible. For example, if a pointer to the owner is included in every member of a DBTG set, then finding the owner would be much faster. The cost, of course, would be the extra disk space required to store those extra pointers.

5.13. RELATIONAL DATABASE STRUCTURES

As stated earlier in this chapter, a relation is essentially the same as a file. Duplicate records are not allowed in a relation. Theoretically, the sequence of records in a relation is immaterial and has no meaning, and we may consider the sequence immaterial in the conceptual model. Practically the records would be arranged in such a way as to facilitate access. A relational database consists simply of a set of relations. Thus, the conceptual model of a relational database is very simple. In particular, there are no pointers. Information about the relationship between records must be contained as data in the records.

Let us consider the same situation as in the previous examples. The relational database might have the same files as the DBTG database. There would be a DEPT file with the department name, and other information such as location, phone number, etc., of which we will show only the phone number. Then there will be the PROF file with the professors' names, and other information such as office location and phone number, which we will not show. This relational database must show which department each professor is in by data (whereas in the DBTG and IMS databases this information is shown by pointers), and this would be done by including the department name in each PROF record. Similarly, the STUDENT file would have to include the students' name, the department name, and the advisor's name. Data on the courses taken by each student can be included in a manner analogous to that used in the DBTG example, that is, by having a file ENROLL that contains records consisting of a student's name and a course name (and perhaps a grade and date) indicating that that student took that course. An example of how this database might look is shown in Figure 5.20.

The word relation is used because this structure corresponds to the general definition of a relation in mathematics. The mathematical term corresponding to a record is *n-tuple* where n is the number of data items in the record. (A record with two items would be called a pair, with three items a triple, with four items a 4-tuple, etc.) The set of all possible values for one data item is called its domain, and the particular value is called

```
DEPT                          STUDENT
DNAME     DPHONE              SNAME      SDEPT      ADVISOR

ART       7292                HIGA       MATH       VILLA
CS        7420                JONES      CS         LIN
MATH      7361                LEE        MATH       MAU
                             PARK       ART        SATO
                             SAITO      CS         LIN
                             SMITH      CS         MEYER


PROF                          ENROLL

PNAME     PDEPT              ENAME      ECOURSE

LIN       CS                 JONES      MATH 210
MAU       MATH               JONES      CS 100
MEYER     CS                 LEE        CS 100
SATO      ART                PARK       MATH 210
VILLA     MATH               SMITH      MATH 210
                             SMITH      MATH 310
                             SMITH      CS 100
```

Figure 5.20 Relational Database Example.

an attribute. For example, the set of all possible department names is the domain of NAME IN DEPT and "MATH" is an example of an attribute. The relation also can be thought of as a table in which the rows are the records or n-tuples. Corresponding to each column there is a domain and all the values in that column are attributes from that domain.

Statements analogous to those shown for DBTG and IMS databases can be used with relational databases. For example, one might provide a GET statement that could find any record in a file that satisfies some specified condition. For example, to find a given student's advisor's phone number, we might write

```
GET STUDENT WHERE (NAME IN STUDENT IS
    EQUAL TO "SMITH")
GET PROF WHERE (NAME IN PROF IS EQUAL TO
    ADVISOR IN STUDENT)
```

and then the advisor's record is in working storage and the phone number, etc. are available. For retrieval where there may be more than one record, one could provide GET FIRST and GET NEXT. Statements similar to ordinary statements in COBOL or PL/I could be provided for inserting, rewriting, or deleting records in any relation.

However, most relational systems use a higher-level approach. It is possible to define operations on relations that give new relations. In general, the result of a query can be considered to be a relation and can be gotten as the result of some of these operations on relations. We will use SEQUEL (Structured English QUEry Language)[G7, Chapter 7] as an example. In SEQUEL, the term *table* is used instead of *relation, column* is used instead of *attribute*, and *row* instead of *n-tuple*.

In SEQUEL, finding and getting data is done using the SELECT statement, which has the form

```
SELECT list of columns
    FROM list of tables
    WHERE logical expression
```

The list of tables may be one or more of the available tables, and the list of columns is a list of one or more of the columns in the tables listed. Conceptually, the system first makes one large table in which the rows are all possible rows that can be made by choosing one row from each table listed (i. e., the Cartesian product of the relations). Then it selects the rows that satisfy the logical expression, and finally it keeps only those columns listed. SEQUEL does not eliminate duplicates unless that is specified (by writing SELECT UNIQUE instead of simply SELECT). It also is possible to specify that the result is to be sorted and on which columns.

The permitted logical expressions include the ordinary comparison operations, AND, OR, and NOT, and parentheses. Set operations IS IN, IS NOT IN, CONTAINS, DOES NOT CONTAIN, UNION, INTERSECTION, and MINUS also are included.

Here are several examples based on the relation examples in Figure 5.20. First, let us make a list of the names of all students whose advisor is Villa:

```
SELECT NAME
    FROM STUDENT
    WHERE ADVISOR = 'VILLA'
```

An asterisk is used as an abbreviation to mean that all columns should be kept. Thus, the following program segment will retrieve all student records of students in the mathematics department whose advisor is Villa:

```
SELECT *
    FROM STUDENT
    WHERE DEPT = 'MATH' AND ADVISOR = 'VILLA'
```

Now let us retrieve a list of students with the department and the department phone number for each:

```
SELECT SNAME, DNAME, DPHONE
    FROM STUDENT, DEPT
    WHERE SDEPT = DNAME
```

The result of a select operation is a table, and it can be assigned to a variable and saved.

```
PALIST(PANAME,PADEPT,PAPHONE)   =
    SELECT SNAME, DNAME, DPHONE
        FROM STUDENT, DEPT
        WHERE SDEPT = DNAME
```

Expressions using the tables produced by SELECT statements also are possible. The following examples use such a set in the logical expression. Let us retrieve a list of students who have taken both Math 210 and Math 310:

```
SELECT SNAME
    FROM STUDENT
    WHERE ('MATH 210', 'MATH 310') IS IN
        (SELECT ECOURSE
            FROM ENROLL
            WHERE ENAME = SNAME)
```

The following expression will retrieve a list of all students who have taken every course taken by a student named Baker:

```
SELECT SNAME
    FROM STUDENT
    WHERE (SELECT ECOURSE
            FROM ENROLL
            WHERE ENAME = 'BAKER')
        CONTAINS
            (SELECT ECOURSE
                FROM ENROLL
                WHERE ENAME = SNAME)
```

Finally, let us retrieve a list of all students who have taken Math 210 but not Math 310:

```
(SELECT SNAME
    FROM STUDENT
    WHERE 'MATH 210' IS IN
        (SELECT ECOURSE
            FROM ENROLL
            WHERE ENAME = SNAME))
MINUS
(SELECT SNAME
    FROM STUDENT
    WHERE 'MATH 310' IS IN
        (SELECT ECOURSE
            FROM ENROLL
            WHERE ENAME = SNAME))
```

In many of these cases, the same retrieval can be done in several different ways because of the richness of the language.

SEQUEL also provides for maintenance of the files. A simple update is done as follows:

```
UPDATE STUDENT
    SET ADVISOR = 'SMITH'
    WHERE SNAME = 'JONES'
```

Insertion may be a single row:

```
INSERT INTO STUDENT:
    <'LEE','ART','OKADA'>
```

Also, a table may be inserted into another table. Suppose that NEWLIST is a list of new course enrollments in the same format as ENROLL. Then one could write

```
INSERT INTO ENROLL:
    NEWLIST
```

The table being inserted also may be an expression. Finally there is a DELETE statement which may delete a row:

```
DELETE STUDENT
    WHERE SNAME = 'SMITH'
```

or it may delete a whole table:

```
    DELETE NEWLIST
```

There are a number of different relational systems with different languages. Another very interesting one is called "Query by Example." It is primarily a query language intended for nontechnical users. The user constructs an "example" of the kind of table he or she wants to see on the video terminal screen using hypothetical data. Then the system examines the example and from it determines how to construct the required table of actual data (which is a relation) from the relations stored in the database.

It is with relational databases that the distinction between the conceptual model and the actual implementation becomes extremely important. The conceptual model is simple and easy to understand. Powerful yet easy to understand and easy to use languages like SEQUEL and Query by Example can be designed. But if the implementation is done in the obvious way from the conceptual model, the system will be neither very efficient in its use of storage, nor very fast. It is possible to use indexes and pointers to facilitate access. The existence of a good theoretical foundation helps make it possible to design good access mechanisms and to be sure that they will work correctly.

There are many ways in which the actual implementation may differ from the conceptual model[G12]. For example, the files may be inverted—there can be an indexed list of all values of an attribute that actually occur, such as a file containing all employee names. In the relations, instead of entering the attribute itself, a pointer might be entered. This would make the relation files smaller and easier to search. There might be pointers with each attribute in the attribute files to the records in the relation files that contain that attribute. There might be pointers in some relation files that point to related tuples in the same or a different relation. Note that these pointers are redundant and are included solely for expediting access.

NOTES

Introductions to data structures are given in [F5], [F7], and [F8]. Related graph theory concepts appear in [F9] and [F10]. Related programming language facilities are described in [F11]. Record handling facilities of languages also are discussed in [K7].

File structures are emphasized in [F1]–[F3]. Database structures are surveyed in [G1]–[G6] and [F4], and are discussed in detail in [G7]–[G11] and [G13]–[G15]. [G13] has an especially extensive bibliography.

EXERCISES

5-1. Show the lists and trees of Figures 5.4 and 5.5, respectively, after Honolulu is inserted in sequence alphabetically.

5-2. Consider Example 5.2. Show what the catalog would look like if the names WWP.PROJA.PROGC.OLD   and WWP.PROJA.PROGC.NEW were added.

5-3. Suppose the data-items A, B, C, and D have probabilities of access equal to 0.10, 0.15, 0.20, and 0.55, respectively. Which of the binary trees shown in Figure 5.21 can be binary-searched in the least time on the average? (Explain!)

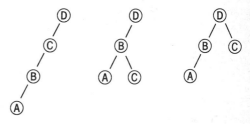

Figure 5.21 Sorted Trees for Exercise 5-3.

5-4(a). Consider Example 5.3 and Figure 5.8. Show what the B-tree would look like after the names MAX, MEL, and NAN are inserted.

5-4(b). Consider Example 5.4 and Figure 5.9. Show what the B$^+$-tree would look like after the names GILES and KATHY are inserted.

5-5(a). Consider Example 5.5. Show what the file and index would look like after the name GILES is inserted.

5-5(b). Consider Example 5.5. Show what the linked multilist and its indexes would look like if the record HALL is deleted from the file.

5-6. Consider Figures 5.12 and 5.13. Show what the
  (a) linked multilist
  (b) inverted multilist
would look like if (ID = 1234,Name = BILBO,Loc = D,Job = ET) were added as the eleventh record (record number = 10).

5-7. Consider the following records:

AB	103
BB	104
AA	102
BF	102
AC	104

which consists of names as primary keys and numbers as secondary keys. Show how these records would be stored on a disk, unblocked, two records per track,

(a) sequentially, in entry order, with an index sorted in primary key order and track-number pointers.

(b) sequentially, in primary key order, with an index of track numbers and high keys.

(c) sequentially, in entry order, and as a multilist, one list chained in primary key order, another list chained in secondary key order.

(d) sequentially, in primary key order, and as an inverted list with an index of secondary key values.

5-8. Consider the following records:

AB	103
BB	104
AA	102
BF	102
AC	104

which consist of names as primary-keys and numbers as secondary keys. Show how these records would be stored on disk, unblocked, two records per track, sequentially in primary-key order, and as a cellular multilist that is partially inverted by secondary-key attributes.

5-9. Consider the following file of six records:

P 102 , S 104 , B 104 , O 103 , H 103 , F 103

Show these records stored as a partially inverted multilist.

5-10. Consider the following file of six records:

O 104 , R 102 , A 102 , N 103 , G 103 , E 103

Show these records stored as a cellular multilist.

5-11. What record type and blocking format would be most appropriate for a file of records whose lengths vary from 50 to 500 bytes with an average length of 70 bytes? Assume a magnetic drum with a fixed 256-byte block length will be used to store the records.

5-12. Using any language implementation available that has a relative file system, write a program to implement one of the multilists shown as an example, including inserting and deleting entries and a few likely types of inquiries. Use simple sequential searching where searching is needed.

5-13. *If a database system is available:* Implement the university database example and make insertions, deletions, modifications, and a variety of inquiries.

5-14. *If a database is not available:* Program a simplified database system and do the preceding exercise to test it.

File Design

6.1. FILES

A file is a collection of data stored outside the main storage of a computer. It can be very large. It is usually impossible or undesirable to put the whole file in main storage, so it is divided into parts, called *records*, that can logically be processed apart from the rest of the file. For example, in a personnel file, all the data pertaining to one person normally should comprise one logical record. Although a file usually contains many records, it may contain as few as one. Note the distinction between a *block* and a *record*. Each read or write operation reads or writes one physical block. However, a call to a read subroutine that results from a **read** statement in a higher level-language program makes one record available, usually from a buffer area in the memory, and causes an actual read when the buffer is emptied. Similarly, a call to a write subroutine that results from a **write** statement in a higher level-language program sends one record to a buffer area with move-mode buffering or makes a new record-size area available in a buffer in locate-mode buffering, and causes an actual write when the buffer becomes full.

A record may be too small or too large to read or write efficiently on auxiliary storage in one step. Thus, a number of records might be grouped to make a block, or a record might be divided into several blocks of a size convenient for the auxiliary storage devices. It is not uncommon to have one record per block, however. In Section 6.10, we discuss record structures, that is, the relationship between records and blocks of various lengths. We also mention, in Section 6.11, how in some cases space for records can be reduced. These aspects of the design of files affect the manner and efficiency with which information in files can be accessed and processed.

Each data record has a physical address in the file by which the record can be accessed. For tapes, this address is its ordinal position on the tape;

131

that is, the number 5 is the address of the fifth record on the tape. For disks and drums, the address of a record consists of its cylinder and/or track number and the ordinal position of the record on the track. Because the addresses are numerical, the records of a file are physically ordered by increasing addresses, whether or not they have any other "logical" ordering.

Because of the nature of tapes, it is very efficient to process records on a tape in sequence by their physical order, but almost invariably it is prohibitively inefficient to process the records in any other sequence. Although it is practical to process records on disk or drum in any sequence, it is much faster to process all records in their physical sequence rather than in random order. Thus, other things being equal, sequential processing is preferred. Let us examine some of the situations where sequential processing is and is not indicated.

6.2. COMMON FILE-ACCESSING REQUIREMENTS

First, if the order in which the records are processed is immaterial, then they should be processed in their physical sequence to minimize the I-O time. This would be the case, for example, for a program that simply counts data or calculates the average, standard deviation, or other statistics independent of the order of the data. Next, in cases where the order of processing is determined, it is natural and efficient to store the records in the order in which they will be processed. An example is a program that prints a report for which the order of printing is specified, perhaps by alphabetical order or date. Another example is a compiler, which must process the statements comprising a program in sequence.

There also are situations in which a particular task can be achieved efficiently using sequential processing if the file is in a specified order. For example, if a file is sorted on a certain key, then it is easy to find all cases of two or more records with the same key by going through the file sequentially once. One of the most common data-processing situations is file updating. There is a *master file*, and a separate file of *transactions* that contains data to be entered into the master file. Each master record has a key such as a name, a social security number, or an account number, and each transaction has a key to indicate to which master record it applies. If both the master file and the transactions are sorted by the key, then updating can be achieved very efficiently by going through the two files together once. File updating is discussed further in Chapter 7.

In other situations, random access, that is, access to any record at any time, is required. This is obviously the case for on-line systems such as airline reservations, point-of-sale systems in retail stores, or a library inquiry system.

It may be that in a given situation, although sequential processing is possible, random access is more efficient. In the updating situation, for example, if every record is to be updated during one update run, sequential processing is more efficient; if only one record is to be updated, random access would be better. There is a crossover point p such that if the percentage of records being updated is less than p, random access is more efficient, whereas if the percentage of records being updated is greater than p, sequential processing is more efficient. The value of p will depend on the hardware characteristics and the size of the file, records, etc. The value of p can be found for a specific situation by calculating the time or costs for both sequential and random processing for various values of p and plotting the two together as graphs.

In still other situations, the same file must be accessed randomly at one time and sequentially at another. For example, in an on-line inventory control system, the daily processing requires random access to the master file to record changes in the inventory as they occur. Periodically, once a day or once a month, a report is printed in sequence by item number or item name. In a time-sharing system for on-line programming, making corrections to a program requires random access to the file containing the program, but compiling requires reading the file in sequence.

There is another independent aspect of files that is very relevant to their structure. Some problems require frequent insertions and/or deletions to the file. Other files do not require such changes. A personnel file, an inventory file, a customer file, or a file containing a program being developed require numerous insertions and deletions. In a dictionary, daily insertions and deletions are not needed. A mathematical table would never change.

If there are not too many deletions and if rewriting of records is allowed, deletions can be handled by simply marking the record as deleted. The main cost is the wasted space occupied by the "deleted" records, which also may result in some lost time. Inserting records is not so easy. Space must be provided for them, but it is nearly always impossible to predict exactly how much space is needed and where. Several techniques for handling this problem are discussed later in this chapter.

One other requirement is worthy of note—it may be necessary with a random-access file to be able to find a record given any one of two or more keys. For example, it may be necessary to be able to find a record given either the name or the social security number.

Chapter 8 describes in some detail the statements provided in the most-used high-level languages for input and output. The actual I-O is done by system I-O subroutines, and the compilers compile calls to these subroutines. Here, we summarize briefly the facilities ordinarily available. For sequential I-O, there are statements that say, "prepare to access the first record," "read the next record," and "write the next record," so that records must be processed in sequence, except that it is possible to go back to the beginning of the file.

For random access, higher-level languages usually handle two distinct file organizations—relative and indexed. For a relative file, the user specifies the record number within the file, for example, "read record number 17" or "write record number N." Note that a relative file can be accessed sequentially by requesting "read record number 1," then "read record number 2," etc. In the conceptual model of an indexed file, the records are stored in sequence by key, although, as we will see, they may not be stored sequentially in the implementation. Subroutines are provided for reading, writing, inserting, and deleting records given the key. Thus, typical statements are "read the record whose key is k," "insert the record whose key is k," "rewrite the record whose key is k," and "delete the record whose key is k." The sequential-access statements, "prepare to access the first record," "read the next record," and "write the next record," also are provided. Thus, both relative and indexed files can be accessed either randomly or sequentially.

6.3. SEQUENTIAL FILES

For sequential files, records are stored so that the desired order of access is the physical order. The only problem is insertions and deletions. Sequential files are commonly processed periodically; each time they are processed, a new master file is produced with the changes, insertions, and deletions. If the file is on tape, the old master file may be kept for backup and perhaps as a permanent record. Alternatively, to handle a relatively few insertions without copying the file, a separate small file of insertions may be kept. If a record is not found in the main file, the insertion file is checked. On a disk file, deletions can be handled by marking the record as deleted. This will not work on tape files because rewriting a record in the middle of a file is not allowed.

A variation of sequential files is a stream file, where data items (as opposed to records) are ordered in physical sequence. These data items can be written individually or in groups. The data items then can be read sequentially, individually, or in groups that need not correspond to the same groups as written. In stream files, physical or logical record boundaries have no significance.

6.4. RANDOM-ACCESS FILES

For random-access files, the user may specify either the relative record number or the key of the record to be read or written. When relative record numbers are used, the records are stored such that their physical sequence corresponds to the relative record numbers. The records must have fixed lengths; then the physical address of a record can be calculated from the relative record number, knowledge of the location of the first record, and the size of each record.

Consider the case where for each access a key is specified, and the record with that key is to be read or written. If, for a file of N records, the keys are the numbers from 0 to $N-1$, then the obvious solution is to store the record whose key is i as relative record number i. If it is possible to calculate a unique integer between 0 and $N-1$ for each key, then the calculated integer can be used as the relative record number. For example, if the file stores mathematical tables and the keys are 0.00, 0.01, 0.02, and so on, then multiplying the key by 100 gives a suitable physical address. For a building with n rooms on each floor and m floors, the formula $n(i-1) + (j-1)$ gives a unique integer between 0 and $mn-1$ for each room, where $1 \leqslant i \leqslant m$ is the floor number and $1 \leqslant j \leqslant n$ is the room number on the floor.

Suppose we have a file of 8000 records that have four-digit keys. Then it is practical to use a relative file with space for 10,000 records and use the key as the record number—the record numbers would range from 0000 to 9999. Only 80% of those numbers are actually in use, so the file space would be only 80% utilized. We will see that, in general, one cannot expect to do better, and that it is a reasonable price to pay for the ability to do random access with random insertion and deletion.

Unfortunately, in the more usual cases, there is no way to calculate a unique relative address for each record. For example, social security numbers are commonly used. For a group of 10,000 people, we would need 10,000 records. But there are 1,000,000,000 different social security numbers. It is out of the question to provide a record space for each possible number. There exist ways to arrange the records so that we can determine the approximate location of each in the file and then do a relatively small amount of searching. The time required is greater than in the case where the exact record location can be determined from the key, but still can be kept within practical limits. There are two very commonly used methods for accomplishing this, and many variations on each. They are usually called *indexed sequential files* and *hashed files*.

6.5. INDEXED SEQUENTIAL FILES

Conceptually, an indexed sequential file is stored in sequential order by key. (The order may not be physically sequential in an actual implementation.) Typically an index or table is kept to aid in locating a record. The index contains the location of every kth record for some suitably chosen k. (Usually it works out well to choose k to be the number of records in a block, so that an index entry points to a block.) Then one searches the index to find the segment (or block) of the file containing the desired record, and then searches that segment to find the record. (Searching and indexing are discussed in more detail later.) This is quite efficient as long as there are no insertions and deletions.

Deletions simply can be flagged. However, insertions cause a serious problem. One must plan where to put them and there is no perfect solution. One solution is to divide the file into segments and leave extra space in each segment to accommodate insertions. Because some segments probably will have more insertions than others, we must plan that the capacity may be exceeded for some. Thus, we might provide an overflow segment for each s segments for a suitably chosen s. Some overflow segments may overflow, too, so a master overflow area also might be provided. We will refer to this file organization as "indexed sequential with overflow areas." This was essentially the method used by IBM in ISAM, which was perhaps the earliest widely used implementation of an indexed file.

There is another method of handling insertions and deletions that has proved to be more efficient and is used in one form or another as the basis for most modern indexed-sequential file systems. This method is based on B^+-trees. The file is divided into segments and some free space is left in each segment. Some unused segments are provided for overflow. When a segment fills and another record must be inserted, then the contents of that segment are divided in half, and the records in one half are put in a new segment. Both the old segment and the new one, being only half full, have room for insertions. The segments are not necessarily in physical sequence, but their locations are kept in the index so the records can be found easily. They also may be chained, that is, each segment may contain a pointer that tells the location of the next segment to facilitate sequential access. We will refer to this indexed file organization as a *segmented file*.

If the file is very large, then the index is very large, and searching it is a problem. It is natural to handle it in the same way as the file, that is, to make a second-level index. Of course, insertions into the index may be necessary. This can be handled by dividing the index into segments of capacity k entries, initially not filling them completely, and when they overflow, splitting them just as with the main file. More than two levels of indexing may be necessary. Most modern indexed sequential file systems, including IBM's VSAM, are organized in this manner; that is, they provide for multiple-level indexes and organize the main file and the indexes as segmented files.

We have arrived at essentially the B^+-tree structure from a different viewpoint. The algorithms for insertion and deletion as described in Chapter 5 are more general and very suitable for a practical implementation.

Also, it was implied that the file is originally set up with a predetermined amount of space left in each segment for insertions. In this way, the initial occupancy percentage can be controlled. In some implementations of COBOL and PL/I, statements for sequential loading of a file will set up the file in this manner. However, in other implementations, the statements for sequential loading will do the kind of insertion described for B$^+$-trees in Chapter 5, that is, the file is built by starting with an empty file and inserting records one by one.

In reading an indexed sequential file sequentially, if it is necessary to read blocks that are not physically adjacent, seek time and latency time are introduced. If the file is first set up by sequential loading, it will be in sequence physically and can be read fast. However, as insertions are made, more and more occurrences of blocks out of physical sequence will occur and sequential read time gradually will increase. Sequential read time can be reduced again by writing the contents of the file out sequentially to a temporary file and then reloading it sequentially into the indexed file.

Example 6.1

We will show in detail a very small indexed sequential file using the segmented-type structure. Each record consists of a name and a phone number, the name being the key. Each segment is a block containing first the pointer (a block number) and space for three records. Initially, two records are put in each block, one space is allowed for overflow, and the blocks are in sequence. Figure 6.1 shows the initial state

```
Block Pointer              Block
 No.

  0      1        ADAMS   2619151   BAKER   3152712
  1      2        CARTER  2616225   CASTRO  4937127
  2      3        CHANG   5162627   DAVIS   7212883
  3      4        HALL    3172939   JORDAN  5169227
  4      5        KAM     6132771   KING    9236956
  5     -1        LEE     7218518   LONG    6443715
  6     -1

Index:
       Last Key in Block                  Block No.
              BAKER                            0
              CASTRO                           1
              DAVIS                            2
              JORDAN                           3
              KING                             4
              LONG                             5
```

Figure 6.1 Example of an Indexed File—Initial State.

of the file. Note that a pointer value of -1 means that it is the last block. Block 6 is an overflow block.

Now assume that FOX is inserted. Comparison with the index shows that it should be inserted into segment 3 with HALL and JORDAN. Next, insert KATO—it will fall into block 4. Next, insert JONES. It should fall into block 3, but block 3 is full. Therefore, we divide block 3 into two blocks, putting JONES and JORDAN in the overflow block (block 6), keeping FOX and HALL in block 3, and adjusting the index accordingly. To locate JONES, for example, we examine the index and find that, being between HALL and JORDAN, it must be in the same block as JORDAN, that is, block 6. The state of the file at this point is shown in Figure 6.2. (In contrast, when using ISAM, JORDAN would be placed in a separate overflow area.)

The example of a B$^+$-tree in Chapter 5 also illustrates insertion and deletion of records from an indexed sequential file.

6.6. SEARCHING SEQUENTIAL AND INDEXED SEQUENTIAL FILES

A file may be searched sequentially from beginning to end no matter how it is arranged. A sequential search for a record with a specified key requires, on the average, going through half the file, about $N/2$ records for a file of N records, if the record is found. If it is not found, the whole file is searched. If the file is in sequence by key, a sequential search may be terminated as soon as a key is found that exceeds the desired key

```
Block  Pointer              Block
No.

0        1       ADAMS   2619151  BAKER   3152712
1        2       CARTER  2616225  CASTRO  4937127
2        3       CHANG   5162627  DAVIS   7212883
3        6       FOX     9234227  HALL    3172939
4        5       KAM     6132771  KATO    2618575  KING  9236956
5       -1       LEE     7218518  LONG    6443715
6        4       JONES   6442484  JORDAN  5169227

Index:
        Last Key in Block              Block No.
        BAKER                             0
        CASTRO                            1
        DAVIS                             2
        HALL                              3
        JORDAN                            6
        KING                              4
        LONG                              5
```

Figure 6.2 Indexed File Example After Insertions.

even if the desired record is not found. In this case, the length of the search is about half the length of the file on the average, whether the record is found or not.

If a file is sorted in sequence by key, then a binary search may be used. One first compares the key of the desired record to the key of the middle record of the file and determines which half of the file the record is in. Another comparison is made to the middle record of that half, which narrows the search to one-fourth of the file. The process continues until the search is narrowed to a single record. For a file of n records, the binary search requires examining about $\log_2(n)$ records.

For large n, the number of accesses saved is substantial—for 1000 records, sequential searching requires examining about 500 records whereas the binary search requires examining about 10. But the binary search is more complicated, requiring more time per record examined. A precise comparison is computer dependent. Typically, if the searches are done in main storage, the two methods are about equal at $n = 20$ with the sequential search faster for smaller n. For a search on disk or drum storage, the binary search requires essentially random access with considerably more seek and latency time than the sequential search. The crossover depends on the characteristics of the disk or drum unit, the record lengths, and the blocking factor, but will be a significantly larger value of n. For a specific situation, points can be calculated for various values of n using the methods described in Chapters 3 and 4, and the crossover can be determined fairly accurately using curves that fit the calculated points.

For a sequential file stored in sequence by key, an index may be used. The index would consist of a table showing the key and location of every kth record for some suitably chosen k. Given the key of the desired record, one can search the index and determine which block of k records contains the desired record. Then this block must be searched. So now we have two searches. The next question is, by what method do we conduct these searches? Both the index and the block of k records will be in sequence by key, so those searches may be done either sequentially or by a binary search, or another index may be used.

It is interesting to note that if both searches of an indexed file are done as binary searches, the total number of accesses required always will be about the same as if there were no index. This can be seen as follows. Assume an index of N_i entries referencing blocks of length N_b. Then $N = N_i \times N_b$. Without an index, this requires about $\log_2(N) = \log_2(N_i) + \log_2(N_b)$ accesses. Searching the index requires about $\log_2(N_i)$ accesses, while searching a block requires about $\log_2(N_b)$ accesses. Still it may be advantageous to have an index. For example, if the index is placed in main storage, it may be searched very quickly, so the overall time would be significantly smaller if the index is used.

Example 6.2

Assume a file of 60,000 records. A simple sequential search would require accessing an average of 30,000 records, a prohibitive value. A binary search would require about $\log_2(60{,}000)$ or about 16 accesses. If we indexed segments of $k = 250$ records, then the index would have $60{,}000/250 = 240$ entries. If both the index and the block are searched sequentially, an average of $250/2 + 240/2 = 245$ accesses will be required—a large, but not prohibitive number. If both are searched by a binary search, each would require about eight accesses, so the total would be 16, just as without the index.

Let us also consider a two-level index. Divide the file into 2000 segments of 30 records each, with a 2000 entry index placed on the disk unit. Then divide the index into segments of 40 entries and provide a second-level index of 50 entries to point to those index segments. Now if we do a sequential search of the second-level index, one segment of the first-level index, and one data segment, the total number of accesses is $50/2 + 40/2 + 30/2 = 60$. Furthermore, if the 50-entry index is in the main storage, then only $40/2 + 30/2 = 35$ disk accesses are required. Taking into account that the file is probably blocked and that the binary search requires an extra seek and latency for each access, a detailed calculation of the average access time should show the two-level index with sequential searches to be faster.

Example 6.5 in Section 6.9 provides a detailed illustration of how an indexed file might be designed.

6.7. HASHED FILES

There are many variations of hashed files. One variation, called *open addressing*, is well adapted to disk files. The space for the file is divided into h *buckets* numbered 0 to $h-1$, of capacity b records per bucket. (Almost invariably, the best choice is to use one block as one bucket.) The designer chooses a *hashing* formula that derives a number, called a *hashed address*, between 0 and $h-1$ from each key. A very frequently used hashing method is to treat the key as a number (for example, by using the numeric value of its binary encoding if it is not a number) and divide the key by h, keeping the remainder as the hashed address. The hashed address is used to find a bucket at which a search for a record key or an open space can be started.

To insert a record with a given key in the file:

1. Calculate the hashed address i from the key.
2. Check buckets $i, i + 1, i + 2$, etc. until an open space for a record

is found. After the last bucket, $h-1$, start from bucket 0 and continue to bucket $i-1$. If no open space is found by then, the file is full and no record can be inserted.

3. When an open space is found, insert the record in it.

To find a record with a given key:

1. Calculate the hashed address i from the key.
2. Search for the record in buckets i, $i + 1$, $i + 2$, etc. After the last bucket, $h-1$, start from bucket 0 and continue to bucket $i-1$. If $i-1$ is reached, the whole file has been searched and the record is not there.

If the record is in the file, it will be found, and usually in the first bucket examined, so the search generally is very fast.

During insertion, it is necessary sometimes to look beyond bucket i for an open space because there is a possibility that too many records have hashed address i. Then bucket i can become full and an additional record would overflow. This is referred to as a *collision*. It generally is impossible to find a hashing formula with which collisions do not occur. With a good hashing method, one can expect to achieve about as few collisions as would occur if one assigned hashed addresses randomly according to a uniform distribution, that is, if the possible addresses $0,1, ..., h-1$ all had equal probability and the addresses were assigned to the records independently.

If a record is in the file, the number of buckets searched to find it will be exactly the same as the number of buckets searched to find the open space to store it when it was originally placed in the file. In many applications, it is necessary to search the file for a record not knowing for certain whether or not the record is in the file. The open-addressing algorithm given would result in searching the whole file every time a search occurred for a nonexistent record. It is possible to do better than that by modifying the algorithm for searching to stop as soon as an open record space is met. When a record is inserted, it is inserted in the first bucket at or beyond its hashed address in which there is space. Therefore, there must be no open space between a record and its hashed address. If we find an open space, we know that the desired record cannot be beyond it and must not be in the file.

Example 6.3

We will show a hashed file using the same records as in the indexed-sequential file example. Again we will assume three records per block and use one block as a bucket. We will assume seven blocks are available, and use the open-addressing algorithm. As a hashing function, we will use the following: Giving A the value 0, B the value 1, C the value 2, etc., add the values of the first two letters in the name, divide by 7, and keep the remainder. (This is too simple to be a good algorithm in a real application—it probably would not lead to an adequately uniform distribution.) The records were inserted in the file in sequence by key. The process is summarized as follows: For ADAMS, the bucket number is A + D = 0 + 3 = 3; for BAKER, B + A = 1 + 0 = 1; for CHANG, C + H = 2 + 7 = 9. Dividing 9 by 7 gives a remainder 2, so CHANG goes in bucket 2. Note also that the number of buckets accessed is equal to one more than the difference between the hashed address and the address of the bucket actually used.

Key	Hashed Address	Bucket	Number of Buckets Accessed
ADAMS	3	3	1
BAKER	1	1	1
CARTER	2	2	1
CASTRO	2	2	1
CHANG	2	2	1
DAVIS	3	3	1
FOX	5	5	1
HALL	0	0	1
JONES	2	3 (2 full)	2
JORDAN	2	4 (2 and 3 full)	3
KAM	3	4 (3 full)	2
KATO	3	4 (3 full)	2
KING	4	5 (4 full)	2
LEE	1	1	1
LONG	4	5 (4 full)	2

Then the file looks like this:

Bucket Number	Bucket Contents						
0	HALL	3172939					
1	BAKER	3152712	LEE	7218518			
2	CARTER	2616225	CASTRO	4937127	CHANG	5162627
3	ADAMS	2619151	DAVIS	7212883	JONES	6442484
4	JORDAN	5169227	KAM	6132771	KATO	2618575
5	FOX	9234227	KING	9236956	LONG	6443715
6						

To search for LONG, for example, first calculate the hashed address. L + O = 11 + 14 = 25, which after dividing by 7 gives remainder 4. We start at bucket 4 and search until we find the record in bucket 5. To search for SMITH, we calculate the hashed address, which comes out to 2, and search starting at block 2. In block 6, we find a space and conclude that if SMITH were there it would have been in some previous space; therefore, SMITH is not in the file.

In this file, JONES, KAM, KATO, KING, and LONG are in the next block after the hashed address and JORDAN is in the second block after its hashed address. The nine others are in the block given by the hashed address. The average length of search is

$$L_{ave} = \frac{(9 \times 1 + 5 \times 2 + 1 \times 3)}{15} = 1.467 \text{ buckets}$$

Note that the records put in the file first usually fall in their proper bucket, although the later ones are more likely to overflow into other buckets. It turns out, however, that the average number of buckets accessed is the same, no matter in what order the records are entered. This can be shown as follows.

Consider a file consisting of records R_1, R_2, ..., R_i, R_{i+1}, ..., R_n, and consider the effect of interchanging only records R_i and R_{i+1}. Suppose that if we enter records $R_1, R_2, ..., R_{i-1}, R_i$, then record R_i goes into bucket B, and that if we enter $R_1, R_2, ..., R_{i-1}, R_{i+1}$, then record R_{i+1} goes into bucket B'. Now B and B' are either the same or different buckets. In the latter case, if we enter $R_1, R_2, ..., R_{i-1}, R_i$, then bucket B' is still open. If we enter R_{i+1} next, then it will go into B'. Similarly, if we enter R_1, $R_2, ..., R_{i-1}, R_{i+1}$, followed by R_i, then R_i will go into bucket B. Therefore, interchanging R_i and R_{i+1} in the file has no effect whatsoever.

Now suppose B and B' are the same. If there is enough space in bucket B for both records, both will go in that bucket, no matter which record is inserted first. On the other hand, suppose that there is only enough space in bucket B for one more record. If we enter $R_1, R_2, ..., R_{i-1}, R_i$, followed by record R_{i+1}, then bucket B will be examined in searching for an open space and the search will continue to the next open bucket, which we denote B''. Similarly, if $R_1, R_2, ..., R_{i-1}, R_{i+1}$ are entered, followed by R_i, then again the search for an open space will examine bucket B and, finding it occupied by R_{i+1}, will continue to the next open space, which again must be B''. Therefore, the result in this case is that exchanging the two records results in exchanging the buckets into which they go. This does not affect where subsequent records go. The number of buckets accessed in searching for R_{i+1} decreases, and the number for R_i increases by exactly the same amount. This leaves the average the same.

Any rearrangement whatsoever of a file can be accomplished by exchanging pairs of successive records, although a large number of exchanges may be necessary. Because each step leaves the average number of buckets accessed unaffected, the average will be the same for any rearrangement of the same records.

Note that there is little relation between the physical sequence of records in a hashed file and their sequence by key. Thus, the records cannot be read in sequence by key. (They can be written out and sorted, of course.) If the records are inserted in sequence by key, then they will be in sequence by key within each bucket, as in the preceding example. If they are stored in sequence by frequency of use, the most-used records first, then they will be in this order within the buckets and the most frequently used records will not overflow, which minimizes searching time.

As long as there are any open spaces in a hashed file, it is possible to insert a record. When the file is nearly full, however, a long search for an open space may occur. Then a long search is also required to retrieve this record. If the file becomes nearly full, the average length of search may become excessive.

The obvious way to handle deletions is simply to flag deleted records. Those flagged records may be used for later insertions. However, there are two difficulties with this method.

First, in searching for a record, the search cannot be terminated when a deleted record is met, because the desired record may be beyond that position. Therefore, one must distinguish between open record spaces resulting from deleted records and record spaces that have never been used. Furthermore, after many insertions and deletions, the never-used spaces gradually will become more and more scarce. Eventually, there may be no never-used spaces even though there may be a lot of open record spaces in the file. A search for a nonexistent record (i.e., one whose key is not in the file) also will become longer and longer and may eventually proceed through the entire file.

Second, records inserted into a hashed file when it is not filled near capacity will be more likely to be in or near the bucket given by the hashed address than records inserted when the file is nearly full. On the average, records require longer and longer access times as they are inserted. If there are many insertions and deletions, even if the total number of records remains almost constant, the average access time gradually will increase because on the average deleted records more likely will have been stored closer to their hashed address than their replacements. The average access time may increase to where the average number of buckets accessed becomes several times the original value. Simulation results showing this effect appear in [H6]. Both these problems can be alleviated by periodically "reorganizing" the file. One simply writes all the records out and then reads them in again in any order, thus restoring the file to the condition in which no insertions and deletions have occurred. However, there is a better method.

Knuth [H1, p.526] suggests a good method for overcoming these problems. When you delete a record and therefore create an open space, you search beyond that record position for a record that would have gone into that space if it had been open at the time that record was inserted. If such a record is found, it is moved to the space vacated by the deleted record. Then a similar search must be made for a record that might have gone into the space just vacated by that record, and so on. This searching can be terminated as soon as a never-used space is found. (Some time can be saved by not moving records backwards within the same bucket. This is done by starting the search at the following bucket.) It is not difficult to verify that if the file was created by inserting all the records in a certain sequence and a certain record was deleted using this algorithm, then the resulting file is essentially the same as it would be if those same records were inserted in the same order without the deleted record. (Records within a bucket may not be in exactly the same sequence.) This algorithm is implemented in the example programs in Chapter 8 and the appendices.

Example 6.4

Let us delete CARTER from the file of Example 6.3 using this algorithm. This leaves a space in bucket 2. Examining succeeding buckets, we find that ADAMS and DAVIS belong in bucket 3, but JONES's hashed address is 2, so JONES should go into the space vacated by CARTER. Proceeding, we find that JORDAN's hashed address is also 2. If it were inserted into the file in its current state, with JONES moved to where CARTER was and JONES's place in bucket 3 open, then JORDAN would be put in bucket 3. Therefore, JORDAN should be moved to bucket 3. Now there is an open space in bucket 4. In bucket 5 we find that KING's hashed address is 4, so that record should be moved into the space left by JORDAN. Finally, we find an open space in bucket 6, so the process terminates.

It is easy to verify that in the resulting file, each record is in the same bucket it would be if all the records were inserted in the same sequence as before, except with CARTER omitted. However, the records are no longer in sequence by key within each bucket.

The open-addressing algorithm is quite complicated, and quite remarkably, Knuth was able to make an analysis that enabled him to calculate the average length of search assuming randomly distributed hashed addresses. His table of values [H1, p.536] is reproduced in Table 6.1. The precise values depend on the file size, but if the file is not too small, the file size has very little effect. The values in Table 6.1 hold except for very small files. These values can be used in file design calculations, as is illustrated in Example 6.5 at the end of this chapter.

Designing a hashed file involves two largely independent steps: (1) Choosing a hashing function, and (2) Choosing a method for handling

Table 6.1 Average Length of Search for Hashed Files [H1]

Bucket Size	Load Factor									
	10%	20%	30%	40%	50%	60%	70%	80%	90%	95%
1	1.0556	1.1250	1.2143	1.3333	1.5000	1.7500	2.167	3.000	5.500	10.5
2	1.0062	1.0242	1.0553	1.1033	1.1767	1.2930	1.494	1.903	3.147	5.6
3	1.0009	1.0066	1.0201	1.0450	1.0872	1.1584	1.286	1.554	2.378	4.0
4	1.0001	1.0021	1.0085	1.0227	1.0497	1.0984	1.190	1.386	2.000	3.2
5	1.0000	1.0007	1.0039	1.0124	1.0307	1.0661	1.136	1.289	1.777	2.7
10	1.0000	1.0000	1.0001	1.0011	1.0047	1.0154	1.042	1.110	1.345	1.8
20	1.0000	1.0000	1.0000	1.0000	1.0003	1.0020	1.010	1.036	1.144	1.4
50	1.0000	1.0000	1.0000	1.0000	1.0000	1.0000	1.001	1.005	1.040	1.1

collisions. Many hashing functions have been devised, used, and studied. Of course, any hashing method that produces for every key a hashed address in the desired range will work, but a bad hashing formula will result in a longer average access time. Methods used in uniform random number generators generally work well. There are two simple methods, one based on division and one on multiplication, that have been found experimentally to be good.

With either hashing method, the first step is to convert the key to a number K, if it is not already a number. We may simply use the binary coding for the key and interpret it as a number. In an assembly language program, this is the obvious solution, but in many high-level languages it is not feasible. If speed is very important, it may be worthwhile to write an assembly language subroutine to call from the higher-level language program. Otherwise, one might consider the character string key to be a number in a radix-r system, where r is the number of possible characters, and convert it to binary or decimal so that it can be used in calculations.

Now suppose we want a hashed address between 0 and $h-1$. Then for the division method, you simply divide the key number K by h and use the remainder. Some choices of h are better than others. For example, if the key is a decimal number and h is chosen to be 1000, then the remainder is simply the last three digits of the key, and in many cases this would be a poor choice. Preferably, h and the number system radix should not have any common factors, that is, for decimal key numbers, h should not be divisible by 2 or 5. Prime numbers seem to be a good choice. Note that if you want to have h buckets and h does not seem to be a good choice as divisor, then it is reasonable to calculate hashed addresses up to some value h' that is slightly smaller than h. No record will go directly into the buckets between h' and $h-1$, but those buckets still will be used for overflows out of bucket $h'-1$, which will reduce the probability of overflow from bucket $h-1$ back to bucket 0.

The multiplication method is not quite as easy to describe. Knuth [H1, p.509] describes it in a mathematical formula. We will describe how it might be programmed in assembly language. The multiply instruction usually multiplies two binary or decimal words, producing a two-word product made up of a left or "most-significant" word and a right or "least-significant" word. Assume that the key number K fits in a word. A constant A is chosen that is quite large and not closely related to the radix of the number system being used. The largest power of 3 or 7 that will fit in a word probably is a good choice, or one might choose a very large prime number. Then the hashed address is calculated as follows:

1. Multiply the key number K by A and keep only the right word of the result.
2. Now multiply that word by h and keep only the left half.

The first step produces a number that appears to be random. If in the second step, we consider the decimal (or binary) point to be at the left of the number obtained from the first step, then that number is less than one. The result of multiplying by h then must be less than h. The decimal (or binary) point in the result is between the resulting words, and in particular at the right of the left result word, so the left word must be between 0 and $h-1$ inclusive as desired.

Quite a number of methods of handling collisions also have been devised and studied. The open-addressing scheme previously described is the simplest, but it suffers from the difficulty that when the file is very nearly full, certain parts of the file tend to become clogged up with too many records although others are relatively open. This occurred in Example 6.3, where buckets 2, 3, 4, and 5 all became full, although adjacent buckets 6, 0, and 1 did not. Methods exist which avoid this problem. One method is to calculate a second hashed address by some predetermined method if the first bucket is full and to try to put the record at that address rather than in the adjacent bucket. If the bucket at the second hashed address is full, you generate a third hashed address and try that bucket, etc. Another method is to have overflow buckets in a separate storage area. A record that overflows a bucket is placed in the overflow area, and a pointer to it is placed in the bucket that overflowed. Overflow from an overflow bucket can be handled in the same way. These methods are mainly used for hashing done in the main memory of a computer, as for table look-up.

When hashing is done on disk or drum storage, there are two differences compared to hashing in main storage, where access to any location takes the same amount of time. First, in main storage one finds that the optimum bucket size is one record per bucket. On drum or disk storage, one usually finds it desirable to block records for efficiency. In this case, one might best always start a search at the beginning of a block. There seems to be no reason to make the bucket size larger than a block. Hence, the bucket size should be chosen equal to the block size. Second, although the refinements described in the previous paragraph usually are advantageous for hashing in main storage, in disk or drum storage, these methods cause the search to deviate from the physical sequence of the device and thereby introduce seek and latency time. Usually the additional delay will exceed the savings, so that the basic open-addressing method is superior.

Finally, consider how to calculate the average access time for a hashed file. There are two common cases. After reading one bucket when the next bucket is in the same cylinder, then (A) because of the processing time required to determine whether another bucket needs to be read, etc., the latency to the next bucket may be one revolution, or (B) it may be possible to access the next bucket, if it is in the same cylinder, without latency, either because negligible processing needs to be done or because buffering is done. Case A is simpler—let us consider it first. To read the first bucket requires seek, latency, and actual read time. Let us denote their total, the average time required to read the first bucket, by t_1, and the time to read each succeeding bucket by t_2. For Case A, always processing, seek, and latency together are one revolution, and

$$t_2 = \left(1 + \frac{1}{n_t}\right) t_r \qquad (6.1)$$

where n_t denotes the number of buckets per track and t_r is the time per revolution.

Let us denote by P_i the probability that i buckets will have to be read. Then the average access time will be

$$
\begin{aligned}
t_h &= t_1 + 1 \times P_2 \times t_2 + 2 \times P_3 \times t_2 + 3 \times P_4 \times t_2 + \cdots \\
&= t_1 + t_2 \times (1 \times P_1 + 2 \times P_2 + 3 \times P_3 + 4 \times P_4 + \cdots) \\
&\quad - t_2 \times (P_1 + P_2 + P_3 + P_4 + \cdots) \\
&= t_1 + L \times t_2 - t_2 \\
t_h &= t_1 + (L-1) \times t_2 \qquad (6.2)
\end{aligned}
$$

where L is the average length of search as given by Table 6.1.

Now let us consider Case B. Suppose there are n_c buckets per cylinder and that we have to read i buckets. On the average, how long will this take? If $i = 1$, then it is t_1. If $i>1$, it depends on exactly which of the n_c buckets in the cylinder was read first. For example, if $i = 2$ and the first bucket read is the last in the cylinder, the time required to read that second bucket will be one revolution for the cylinder change plus the time to read one bucket; for all other buckets in the cylinder, the time is simply the time it takes to read a bucket. The time to read a bucket is $1/n_t$ revolutions. Then the average time required to read the second bucket will be

$$\left(\frac{1}{n_c}\right)\left(\frac{1}{n_t} + 1\right) + \frac{(n_c - 1)}{n_c}\left(\frac{1}{n_t}\right) = \frac{1}{n_t} + \frac{1}{n_c} \text{ revolutions}$$

for the case $i = 2$. For $i = 3$, a revolution will be needed for a cylinder change if the first bucket read is one of the last two; therefore, the average time required to read the two additional buckets, averaged over all possible places where the first bucket might be, will be $2/n_t + 2/n_c$. Similarly, for any value of i, the average time required to read the $i-1$ additional buckets will be $(i-1)/n_t + (i-1)/n_c$ revolutions. It is not difficult to verify that this is true even when i is larger than n_c, the number of buckets per cylinder, so that a whole cylinder and more have to be read.

The total time required, on the average, to read all i buckets will be

$$f(i) = t_1 + (i-1) \times \left(\frac{1}{n_t} + \frac{1}{n_c}\right) t_r \tag{6.3}$$

where t_r is the time per revolution. Now we average this over all possible values of i:

$$t_h = P_1 \times f(1) + P_2 \times f(2) + P_3 \times f(3) + \cdots$$

$$= \left(t_1 - \frac{t_r}{n_t} - \frac{t_r}{n_c}\right) \times (P_1 + P_2 + P_3 + \cdots)$$

$$+ \left(\frac{t_r}{n_t} + \frac{t_r}{n_c}\right) \times (P_1 + 2 \times P_2 + 3 \times P_3 + \cdots)$$

$$= \left(t_1 - \frac{t_r}{n_t} - \frac{t_r}{n_c}\right) + \left(\frac{t_r}{n_t} + \frac{t_r}{n_c}\right) \times L$$

$$t_h = t_1 + (L-1) \times \left(\frac{1}{n_t} + \frac{1}{n_c}\right) t_r \tag{6.4}$$

where L is the average length of search given in Table 6.1. This equation applies in the case where successive buckets after the first can be read without latency except for cylinder changes. Note that the form of this equation is the same as that of Eq. 6.2, with

$$t_2 = \left(\frac{1}{n_t} + \frac{1}{n_c}\right) t_r$$

It can be interpreted to mean that, on the average, there are $L-1$ buckets to read after the first. For each, the time required is, on the average, the read time, t_r/n_t, plus the average time for cylinder changes, which is t_r/n_c, because a cylinder change requires one revolution, and it occurs a fraction $1/n_c$ of the time.

6.8. COMPARISON OF INDEXED SEQUENTIAL AND HASHED FILES

For an indexed sequential file that does not require insertions and deletions, the space required is that for the file plus that for the index. A hashed file that does not require insertions could be put in exactly the space required for the records, but the last records stored would, on the average, require prohibitively long access times, so that in practice the file should not be made more than 90% to 95% full. Both systems will be very efficient—the indexed sequential file will probably require slightly less space. The hashed file will generally be faster, if it is not too full.

When there are insertions and deletions, if both systems are provided equal resources, in general the average access time will be smaller with a hashed addressing system. On the other hand, the indexed system can easily provide sequential access, whereas the hashed system cannot—there is just no easy way to locate the next sequential record by key in the hashed system if you do not know the key. A hashed addressing system can be programmed much more simply than an indexed system. Partly for this reason, subroutines for indexed files are available for many computers as a part of the operating system or as separate software packages to perform the complex indexing and maintenance functions, whereas software packages for hashed addressing are not widely available. (Programming examples are given in Chapter 8.)

In general, an application requiring random access but never requiring sequential access would be best handled by a hashed file. On the other hand, where frequent sequential access as well as random access is required, then an indexed file is indicated. For example, programs in a time-sharing programming system typically are accessed randomly a few times for corrections and then sequentially for compiling. Clearly, an indexed file is indicated.

It is difficult to imagine a situation in which a file is never accessed sequentially, but it is common to access files much more often randomly than sequentially. For example, an on-line inventory system for a retail store might be accessed thousands of times each day, and then a report in sequence by key might be produced at the end of each week. This could be handled as an indexed file. Alternatively, it could be handled as a hashed file and sorted, using a utility sort program, once each week to produce the report. Which alternative is better depends on the ratio of random to sequential accesses, and on other considerations such as the fact that the random accesses probably occur during prime time, whereas the weekly report may be produced on nonprime time late at night or during the weekend.

6.9. DESIGNING A RANDOM-ACCESS FILE

Either an indexed sequential file or a hashed file may be designed along the lines described in the several preceding sections; either will work fairly well if it is not too full. For any situation where much computer time will be used or high efficiency is important for any reason, the following procedure is suggested:

1. Carefully review the available literature on potentially applicable methods. The relevant references listed in this chapter should suffice or at least provide a good starting point.

2. Repeat steps (3) to (5) until a satisfactory design is found.

3. Choose one or more possible file designs.

4. Determine relevant parameters such as average length of search for an open-addressing system, or average number of records in overflow areas, utilizing theory, equations, and data found in references, original analysis, or simulation. (Random-access files can be simulated quite readily.)

5. Using specifications for the proposed hardware, calculate average access time and other required data.

Example 6.5

Let us consider using the Miniscribe 4012 fixed-disk drive for a random access file with several tens of thousands of 200-character records. The drive characteristics (formatted as we will use it) are as follows:

Sector	512 bytes
Track	17 sectors
Number of cylinders	306
Tracks per cylinder	4
Rotational speed	3600 rpm
	(16.7 msec/revolution)
Seek time:	
Track-to-track	3 msec
Settling time	15 msec
Average (including settling)	85 msec
Maximum (including settling)	205 msec

Let us assume that seek time is reasonably well approximated by the straight line

$$t = 15 + 0.66n \text{ msec} \tag{6.5}$$

for moving a distance of n cylinders. This agrees within 15% of the quoted figures for track-to-track, average, and maximum seek time, which is about as good as we can expect for a straight-line approximation to the seek time curve of a disk system with a variable-step-rate motor.

Assume a file of 200-character records with nine-character keys. Assume that we wish to use 300 cylinders for our file and reserve five cylinders of this disk drive for other purposes. Storing two records per 512-byte sector is not very efficient. However, if we make blocks consisting of two sectors or 1024 bytes, each will hold five records with only 24 bytes left over. The total capacity of the file will be $17 \times 300 \times \frac{4}{2} = 10,200$ blocks, or 51,000 records, although we cannot use all this space for data records in a practical file system.

Now let us consider an indexed sequential file system structured as a B^+-tree. It seems reasonable to make the index blocks the same size as the data blocks, that is, 1024 characters. Each index entry requires nine bytes for a key and a pointer to a block. Assume that the pointers are block numbers each having five decimal digits stored as a character string. Then an index entry requires $9 + 5 = 14$ bytes. A 1024-byte block will hold $1024/14 = 73$ entries. Because of the structure of the B^+-tree, all index blocks will be at least half full. We can expect, if the file is made by random insertions, that there will be a fairly uniform distribution of index-block contents between half-full and full; and therefore we anticipate an average of 75% full or about 55 entries per index block. Data blocks will have at least three records and at most five, and can be expected to have an average of four records, that is, to be 80% full on the average.

To get an estimate of the number of index blocks required, let n_i denote the number of index blocks. Then the number of data blocks is $10,200 - n_i$. Neglecting second-level index blocks for the moment, we must have one index entry for every data block; therefore, we have the approximate equation

$$55n_i = 10,200 - n_i \tag{6.6}$$

Solving this, we find that we need approximately 182 index blocks for the first-level index. We need a second-level index of 182/55 or about four blocks, and finally a third-level index (the B^+-tree root node) of about four entries. Since it is small, let us keep the third-level index in main memory. Then there are about $10,200 - 182 - 4 = 10,014$ blocks available for the data-record blocks. If we start out and insert records randomly, we would expect to run out of blocks to use for inserting new records when the data-block portion of the file is about 80% full, that is, this file system would have a capacity of about 80% of 10,014, or about 8000 blocks or 8000 × 5 = 40,000 records. Each block contains an average of four records.

Now let us consider access time. To find a record, we must search the third-level index (in main memory) to find a pointer to the correct block of the second-level index. Next we must read that block and search it for a pointer to the correct block in the first-level index. Then we must read that block and search for a pointer to the correct data-record block. Finally, we read the data block and search it. Thus, we must read three blocks from the file.

Assume that the data blocks and index blocks are mixed randomly throughout the entire file of 300 cylinders. On each read, the seek time is given by Eq. 3.10 or 3.11:

$$\text{Seek time} = 15 + 0.66 \times \frac{300}{3} = 81.00 \text{ msec}$$

$$\text{Latency} = \frac{1}{2} \text{ revolution} = 8.33 \text{ msec}$$

$$\text{Read time} = \frac{2}{17} \text{ revolution} = 1.96 \text{ msec}$$

$$\text{Total average read time} = 91.29 \text{ msec} \qquad (6.7)$$

and each read requires the same time. Therefore, locating and reading one record requires an average of 3 × 91.29 = 273.87 msec.

Access time will be reduced a little if the index is placed in the middle of the file. The index requires about 186 blocks. This is about 5.5 cylinders. Assume that the center six cylinders are reserved for the index. Then Eq. 3.18 applies to the first and last seeks, Eq. 3.10 to the second:

$$\text{First seek time} = 15 + 0.66 \times \left(\frac{6}{2} + \frac{294}{4} \right) = 65.49 \text{ msec}$$

$$\text{Second seek time} = \frac{5}{6} \times \left(15 + 0.66 \times \frac{7}{3} \right) = 13.78$$

$$\text{Third seek time} = \text{same as first} = 65.49 \text{ msec} \quad (6.8)$$

Adding three half-revolutions for latency and three times the time to read one block, we get a total of 175.64 msec per access, an improvement of about 35%.

Note that unless the file contains only a small fraction of its capacity, three levels of index will be needed and three accesses to the file will be required (assuming that the third-level index is in main memory). If a significant amount of empty space remains, these could be placed at the extremes of the file, and seek times would be shortened a little. However, the average access time does not depend strongly on how many records are in the file. The absolute maximum seek time would be no more than double the calculated time where Eq. 3.18 was used, no more than triple the calculated value where Eq. 3.10 or 3.11 was used, the latency time would never be more than double the nominal half-revolution, and the actual read time is fixed. Therefore, the maximum access time always will be less than three times the calculated average value, and rarely will be that large.

Note also that we used blocks of 1024 bytes to store five records of 200 characters. That leaves 24 bytes unused. Thus, there is space in the data-record blocks for some pointers. One might well include in each data block a pointer to the next sequential block (and perhaps a pointer to the previous block) to facilitate sequential access. Let us assume as above that the 40,000 data records have been inserted in random sequence into 10,000 data-record blocks. The time required to read the file sequentially is the time to read 10,000 blocks at 91.29 msec each, as calculated in Eq. 6.7. The total is 912.9 sec or about 15 min.

Reading will be considerably faster if the records are in the proper physical sequence. Suppose we have a utility program that loads the records four to a block in the proper physical sequence and makes the index. Let us assume 40,000 records again and that we have placed the index in the middle of the file. Again, there will be 10,000 blocks, which will require about 294 cylinders. Neglecting initial seek and latency, reading this entire file sequentially will require four revolutions to read each cylinder and one revolution for each cylinder change. Crossing the index requires a seek of $15 + 0.66 \times 6 = 18.96$ msec; this time being between one and two revolutions, crossing the index will require seek and latency of exactly two revolutions. The total will be 1470 revolutions or $1470/60 = 24.5$ sec. This is about 30 times faster than when the data blocks are in random physical sequence. As records are inserted and deleted, gradually more and more data-record blocks would be out of physical sequence and the average time to read the file sequentially gradually would increase. It could be reduced periodically as needed by copying the file sequentially to a temporary file and then loading it again in sequence.

Now let us consider a hashed file for the same system. Using blocks of five records stored in two sectors on the disk and considering a block to be a bucket appears to be a reasonable plan. Assume again that there are 300 cylinders available. With hashing, it is possible to fill the file completely. The capacity is 10,200 buckets as before, so we can store $5 \times 10,200 = 51,000$ records. However, when the hashed file is very nearly full, the access time becomes excessive. The calculation of access time is straightforward: use Eq. 6.2 if a revolution of seek and latency is required for each successive bucket read after the first, or Eq. 6.4 if latency is needed only on cylinder changes. For our case, n_t = 17/2, n_c = 34, t_r = 16.67 msec, and t_l = 91.29 msec, as calculated in Eq. 6.7. We find the average length of search L from Table 6.1. Calculations are summarized in Table 6.2.

Note that these times for the hashed file are significantly shorter than those required for the indexed file, even though more records can be handled with the same resources with the hashed file than with the indexed file. Of course, sequential access cannot be done. Note that we have calculated the average access times. When the file is nearly full, the actual search for most records is not greater than this, but for a few records it may be very large, a significant fraction of the time to read the whole file in physical sequence, which we found to be about 25 sec. Therefore, it is a good idea not to fill the file too much. We do not have any concrete guidelines on how much is too much, however.

Consider one more possibility. Give the file have a hashed index with an index entry for every record and place the index in the middle of the file. Assume the same block size again, both for the index and the data-record blocks. Then the bucket size will be the same as the block size, that is, 73 index entries per bucket. Assume that the hashed index is to be at most 95% full. If we denote by n_i the number of index blocks, then the number of data blocks will be 10,200 $-$ n_i, that is, all the rest of the blocks. Then when the index is 95% full, there should be one entry for each record that can fit in the data-record blocks, that is,

$$5 \times (10200 - n_i) = 0.95 \times 73 \times n_i$$

Solving this equation, we find that we need 686 index blocks; hence, there are 9514 data-record blocks, which provides space for 47,570 records. According to Table 6.1, the average length of search will be less than 1.1. Accessing the first index block will take the same seek time as calculated in Eq. 6.8; adding latency and actual read time, we find that

Table 6.2 Calculated Access Times for Hashed File Example

Percent Full	L	Number of Records	T_h (Eq. 6.2)	T_h (Eq. 6.4)
70%	1.136	35,700	93.8 msec	91.6 msec
80%	1.289	40,800	96.7 msec	92.0 msec
90%	1.777	45,900	105.8 msec	95.5 msec
95%	2.7	48,450	123.0 msec	95.5 msec

$$t_1 = 65.49 + 8.33 + 1.96 = 75.78 \text{ msec}$$

If we take the pessimistic view that Eq. 6.2 applies, then the average access time to the index will be

$$t_h = 75.78 + (1.1 - 1) \times \left(\frac{2}{17} + 1\right) = 77.64 \text{ msec}$$

and if Eq. 6.4 applies, then the time is a little shorter. However, now we must access the main file. The time required for that will be the same as t_1 in Eq. 6.9. Therefore, the total access time to the record via the index will be $75.78 + 77.64 = 153.42$.

 With very large records and a very nearly full file, having the hashed index may provide faster average access. There is another advantage, however. The absolute maximum access time, if the index were full, would be the time to read the whole index, and that would be much smaller than the longest time that could occur with a hashed main file.

6.10. RECORD STRUCTURES

The most common way to structure the attributes of an individual record is serially as a list of value fields. The value fields may be of different types (e.g., numerical or character-string) and different lengths. Value-fields also may be grouped together so that a record has a tree structure: for example, using COBOL or PL/I notation,

```
1    RECORD R
     2    GROUP A
          3    VALUE-FIELD 1
          3    VALUE-FIELD 2
     2    VALUE-FIELD 3
     2    GROUP B
          3    GROUP C
               4    VALUE-FIELD 4
               4    VALUE-FIELD 5
          3    VALUE-FIELD 6
```

The corresponding tree is depicted graphically in Figure 6.3. Each of the "groups" may be an array of values. Note that some data items might be pointers. The tree structure of the record is useful to the programmer— the whole record, any subtree, or any single data item can be referenced by a single name. However, if the n value fields are simply stored as a list or n-tuple, the file is essentially a relation. Determination of the length of a record requires specific knowledge of how data values of different types are encoded. See Appendix A for a discussion of this subject.

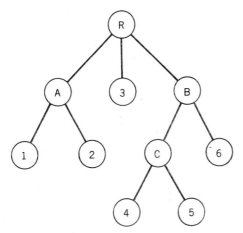

Figure 6.3 A Record Structure.

A file consists of a sequence or list of records. Ordinarily it will be stored in physical sequence, but it also may be stored as a linked list with a pointer in each record to the next record, or in blocks with a pointer in each block to the next block. Very commonly, all records in a file have the same length, but it also is common to have variable-length data in the records, usually either variable-length character data or variable-length arrays. It also is possible to have records of two or more different formats of the same or different lengths in the same file. There are two ways to handle variable-length data. All records can be made the same length by providing space in every record for the maximum amount of data. Alternatively, we may allow the record lengths to be variable. Fixed-length records are easier to process, but the use of variable-length records saves storage space for the file. Main-memory space will generally not be saved using variable-length records because the work area reserved in memory must accommodate the largest possible record.

With variable-length records, it should be possible to determine where one record ends and the next one starts. This can be done either by including the record length (byte count) in the record or by putting a special end-of-record mark at the end of each record. If the operating system does not provide either this count or marker, then the programmer must. Note also that variable-length records affect blocking. If there are going to be a number of whole records per block—even if there are not the same number in each block—then the blocks will have variable lengths. Alternatively, the block length may be fixed, with whole records or portions of records if necessary filling up each block completely. Portions of a record that do not fit in one block are put in one or more subsequent blocks. In this case, we say that the record *spans* the blocks.

Example 6.6

Figure 6.4 illustrates the five common kinds of sequential file record formats. "F" stands for fixed-length records, "V" for variable length records, "B" for blocking, and "S" for spanning. Case F shows five fixed-length records, with one record per block, each record and block of length two. (The record lengths and block sizes are shown in parentheses.) Case FB shows these five records blocked, two records per block. The odd record is shown as a short block, which is conventional—an alternative would be to pad the last block with a dummy record. Case V shows five variable-length records with one record per variable-length block. Case VB shows these five records blocked in such a way that the maximum block size is four. The first block B1 is not of maximum size because adding the next record R3 would make it too large. If we wish the blocks to be the same size, each block could

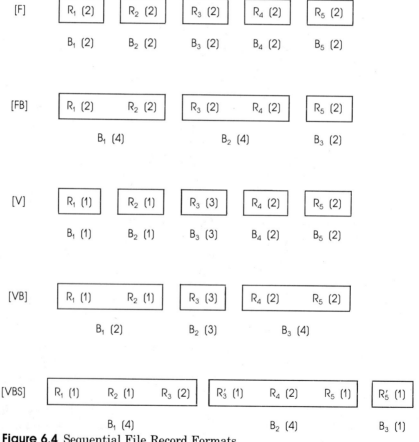

Figure 6.4 Sequential File Record Formats.

be padded to the maximum length. Alternatively, by allowing the records to span the blocks, as is shown in case VBS, then every block except the last may be exactly the maximum size with no padding.

Accessing problems are more severe with variable-length records in random-access files, in that it is not possible to calculate the location of the ith record from knowledge of i alone, as with fixed-length records. It is possible, however, to create an index showing, for example, the number of the first record in each block. We can locate any record by first reading this index, then the one block to which it points, and finally searching that block.

The total length of a file with N records, if the maximum length L_{max} is used for every record, is $N \times L_{max}$. Suppose the total length of a file stored using variable-length records is L_{vt}. Then the average length of a record is

$$L_{ave} = \frac{L_{vt}}{N}$$

The percentage reduction in the file resulting from using variable-length records is

$$\text{percent compression} = 100 \times \left(1 - \frac{L_{vt}}{N \times L_{max}}\right)$$

$$= 100 \times \left(1 - \frac{L_{ave}}{L_{max}}\right)$$

where L_{ave} is the average length of a record including the byte count or end-of-record marker.

Example 6.7

Typically, program source files have a maximum length of about 80 characters. Even if the actual source code is never this long, the documentation and comments will be in this range. The average length of a record is likely to be 20 characters or less. This indicates a saving of 75%—files stored using variable-length records will be about one-fourth as large as the same file stored with fixed-length records. If source files occupy a significant part of a file system, there is a strong motivation to use variable-length records.

The CP/M operating system uses the VBS file format. CP/M stores data on disks in sectors of 128 bytes that may be thought of as blocks. If a file consists of ASCII characters, it is very common to use a carriage return and a line-feed character together as an end-of-record marker and to allow variable-length records with essentially no limits on record length. A single record may span several sectors or, more commonly, there may be several records in a single sector. (Such a file can be sent to a printer as a stream and will print one record per line, as long as records are less than the printer line lengths.) This system is very simple, easy to use, and very efficient for program source files.

6.11. FILE COMPRESSION

We have noted previously that files can be stored in substantially less space by blocking, which reduces the number of gaps between records, and by using variable-length records. Space for the records themselves can be reduced in several ways. It should be emphasized at the outset that space usually can be saved only at the expense of time.

Redundancy in files may exist in various forms, for example, data may be inefficiently coded, records may be duplicated, data-items may be duplicated, and characters may be repeated. The main reason that more than one copy of a record may exist is that the record may belong to numerous files or subfiles. For example, a record containing a person's name, address, and telephone number may appear in a standard telephone directory file, a street-address directory file, and a monthly billing file. Separate files, physically organized in different ways, permit the different functions taken independently to be performed in the most efficient fashion. However, some compromise between time and space may be warranted.

One way of reducing space requirements, at the expense of added access time, is to keep only one copy of each record in a file ordered by a primary key (say, the name) and to have another file, consisting solely of secondary keys (say, addresses) and pointers to the records in the primary file. Note that the secondary key is duplicated, but the primary key is not. Pointers usually are shorter than the primary keys, and tertiary information (say, telephone numbers) need not be replicated. Sequential access by the secondary key is efficient only if the primary-key file is organized as a random-access file.

Data-items frequently appear as part of several records in a single file, as well as in a number of different files. When the data items are sizable, it may save much space to have one copy of the data item pointed to by each of the different records. The disadvantage of this scheme is that a record cannot be read or written in a single physical I-O operation.

When a data-item has numerous repeated characters, for example, leading zeroes or trailing blanks, these characters can be replaced by a single such character and repetition factor. Trailing blanks at the end of a field can be replaced by a "tab" character. If records have missing or unused data fields, these fields can be omitted or replaced by a concise missing-data code. These techniques can save a considerable amount of space, but they result in variable-length records.

A record also may contain several copies of the same data-item or sub-record. When they are adjacent, repetition factors may be used. Otherwise, pointers to a single copy may be used.

In many situations, data-items are assigned values that are meaningful to users, especially complete words (such as MALE and FEMALE, or HAWAII and MAINE). Abbreviations (M and F, or HI and ME) can result in much space reduction, but also can lead to mistakes if the user must translate them. (For example, the user may erroneously code MA for Maine or decode MI as Minnesota.) To prevent such mistakes, the full words may be used by the user, and I-O procedures would translate them as needed to and from their internal codes for storage. Other internal codes may result in even greater compression. For example, M and F may be represented by a single bit; a state abbreviation may be represented by a six-bit integer. Numerical coding, especially binary coding, of this sort usually is advantageous when the values of a data-item are very long and from a small known set.

When alphanumeric strings have no predeterminable set of values, the strings usually are encoded one character at a time using ASCII seven-bit code or EBCDIC eight-bit code. Numerical strings may be more compactly represented coded as binary numbers than in character code.

Character codes need not be a fixed number of bits in length. If some characters are much more likely than others and the various occurrence probabilities are known, then the more likely characters may be given shorter codes and the less likely characters may be given longer codes. The result will be shorter encoded strings, on the average. For example, using the Huffman code to code single letters for English text into variable-length binary codes requires an average of 4.2 bits per letter compared to 5 for a fixed-length code [K2]. This type of encoding seldom has been used in practical applications, probably because of the processing required to encode and decode. This and other sophisticated encodings may become attractive as the cost of processing decreases.

6.12. FILE SYSTEM ALLOCATION

A file system typically contains many files. In general, a program can use many different files and a file can be used by many different programs. The auxiliary storage locations (e.g., the unit, cylinder, track, and sector numbers) of each file referenced by a program must be readily available. These locations commonly are stored in a system file called a *directory* or *catalog*. Often, only the volume (e.g., reel of tape or disk pack) in which the file is stored is identified in the system directory. The system may allow for the volume to be mounted on any one of several drives. The volume itself contains another directory, called a *volume index* or table of contents, that lists the names and locations of each of its files.

If a file is stored physically contiguously, it is necessary to place only its beginning address and length in the volume index. If a file is stored physically in several scattered segments, then the locations and lengths of each segment must be known. This information is of indefinite size. If this information is in the index, then the index either must be of variable size or it must allow for the maximum amount of such information for a file. Alternatively, each segment of a file may contain a pointer, chaining it to the next segment. Another possibility is for each file to have a small file directory listing its segments and to have the volume index contain pointers to these directories.

If a new file is to be placed on a given auxiliary storage device or volume, space for it must be allocated. In some systems, the maximum size of a file must be declared and enough space reserved for it when it is created. Some provision may be made for acquiring more space, if needed. In other systems, space for files is allocated only as needed. In any case, some means of locating unused space in auxiliary storage is required. A common approach is to have each volume include a *free space list* that identifies each segment of unused space. This can be implemented by chaining available segments together or by keeping a list of their locations and sizes.

Space for files normally is allocated in multiples of some minimum-size unit, usually sectors for small systems and tracks for large ones. After a file system is used for some time with space alternately allocated, freed, and reallocated, it becomes fragmented so that there are few contiguous units of free space available. If the size of the allocation unit is large, then space is wasted because a large unit must be allocated even in cases where a very small amount of space is required. On the other hand, if the allocation unit is very small, then time is wasted because the fragmentation problem is serious—files allocated when the file system is fragmented badly will consist of a very large number of very small allocations that may be widely separated. Some reasonable compromise must be struck.

Our calculations of access time for random-access files were based on the assumption that the file in question consisted of one contiguous allocation. Obviously, if the file consists of a number of noncontiguous allocations scattered on different cylinders, then seek time will be longer. This situation should be avoided in cases where timing is critical. In some systems, it is possible for a user to request a contiguous allocation;

if enough contiguous space is available, the system will allocate it, but if not the user must wait. It is common also to "reorganize" the file system by writing out all files and then reading the files back into the file system while allocating them contiguous space.

Example 6.8 (CP/M)

The CP/M disk operating system was originally designed to use an 8 in. floppy diskette in the de facto "standard IBM format." Later, the system was modified to make it adaptable to various other formats, such as the 5¼ in. diskettes, double density and/or double-sided diskettes, and the various fixed-disk drives that have come into common use. The basic structure of the file system is the same, but some of the parameters may be changed to effect these adaptations. As a very specific example, we will describe the original system and comment briefly on some variations.

The single-density standard IBM 8 in. diskette has 77 tracks with 26 128-byte sectors in each track. CP/M uses the first two tracks to store the operating system, which leaves the rest for the file system. The allocation block size (the minimum unit of allocation) is eight sectors, and allocation blocks consist of successive sets of eight contiguous sectors. There are a total of $26 \times 75 = 1950$ sectors and, thus, there are $1950/8 = 243$ allocation blocks with six sectors left over. These blocks are numbered 0 through 242 and, thus, an allocation block number fits in one byte.

Each directory entry consists of 32 bytes. Of those, 11 are used for the name and type of the file. Sixteen bytes store the numbers of up to 16 allocation blocks allocated to this file, and the remaining five bytes store other information about the file. Thus, one directory entry can specify the location of sixteen allocation blocks, each consisting of eight 128-byte sectors, for a total of 16,384 bytes.

Files may be larger than 16,384 bytes. Larger files are made up of several *extents* of up to 16,384 bytes; for each extent, there is a directory entry showing which allocation blocks have been allocated to it. Each directory entry contains the file name and type, and one byte in it contains the extent number.

The directory uses the first two allocation blocks and, thus, has space for 64 directory entries. When a file is created, the first available space in the directory is used, and a directory entry is created, but no space is allocated to the file. Space is allocated, one allocation block at a time, as it is called for by write commands. When a file is deleted, the directory entry is simply marked as unused. The directory is searched sequentially from the beginning for any desired entry.

When a diskette is first "logged in," an *allocation vector* is constructed that has one bit for each allocation block. The entire directory is read and each bit in the allocation vector is set to one if that block is allocated to some file, to zero if it is not. When a block is allocated, the first available block is used.

The result is a system that is very easy to use, because the user does not need to be concerned with any details about file characteristics. After a considerable number of files have been created and deleted, the space becomes very fragmented and the allocation blocks allocated to a file are scattered all over the disk. However, the disk can be reorganized by simply copying it, file by file, to an empty diskette. Then all files will occupy contiguous space.

(It was implied above that eight contiguous sectors make up an allocation block. This is not strictly true. The sectors are given a logical sequencing such that the successive logical sectors are separated by five physical sectors to reduce latency time, as shown in Example 4.5, that is, an offset of six is used. Each allocation block consists of eight logically contiguous sectors. Note that these may span tracks.)

To accommodate different disk systems, CP/M2.2 provides for some of the parameters to be specified. The allocation block size may be any power of two from 1024 (as in the above example) to 16,384. The total number of blocks may be larger than 255—if so, then the directory entry is kept at the same size and 16 bytes are still used to indicate which allocation blocks are allocated to this extent. However, two bytes are used for each allocation block number, and therefore one extent may have only eight blocks allocated to it. Any number of allocation blocks up to 16 may be allocated to the directory.

Example 6.9 (IBM/OS)

Many operating systems have been designed for the IBM computers. One family of operating systems is known as "OS," which exists in numerous variations. We will not describe any specific version, but will discuss general characteristics here and in Appendix E. (Actual job control language specifications, which are made in file-defining DD statements, will be shown in square brackets below. Some more detailed examples are given in Appendix E.)

OS was designed to support a wide variety of file-storage devices. These devices are grouped in various ways, for example, by device model (such as the IBM 3330 disk unit) or device class (such as direct-access or tape). One direct-access device is designated as the "system" device, wherein resides the main directory file from which all other system files can be found. This main directory, which is called the system catalog, may be thought of as the root of a hierarchical file system (see Example 5.2). Portions of this catalog may be placed on other devices. When a new file is created on any device or volume, the user may request that an entry for it be made in the catalog system. [This request is made by specifying CATLG in the DISP parameter.] The volume on which the file resides is then identified in the catalog entry. Although it is possible to specify a particular volume by giving its name [in the VOLUME parameter], it is only necessary to specify a device model or class [in the UNIT parameter], which leaves the system free to make the selection of a particular volume at its discretion.

Each direct-access volume must include an index or table of contents describing the files residing in that volume. The volume table of contents (VTOC) is a file whose size and location need not be fixed; however, its size is limited to one cylinder. The address of the VTOC is placed in a designated location on each volume, specifically, in the *volume label* area (by convention, at cylinder 0, track 0, sector 0). The volume label also contains an identifier, which serves as the name of the volume and hence must be distinguishable from all other volume identifiers. It is this volume identifier that appears in the catalog system.

Each tape volume (i. e., each individual reel of tape) also has a volume identifier located in a designated label area at the beginning of the tape. There is no separate VTOC for tapes. However, each file on a tape is headed by its name, so that the sequence of headers may be regarded as a noncontiguous volume index.

Unlike the case for most small microcomputer systems, in the IBM system when a new volume is mounted on a device, an interrupt is generated and the volume is automatically recognized. OS, in servicing such interrupts, reads the volume label and stores the volume identifier in a system *device table*. The device table provides the system with the identities of each currently accessible volume.

When a file is requested by name, the catalog system is consulted to determine the volume on which the file resides and the device table is consulted to determine the device on which the volume is currently mounted. Of course, "unknown file" and "unmounted volume" errors must be handled. If the file name and its volume are found, the appropriate VTOC is searched to determine the precise location of the requested file. OS also permits users to specify volume identifiers in job control statements, bypassing the system catalog.

When a new file is created on a direct-access device, it is necessary to request a specific amount of space. The unit of space may be cylinders, tracks, or blocks of designated size b. To permit dynamic space allocation, at least in part, the space request may be made by specifying an initial amount p and an incremental amount s. [In the job control language, we would write SPACE $= (b,(p,s))$.] The "primary" allocation of p units of size b would be made initially, and additional "secondary" allocations of s units of size b would be made as needed. The number of secondary allocations is limited to 15, fewer if contiguous space is not available. This limitation is associated with the size allocated to each entry in the VTOC.

If contiguous space is desired, it must be requested explicitly [as part of the SPACE parameter]; the default is noncontiguity. Contiguous files, of course, result in faster processing times and should be requested when this is of importance. Contiguous space should not routinely be requested because execution of a program may be delayed until enough contiguous space becomes available. This penalty encourages users to accept the smaller blocks of free space that usually are scattered about the volume.

A list of available space is kept in the VTOC. This list contains an entry for each *extent*, which is a contiguous block of free space. The minimum size of an extent is one track. Track capacities for various disk units are given in Table 3.1.

An important OS facility permits space allocated to one file to be suballocated to other files [using the SUBALLOC parameter]. It also is possible to share a group of cylinders among several files [using the SPLIT parameter]. Thus, a user may place files A, B, and C in adjacent cylinders by suballocating space in A to B and C, or may split several cylinders, giving, say, 50% of the tracks in each cylinder to A and 25% each to B and C. These facilities allow users to control to a large extent where their files are located, as may be necessary to reduce seek times, for example.

For sequential files in direct-access devices, space allocation is straightforward. If a file is not contiguous, the VTOC must identify the beginning and end of each extent. With this information, it is not difficult to go from one extent to the next one during sequential processing. The problem is more complex for relative files. Given a relative record number, the system must determine the extent in which the record resides; a simple formula is not possible if the extents are not of equal size. Nevertheless, although address calculations require more effort, access is still direct, that is, no search is required.

The problem for indexed files is complicated by the need to allocate space for the index and overflow areas as well as for the data records. An overall minimum of one contiguous cylinder is required for ISAM files. OS permits users to allocate index space separately [i.e., in another DD statement], perhaps even on a different volume [using the SEP parameter]. This results in reduced access times by eliminating seeks between the index and the data area. However, users need not explicitly allocate index space at all; the system by default will allocate sufficient space at the beginning of the data area for the index. To allocate space for overflows from the data area, which is required if insertions are anticipated, users must specify the number of tracks per cylinder to be reserved for overflows within each cylinder [using the CYLOFL parameter]. In addition, if overflows from these "cylinder overflow" areas are to be accommodated, users must allocate a separate "independent overflow" area [using another DD statement].

NOTES

For in-depth analyses of search methods for various data and file structures, see [H1], which was our primary reference. Analyses of search techniques also appear in the literature on the "analysis of algorithms." For an introduction, see [H9] and, for more detail see [H10]. Binary trees also are surveyed in [F6] and [H11]. Hashing is surveyed in [H1], [H5], and [H7]; hashing functions are discussed in [H12]. Some file systems analysis techniques also are introduced in [A2], [A9], and [A13].

For a description of data compression techniques, see [K1]. More detail may be found in [K3]. Some books that contain a chapter on file compression include [F3] and [A11]. An introduction to some of the relevant concepts of information theory is given in [A8] and [A10], but for additional information see [K2].

File allocation procedures are discussed in [A5] and [J1]. CP/M is discussed in greater detail in [J10]. Further information on the IBM file system appears in [J8]; ISAM is described further in [J9] and VSAM in [H15].

EXERCISES

6-1. Example 6.1 illustrates a segmented indexed-sequential file (B$^+$-tree).

(a) Show the state of the file and its index after insertion of KELLY.

(b) Suppose that separate overflow areas instead of chained segments are used. For the same initial state, show the state of the file and its index after insertion of FOX, JONES, and KATO.

6-2. Consider the hashed file in Example 6.3. Show what the file would look like after the name SMITH is inserted. Show what it would look like after JONES is deleted.

6-3. In Example 6.5, the approximation $t = 15 + 0.66N$ was stated to be within 15% of the quoted figures. Is the approximation within 15% on the high side or the low side (or both)?

6-4. Consider Example 6.5. How much space (in characters) would be needed for the third-level index mentioned in the example?

For the next two exercises, let us assume a "double-sided double-track double density" 5¼ in. floppy disk drive. These drives have the following characteristics (these data are taken from the manual for a TEAC Model FD-55F half-height drive):

Number of cylinders	80
Number of tracks per cylinder	2
Number of sectors per track	16
Number of bytes per sector	256
Rotational speed	300 rpm
Seek time	3 msec per cylinder
Settling time	15 msec

The head is driven by a stepping motor, and Eq. 3.4 in the text is accurate. Tracks 0 and 1 make up the first cylinder, tracks 2 and 3 the second cylinder, etc. Assume that the sectors are written in sequence on the disk, that is, there is no offset.

6-5. Assume we have a file of 3200 records with a length of 64 bytes. Each record has a 20-byte name, 37-byte address, and a 7-byte phone number. The file is organized as an indexed sequential file with a two-level index with index entries consisting of a 20-byte name and a 4-byte pointer. The second-level index is stored in the main memory. Assume that the file occupies 40 cylinders and the middle two cylinders of the file are reserved for the index. On the average, how long will it take to access one record, assuming successive accesses to the same file?

6-6. Assume a file of 3200 records with a length of 64 bytes. Each record has a 20-byte name, 37-byte address, and a 7-byte phone number. This time the file is organized as a hashed file with bucket size equal to one sector, and uses 30 cylinders. Again assuming successive accesses to this same file, what is the average access time for each record?

For the next three problems, let us assume that (1) we have a file of 6000 records of length 1000 characters each, with a 12-character key, and (2) half of a Miniscribe 4020 fixed-disk drive is available for storing the data. We need random access to the data. Given the key we must be able to find the record, the quicker the better. Let us explore several ways of achieving this. On this kind of drive, one choice is to format each track with nine blocks of 1024 characters. Do this and store the records one record per block. The drive has 1920 tracks—assume that 960 tracks are available for this application. Thus, there are 960 × 9 = 8640 blocks. When we use an index, an index entry will require 12 bytes for the key and four bytes for a pointer to a block, or a total of 16 bytes. (We could save a couple of bytes by storing the key in binary, but do not assume that.)

6-7. Use an indexed file organized as a B^+-tree with one record per block in the leaf nodes. $1024/16 = 64$, so each internal node may contain as many as 64 pointers. Assuming that internal nodes will become about ¾ full on the average, they will contain about 48 pointers each. Thus, with 6000 records in the file, one per block, we will need 6000/48 = about 125 first-level index

blocks. Then we will need a second-level index of about three blocks, and a third-level index (the root node) with about three entries in it. The root node is very small—assume that we keep it in the main memory, and accessing it will require a negligible amount of time.

(a) Assuming that the internal (index) nodes are mixed randomly with the leaf nodes (records) in the file, calculate the average time required to find and read a randomly chosen record given the key. Assume that just prior to this access, another access was made to a randomly chosen record in this same file, so that the read head is on a track in this file.

(b) Assume that the file was created in such a way that the records are physically arranged in order by key, and that each block containing a record has a pointer to the next one. Assume you know where the first record is, so the others can be read sequentially without using the index. How long will it take to read the file sequentially?

(c) Now assume that the records are randomly placed, with no obvious relation between their location and the order of their keys, as would be the case if the records are inserted in random order. Assume again that each block has a pointer to the next one and you know where the first one is. How long will it take to read the file sequentially?

6-8. Assume a hashed file with a bucket-size of one record using all available space. Assume that the hashing function is a good one so that you can use Table 6.1 to determine the average length of search. What is the average time required to find and read a record?

6-9. Finally, assume that we have a hashed index. Each index entry is 16 characters, and the index entries are stored in 1024-byte blocks. Thus, the index is a hashed file with bucket size 64. Assume that we allocate 200 blocks to the index, leaving 8440 blocks for records. Again, assume that the hash function is as good as random. How long will it take, on the average, to locate and read a randomly chosen record given the key?

6-10. The IBM 3330 has 400 cylinders and 19 tracks per cylinder, so disk addresses go from 00000 to 39918. Suppose you had a file having 1000 blocks stored in four extents according to the table below:

Extent	Beginning block numbers	Beginning disk address
1	1	00103
2	170	02201
3	628	04000
4	988	08609

(a) Assume two blocks per track. Determine the ending disk addresses of each extent.

(b) Assume two blocks per track. Calculate the beginning disk address of block number 623.

(c) What upper and lower limits on the number of blocks per track are imposed by the foregoing table?

6-11. (a) Describe two different ways to generate addresses from keys.

(b) Describe circumstances under which one way is better than the other, and vice versa.

6-12. Does increasing bucket size tend to increase or decrease record retrieval time? Explain!

6-13. Deletion of a record from a file often is accomplished by simply marking the deleted record with an "absent" flag. For each of the following organizations,

(a) sequential

(b) relative/hashed

(c) indexed-sequential

(d) linked-list

specify whether deletion by marking is possible: If possible, what difficulties or disadvantages unique to that file organization could there be; otherwise, if not possible, explain why not.

6-14. Assume a random distribution of bucket numbers. How many records can be loaded into a hashed file having 1000 buckets containing 20 records each, with an overflow rate of 5%?

6-15. (a) The following question relates to hashing with a separate overflow area. Assuming a random distribution of bucket numbers and a maximum allowable overflow rate of 4.5%, which of the following will accommodate the greatest number of records?

(i) 2000 buckets of size 2

(ii) 500 buckets of size 5

(iii) 18 buckets of size 80

(Note: round-off load factors to the nearest tenth.)

(b) For the answer given above, how much space should be allocated for the overflow area?

6-16. Consider a hashed file using open addressing. Assume it has 50 buckets, each of which can hold two records. Suppose we randomly insert 88 records into the file. How many buckets, on the average, do we have to search to retrieve an arbitrary given record?

6-17. Illustrate the case where the record format = VS by drawing a picture similar to Figure 6.4. Be careful to distinguish it from other cases (especially VB and VBS).

File Processing and Programming

7

File Processes: Sorting and File Maintenance

7.1. INTRODUCTION

Two of the most important file-processing problems are (1) sorting and (2) file maintenance. An inefficient sort program can be very wasteful of computer resources. Writing an efficient sort program is a complicated job. Good sort utilities are available on most computer systems and it is generally better to use library utility sort programs than to write custom programs for every application. COBOL encourages this by providing a SORT statement that compiles a call to a library sort routine.

File-maintenance systems, on the other hand, are the principal responsibility of many, many programmers and analysts, and detailed discussions of file-maintenance algorithms are very appropriate. The main file-maintenance tasks are edit checking of transactions, file updating, and report writing. In a top-down type of approach, this chapter gives an overview, and the examples include calls to file I-O procedures. Chapter 8 includes the actual detailed coding of the I-O procedures needed to complete the examples of this chapter.

7.2. FILE SORTING

File sorting is the process of rearranging the records of the file in either ascending or descending order with respect to a record key. Sorting has been studied extensively and productively. Two excellent books on sorting are [H1] and [H2]. These publications include many references to other work. In addition, there is an extensive bibliography [H8]. This section provides, within the space of a few pages, some perspective on sorting. We also intend it as a guide to further information on sorting as it may be needed by the reader.

Sorting is a very important part of data processing. According to Knuth[H1],

Computer manufacturers estimate that over 25 percent of the running time on their computers is currently being spent on sorting, when all their customers are taken into account. There are many installations in which sorting uses more than half of the computing time. From these statistics we may conclude either that (*i*) there are many important applications of sorting, or (*ii*) many people sort when they shouldn't, or (*iii*) inefficient sorting algorithms are in common use. The real truth probably involves some of all three alternatives. In any event we can see that sorting is worthy of serious study, as a practical matter.

The comments on sorting being done inefficiently should not be taken lightly. There are many ways to sort, and they differ greatly. Some methods are practical for sorting files in auxiliary storage, but others only are practical for sorting in main memory. For example, consider two sorting methods: sorting by merging and sorting by insertion.

In our discussion of sorting, we will refer to a group of successive records that are a part of a file and that are in sequence by key as a *run*. Some sorting methods produce longer and longer runs as the process continues, until finally the whole file consists of a single run, and therefore is sorted. Some sorting methods start at the beginning of the file and go sequentially through it, doing some processing but not completely sorting it. Then they start at the beginning and go through it completely again—perhaps a number of times. With such methods, each time through is called a *pass*. Sorting by merging is a multiple-pass method, producing longer and longer runs on successive passes.

In sorting by insertion, there are two lists at each point: a list of all items sorted so far and a list of unsorted items. Initially, one item is placed in the sorted list, the rest in the unsorted list. On each pass, one item is taken from the unsorted list and a search for a place to insert the item is made starting from the end of the sorted list. Each item greater than the new one is moved down one place, and when the proper place for the new item is found, it is put there. For N items, the number of passes is $N-1$. The length of the sorted file grows from 1 to N, and the average length is $N/2$. On the average, it is necessary to search about halfway through the file to find where to put the next record. Thus, on the average, it is necessary to examine and move $N/4$ records on each pass. The amount of processing is proportional to $N(N-1)/4$. Figure 7.1 shows the lists after each pass for an example of sorting by insertion with eight items.

	Initial	1st	2nd	3rd	4th	5th	6th	7th
Sorted List	7	2	2	2	2	2	1	1
		7	5	5	3	3	2	2
	2		7	7	5	5	3	3
	5	5		9	7	7	5	5
	9	9	9		9	8	7	6
	3	3	3	3		9	8	7
	8	8	8	8	8		9	8
	1	1	1	1	1	1		9
Unsorted List	6	6	6	6	6	6	6	

Figure 7.1 An Example of Sorting by Insertion.

In the simplest form of sorting by merging, the initial list is divided into two equal parts and space is provided for temporary storage of two more lists. Let us call these lists L1, L2, L3, and L4, respectively. First, one item is taken from each list L1 and L2, and they are put in sequence and placed on L3. The next item is taken from each L1 and L2, and they are placed in order on L4. Then two more items are taken, placed in order, and put on L3 again, and so on. After the first pass, lists L1 and L2 are empty and lists L3 and L4 contain an equal number of runs of length 2. On the second pass, a pair taken from each list L3 and L4 are "merged" (reordered in the fashion described below) into a run of length 4 and placed on list L1. Then another pair is taken from each list L3 and L4, merged into a run of length 4, placed on L2, and so on. After the second pass, lists L3 and L4 are empty and L1 and L2 contain an equal number of runs of length 4. The succeeding passes similarly produce runs of length 8, 16, 32, etc. The process continues until there is just one run. (This works perfectly if the number of records is a power of 2, but even if it is not, the process can be done, with shorter runs and/or missing runs at the end of the lists.) Figure 7.2 shows the contents of each non-empty list at the end of each pass for a merge sort of 16 items.

Sorting by merging can be programmed in such a way that items are taken from each list one at a time in sequence from beginning to end, and thus is well adapted to sorting magnetic tapes. In the previous example, on the second pass, the run (3,9,10,15) can be produced from runs

Initial		1st Pass		2nd Pass		3rd Pass		4th Pass	
									L1
L1	L2	L3	L4	L1	L2	L3	L4	L1	(cont.)
9	10	9	3	3	6	3	1	1	9
3	15	10	15	9	8	6	2	2	10
12	8	8	6	10	12	8	4	3	11
6	19	12	19	15	19	9	5	4	12
4	5	4	1	1	2	10	7	5	13
17	1	5	17	4	7	12	11	6	15
11	13	11	2	5	11	15	13	7	17
2	7	13	7	17	13	19	17	8	19

Figure 7.2 An Example of Sorting by Merging.

(9,10) on L3 and (3,15) on L4 as follows: First 9 is read from L3 and 3 from L4; the smaller one, 3, is written out on L1 and the next item, 15, is read from L4 to replace it; then 9, the smaller remaining item, is written out on L1 and the next item, 10, is read from L3 to replace it; finally, 10 is the smaller of the remaining items and is written out next followed by 15 to conclude the run. Note that L3 and L4 are not read from again until the later runs are merged in the same pass. Because the length of runs doubles on each pass, a file of length $N = 2^p$ can be sorted in p passes. Thus, the number of passes is the base 2 logarithm of N. (If N is not an even power of 2, then $\log_2(N)$ is not a whole number. The number of passes required is the smallest whole number larger than this.) On each pass it is necessary to examine and move every item, so the amount of processing is proportional to $N \times \log_2(N)$.

In a variation called *natural* merging, the runs that naturally occur in the input are used instead of fixed-length runs. This method has the advantage of requiring fewer passes—if the input records are in random order, one fewer pass is required on the average. For files that are almost in sequence, even fewer passes are required. Natural merging is a little harder to program, and it is a little harder to analyze. Figure 7.3 shows an example of natural merging. The ends of runs are marked. Note that (5,6) and (7,11), produced separately during the first pass, are treated as a single run during the second pass.

Now let us compare sorting by merging with sorting by insertion. Some values of $(N-1) \times N/4$ and $N \times \log_2(N)$ are given in Table 7.1. Because sorting by merging requires a more complicated program, examining one item will take more time in a merge-sort program than in an insertion-sort program. The difference will depend on the program and the machine. For sorting up to 16 items, the insertion sort will be faster, even

Initial		1st Pass		2nd Pass		3rd Pass		4th Pass
L1	L2	L3	L4	L1	L2	L3	L4	L1
9	10	9	3	3	1	1	2	1
3	15	10	8	8	4	3		2
12	8	15	12	9	5	4		3
6	19	5	19	10	6	5		4
4	5	6	1	12	7	6		5
17	1	7	4	15	11	7		6
11	13	11	13	19	13	8		7
2	7		17	2	17	9		8
			2			10		9
						11		10
						12		11
						13		12
						15		13
						17		15
						19		17
								19

Figure 7.3 An Example of Sorting by Natural Merging.

Table 7.1 Comparison of $(N-1)N/4$ and $N\times\log_2(N)$

N	$(N-1)N/4$	$N\log_2 N$	Ratio
4	3	8	.375
8	14	24	.583
16	60	64	.938
32	248	160	1.55
64	1008	384	2.63
128	4064	896	4.54
256	16320	2048	7.96
$1024 = 2^{10}$	261888	10240	25.6
$65536 = 2^{16}$	$1.073*10^9$	$1.049*10^6$	$1.02*10^3$
$1048576 = 2^{20}$	$2.746*10^{11}$	$2.097*10^7$	$1.31*10^4$

if examining one item takes the same time with either program. If sorting by merging is three times slower per item, then sorting by insertion is faster at $N = 64$, but slower at 128. At $N = 1024$, sorting by merging will be faster by a factor somewhere between 5 and 25, which would be significant if it is done many times. If there are a million items, they almost certainly will be on tape or disk. Examining one item probably will require a few milliseconds at least. If we assume one millisecond per item, then sorting by merging would require about 20,970 sec = 5.82 hours, whereas sorting by insertion would require about 274,600,000 sec = 8.7 years! Even though these timing estimates are only approximate, we may safely conclude that it is practical to sort a million records using sorting by merging, but not using insertion sorting. Clearly, one must take some care in choosing a sorting algorithm for sorting a large number of items!

With respect to the amount of storage required, insertion sorting is optimal in that to sort N items requires space to store just $N + 1$ items. (If the sorted list is placed in front of the unsorted list in the same array, then an array of length N plus a space to store the next record to be inserted is all that is needed.) To sort N items by merging requires storage for $2N$ items. On the other hand, sorting by merging is near optimal with respect to speed in that for large N no sorting method requires processing time that increases significantly slower as N is increased than $N \times \log_2(N)$. There exist methods that are near optimal with respect to both speed and storage requirements[H1]. "Batcher's method" requires the same space as sorting by insertion, $N + 1$ spaces to sort N items. It requires about the same amount of processing as sorting by merging, but requires some bit string operations. "Quicksort" requires little more than N storage spaces and processing proportional to $N \times \log_2(N)$ on the average. This algorithm can be programmed quite easily in any common higher-level language in about 20 to 40 statements. These algorithms are described in [H1] and [H2].

Next, let us consider some practical problems that arise when files are to be sorted. If the file to be sorted will fit entirely in main storage, then almost invariably it is best sorted there. Sorting within main memory is called *internal sorting*. In contrast, sorting that uses auxiliary storage devices such as tapes and/or disks is called *external sorting*. Knuth ([H1], p. 181 et seq.) discusses many methods of internal and external sorting. In his summary of internal sorting, he lists 14 of the "most significant algorithms for internal sorting," each of which is best under some circumstances; Batcher's method and Quicksort are two of the best algorithms overall.

Special conditions often dictate special methods. For example, suppose we want to sort a personnel file of records by sex, placing all records marked F before the records marked M. Any sorting method, such as insertion or merging, could be used, but the obvious way to do this is simply to make two lists and "distribute" each record to its appropriate list. This is simpler and faster than the more general methods. The same applies if there are more than two but not too many categories. It also applies if there are N items numbered 1 to N.

For the more common situation, where the number of possible keys is much larger than the number of records, if one wants to sort only a few records at a time, then sorting by insertion is as fast and simple as any method. Internal sorts frequently are done on 1000 records or more, but then insertion sorting is too slow, unless it is to be done very infrequently. Quicksort or Batcher's method would be suitable. The crossover point below which insertion sorting is faster and above which Quicksort or Batcher's method would be faster is typically in the range of $N = 30$ to 100 items, depending on the details of the program and the hardware.

Now let us consider external sorting briefly. As with internal sorting, if the number of distinct keys is small, as with sorting by sex, a distribution sort may be best. If there are N records numbered 1 to N to be sorted, this cannot be done easily with tape, but it can with disk. With disks, distribution sorting may or may not be faster than conventional methods because reading and writing records in sequence is faster than reading or writing in random order on a disk unit.

In the more usual case where the number of possible keys is much larger than the number of records, sorting by merging is almost invariably best. However, there are many possible variations. As a preliminary step, it is advantageous to repeatedly read a number $N1$ of records into the main storage, sort them using an internal sort, and write them out. Thus, on the first pass, files made up of runs of $N1$ records are produced. The larger $N1$ is, the fewer additional passes will be required to complete the sort.

It might seem that if you have main storage large enough to store K

records (plus space for buffers and a little more), the optimum strategy would be to choose $N1 = K$ and use Quicksort or Batcher's method to produce runs of length K. However, it is possible to do even better, by a method called *replacement selection*. The idea is as follows: You place K records in main storage. Then you write out (to the output buffer) the one with the lowest key and immediately read in (from the input buffer) a new one to replace it, so you still have K records in main storage. You write out the one of these with lowest key not lower than the key on last record written, then replace it, and so on. When there is no record with a key not lower than the key on the last record written, you start a new run by writing out the lowest record.

Figure 7.4 shows how replacement selection would work with the same file of 16 numbers as was used for merge sorting. Line 0 shows the data with the last to be read at the left, and with a work space that holds four numbers shown in parentheses. The first step is to write out the smallest number, 3, and replace it immediately with the 4 from the input stream. Next write out the smallest number again, 4, and replace it with the 17 from the input stream. Note that at step 5 we do not write out the smallest number, 2, but rather the smallest number that continues the run, which is 11. At step 10, it is no longer possible to continue the run, so we start a new run, writing out the 2. We end up with three runs of average length 5.33.

Clearly, the minimum length of runs is the size of the work space, K, and there is a possibility for runs much longer than K. It can be shown that if the records are in random order, the average length of runs produced will be $2K$ [H1, H2]. If the file is initially almost in sequence, even longer runs will result, which will greatly reduce the number of addi-

```
 0.  7  13   1    5   19    8   15   10    2   11   17    4  (6   12    3   9)
 1.  7  13   1    5   19    8   15   10    2   11   17   (6   12    4   9)   3
 2.  7  13   1    5   19    8   15   10    2   11   (6   12   17   9)   4    3
 3.  7  13   1    5   19    8   15   10    2  (11   12   17   9)   6    4    3
 4.  7  13   1    5   19    8   15   10  (11   12   17   2)   9    6    4    3
 5.  7  13   1    5   19    8   15  (10   12   17   2)  11    9    6    4    3
 6.  7  13   1    5   19    8  (10   15   17   2)  12   11    9    6    4    3
 7.  7  13   1    5   19  (10    8   17   2)  15   12   11    9    6    4    3
 8.  7  13   1    5  (10    8   19   2)  17   15   12   11    9    6    4    3
 9.  7  13   1  (10    8    5   2)  19   17   15   12   11    9    6    4    3
10.  7  13  (10   8    5   1)   2  |19   17   15   12   11    9    6    4    3
11.  7  (10   8   13   1)   5    2  |19   17   15   12   11    9    6    4    3
12.  (10   7  13   1)   8    5    2  |19   17   15   12   11    9    6    4    3
13.  (7   13   1)  10    8    5    2  |19   17   15   12   11    9    6    4    3
14.  (7    1)  13   10    8    5    2  |19   17   15   12   11    9    6    4    3
15.  (7)   1  |13   10    8    5    2  |19   17   15   12   11    9    6    4    3
16.  7    1  |13   10    8    5    2  |19   17   15   12   11    9    6    4    3
```

Figure 7.4 An Example of Replacement Selection.

tional passes required. Note that since the runs produced are of variable length, natural merging is needed on the succeeding passes.

In programming replacement selection, the most obvious way is to search through all K records to find the one of lowest key on each step. This requires $K - 1$ comparisons per record. Essentially by saving information about previous comparisons, it is possible to reduce this to about $\log_2(K)$ comparisons per record. This represents a substantial saving in processing time, at the cost of a somewhat more complicated program.

The runs of modest length that result from replacement selection can be distributed nearly evenly onto M files. Then these M files can be sorted by merging them into fewer and longer runs until there is only one run consisting of the whole file. On each pass of this M-way merge procedure, M runs are merged into one, so that the number of runs is divided by M. After each merge pass except the last, the resulting runs should be distributed onto M files again to prepare for the next pass. If, after the first pass, there are $N2$ runs in all, then the number of additional passes required is the smallest integer not less than $\log_M(N2)$. For example, with 1000 runs, a two-way merge requires 10 merge passes, a three-way merge requires 7, and a four-way merge requires 5.

Since one pass requires reading and writing each record in the file, the amount of time required for a pass is independent of M, and the larger M is, the less time the sort will require. However, an M-way merge using tape requires M input units and M output units, a total of $2M$ tape drives. On disk units, unless each I-O unit is on a separate drive, seek time will be very large, so in practice $2M$ disk drives are generally used for an M-way merge, if available.

Up to this point, we tacitly have assumed a *balanced merge*. On each pass the output is distributed equally on M output units. Note that if N I-O units are available, rather than performing a balanced $(N/2)$-way merge, we may perform an $(N - 1)$-way merge onto a single I-O unit and distribute the runs back onto the $N - 1$ other units for the next pass. There are a number of other merge patterns that may be more efficient under certain circumstances than the balanced merge. As a simple and very practical example, suppose you have only three tapes. Then you cannot do a balanced two-way merge without some modification. Suppose you have 13 runs after the first pass. Put eight runs on tape 1 and five on tape 2. Now merge five pairs of runs from tape 1 and tape 2 onto tape 3—now there are three runs on tape 1, five on tape 3, and none on tape 2. Next merge three pairs from each tape 1 and tape 3 onto tape 2. Now tape 1 is empty, tape 2 has three runs, and tape 3 has two. Next merge two runs from 2 and 3 onto 1. Now tape 1 has two runs, tape 3 has none, and tape 2 has one. Next merge one run from each tape 1 and 2 onto tape 3. Now tape 1 and tape 3 have one run each and tape 2 has none. One more merge finishes the job. An analysis of this so-called *polyphase merge* shows it to be only slightly less efficient than a balanced two-way merge, even though it requires one fewer tape unit. There are a number of other patterns also possible that under certain circumstances offer advantages over balanced merges.

One can conclude from the preceding discussion that designing and producing an efficient program to do an external sort is a major undertaking. Doing it well requires a careful study of known sorting techniques, because there can be a very great difference in efficiency between a poorly designed sorting system and one that makes good use of modern techniques. Fortunately, excellent literature is available, such as those cited at the end of the chapter. We recommend the example by Bentley[H13], which shows the importance of a careful design when an application has special characteristics.

There is a practical alternative that is usually available. One can expect a good sort-merge utility program to be available for any well-supported computer system. Although some compromises must be made to produce a general-purpose system, reasonable efficiency can be expected. Utility programs probably can handle more than 99% of sorting requirements conveniently and with entirely satisfactory efficiency. Using a utility sort certainly is preferable to just reusing a sort program designed for some other application.

For a typical sort-merge utility, the user first specifies whether a sort of one file or a merge of several files is required. The user then specifies a primary key and optionally one or more secondary keys, and in each case whether the key is to be ascending or descending in the final file. In sorting or merging, the program compares primary keys. If they are equal, the first secondary keys are compared. If they are equal also, the next secondary keys are compared, and so on. (If all keys are equal on a pair of records, their order in the output file may or may not be preserved. A system that preserves the order of equal records is called *stable*.) The user also specifies the record size, the locations of keys in the record, and other file characteristics, as well as an output file and files for intermediate storage for merging. (Formulas usually are provided for estimating the size required for the files for intermediate storage.) Finally, the user may specify an estimated file size (which enables the utility to do some optimizing) and may be able to choose among several sorting methods.

Some systems also provide for the user to insert an input procedure to be executed each time a record is read from the original file and an output procedure to be executed each time a record is to be written on the output file. This allows reformatting of records to simplify sorting by eliminating unneeded data or records, or to compress data on input and restore it after, or to do whatever else the user might wish.

Details on sort-merge utilities are available in manuals provided by the vendors. Some early systems are mentioned in [H14]. The use of

IBM's package is described in [J9]. Some information is also available in books on data-processing practice.

The above discussion of sorting is sufficient for making fairly accurate estimates of the time required to sort a file, as is illustrated by Example 7.1.

Example 7.1

Assume we want to sort a file of 1,000,000 records on tape. Assume a standard 6250 cpi tape and blocks of 250 80-character records. Then the blocks will require $250 \times 80 = 20,000$ characters and $20,000/6250 = 3.2$ in. The gap is 0.3 in., so each block requires a total of 3.5 in. A million records will require 4000 blocks or 14,000 in., which is somewhat more than one-half of one 2400 ft. reel.

Assume that there is a work space of a little more than 100,000 characters in memory for the first pass of the sort and that it will use replacement selection. Then the memory can hold 1250 records at one time, and replacement selection will produce runs having an average length of 2500 records. The 1,000,000 records will comprise about 400 runs.

Assume that we finish the sort using a balanced two-way merge. The number of passes required will be the next integer greater than $\log_2(400)$, which is nine. (The number of runs will halve on each pass, becoming 200, 100, 50, 25, 13, 7, 4, 2, and finally 1.) On the first pass, half of the runs will be put on each of the two output tapes. On each of the eight intermediate passes, a run from one input tape will be merged with a run from the other, and half of the resulting runs will be written on each output tape. On the last pass, there will be one run on each input tape, and they will be merged to produce a single run on the final output tape.

On the first pass, the processing time can be overlapped with the read time. On a fast computer, the processing time will be less than the read time and the total time will equal the I-O time. On the other passes, the processing time is very small and almost always will be smaller than the I-O time. We will calculate time on the assumption that processing time all can be overlapped with I-O.

The time required will depend on how many I-O processors are available. First, assume that one I-O processor is available. Then it is possible to read or write, but not to do both at once. Each pass will require reading and writing each block, a total of 14,000 in. of reading and 14,000 in. of writing. At a speed of 200 ips, this will require 140 sec. Ten passes are required, so the total will be 1400 sec or 23.3 min. If we have two I-O processors, then the best plan is to use one for input and the other for output. The time for input is equal to the time for output, and input and output can be done simultaneously, so the time required will be half that required with one processor, 700 sec or 11.7 min.

If there are four I-O processors, then the total time for the first and last pass is still the time required to read the input tape and write the final output tape, respectively, which is 70 sec each. With these parameters, the runs produced on the initial pass are considerably more than one block—an average of 10 blocks on the input for the second pass and doubling on every pass. Therefore, it is necessary to write 10 or more blocks to one tape, then 10 or more to the other, and so on. Very little overlapping can occur, so no more than a few percent of the required time can be saved.

Similar calculations can be made for disk files. Note that one cannot predict in what order blocks will be read, and unlike the case for tapes, this affects the time required because it affects the latency and possibly seek times. In general, blocks will be read alternately from one input file and then the other, at least most of the time. Similarly, one would expect that after an input operation, the next operation would most likely be an output operation, and vice versa. As far as the authors know, no theoretical studies of these matters have been made. This makes estimates of latency time uncertain, and if two files are on the same disk unit, then estimates of seek time also are uncertain. If we assume that the latency is, on the average, $\frac{1}{2}$ revolution and that seek is required every time if files share a disk drive, the resulting estimates should be conservative but only by a modest percentage.

7.3. FILE MAINTENANCE

Recordkeeping for business or government operations (as contrasted to detailed analysis, forecasting, and decision making) is simply file maintenance, which probably accounts for more than half of all use of computer resources and programming and analysis. There are strong similarities among almost all file-maintenance processes. The remainder of this chapter describes the most important of these processes and presents algorithms for doing them.

In file maintenance, the main file that is being maintained is called the *master file*. The input data are called *transactions*. The transactions contain information that affects the contents of the master file. The output of the system consists of *reports* and an updated master file.

File-maintenance systems typically include three tasks, which may be done by separate programs or combined:

1. Edit checking of transactions,
2. Actual file updating, and
3. Report writing.

There are two fundamentally different ways of doing file updating—batch and on-line. In batch processing, transactions are collected, and periodically (daily, weekly, or monthly, for example) an update program is run that processes all these transactions, making the indicated changes in the master file, and possibly, at the same time, producing desired reports. With an on-line system, transactions are entered from a terminal and processed, updating the master file almost immediately. In the past, computers were used almost entirely for batch processing, but in recent years, advances in technology of terminals, data communications, and most of all, disk storage have made on-line systems more and more economically attractive. They are now very widely used.

Certain applications, such as airline reservations, are practical only as on-line systems. Others, payroll, for example, gain almost nothing from on-line processing, because they are by nature done periodically. In still other cases, although batch processing has proved practical, on-line processing offers important advantages. For example, retail sales charge accounts can be handled very satisfactorily in a batch system, but an on-line system offers important advantages such as the ability to check the status of the customer account at the time of the sale and to refuse the sale if the customer is not in good standing.

Example 7.2

In a retail sales system, the master file will include one record for each customer, with the account number, name, address, account balance, possibly a list of purchases and payments since the last statement, and probably some other data such as credit limit, overdue payments, if any, and payment plan. Transactions would include purchases, payments, and changes in all other data, and orders to create a new master record for a new customer or to delete a record for a closed account.

In a simple reservation system such as for a hotel or a concert hall, the master file would include records of the resources to be reserved, the name of the party who made the reservation, and whether or not a payment was made. The transactions would include reservations, reservation cancellations, and payments. An airline reservation system might include two files—one for the passengers' names, itineraries, and the status of each, and the other would include a listing of space on planes, showing whether or not it is reserved, and if so, referring to the itinerary.

In a student records system in a school or university, the master file would contain the student's name, address, a complete list of all courses taken along with their grades, and other facts. Transactions would include entry of courses, grades, grade changes, record insertion and deletion, and provisions for making changes in other data. It is practical to maintain student records as a batch system and to update as seldom as once or twice per school term.

We will use a simple inventory system for example programs in this chapter and the next. It will be simplified to make the programs as short as possible while still illustrating the important concepts. Segments of programs will be used throughout the rest of this chapter in examples, and those example programs will be in COBOL. (COBOL is quite easy to read and understand, even for persons who do not know COBOL, although it is not easier to write than other common languages.) The complete COBOL programs are in Appendix B, and similar complete example programs in PL/I and FORTRAN are included in Appendix C and Appendix D, respectively.

Example 7.3

In the example programs in the rest of this chapter and in the next one, we assume a simple inventory system. We will assume the master records have the following format:

Column 1–6	Stock ID or part number (all digits)
Column 7–10	Quantity
Column 11–25	Description

We will assume four kinds of transactions with codes A, B, C, and D.

A	Add new item (insert)
B	Stock added to inventory (receive)
C	Stock removed from inventory (disburse)
D	Delete item

We will assume the following format for transactions:

Column 1–6	Stock part number
Column 7	Transaction code (A,B,C, or D)
Column 8–11	Quantity
Column 12–26	Description

Part number and transaction code are required on all transactions. Quantity is required on A, B, and C. Description is required on A only. We will consider both an on-line system and a batch system. On the batch system, a run is made once a week and a report is prepared during the batch run.

In COBOL, one might declare the input records as follows:

```
DATA DIVISION.
FILE SECTION.
FD  OLD-MASTER.
01  OLD-MASTER-RECORD.
    02 PART-NO PICTURE XXXXX.
    02 QUANTITY PICTURE 9999.
    02 DESCRIPTION PICTURE X(15).

FD  NEW-MASTER.
01  NEW-MASTER-RECORD.
    02 PART-NO PICTURE XXXXX.
    02 QUANTITY PICTURE 9999.
    02 DESCRIPTION PICTURE X(15).

FD  TRANSACTIONS.
01  TRANSACTION-RECORD.
    02 PART-NO PICTURE XXXXX.
    02 T-CODE PICTURE X.
       88 INSERT-RECORD VALUE IS "A".
       88 RECEIVE-GOODS VALUE IS "B".
       88 DISBURSE-GOODS VALUE IS "C".
       88 DELETE-RECORD VALUE IS "D".
       88 VALID-CODE VALUE IS "A" THRU "D".
       88 NEED-QUANTITY VALUE IS "A" THRU "C".
    02 QUANTITY PICTURE 9999.
    02 DESCRIPTION PICTURE X(15).
```

Each file description (FD) describes the record format (specifying fields and their types) for that file. An "88" declares a variable (called a condition name) to be true if a field has a specified value; e.g., INSERT-RECORD is true if T-CODE = "A".

7.4. EDIT CHECKING

Edit checking is simply the checking of transactions for errors. It is needed because the transactions come from outside the system—they usually are generated by humans and entered into the computer directly or indirectly by humans. The probability of error in a single transaction may be very small, but when there are thousands of transactions it is extremely unlikely that they will all be correct. Proper edit checking (1) will assure that the system does not "bomb out" because of bad data, and (2) will assure to as great an extent as possible the integrity of the file by preventing the entry of invalid data into the system.

This is the simplest of the three aspects of file processing—seemingly trivial. Its seeming triviality is likely to result in its not being given the attention it deserves. It is the responsibility of every systems analyst and programmer to see that edit checking is done thoroughly.

There are several points that deserve some discussion. Most checks can be made on transactions without referring to the master file—you can check that all fields that are supposed to be numbers are actually numbers and whether their values are within acceptable limits. You can check for the presence of all required data. There are also certain errors that cannot be checked without referring to the master file, notably if the transaction is an insertion, there must not already be a record in the file with that key, and in all other cases, there must be a master record with that key. As other examples, an accounts-receivable or an accounts-payable record generally should not be deleted if its balance is not zero, and an order should not be processed if there is not enough of an item in the inventory to fill it; these facts are available only in the master file. Even if an edit-check run checking every transaction against the master file is made, errors still may occur. For example, if there are two transactions to delete a certain record, only one can be processed, the other must be an error. Checking a batch of transactions before processing any of them will not reveal that error, because although each transaction is valid itself, as soon as one is processed, the other becomes invalid.

With a batch system, there are two possible approaches:

(a) *Make an edit-checking program separately from the update program.* First you run the transactions through the edit checking. If any errors are found, try to correct them and reject any transactions that cannot be corrected. Then use the corrected transactions for the update program. Using this method, you catch most errors on the edit run, but not all. Then you must at least provide for occasionally running the update program again with the transactions resulting from correcting errors found on the update run. Edit checking should be incorporated in the update program to insure against accidental runs with nonchecked data or erroneously corrected data.

(b) *Incorporate edit checking into the update program.* In this case, it probably will be normal for transaction errors to be found and at least a second update run will be needed to make the corrections. (For some applications, it may be acceptable to let the corrections wait until the next regular update run.)

Each of these alternatives has advantages and disadvantages and either may be better in given circumstances.

The problem of additional update runs does not occur with an on-line system. When each transaction comes from a terminal, it is checked independently and then against the master file. If it is erroneous, the operator is notified and may enter a corrected transaction. Each good transaction is processed immediately.

Program logic for the edit-checking program should be simple and clear. Typically, there will be a list of things to check. In some cases, a check is made only if a previous check succeeds. For example, if a certain field is supposed to be a number between 1 and 18, a check should be made to see that it is actually a number and then only if it is a number should the range be checked. Otherwise, checking should not stop when the first error is found—the edit checking should find as many errors as possible and print error messages for all.

Suppose that the list of checks consists of test #1, test #2, and test #3, and test #2 is done only if test #1 succeeds. Then the program should be organized something like this: (Note the significance of the word "else.")

```
set error flag false.

if test #1 fails then set error flag true and
      print an error message

else if test #2 fails then set error flag true
      and print an error message.

if test #3 fails then set error flag true and
      print an error message.
```

In PL/I there is a language feature, the CONVERSION ON condition, that only applies to checking whether data are numeric. However, programs that use this feature have a complicated control structure and are very error prone, so it is better to avoid it and simply use the ordinary string-processing features of PL/I—especially VERIFY, INDEX, and SUBSTR—to verify the format of the input data in a simple and straightforward manner. This method is illustrated in the examples in Appendix C. COBOL has built-in functions that check for NUMERIC or ALPHABETIC data.

Example 7.4

The following COBOL paragraphs could be used for edit checking for the simple inventory example:

```
EDIT-CHECK.
      MOVE FALSE TO ERROR-FLAG.
*  MOVING FALSE TO ERROR-FLAG MAKES OK TRUE.
         IF PART-NO IN TRANSACTION-RECORD IS NOT NUMERIC
            MOVE TRUE TO ERROR-FLAG
            DISPLAY  "--PART-NO NOT NUMERIC".
```

```
* NOTE THAT THE FOLLOWING TWO CHECKS CAN BE INCLUDED
* ONLY IF THIS EDIT PROGRAM IS A PART OF THE UPDATE
* PROGRAM, AND THEREFORE THE MASTER RECORD IS AVAILABLE.

    IF OK AND INSERT-RECORD AND PART-NO IN
        TRANSACTION-RECORD IS EQUAL TO PART-NO IN
        NEW-MASTER-RECORD
        MOVE TRUE TO ERROR-FLAG
        DISPLAY "--DUPLICATE PART-NO"
    ELSE IF OK AND NOT INSERT-RECORD AND PART-NO IN
        TRANSACTION-RECORD IS NOT EQUAL TO PART-NO IN
        NEW-MASTER-RECORD
        MOVE TRUE TO ERROR-FLAG
        DISPLAY "--MASTER RECORD NOT FOUND".

* FOR THE FOLLOWING, VALID CODE IS A CONDITION NAME
* THAT IS TRUE FOR CODES A THROUGH D, AND NEED-QUANTITY
* IS A CONDITION NAME TRUE FOR A THROUGH C.

    IF NOT VALID-CODE
        MOVE TRUE TO ERROR-FLAG
        DISPLAY "--INVALID CODE".
    IF NEED-QUANTITY AND QUANTITY IN
        TRANSACTION-RECORD IS NOT NUMERIC
        MOVE TRUE TO ERROR-FLAG
        DISPLAY "--QUANTITY NOT NUMERIC"
    ELSE IF DISBURSE-GOODS AND OK AND QUANTITY IN
        TRANSACTION-RECORD IS GREATER THAN QUANTITY
        IN NEW-MASTER-RECORD
        MOVE TRUE TO ERROR-FLAG
        DISPLAY "--NOT ENOUGH IN STOCK".
    IF INSERT-RECORD AND DESCRIPTION IN
        TRANSACTION-RECORD IS EQUAL TO SPACES
        MOVE TRUE TO ERROR-FLAG
        DISPLAY "--DESCRIPTION MISSING".
    IF DELETE-RECORD AND OK AND QUANTITY IN
        NEW-MASTER-RECORD IS NOT EQUAL TO ZERO
        MOVE TRUE TO ERROR-FLAG
        DISPLAY "QUANTITY NOT ZERO ON DELETE".
```

7.5. BATCH UPDATE PROCESSING

We will assume that each record has a key. Names, social security numbers, part numbers, and account numbers are examples of data-items often used as keys. We assume that no two master records have the same key. The key on a transaction indicates to which master record it applies, and for a given master record there may be no transactions or several transactions. It was pointed out in Chapter 6 that updating can be done very efficiently if both the master file and the transactions file are sorted in sequence by key. The essential idea is to process all transactions that match the first master record, then all that match the second, and so on. This can be accomplished by first reading a master record, then reading and processing all associated transactions, then reading the next master record, and so on. The records will show up in the order that they are needed if both files are sorted by key. The details needed to make this work out well are not trivial. For example, it should be possible to insert a new master record and process its associated transactions on the same run.

Usually with a batch system—always if the master file is on tape—no attempt is made to change the old master file, but instead a completely new updated copy of the master file is produced. With tape systems, it is generally not possible to change a record unless all the following records are rewritten. It is common to keep the old master file and the transactions file as permanent records and as backup against the loss of a file.

There may be things that have to be done when we first start on another master record before we process any associated transactions, such as initializing some variables or, if we are simultaneously preparing a report, printing a heading for the data pertaining to this master record. We will assume these tasks are done by a procedure called do-initial-processing. For each transaction, certain other things must be done. We will assume these tasks are included in a procedure called process-transaction. After the last transaction for a given master record has been processed, there may be still other things that must be done, such as routine changes in the master file or printing footing lines for the group of data pertaining to this master record in a concurrently prepared report. We will assume that these tasks are included in a procedure called do-final-processing.

Obviously, we need a work area in memory for the master-file record being processed and one for the transaction being processed. If the update system is going to handle insertions, then two master records must be in the memory at the same time, because it is impossible to know where the new master record should be inserted until the one following it has been read. For example, suppose we are to insert a record for LIN and the record just processed was LAM. We cannot be sure LIN is next. Next we read LEE. We still can not be sure LIN is next. Next we read LEW. We still do not know. Next we read LIU. Now we know—LIN should be inserted between LEW and LIU, so we should process LIN after processing LEW but before processing LIU, even though LIU has already been read. Because we must handle some cases this way, it is simplest to handle all this way, that is, always to keep in memory the record we are working on, which we will refer to as the new-master-record, and the next record on the old master file, which we will call the old-master-record. Old-master-record may be thought of as associated with the old master file, and new-master-record as associated with the new master file. We will do all processing on a record when it is in the new-master-record position.

There is a technique for handling end conditions whose use predates computers—it was commonly used in the old card systems. Its use simplifies programs very significantly, so we will use it in our examples. In card systems, a dummy record with a key value (called high-values) higher than any real key was inserted at the end of the file. For example, if the key is alphabetic, a value of all Z's would be used; if the key is numeric, generally a value of all 9's is suitable. (No person may have 999-99-9999 as his social security number or ZZZZZZZZZZZZZ as her name.) When the record with this key comes up for processing, we know that all real records have been processed and terminate the program. This is an oversimplification—we will check the details when we have a complete algorithm. With modern languages, the dummy record usually is not included in the file. Instead, it is inserted in the memory when an end-of-file condition is met. For example, in PL/I, we may use

```
ON ENDFILE(OLDMASTER)
    OLD_MASTER_RECORD.NAME = 'ZZZZZZZZZZZZ';
```

or in COBOL,

```
READ TRANSACTIONS AT END MOVE 'ZZZZZZZZZZZZ'
    TO NAME IN TRANSACTION-RECORD.
```

COBOL has a built-in constant called HIGH-VALUES that is the highest value that can be represented in the computer, and a similar constant called LOW-VALUES that is the lowest value that can be represented. PL/I also has similar constants, HIGH(n) and LOW(n), which are character strings of length n. The PL/I standard regards them as built-in functions. It is preferable to use these values rather than the values suggested in the preceding paragraph, because it is possible to have invalid nonalphabetic values greater than all Z's in a field that is supposed to be alphabetic or nonnumeric values greater than all 9's in a field that is supposed to be numeric. Such data will cause problems with many algorithms if the values all Z's for alphabetic fields or all 9's for numeric fields are used as the highest possible values.

When we start processing, there is a possibility that the first transaction inserts a new master record before the first old master record. Therefore, we do not know which record goes into new-master-record initially. We propose to solve this problem in a way analogous to the handling of the end of the file—we will initially put a key lower than any valid key in the new-master-record to form another kind of dummy record. (We might use all zeros for a numeric key, all blanks for an alphabetic key, but it is better to use LOW-VALUES in COBOL or LOW(n) in PL/I.) Also, to delete a record, we will change its key to this low value. Again we will check details when we have a complete algorithm.

We will assume that we have a procedure called read-master that reads the next master record into the area called old-master-record and on end-of-file sets the key in that area to high-values. Similarly, we will assume that we have a procedure read-transaction that reads the next trans-action into the area called transaction and on end-of-file sets the key in that area to high-values. Finally, we will assume a procedure called write-master that writes a new master record on the new master file from the area called new-master-record.

There are two commonly used algorithms for batch update programs (and many small variations, of course). We will present both. The first uses a single loop and is a little shorter. but some persons may find the second, which uses two nested loops, a little easier to understand. They are equivalent.

With the first approach, each time through the single loop, one record, either a transaction or a master record, is processed. If the choice is to process a master record, this means to move the next record from the old-master-record into the new-master-record, read another old master record, and execute do-initial-processing. The algorithm looks like this:

```
set key in new-master-record to low-values;
read-transaction;
read-master;
while key in new-master-record is less than high-values do begin
   if key in new-master-record is less than key in
      transaction-record and not equal to low-values then begin
{a}   do-final-processing;
      write-master;
      set key in new-master-record to low-values
      end;

   if key in old-master-record is not greater than key in
      transaction-record then begin
      move old-master-record to new-master-record;
      if key in new-master-record is less than high-values then
{b}      begin
         read-master;
         do-initial-processing
         end
      end

   else begin
      do-edit-check;
{c}   if OK then process-transaction;
      read-transaction
      end;
   end {of while loop}
```

The first three statements establish proper initial conditions. Then the loop is repeated until the new-master-record has its key equal to high-values. Within that loop, there are three parts. Part {a} states that if the current transaction key is greater than the new-master-record key, there are no more transactions for this master record, and it should be written out. Setting the key to zero makes it clear that that record is no longer in new-master-record.

Part {b} of the loop states that if the old-master-record key is less than or equal to the transaction key, we are ready to use that record; it should be moved to the new-master-record position, do-initial-processing should be executed, and the next master record should be read into old-master-record. There are two cases. If equality holds, then the transaction applies to this master record. If not, there must be no transactions that match this master record. In either case, note that the new-master-record key must have been less than the old-master-record key and so must have been less than the transaction key, so that if there was a master record (with nonzero key) in the new-master-record it would have been written out in part {a}.

Note also that the last time the loop is entered, the keys in both the transaction and the old-master-record will be high-values and no attempt should be made to either read the next master (because end-of-file already has been met) or to do-initial-processing on this record (because it is not a real record). This is shown in the preceding algorithm.

Finally, if part {b} is not done, then the transaction key must be less than the old-master-record key. It might be equal to the new-master-record key—that is the usual case. No action ever results in a new-master-record key greater than the transaction key. So if the keys are not equal, the transaction key must be greater, and if the new-master-record key was not zero when the loop was entered, it was set to zero at part {a}. This case is an insertion, if it is a valid transaction.

Note that with the edit check deferred until just before processing, if there exists a matching master record, it will be in the new-master-record and those checks requiring information about the master record can be done. One might worry about invalid ID fields. If the transactions are properly sorted, for example, by computer, this will cause no problems.

Now let us check whether we start properly. If the first transaction is an insertion to precede the first old-master-record, it is inserted at part {c} the first time through the loop. Otherwise, the first old-master-record is moved into new-master-record on the first time through the loop.

At the end, either file may become empty first. If the transaction file empties first, then the transaction key becomes high-values and both parts {a} and {b} of the loop are repeated until the last real master record has been written, at which time the new-master-record key becomes high-values and the loop terminates. On the other hand, if the old-master-file empties first, then the old-master-record key becomes high-values and part {c} (and possibly {a}) is done every time through the loop until all transactions have been read. When the transaction key becomes high-values also, part {b} is done once, new-master-record key becomes high-values, and the program terminates.

Example 7.5

In COBOL, the simple inventory program might look like this:

```
PROCEDURE DIVISION.
MAIN-PROGRAM.
    OPEN INPUT OLD-MASTER TRANSACTIONS.
    OPEN OUTPUT NEW-MASTER.
    MOVE LOW-VALUES TO PART-NO IN NEW-MASTER.
    PERFORM READ-TRANSACTION.
    PERFORM READ-MASTER.
    DISPLAY "PART-NO  DESCRIPTION    QUANTITY"
    DISPLAY
       "                    OLD  IN   OUT  NEW".
    PERFORM MAIN-LOOP UNTIL PART-NO IN NEW-MASTER-
        RECORD IS EQUAL TO HIGH-VALUES.
    CLOSE OLD-MASTER NEW-MASTER TRANSACTIONS.
    DISPLAY "PROCESSING FINISHED".
    STOP RUN.

MAIN-LOOP.

* IF THERE ARE NO MORE TRANSACTIONS FOR THE
* CURRENT NEW-MASTER-RECORD, FINISH PROCESSING IT
* AND WRITE IT OUT.

    IF PART-NO IN NEW-MASTER-RECORD IS LESS THAN PART-NO
        IN TRANSACTION-RECORD AND NOT EQUAL TO LOW-VALUES
        PERFORM FINAL-PROCESSING
        PERFORM WRITE-MASTER
        MOVE LOW-VALUES TO PART-NO IN NEW-MASTER-RECORD.

* IF THE NEXT PROCESSING IS TO APPLY TO THE RECORD
* IN OLD-MASTER-RECORD, MOVE IT TO NEW-MASTER-RECORD.

    IF PART-NO IN OLD-MASTER-RECORD IS NOT GREATER THAN
        PART-NO IN TRANSACTION-RECORD
        MOVE OLD-MASTER-RECORD TO NEW-MASTER-RECORD
        PERFORM READ-MASTER
        PERFORM INITIAL-PROCESSING

* OTHERWISE WE ARE READY TO PROCESS THE NEXT
* TRANSACTION.
```

```
      ELSE PERFORM EDIT-CHECK
          PERFORM PROCESS-TRANSACTION
          PERFORM READ-TRANSACTION.
```

   The other needed paragraphs, INITIAL-PROCESSING, FINAL-PROCESSING, and PROCESS-TRANSACTION follow. READ-MASTER, READ-TRANSACTION, and WRITE-MASTER are given in the next chapter.

```
INITIAL-PROCESSING.
    IF PART-NO IN NEW-MASTER-RECORD
       IS NOT EQUAL TO HIGH-VALUES
       MOVE QUANTITY IN NEW-MASTER-RECORD
           TO OLD-QUANTITY.
    MOVE ZERO TO RECEIVE-COUNT DISBURSE-COUNT.

FINAL-PROCESSING.
    DISPLAY PART-NO IN NEW-MASTER-RECORD " "
            DESCRIPTION IN NEW-MASTER-RECORD
            OLD-QUANTITY " "
            RECEIVE-COUNT " "
            DISBURSE-COUNT " "
            QUANTITY IN NEW-MASTER-RECORD.

PROCESS-TRANSACTION.
    IF NOT OK DISPLAY "TRANSACTION NOT PROCESSED"
    ELSE IF INSERT-RECORD PERFORM INSERTION
    ELSE IF RECEIVE-GOODS PERFORM RECEPTION
    ELSE IF DISBURSE-GOODS PERFORM DISBURSAL
    ELSE PERFORM DELETION.

INSERTION.
    MOVE PART-NO IN TRANSACTION-RECORD TO PART-NO IN
        NEW-MASTER-RECORD.
    MOVE ZEROS TO QUANTITY IN NEW-MASTER-RECORD.
    MOVE DESCRIPTION IN TRANSACTION-RECORD TO
        DESCRIPTION IN NEW-MASTER-RECORD.
    PERFORM INITIAL-PROCESSING.
    PERFORM RECEPTION.

RECEPTION.
    ADD QUANTITY IN TRANSACTION-RECORD TO
        QUANTITY IN NEW-MASTER-RECORD.
    ADD QUANTITY IN TRANSACTION-RECORD TO RECEIVE-COUNT.
```

```
DISBURSAL.
    SUBTRACT QUANTITY IN TRANSACTION-RECORD FROM
        QUANTITY IN NEW-MASTER-RECORD.
    ADD QUANTITY IN TRANSACTION-RECORD TO DISBURSE-COUNT.

DELETION.
    DISPLAY PART-NO IN TRANSACTION-RECORD " DELETED".
    PERFORM FINAL-PROCESSING.
    MOVE LOW-VALUES TO PART-NO IN NEW-MASTER-RECORD.
* WITH LOW-VALUES IN THE PART-NO, IT WILL NOT BE WRITTEN
* ONTO THE NEW MASTER FILE.
```

The other commonly used batch-update algorithm uses nested loops. The outside loop is done once for each master record and the inner loop is repeated once for each transaction that applies to that master record. Thus, the inner loop may be executed no time, one time, or more than one time for a given master record. Again, the insertion of new records introduces some minor complications because the outer loop must be executed once for each insertion as well as for each previously existing old-master-record. Using, to as great an extent as possible, the previous terminology, here is the algorithm:

```
set key in new-master-record to low-values;
read-transaction;
read-master;
while key in new-master-record is less than high-values do begin

    if key in transaction-record is not less than
        key in old-master-record then begin
        move old-master-record to new-master-record;
        if key in new-master-record is less than high-values
            then read master;
        end
    else do-insertion;

    do-initial-processing;
    while key in transaction-record is equal to key in
        new-master-record do begin
        do-edit-check;
        if OK then process-transaction;
        read-transaction
        end; (of transaction while loop)

    do-final-processing;
    write-master
end (of master-record while loop)
```

In the main loop, the decision whether to process an old master record or to insert a new one must be made and the appropriate record must be put in the new-master-record. After executing do-initial-processing, all transactions that apply to that master record are done by the inner loop.

Then executing do-final-processing and writing out the master record completes processing of that master record and the outer loop is repeated for the next master record. Note that the procedure insertion, which is not shown, must check whether the current transaction is a valid insertion-type transaction. The do-edit-check performed in the inner loop, on the other hand, should never find an insertion—if it does, that is an error.

7.6. ON-LINE UPDATE PROCESSING

On-line updating is significantly simpler than batch updating, because we can limit our attention to a single transaction and a single master record. However, it requires the use of a random-access file system. The following algorithm will serve:

```
repeat indefinitely:
    write a cue message;
    read a transaction from the terminal;
    do the first edit check;
    if there is no error then
        read the master record and
        do the second edit check;
    if still no error then
        process the transaction.
```

First we print a cue message requesting a transaction from the operator. The computer then waits until a command or transaction has been entered into a terminal and then reads it. The first edit check makes the checks that do not require reading the master record. If there is no error, then an attempt should be made to read the matching master record, whether or not you expect it to be there. The read-master procedure must tell whether it is successful or not, for example, by setting a logical variable **true** or **false**. Then the second edit check makes the checks that need knowledge about the master record. In particular, if the transaction is an insertion and reading the master file is successful, then there is a duplicate-record type error. Finally, if still there is no error, the transaction can be processed and a response made to the terminal, if required.

In implementing any on-line system, one should take great care to make the interface with the user very convenient, easy to use, and well matched to the users' level of skill and familiarity with the system. This dictates some variation in the preceding algorithm. For example, one should cue, input, and check each of several data items individually, rather than to input all the transaction data at once. In the case of an error, one may want to provide for reentering only the erroneous data item and then continuing. In some systems that are implemented in this way, the program requests that the user reenter the erroneous data, but presents no obvious way for the user to decline to do that and abort the transaction—it would be preferable to require reentering the entire transaction. The best plan is to present to the user a menu on which one of the alternatives is to reenter the erroneous data and another is to abort the transaction.

Example 7.6

Assume that the format of the master record is the same as before. One new command or transaction type should be added—it should be possible to inquire about the quantity in stock for any ID. Assume that the code for this command is "Q." Also include a command "S" to stop the system and a command "H" for help. For simplicity, when an error occurs, we abort the transaction.

This program is written using a separately compiled module for all I-O operations. The module has an entry point for each file operation. The details of how these operations are done are discussed in Chapter 8. FORTRAN and PL/I examples are given in the appendices. In COBOL, the program might look as follows:

```
PROCEDURE DIVISION.

*THERE ARE SIX ENTRIES TO THE FILE-HANDLING SUBPROGRAM:
*    OPENM     OPEN THE MASTER FILE
*    CLOSEM    CLOSE THE MASTER FILE
*    READM     IF THE RECORD WITH THE KEY IN THE MASTER
*              RECORD IS FOUND, SET THE RECORD FLAG TRUE
*              AND READ THE MASTER FILE INTO MASTER-RECORD
*    WRITEM    WRITE A NEW RECORD FROM MASTER-RECORD
*    REWRM     REWRITE FROM THE MASTER-RECORD
*    DELM      DELETE THE RECORD LAST READ.

  MAIN-PROGRAM.
      DISPLAY "INVENTORY SYSTEM--COMMAND H FOR HELP".
      CALL OPENM.
      PERFORM MAIN-LOOP UNTIL STOP-RUN.
      CALL CLOSEM.
      DISPLAY "INVENTORY SYSTEM--END OF RUN".
      STOP RUN.

  MAIN-LOOP.
*     THIS LOOP IS PERFORMED ONCE FOR EACH
*     TRANSACTION READ FROM THE TERMINAL.
      MOVE FALSE TO ERROR-FLAG.
      PERFORM GET-COMMAND.
```

```
    IF NEED-TO-READ PERFORM GET-PART-NO,
    IF OK AND NEED-TO-READ CALL READM
        USING MASTER-RECORD RECORD-FLAG
        PERFORM CHECKING,

    IF OK AND NEED-QUANTITY PERFORM GET-QUANTITY,
    IF OK AND INSERT-RECORD PERFORM GET-DESCRIPTION,

    IF NOT OK DISPLAY "NOT DONE BECAUSE OF ERROR"
    ELSE IF INSERT-RECORD PERFORM INSERTION
    ELSE IF RECEIVE-GOODS PERFORM RECEPTION
    ELSE IF DISBURSE-GOODS PERFORM DISBURSAL
    ELSE IF DELETE-RECORD PERFORM DELETION
    ELSE IF HELP PERFORM HELP-LISTING,

    IF OK AND DELETE-RECORD DISPLAY "RECORD DELETED"
    ELSE IF OK AND NEED-TO-READ
        DISPLAY PART-NO IN MASTER-RECORD " "
                DESCRIPTION IN MASTER-RECORD
                " QUANTITY ON HAND "
                QUANTITY IN MASTER-RECORD,

GET-COMMAND,
    DISPLAY "ENTER COMMAND",
    ACCEPT COMMAND,
    IF NOT VALID-COMMAND MOVE TRUE TO ERROR-FLAG
        DISPLAY "INVALID COMMAND",

GET-PART-NO,
    DISPLAY "ENTER PART-NO (6 DIGITS)",
    ACCEPT INPUT-PART-NO,
    IF INPUT-PART-NO IS NOT NUMERIC
        MOVE TRUE TO ERROR-FLAG
        DISPLAY "PART-NO NOT ALL DIGITS"
    ELSE IF INPUT-PART-NO IS EQUAL TO 000000
        MOVE TRUE TO ERROR-FLAG
        DISPLAY "NOT ALLOWED AS PART-NO"
    ELSE MOVE INPUT-PART-NO TO PART-NO IN MASTER-RECORD,
*    TO SEND TO THE SUB-PROGRAM TO USE AS KEY IN READING,

CHECKING,
    IF INSERT-RECORD AND RECORD-FOUND
        MOVE TRUE TO ERROR-FLAG
        DISPLAY "DUPLICATE PART-NO FOUND"
    ELSE IF NOT INSERT-RECORD AND NOT RECORD-FOUND
        MOVE TRUE TO ERROR-FLAG
        DISPLAY "RECORD NOT FOUND",
```

```
GET-DESCRIPTION.
    DISPLAY "ENTER DESCRIPTION--MAX 15 CHAR".
    ACCEPT INPUT-DESCRIPTION.
    IF INPUT-DESCRIPTION IS EQUAL TO SPACES
        MOVE TRUE TO ERROR-FLAG
        DISPLAY "NOT ENTERED".

GET-QUANTITY.
    DISPLAY "ENTER QUANTITY (4 DIGITS)".
    ACCEPT INPUT-QUANTITY.
    IF INPUT-QUANTITY IS NOT NUMERIC
        MOVE TRUE TO ERROR-FLAG
        DISPLAY "NOT NUMERIC"
    ELSE IF DISBURSE-GOODS AND INPUT-QUANTITY
        IS GREATER THAN QUANTITY IN MASTER-RECORD
        MOVE TRUE TO ERROR-FLAG
        DISPLAY "NOT ENOUGH IN STOCK".

INSERTION.
*   NOTE THAT WE HAVE PREVIOUSLY SEARCHED FOR A
*   RECORD WITH THIS PART-NO IN THE MASTER FILE, AND
*   HAVE FOUND NO RECORD WITH THIS PART-NO IN THE FILE.
    MOVE INPUT-QUANTITY TO QUANTITY IN MASTER-RECORD.
    MOVE INPUT-DESCRIPTION TO DESCRIPTION IN MASTER-RECORD.
    CALL WRITEM USING MASTER-RECORD.

RECEPTION.
    ADD INPUT-QUANTITY TO QUANTITY IN MASTER-RECORD.
    CALL REWRM USING MASTER-RECORD.

DISBURSAL.
    SUBTRACT INPUT-QUANTITY FROM
        QUANTITY IN MASTER-RECORD.
    CALL REWRM USING MASTER-RECORD.

HELP-LISTING.
    DISPLAY "COMMANDS:".
    DISPLAY "A   INSERT RECORD".
    DISPLAY "B   RECEIVE GOODS".
    DISPLAY "C   DISBURSE GOODS".
    DISPLAY "D   DELETE RECORD".
    DISPLAY "Q   INQUIRY".
    DISPLAY "H   HELP-LIST COMMANDS".
    DISPLAY "S   STOP RUN".

DELETION.
    CALL DELM.
```

The remaining four paragraphs, READ-MASTER, WRITE-MASTER, REWRITE-MASTER, and DELETE-MASTER, are presented in Chapter 8. Note that for random-access files, one must make a distinction between writing a new record and rewriting an old one. Also, deleting a record requires more than simply not writing it. These matters are discussed in detail in the next chapter.

Typically, there are small differences in the implementation of I-O operations with terminals that make it necessary to adapt to each compiler and operating system—the standards do not define interaction with terminals clearly enough to make machine-independent programming possible for terminal I-O.

7.7. REPORT WRITING

By and large, report writing is quite simple and straightforward. Frequently, utility sort programs are used to sort records into the sequence required in the report before the report-writing program is used.

There is one requirement in reports that occurs often enough to deserve discussion and a carefully thought out algorithm. That is the grouping of data with headings and footings on each group.

A report often has a heading and a footing, and a body consisting of some data from each of the records of a file. The part of the report associated with a single record is usually called a *detail*. The following algorithm will write such a report:

```
open the file;
read the first record;
do the heading;
repeat the following
     do the detail for one record;
     read the next record
until end of file;
do the footing.
```

Example 7.7

For our on-line inventory system, the periodic reports must be produced by a separate program, in contrast to the batch system where the report was most conveniently produced at the time of the batch run. This might be done as follows in COBOL:

```
PROCEDURE DIVISION.
MAIN-PROGRAM.
    DISPLAY "INVENTORY REPORT".
```

```
DISPLAY "ID        DESCRIPTION      OLD   REC   DIS   NEW".
OPEN I-O MASTER-FILE.
MOVE FALSE TO END-FLAG.
READ MASTER-FILE
AT END MOVE TRUE TO END-FLAG.
PERFORM MAIN-LOOP
UNTIL END-FLAG IS EQUAL TO TRUE.
CLOSE MASTER-FILE.
DISPLAY "INVENTORY SYSTEM--END OF RUN".
STOP RUN.


MAIN-LOOP.
    DISPLAY ID " "
            DESCRIPTION
            OLD-QUANTITY " "
            RECEIVE-COUNT " "
            DISBURSE-COUNT " "
            QUANTITY.
    READ MASTER-FILE
    AT END MOVE TRUE TO END-FLAG.
```

In the above case, the report consists of a heading, a body, and a footing, and the body consists of a number of details. Frequently, the body of a report consists of a number of groups, each containing a heading, a body, and a footing. Furthermore, that body may consist of details or of still another set of groups with a heading, a body, and a footing, and so on. The following are a set of records and a report of this type that might be produced from them:

Data:

```
HAWAII      HONOLULU       DOWNTOWN        10
HAWAII      HONOLULU       MOILIILI        12
HAWAII      HONOLULU       HAWAII KAI       8
HAWAII      HONOLULU       KALIHI          10
HAWAII      LAHAINA        DOWNTOWN         6
HAWAII      KONA           DOWNTOWN         5
HAWAII      KONA           AIRPORT          6
CALIFORNIA  LOS ANGELES    DOWNTOWN        15
CALIFORNIA  LOS ANGELES    HOLLYWOOD       21
CALIFORNIA  SAN FRANCISCO  DOWNTOWN        18
CALIFORNIA  SAN FRANCISCO  AIRPORT         15
```

Report:

```
NUMBER OF EMPLOYEES AT EACH BRANCH
HAWAII
        HONOLULU
                DOWNTOWN        10
                MOILIILI        12
                HAWAII KAI       8
                KALIHI          10
                TOTAL FOR HONOLULU IS           40

        LAHAINA
                DOWNTOWN         6
                TOTAL FOR LAHAINA IS            6

        KONA
                DOWNTOWN         5
                AIRPORT          6
                TOTAL FOR KONA IS             11

        TOTAL FOR HAWAII IS              57
CALIFORNIA
        LOS ANGELES
                DOWNTOWN        15
                HOLLYWOOD       21
                TOTAL FOR LOS ANGELES IS     36

        SAN FRANCISCO
                DOWNTOWN        18
                AIRPORT         15
                TOTAL FOR SAN FRANCISCO IS   33

        TOTAL FOR CALIFORNIA IS          69
GRAND TOTAL                             126
```

The following algorithm implements this type of report. We consider the whole report to be the highest level and number it level-0. The next lower level is level-1, and so on. For each level, level-i, there is a key key-i in the master record and a variable level-i-key that saves the key for that level for the current group at that level. Each time a new master record is read, a variable change-level is set to the number of the highest level that has changed. Each group whose level number is higher than this has to end. (When a group ends, then every group that it contains also must end.) For simplicity, the following algorithm is written for three levels, like the preceding example, but the generalization should be clear.

```
read-master;
print-level-0-heading;

repeat; {start of level-1 loop}
   print-level-1-heading;
   move key-1 to level-1-key;

   repeat; {start of level-2 loop}
      print-level-2-heading;
      move key-2 to level-2-key;

      repeat {start of detail loop}
         print-detail;
         read-master;
         if key-1≠high-values then {end of file}
            set change-level to 0
         else if key-1≠level-1-key then
            set change-level to 1
         else if key-2≠level-2-key then
            set change-level to 2
         else set change-level to 3
      until change-level<3; {end of detail loop}

      print-level-2-footing
   until change-level<2; {end of level-2 loop}

   print-level-1-footing
until change-level<1; {end of level-1 loop}

print-level-0-footing.
```

Example 7.8

For the preceding example, LEVEL-0 is the whole report. LEVEL-1 is the grouping by states, LEVEL-2 is the grouping by cities, and LEVEL-3 is the detail for one record. In COBOL, the programs could be written as follows:

```
PROGRAM-ID, "REPORT",
AUTHOR, W W PETERSON,
DATE-WRITTEN, 4 FEB,1982,

ENVIRONMENT DIVISION,
CONFIGURATION SECTION,
SOURCE-COMPUTER, HARRIS-135,
OBJECT-COMPUTER, HARRIS-135,
```

```
INPUT-OUTPUT SECTION.
FILE-CONTROL.
     SELECT MASTER-FILE ASSIGN TO "REPDATA".
DATA DIVISION.
FILE SECTION.
FD   MASTER-FILE
     DATA RECORD IS REPORT-DATA.
01   REPORT-DATA.
     02   STATE PICTURE X(11).
     02   CITY PICTURE X(14).
     02   BRANCH PICTURE X(15).
     02   DATA-COUNT PICTURE 99.

WORKING-STORAGE SECTION.
77   GRAND-TOTAL PICTURE 9(3).
77   STATE-TOTAL PICTURE 9(2).
77   CITY-TOTAL PICTURE 9(2).
77   LEVEL PICTURE 9.
77   LEVEL-1-KEY PICTURE X(11).
77   LEVEL-2-KEY PICTURE X(14).

PROCEDURE DIVISION.
INITIALIZATION.
     OPEN INPUT MASTER-FILE.
     PERFORM READ-MASTER.
     MOVE ZERO TO GRAND-TOTAL.

LEVEL-0.
     DISPLAY "NUMBER OF EMPLOYEES AT EACH BRANCH".
     MOVE 1 TO LEVEL.
     PERFORM LEVEL-1 UNTIL LEVEL IS LESS THAN 1.
     DISPLAY "GRAND TOTAL
               GRAND-TOTAL
     STOP RUN.

LEVEL-1.
     DISPLAY STATE.
     MOVE STATE TO LEVEL-1-KEY.
     MOVE ZERO TO STATE-TOTAL.
     MOVE 2 TO LEVEL
     PERFORM LEVEL-2
         UNTIL LEVEL IS LESS THAN 2.
     DISPLAY "     TOTAL FOR " LEVEL-1-KEY
         "IS           " STATE-TOTAL.
     DISPLAY " ".
     ADD STATE-TOTAL TO GRAND-TOTAL.
```

```
LEVEL-2.
    DISPLAY "       " CITY.
    MOVE CITY TO LEVEL-2-KEY.
    MOVE ZERO TO CITY-TOTAL
    MOVE 3 TO LEVEL.
    PERFORM LEVEL-3
        UNTIL LEVEL IS LESS THAN 3.
    DISPLAY "            TOTAL FOR " LEVEL-2-KEY
        "IS    " CITY-TOTAL.
    DISPLAY " ".
    ADD CITY-TOTAL TO STATE-TOTAL.
LEVEL-3.
    DISPLAY "            " BRANCH " " DATA-COUNT.
    ADD DATA-COUNT TO CITY-TOTAL.
    PERFORM READ-MASTER.
    IF STATE IS EQUAL TO "ZZZZZZ" MOVE 0 TO LEVEL
    ELSE IF STATE IS NOT EQUAL TO LEVEL-1-KEY
        MOVE 1 TO LEVEL
    ELSE IF CITY IS NOT EQUAL TO LEVEL-2-KEY
        MOVE 2 TO LEVEL
    ELSE MOVE 3 TO LEVEL.
READ-MASTER.
    READ MASTER-FILE AT END MOVE "ZZZZZZ" TO STATE.
```

It should be noted that by the time a footing is printed, the record in memory is the first record for the next group. All information in a record that may be needed in footings must be saved in other memory locations.

Example 7.8 (continued)

In the preceding example, the footing for a state was printed by the statement

```
DISPLAY "TOTAL FOR" LEVEL-1-KEY "IS" STATE-TOTAL.
```

If the word LEVEL-1-KEY were replaced by STATE, then the data would be taken from the last record read, and this record belongs to the next group, so that the wrong state name would be printed in the footing. LEVEL-1-KEY still contains the state name for the just-finished group, however, and that is what we want in the footing.

The fact that these algorithms will handle a very broad class of data-processing applications makes it possible to automate their implementation to a large extent. The COBOL Report-Writer feature implements this type of report writing in a reasonably convenient way. RPG (Report Program Generator) implements both the file update and the report-writing algorithms in a convenient way, but RPG's style is archaic. A system based on the same concept, but implemented in a modern-style language would be very attractive for most file-processing applications.

NOTES

Analyses of sorting techniques also appear in the literature on the "analysis of algorithms." See [H9] and [H10]. An example illustrating the importance of the design of a sort algorithm appears in [H13]. Books devoted entirely to sorting and searching include [H1–H3]. See [H4] or [H14] for a survey and [H8] for a bibliography. [H14] describes early sort/merge packages; [J9] discusses the use of a contemporary one. COBOL includes a SORT statement as part of the language; for a description, see [I9].

Edit checking for the validation of data is described in [A8]. The file-updating problem was treated rather haphazardly until Dijkstra discussed it in [K8]. Subsequent discussions appear in [K9] and [K10]. The first algorithm presented here is essentially the one used in RPG, and therefore dates back at least to the 1960s. COBOL's report writing features are described in [I9]; for details on RPG, see [I14].

EXERCISES

7-1. Make a deck of about 50 numbered cards or use a deck of playing cards. Shuffle them so that they are in random order.
(a) Count the natural runs. (Theory predicts that the average run length will be 2 and that there will be about one-half as many runs as cards.)
(b) By hand, do a replacement-selection pass using working storage for three cards.

Count the resulting number of runs. (Theory predicts that with a large file the average length of runs will be six, so the number of runs will be one-sixth of the number of cards. With a short file, there may be a few short runs at the end.)

7-2. Assume a file of 6000 records of 1000 bytes each stored on standard 6250 cpi magnetic tape, five records per block. Assume you have four tape units available, with 200 ips tape speed and start time equal to 1.5 msec. Assume sorting is done using a replacement-selection pass with a 64,000 byte work area (plus buffers), followed by two-way balanced merge passes. Assume that the I-O is buffered and the processing time is less than the I-O time. Estimate the time required to sort the file,
(a) assuming that there is one I-O processor shared between input and output, so that input and output cannot be done simultaneously, and
(b) assuming two I-O processors.

7-3. Let us assume that we wish to sort a sequential file of 6000 1000-byte records stored on a Miniscribe 4020 disk drive formatted with nine 1024-byte sectors per track. On the first we will use replacement selection with a 64,000 byte work area (plus the required buffers) and two-way merges on the succeeding passes. Also, to keep seek time down, assume that every time we read or write, we read or write a full track (a block of nine records). Also, assume that the I-O is buffered and that all processing time is overlapped with reading and writing, so that we only have to calculate the time to read and write. Assume that we do all I-O on the same disk drive with a single I-O processor.

At the start of each pass, the 6000 records will be in one file of 6000 records (on the first pass) or in two adjacent files of approximately 3000 records (on all other passes). The output will go into two approximately equal adjacent files (on the first and intermediate passes) or into one file (on the last pass). The input files will be adjacent to the output files. It is not easy to predict how often there will be two reads or two writes in a row and how often a read will be followed by a write and vice versa. Take the pessimistic view that a read is always followed by a write and vice versa.

The 4020 rotates at 3600 rpm. Assume that its seek time is given by $t = 3 + n$ msec to seek a distance of n cylinders. There are four tracks per cylinder.

(a) Show that with the preceding assumptions, the average seek will be across half the portion of the disk that is used.

(b) Estimate the time required to sort this file.

7-4. Let us assume that we have a system with tape drives and a file to be sorted. Assume that the tape rewind speed is the same as the forward speed. As a result of a replacement-selection pass, the file consists of eight runs. Assume that each run has n_b blocks and the time required to read or write a block is t_b.

(a) How long will it take to finish the sort using a balanced two-way merge?

(b) How long will it take to complete the sort using the polyphase three-tape merge strategy described in Section 7.2?

(c) For a four-tape polyphase sort, the eight runs of the above file should be distributed onto three tapes as follows: the first two runs should go on tape A, the next three runs should go on tape B, and the last three runs should go on tape C. Apply the polyphase sort procedure until completion, showing the result of each pass. Then calculate the time required to complete the sort using this strategy.

7-5. Suppose you wish to sort a telephone directory file so that the entries are ordered by last name, then among those with the same last name, by first name. One way to proceed is to first sort the file using only the first name as the key and then to sort the file again using only the last name as the key. For this to work, for two records with equal keys, the one that comes first in the input file must come first in the output file. An algorithm that preserves the order of records with equal keys is said to have the *stability* property.

(a) Does replacement selection have this property?

(b) Does insertion sorting have this property?

(c) Does the simple balanced two-way merge have this property?

(d) Suppose you have a sorting algorithm that does not have this property. Devise a way to modify it so that it does.

7-6. Suppose we have a dormitory with four floors, thirteen rooms on each floor, numbered 101 to 113, 201 to 213, 301 to 313, and 401 to 413, and one resident in each room. Assume we have a file containing the names and room numbers, arranged alphabetically by name. Is it possible to sort this file with fewer record moves than $n \times \log_2 n$? Describe the best algorithm you can find, and count the number of record moves it requires.

7-7. Suppose you had a sorted telephone directory file (File A) in name-key order and another unsorted file (File B) that consists of names. Assume File B has about 10% as many entries as File A. The problem is to print out all the entries in File A whose names are in File B. How would you proceed?

7-8. Suppose you have two mailing lists that are alphabetically arranged. Devise an efficient algorithm to produce each of the following: (In each case, the resulting list should be in sequence alphabetically.)

(a) A list that includes all the names on both lists with duplicates eliminated. (The set union of the lists.)

(b) A list of all names that are on both lists. (The set intersection of the two lists.)

(c) A list of all the names on list A that are not on list B. (The set difference of the two lists.)

7-9. Consider the following data records, which have probabilities of access as shown.

CCCCC33333	5%
CDCDC34343	25%
DDDDD44444	25%
FFFFF66666	45%

Suppose you wanted to minimize expected access time.

(a) How would you store the records in a sequential file?

(b) How would you store the records in a sorted binary tree?

Note that there are some suggested programming projects at the end of Chapter 8 that relate to the contents of both Chapter 7 and Chapter 8.

File Programming

8.1. INTRODUCTION

We discuss here ways that files are handled using general-purpose programming languages, such as FORTRAN, COBOL, and PL/I. In these languages, I-O instructions direct the transfer of information between the internal main memory of the computer and external I-O units. Other instructions specify control operations, such as rewinding a tape unit.

BASIC, Pascal, Ada, and C are other important, widely used computer languages. There is a standard defined for "Standard Minimal BASIC" that does not include file operations. Most BASIC systems include sequential and/or relative file operations, but they differ from one implementation to the next. They usually are quite easy to use. Pascal, Ada, Modula 2, and C all treat files in essentially the same way. These languages contain no special statements for I-O, but rather expect it to be done by procedures, some of which may have to be written in assembly language. For sequential I-O, which is rather straightforward, procedures of more or less standard format are in common use, but there is no standard for random-access I-O. There seems to be little that can be said about random-access I-O for these languages that will apply generally, not simply to specific implementations. However, the more interesting and significant questions relate to random-access files.

From the viewpoint of the programmer, I-O units may be classified according to whether their use is communication with the computer or storage of information. Communication units include card readers, line printers, printing and video display terminals, graphics terminals, and a wide variety of sensing and measuring devices and apparatus that may be turned on or off or controlled in other ways. Storage units include magnetic tapes, disks, and drums. The two classes of units differ in that the latter class allows both writing and reading of information. The former class may not allow both writing or reading, or if both are allowed, then information written cannot be read back.

We are primarily concerned with storage units. Insofar as the programming of I-O operations is concerned, both classes of I-O units are treated similarly. To transfer information from the unit to main memory, a READ (or INPUT, GET, or ACCEPT) instruction must be executed. To transfer information from main memory to the unit, a WRITE (or OUTPUT, PRINT, PUT, or DISPLAY) instruction must be executed. For both purposes, a number of parameters must be specified, either explicitly or implicitly:

1. The identification and type of I-O unit, and, for addressable storage units, the physical location in the unit from/to which information is transferred.

2. A list of main memory locations (names or addresses) to/from which information is transferred.

3. The amount of information to be transferred.

4. How information is organized (structured, formatted) in both main memory and the I-O unit, and, hence, any conversion that may be required.

This information may be furnished in various ways, depending on the operating system and the language used.

8.2. FILE CREATION AND DELETION

Creation of a file means making an entry in the directory, which is usually stored on the same I-O unit as the file. This entry must include the file name and the information required to find the file data. Other data such as maximum size, file organization or type, block size, and record size may be included. Usually creation of the file changes only the directory—data are entered by write statements that are executed later. Space may or may not be allocated to the file at the time it is created. For example, IBM OS/VS allocates the requested amount of space at the time of creation and provides for later allocation of additional extents of space as needed. Digital Research's CP/M, on the other hand, allocates space only as needed during writing.

Files can be created by the use of a command from a terminal or, for batch use, a job control language statement. Alternatively, they may be created during program execution by the use of a subroutine call to an operating system routine. Most modern operating systems provide both methods. Terminal-operated systems usually provide a text editor for entering or altering files from a terminal. Most edit programs are capable of creating files for that purpose.

Deletion of a file involves deallocation of the physical space, which makes it available for other files, and deletion of the name and any other data from the directory or other system tables.

It is very convenient to have a program create any new files it needs as it executes. Although this is possible in any operating system that provides system subroutine calls for allocations, some operating systems still require that all new files needed by a program be created before the program starts to execute.

8.3. FILE DECLARATIONS AND OPEN STATEMENTS

The names (or ID numbers) by which the files are referenced within the program need not correspond to the names under which they were created and entered in the system directories or *catalogs*. Naming conventions for file names in the directory are operating-system-dependent, hence, they are less standardized than the names used in programs, which are programming-language-dependent. We will refer to the name(s) used in the program as the *logical* file name(s) and the name in the directory as the *physical* file name.

In some languages, there are two logical file names, an *internal* name that is only used within the program (usually in actual read and write statements), and an *external* name by which the logical file is referenced outside the program in job control or command statements. In other languages, or by default, these two logical names may coincide. We emphasize that, from the viewpoint of the operating system, the two logical names may or may not coincide because only the external name is visible. On the other hand, from the viewpoint of the program, only the external name is visible, so it may or may not coincide with the physical name.

Some way must be provided to associate a logical file name with a physical file name. One way is to use a statement within the program, such as the COBOL statement

```
SELECT A ASSIGN TO B
```

where A is the internal logical file name and B is the external file name. In some implementations, the external name coincides with the physical name. In other systems, the association of external names with physical names is made by a command or job control language statement. For example, on the Harris Vulcan Operating System, the command is

```
ASSIGN n = X
```

where n is the external file name (which here also coincides with the file identification number used in the program, i.e., with the internal file name) and X is the physical file name. In the IBM COBOL system, the ASSIGN statement assigns an internal logical name to an external name (called the DDNAME) and the allocate command or "data definition" job control statement assigns this external name to a physical file name (called the DSNAME). Similarly, there is a TITLE parameter in PL/I that may appear in the OPEN statement for an internal logical file and specify an external name that, in some implementations, coincides with the physical file name.

One advantage of having internal logical names is portability. Internal names need not conform to operating system conventions or the conventions of a particular installation for naming files. Also, using a command or job control statement to associate a logical file name with a physical file name permits running a program more than once with different files on each run without making any changes to the program. On some systems, the association of a logical file name with a physical file name may be done by subroutine call, which permits the physical file name to be presented by the user as input data (and entered from a terminal, for example) as an alternative way of permitting the same program to process different files.

In some languages, the logical file name must be explicitly declared. In others, declaration is optional; there may be an implicit declaration when the file is opened (as explained below). Read and write statements which do not name a file usually refer, by default, to system input and output files.

Before a file can be used by a program, a few preparatory actions must be taken, such as:

1. Verification that the file has been created and is available (i. e., operational, not protected, mounted, and so on).

2. Location of the physical beginning of the file, and the setting of a "pointer" thereto; this may require repositioning or rewinding operations.

3. Initialization of run-time tables containing various file parameters either (a) supplied when the file was created, (b) found in the file itself (for example, in *labels*), (c) specified in control statements for the current job, or (d) specified within the program itself in a declaration or an executable statement.

The process of completing the preceding actions (and perhaps other system-dependent actions) is called *opening* the file. In some systems, a file is automatically opened at the time of its first access (read or write) in a program. In other systems, a file must be explicitly opened using an executable OPEN statement prior to its first access (read or write). Some preparatory actions may be performed instead prior to program execution, for example, by the system loader.

Generally, when a program has completed the last use (or use for the specified function) of a file, the file should be closed. In some languages there is a CLOSE statement. In others, files are closed automatically when programs terminate normally or even abnormally. This will force completion of any pending operations on the file, such as writing out a partially filled buffer, and permit use of the file by others or reuse of the file for a different function within the same program. Reuse within the same program requires that the file be reopened with the specification of new parameters. Thus, for example, it is possible to restrict use of a file to sequential "write-only" and random-access "read-only" at different points within the same program. The CLOSE statement also may *lock* the file, which prevents its reuse. For sequential access, closing a file and then reopening it also serves the purpose of moving the file pointer back to the beginning of the file so that it can be reread or rewritten from the beginning.

The various parameters needed for use of a file include (1) record size, (2) file structure, (3) association of the internal logical file name with the external or physical file name, (4) whether the file is to be used for input, output, or both (update), and (5) whether the file is to be accessed sequentially or randomly. These parameters may be furnished with the declaration for the file or with the open statement. Parameters also may be saved with the file or in the directory, or specified in commands or job control statements, or fixed in a given system. There is no uniform practice. Generally, the file function—input, output, or update—and the type of access—sequential or direct—are included in the open statement. This permits opening a file for output, for example, and writing some data into it, and then closing it and opening it for input and reading the data just written. In some systems a direct-access file must be written full of records sequentially before direct access can take place. In that case, one opens the file for sequential access, writes the records, closes it, and reopens it for direct access.

8.4. STREAM FILE PROCESSING

A stream file consists simply of a stream of data-items. From the programmer's viewpoint, a file pointer is maintained by the system that always points to the "next" location in the file from or to which a data value is to be transferred. This pointer is moved automatically by the system each time a data value is transferred; at the time the file is opened, the pointer is initially set to point to the first physical storage location. At the completion of a read statement, the file pointer points to the next data value that will be read. At the completion of a write statement, the file pointer points one physical storage location past the last data value written. When the file is closed, a logical end-of-file mark is written at this location. There are no logical record delimiters within the files. The main difference between stream files and record files is that in the latter the file pointer always points to the beginning of a record. In stream files the pointer may point to any data-item and the concept of "record" has no meaning. Few languages permit stream processing facilities in precisely this sense; the *list-directed* I-O facilities offered by some languages approximate stream processing.

For stream file processing, within program read or write statements, it is generally sufficient to specify only the logical name of the file and a list of data-items (variables for input or expressions for output) whose values are to be read or written. From this data-list and the declared or implicit attributes of the variables named in the list, data conversion information for variables to be transmitted can be deduced. In particular, the number of physical memory locations associated with each data-item depends upon its attributes; there is therefore a clear danger on stream input of mismatching when all data-items (variables and values) do not have the same attributes. It is usually the programmer's responsibility to guard against this danger.

In addition to a logical end, all stream files have a physical end, which may be associated with the size specified at the time the file was created or the physical limitations of a particular I-O unit (e.g., the length of a reel of magnetic tape). Attempts to read or write data past the physical end of a stream file result in an error condition. Of course, each file also has a physical beginning, that is, its first physical storage location. It is possible to reset the file pointer to this physical beginning by the use of a "rewind" instruction or by closing and reopening the file.

Stream files are used ordinarily for input or output alone. Hence, special facilities for inserting, deleting, or altering data-items generally are not provided. Changes can be made by making a new updated "master" copy of the file.

8.5. SEQUENTIAL PROCESSING OF RECORDS

Sequential files differ from stream files in that they are composed of logical records. The size and contents of a logical record are chosen by the programmer for convenience during processing. Typically, a record consists of a set of data-items that will be processed together, such as all data for one employee in a payroll program. Ordinarily, a read or write statement reads or writes the next sequential record. (There are exceptions, for example, the formatted read and write statements in FORTRAN may read or write a number of records.) As in stream processing, the system maintains a sequential file pointer that initially points to the first record and is moved by the system each time a record is read or written to the following record position, which may or may not contain a record. The only information in the sequential read or write statement normally is the logical file name and the list of data-items to be transmitted.

There also are end-of-file marks to indicate the logical end of a file, generally written when the file is closed. In some systems, it is possible to write an end-of-file mark without closing the file using a **write-EOF** statement. When a read operation is attempted with the file-pointer at an end-of-file mark, an end-of-file condition is detected by the computer. This information may be made available to the programmer or the program may be terminated. In general, it is possible to reset the file-pointer to the first record of a sequential file. This may be done by closing the file and then reopening it. In addition, some languages also provide a **rewind** statement for that purpose. Some languages also provide a **back-space** statement to reset the file-pointer to the immediately preceding record. Finally, a sequential file may be opened for either input or output, but usually not both.

Updating and deleting records in a sequential file require that the file be opened for both input and output. In systems that do not permit a sequential file to be opened for both input and output, records cannot be inserted, deleted, or altered directly. A new updated copy of the file must be made instead. Systems that do permit updating records in a sequential file have a **sequential-rewrite** statement that alters the record just read. Note that this requires a backspacing capability, as well as the ability to write a record without erasing subsequent records, which is possible on disk units but not ordinarily with tape. The rewriting capability also enables records to be deleted if a convention is adopted that (say) the leading bit(s) of each record specifies whether the record exists or is *deleted*. Some systems provide a separate **sequential-delete** statement that deletes the record just previously read in this way. Unfortunately, records cannot be inserted into sequential files; additional records may be maintained separately until a complete updated copy of the file is made.

8.6. RANDOM PROCESSING OF RECORDS

Most systems provide for relative files, in which any record can be accessed by giving its record number, which often is called its *relative key*. Many systems also provide a built-in indexed sequential file system. Records can be accessed by giving the record key, which is usually a part of the record data. In both cases, the key must either be included in a **random-read** or **random-write** statement, or in a separate statement that sets the file pointer.

For both relative files and indexed sequential files, sequential processing of random-access files is possible. This certainly is the case for relative files, where the records can be processed (read or written) in relative-record-number order quite naturally by using the ordinary random read and write statements and supplying successive integers as keys. Many systems, however, also provide sequential read and write statements for this purpose; the latter may be preferable because they can include buffering.

Indexed files may be processed sequentially, too. Unlike the situation for relative files, however, the programmer usually cannot use the ordinary random-read statement because the keys recorded in the file generally are not known. Therefore, it is most common to provide a sequential read statement or perhaps a special **read-next** statement to read the next record in sequence whatever its key may be. To write an indexed file sequentially the ordinary random-write statement may be used, but to gain efficiency, a sequential-write statement usually is provided and may be used if the records are already sorted in the desired sequence.

8.7. ERROR CONDITIONS

When using I-O program instructions, a number of error conditions or *exceptions* can occur. For example, when a request to open a file is made, the file may be inaccessible for a variety of reasons (e.g., nonexistent or misspelled file name, lack of authorization, inconsistent specification of parameters, and so on). Or when a read request is made for a record, the record may not be defined (e.g., because the end of a sequential file was reached or a specified key was invalid). Many programming languages incorporate clauses in their I-O statements that specify some action (either an executable statement or a statement number or label to go to) that is to be conditionally performed if the I-O statement results in a given error. Other languages have *trap*-setting statements that specify some action should a given error occur in any I-O statement. Finally, some languages have facilities by which file-status flags set by I-O statements may be explicitly interrogated. Examples of specific language facilities appear in subsequent sample programs.

8.8. BLOCKING AND BUFFERING

In most systems, blocking and buffering of sequential files is performed by the operating system so that the programmer need not be concerned with the details. In fact, most high-level languages do not have special statements associated with these tasks. Instead, the programmer only needs to supply relevant information (e.g., block sizes and blocking factors, and the number of buffers desired) in job control commands or the program. In PL/I, blocking information can be specified in the ENVIRONMENT clause of the DECLARE statement; in COBOL, it may be specified in the BLOCK CONTAINS clause. Unless otherwise specified, default values are assumed (commonly, block size = record size, number of buffers = 2). Blocking and buffering for random-access files normally are not provided.

Blocking can be performed totally under the control of the programmer at some inconvenience. Each read and write would have to specify a block of data rather than a logical record. On the other hand, buffering cannot be performed under the direct control of most high-level languages, because facilities for explicitly specifying concurrent I-O and computing are not available. Generally, the I-O operation specified by a read or write statement is completed before control passes to the subsequent statements; in effect, the read and write statements include a wait operation. (PL/I implementations that include multitasking, Ada, Concurrent Pascal, and C can do concurrent processing, and buffering can be implemented using them.)

Assembly languages may provide a **check** statement, in lieu of interrupt-handling statements, to test whether an I-O operation has been completed. (The system handles the interrupts and sets the flags checked.) For languages having such a statement, a read or write statement initiates an I-O operation, and then control passes to the subsequent statement without waiting for the operation to be completed. Before using the data variables read or changing the variables to be written, the programmer must employ the check statement to ensure that the read or write operation has been completed; if not, completion must be awaited by looping on the check statement or executing a **wait** statement. The point is that useful processing can now take place between the time an I-O operation is initiated and the time it is completed; specifically, the contents of a buffer read in previously may be processed in this interval.

Although timing or synchronization facilities are not common in high-level languages, both PL/I and COBOL permit either the *move* or *locate* mode of buffering to be used. (See Section 4.7.) In PL/I and COBOL, for the move mode, the INTO or FROM clause is used in the READ or WRITE statement. In COBOL, omission of this clause specifies the locate mode. In PL/I, the READ-SET and LOCATE statements are used instead for locate-mode buffering.

8.9. I-O STATEMENTS IN COBOL

We will describe the most important features of statements required to do I-O using 1974 ANSI Standard COBOL [I3]. For further details, the reader should consult the standard and the documentation for the particular compiler that will be used. The older standard [I4] is not compatible with the 1974 standard. Familiarity with COBOL is assumed.

The standard describes two levels of I-O features. Level 1 is a subset, and level 2 includes the full standard COBOL. Except where explicitly stated to the contrary, everything described in detail here is in the basic subset, level 1.

In the ENVIRONMENT DIVISION, INPUT-OUTPUT SECTION, there is a paragraph called FILE-CONTROL. It consists of one sentence for each file used by the program. The first statement in each sentence is

```
SELECT file-name ASSIGN TO literal
```

The meaning of the *literal* is dependent on the implementation and the documentation for the system actually being used must be consulted. Commonly, the *file-name* is the internal logical file name, and the literal is the external name of the file to be used. Following this statement, there are several optional statements. One of the following may be included, with obvious meaning:

```
ORGANIZATION IS SEQUENTIAL
ORGANIZATION IS RELATIVE
ORGANIZATION IS INDEXED
```

INDEXED means indexed sequential. If none of these statements is included, sequential organization is assumed. Next, one of the following statements may be included:

```
ACCESS IS SEQUENTIAL
ACCESS IS RANDOM
ACCESS IS DYNAMIC
```

If none is included, then sequential access is assumed. RANDOM means that the record number (for relative files) or the record key (for indexed files) is specified and the appropriate record is to be accessed. DYNAMIC (which is a level-2 feature) means that both random and sequential access may be used, the type of access being determined by the form of read or write statement used. For relative files, the statement

```
RELATIVE KEY IS data-name
```

must be included, where the data-name is defined as a numerical (PIC 9) string in the WORKING-STORAGE SECTION of the DATA DIVISION and is used for storing the record number. (Note: In at least one common nonstandard implementation, data-name must be a signed COMPUTATIONAL variable.) For indexed sequential files, the statement

```
RECORD KEY IS data-name
```

must be included, and the data-name is the alphanumeric field used to store the record key. This key must be within the data record given in the file description. If the statement

```
FILE STATUS IS data-name
```

is included, where data-name is the name of a two-character alpha-numeric data-item in working storage, then after each I-O operation, status information is put into that data-item. The first digit has one of the following meanings:

0   I-O operation successfully completed.
1   End-of-file, that is, an attempt was made to read sequentially and no next record was found.
2   Invalid key, that is, a sequence error in an indexed file, a duplicate key, no record found for specified key, or a relative key outside the defined range.
3   A permanent read error.
9   Special implementation-dependent information.

The second digit has one of the following meanings, if the first digit is not 9:

0   No further information.
1   Sequence error in indexed file.
2   Duplicate key.
3   No record found.
4   Relative key outside defined range.

In the DATA DIVISION, FILE SECTION, there is a file description entry for each file. The first sentence in each entry has the word FD followed by the internal logical file name and a number of optional statements. These statements include

```
BLOCK CONTAINS integer RECORDS
```

which must be included if blocking is used. The integer specifies a blocking factor. Blocking is permitted by the standard for indexed and relative files as well as sequential files. The statement

```
RECORD CONTAINS integer CHARACTERS
```

may be included, but is always optional, because the record size can be determined from the record description. The statement

```
LABEL RECORDS ARE STANDARD, or
LABEL RECORDS ARE OMITTED
```

may be included. The label statements apply to tape files, on which it is common practice to record label records on the tape and to use them to help assure that the correct tape is being used at all times, as noted in Chapter 2. If all of the data are not written in the alphanumeric code, that is, if COMPUTATIONAL items are included, then the statement

```
MODE IS BINARY
```

must be included. Level-2 COBOL also includes a LINAGE statement that is used only for printed output files, and is used to specify how many lines per page and the placement of the headings and footings. Finally, the statement

```
DATA RECORD IS data-name
```

may be included, where data-name is the name of a COBOL data-item or structure whose description follows immediately. Alternatively, this statement may read DATA RECORDS ARE followed by a list of data-names. Whether or not the statement is included, COBOL descriptions for one or more data records must follow. If there are more than one, there is still only one data storage area for this file, but these data records provide several descriptions of the fields for that same area, any of which may be used at any time. (The same feature in other languages is called "aliasing" or "overlaying," and is provided by EQUIVALENCE and BASED-variable statements, for example.)

COBOL I-O is commonly implemented with double-buffering in the locate mode, blocked or unblocked. The data record *data-name* is a buffer if there is no blocking, or is a part of a buffer if there is blocking. Thus, a COBOL data record for a file is not a fixed area of memory; data-name is always accessed indirectly using a pointer. On input, when a read statement is given, this pointer is set to point to the position in the buffers containing the next input record to be processed. On output, when a write statement is given, this pointer is set to point to the next available open area in the buffers, making the previous output record unavailable for further processing; this output record is given to the system write procedure and new output data can then be assembled into the buffer area pointed to now. For either input or output, data records can also be moved between work areas declared in working-storage and the buffers.

8.10. PROCEDURE DIVISION STATEMENTS FOR SEQUENTIAL FILES

In COBOL, every file must be opened before it is used. For sequential files, the open statement has the form

```
OPEN INPUT file-name,
OPEN OUTPUT file-name,
OPEN I-O file-name, or
OPEN EXTEND file-name
```

OPEN INPUT is used for reading and OPEN OUTPUT for writing. OPEN I-O is used only for files that already exist on disk storage, and allows the use of both READ and REWRITE statements. OPEN EXTEND, which is a level-2 feature, opens the file for writing and positions the file pointer at the end instead of at the usual beginning. This permits adding data at the end of an existing file. A file may be opened by any one of these statements, closed, and then reopened using any of these statements, not necessarily the same one.

The CLOSE statement has the form

```
CLOSE file-name
```

The CLOSE statement is required for all files. (The COBOL standard does not specify what will happen if you do not close a file—in some implementations the system may close the file anyway, although in others, there may be no error message and the file may not be correct.) In either OPEN or CLOSE, a list of file names may be used to open or close several files with one statement.

The sequential output statement has the form

```
WRITE record-name, or
WRITE record-name FROM identifier
```

The second form is equivalent to the pair of statements

```
MOVE identifier TO record-name
WRITE record-name
```

There are two statements that may be added to the write statement to facilitate formatting data for printing. One, AFTER ADVANCING or BEFORE ADVANCING, provides for advancing a specified number of lines or to the next page before or after writing. The other, AT END-OF-PAGE, which is a level-2 feature, provides for executing specified statements at the end of a page, usually to print a footing on that page and/or a heading on the next.

There also is a statement

```
REWRITE record-name, or
REWRITE record-name FROM identifier
```

The file must be on disk—rewriting records on tape files is not allowed. The previously executed I-O statement must have been a successful READ statement. The REWRITE causes that record to be replaced. Again, the second statement is equivalent to the pair of statements

```
MOVE identifier TO record-name
REWRITE record-name
```

Finally, the sequential input statements have the form

```
READ file-name, or
READ file-name INTO identifier
```

where the second statement is equivalent to the pair of statements

```
READ file-name
MOVE record-name TO identifier
```

The action to be taken on end-of-file must be specified. There are three alternatives:

1. There may be an AT END clause following each READ statement. The words AT END are followed by a sentence, which will be executed whenever the READ statement is executed and the end-of-file condition occurs, that is, when there are no more records to read.

2. There may be a USE statement in the DECLARATIVES section at the beginning of the PROCEDURE division specifying the action to be taken on end-of-file.

3. Otherwise, there must be some default system action, such as printing an error message and terminating the program execution.

Example 8.1

In Chapter 7, a simple inventory system was designed to illustrate certain file processing concepts. Details of the I-O programming required were not included. The necessary programming statements to complete the example are given here.

First, consider the batch system. In the ENVIRONMENT DIVISION, INPUT-OUTPUT SECTION, we need the statements

```
SELECT OLD-MASTER ASSIGN TO "OLDMAST",
SELECT NEW-MASTER ASSIGN TO "NEWMAST",
SELECT TRANSACTIONS ASSIGN TO "TRANS",
```

The ASSIGN TO part is implementation-dependent—it furnishes to the operating system the information necessary to associate the logical file names OLD-MASTER, TRANSACTIONS, and NEW-MASTER with appropriate real files. (In fact, the examples in Appendix B actually were run on a DEC-20 computer; the statements for that system differ somewhat from what is shown here. What is shown here is more typical.) We may omit clauses specifying file organization and access mode because these default to SEQUENTIAL in the absence of an explicit declaration.

Next, the file description entries are needed. Those given in Example 7.3 are suitable. The OPEN and CLOSE statements in Example 7.5 are also required and suitable.

Finally we need the paragraphs to do the actual reading and writing, and the following will do the job:

```
READ-MASTER.
    IF PART-NO IN NEW-MASTER-RECORD IS NOT EQUAL
        TO HIGH-VALUES
        READ OLD-MASTER AT END MOVE HIGH-VALUES
            TO PART-NO IN OLD-MASTER-RECORD.

READ-TRANSACTION.
    READ TRANSACTIONS AT END MOVE HIGH-VALUES
        TO PART-NO IN TRANSACTION-RECORD.


WRITE-MASTER.
    WRITE NEW-MASTER-RECORD.
```

8.11. RELATIVE FILES IN COBOL

For relative files, the relative organization must be specified in the SE-LECT statement, and the ACCESS MODE may be specified SEQUEN-TIAL, RANDOM, or DYNAMIC; if it is not specified, SEQUENTIAL is assumed. (Note that DYNAMIC is a level-2 feature.) The file description paragraph and the OPEN and CLOSE statements are the same as for sequential files.

For sequential access, the statements are the same as for sequential files. In addition, the data-item specified as the RELATIVE KEY in the SELECT statement is updated on each read or write to contain the record number of the record just read or written.

For RANDOM access, the read statement has the form

```
READ file-name
READ file-name INVALID KEY sentence
READ file-name INTO identifier, or
READ file-name INTO identifier INVALID KEY sentence
```

Before the statement is executed, the number of the desired record must be put into the data-item specified in the SELECT sentence as the REL-ATIVE KEY, which is the key field in the data record declared for that file. If the number specified is outside the valid range (too small or too large) or if no record has ever been stored in the specified record position, then the key is considered invalid and the sentence following the words INVALID KEY is executed. If the read is successful, then the record goes into the data record area specified in the FD paragraph for that file. If the INTO is included, the record is moved into that work area.

The WRITE statement has the form

```
WRITE record-name
WRITE record-name INVALID KEY sentence
WRITE record-name FROM identifier, or
WRITE record-name FROM identifier INVALID KEY sentence
```

As in the case of the READ statement, the number of the record position where the record is to be written must be placed into the data-item specified as the RELATIVE KEY in the SELECT sentence. The WRITE statement is used for writing records into unused record positions in the file. The INVALID KEY sentence is executed if the specified record number is out of range or if the record already exists on WRITE. Otherwise, if the FROM is included, the contents for the specified work area are copied into the output data record, and then in either case, the data record is written into the file.

The REWRITE statement has exactly the same form as the WRITE statement, with the word WRITE replaced by REWRITE. REWRITE is used for replacing records already in the file. The INVALID KEY statement is allowed only for indexed files. REWRITE should only be used if the record to be rewritten is the last record read,

There is also a DELETE statement:

```
DELETE file-name RECORD, or
DELETE file-name RECORD INVALID KEY sentence
```

Again, the RELATIVE KEY data-item must be set to the record number of the record to be deleted. If the specified record does not exist, the INVALID KEY condition occurs.

If the file is specified for DYNAMIC access (which is a level-2 COBOL I-O feature), then both random and sequential input and output statements may be used. The sequential read statement must include the word NEXT:

```
READ file-name NEXT RECORD
```

and may include the INTO and/or AT END. In addition, there is a START statement for use only in the DYNAMIC mode that positions the pointer for subsequent retrieval of records:

```
START file-name
START file-name KEY IS data-name
START file-name KEY IS EQUAL TO data-name
START file-name KEY IS GREATER THAN data-name, or
START file-name KEY IS NOT LESS THAN data-name
```

The data-name must be the specified RELATIVE KEY data-item. An INVALID KEY clause may be included. The first three forms have the same meaning. This positions the pointer to the first existing record that satisfies the specified condition. If no such record exists, then the IN-VALID KEY sentence is executed.

The COBOL standard is not clear on what must be done to create a relative file; it differs from one implementation to another. It may be sufficient to create the file by a terminal command or a job control statement that specifies its size. It may be necessary to at least open the file for output and then close it to get the file created. It may be necessary to open the file for sequential output and actually write it full of records—at least dummy records of a chosen format. No standard has been adopted for undefined records, and unless each relative record is marked in some fashion on creation of the file, its contents may appear to be valid data.

Example 8.2

In Example 7.6 and Appendix B, there is a program for an on-line version of the inventory system. We will discuss three different ways that might be used to implement the master file for this system. Note that if the keys are not numbers, they certainly can be converted to numbers by some simple process such as using the value of the binary representation of the keys. Here we will consider the keys to be numbers.

(a) It is certainly possible to use a relative file system, using the numeric value of the record key as the relative key. This will be practical only if most of the possible key values are actually in use. For example, we assumed six-digit ID numbers as keys. If we had 9000 records with keys scattered through the entire range of possible values, the file would have to provide space for 1,000,000 records and would be only 0.9% full. That is not practical. However, if we assume that the first two digits of each key are zeros and that there are 9000 records, then all the keys are numbers between 0 and 9999, a total of 10,000 keys, and 90% of all possible keys are actually in use. In this case, a relative file would be reasonably efficient in its use of space. It is, in fact, unlikely that an indexed or a hashed system could make better use of storage space. Furthermore, access in a relative file is faster than access in either a hashed or an indexed file.

(b) More often than not, the keys do not satisfy conditions that make direct use of a relative file practical. If an indexed sequential file system is available, then the master file for the inventory system can be so implemented. Indexed sequential files in COBOL are discussed in the next section.

(c) It is also possible to implement either a hashed file system or an indexed sequential file system using a relative file system for the actual I-O. We show how to implement a hashed file system using relative I-O in Section 8.19.

The example programs illustrating random access in Appendix B are divided into two modules—a main program that implements the required algorithm, and a subprogram that contains all the statements associated with the file I-O operations. A record and a flag indicating whether or not a record was found are put in the *linkage section* (a data area for passing parameters between programs and subprograms) to be passed between the modules, and the key is passed to the subprogram in the PART-NO field in the linkage record. Three versions of the I-O module are included, one using a relative file, one an indexed file, and one a hashed file. In the relative-file version, the following statements directly related to file operations are included in the subprogram.

First, the file-control entry in the ENVIRONMENT DIVISION must indicate that the master file is a relative file:

```
SELECT MASTER-FILE ASSIGN TO "MASTER"
     ORGANIZATION IS RELATIVE
     ACCESS IS RANDOM
     RELATIVE KEY IS PART-NO-KEY.
```

(Again, this differs slightly from the example program in Appendix B, which was run on the DEC-20 and for which the ASSIGN clause is not typical.) The file description entry can be the same as in Example 7.3. The key of the desired record must be in working storage, so PART-NO-KEY is declared in working storage and the key is moved there from the linkage record before reading. The flag RECORD-FLAG, which is set in the READ statement, is declared in the linkage section.

```
77   PART-NO-KEY PICTURE 999999.

77   RECORD-FLAG PICTURE 9.
     88 RECORD-FOUND VALUE IS 1.
```

Next, the open and close statements shown in Example 7.5 are suitable. Finally, we need only the following statements to complete the program:

```
TO READ A RECORD
MOVE PART-NO IN LINK-RECORD TO PART-NO-KEY.
MOVE TRUE TO RECORD-FLAG.
READ MASTER-FILE INTO LINK-RECORD
     INVALID KEY MOVE FALSE TO RECORD-FLAG.
```

```
*    TO WRITE A RECORD
     WRITE MASTER-RECORD FROM LINK-RECORD
        INVALID KEY DISPLAY "INVALID KEY ON WRITE".

*    TO REWRITE A RECORD
     REWRITE MASTER-RECORD
        INVALID KEY DISPLAY "INVALID KEY ON REWRITE".

*    TO DELETE A RECORD
     DELETE MASTER-FILE
        INVALID KEY DISPLAY "INVALID KEY ON DELETE".
```

The program logic assures that an invalid key will not occur in these last three cases, but the INVALID KEY clause is required by standard COBOL.

8.12. INDEXED SEQUENTIAL FILES IN COBOL

For indexed sequential files, ORGANIZATION IS INDEXED must be specified in the SELECT sentence, and the ACCESS MODE must be specified to be SEQUENTIAL, RANDOM, or DYNAMIC; if it is not specified, SEQUENTIAL is assumed. (Note that DYNAMIC is a level-2 feature.) The file description paragraph and the OPEN and CLOSE statements are the same as for the previous cases.

For sequential access, the statements are the same as for sequential files. In addition, the data-item specified as the RECORD KEY in the SELECT statement is updated on each read to contain the key found in the record just read.

For RANDOM access, the read statement has the form

```
READ file-name
READ file-name INVALID KEY sentence
READ file-name INTO identifier, or
READ file-name INTO identifier INVALID KEY sentence
```

Before the statement is executed, the value of the key of the desired record must be put into the data-item specified in the SELECT sentence as the RECORD KEY, which is the key field in the data record declared for that file. If no record has ever been stored with the specified key value, then the key is considered invalid and the sentence following the words INVALID KEY is executed. If the read is successful, then the record goes into the data record area specified in the FD paragraph for that file. If the INTO is included, the record is moved into that work area.

The WRITE statement has the form

```
WRITE  record-name
WRITE  record-name INVALID KEY sentence
WRITE  record-name FROM identifier, or
WRITE  record-name FROM identifier INVALID KEY sentence
```

and the REWRITE statement has exactly the same form, with the word WRITE replaced by REWRITE. As in the case of the READ statement, the value of the key of the record to be written must be placed into the data-item specified as the RECORD KEY in the SELECT sentence. The WRITE statement is used for writing a new record (i. e., a record whose key is different from that of any record in the file), and REWRITE is used for replacing the record already in the file that has the same key. The INVALID KEY sentence is executed if on WRITE there is already a record in the file with the specified key value. On REWRITE, if there is not a record in the file with the specified key, the INVALID KEY sentence is executed. Otherwise, if the FROM is included, the contents for the specified work area are copied into the output data record, and then, in either case, the data record is written into the file.

There is also a DELETE statement:

```
DELETE file-name RECORD, or
DELETE file-name RECORD INVALID KEY sentence
```

Again, the RECORD KEY data-item must be set to the key value of the record to be deleted. If the specified record does not exist, the INVALID KEY condition occurs.

If the file is specified for DYNAMIC access (which is a level-2 COBOL I-O feature), then both random and sequential I-O statements may be used. The sequential read statement must include the word NEXT:

```
READ file-name NEXT RECORD
```

and may include the INTO and/or AT END. In addition, there is a START statement for use only in the DYNAMIC mode that positions the pointer for subsequent retrieval of records:

```
START  file-name
START  file-name KEY IS data-name
START  file-name KEY IS EQUAL TO data-name
START  file-name KEY IS GREATER THAN data-name, or
START  file-name KEY IS NOT LESS THAN data-name
```

The data-name must be the specified RECORD KEY data-item. An INVALID KEY clause may be included. The first three forms have the same meaning. This positions the pointer to the first existing record that satisfies the specified condition. If no such record exists, then the INVALID KEY sentence is executed.

The COBOL standard is not clear on what must be done to create an indexed sequential file; it differs from one implementation to another. One normally would expect to use one of the following procedures:

(a) Open the file for sequential output and write all the records that are to be in the file initially, in sequence by key, and then close the file. Now the file exists and can be opened for random access and records can be read, inserted, changed (rewritten), or deleted.

(b) Create an empty indexed file, possibly by opening the file for sequential output and immediately closing it again. Then the file can be opened for random access and records can be inserted, read, changed, and deleted. Records may be inserted in any sequence whatsoever, and they will be stored logically in sequence so that when they are read sequentially, they will come out in sequence by key.

(c) A utility program may be provided for creating and initially loading an indexed file; its use may be required in some systems.

One or more of these alternatives may be possible. In some systems, loading the file sequentially as in (a) or (c) would result in a more efficient placement of the records in the file, such as an equal number of records per segment. In others, all alternatives would give essentially the same results.

Example 8.3

In Example 8.2, we stated that Appendix B includes a main program for an example of an on-line system and three versions of an I-O subprogram that may be used with it. The relative-file version was discussed in the previous example; here we discuss the indexed-file version.

Of course, the file-control entry in the ENVIRONMENT DIVISION must indicate that the master file is an indexed sequential file:

```
SELECT MASTER-FILE ASSIGN TO "OLDMAST"
      ORGANIZATION IS INDEXED
      ACCESS IS RANDOM
      RECORD KEY IS PART-NO IN MASTER-RECORD.
```

(Again, this differs slightly from the example program shown in Appendix B, run on the DEC-20, but the above is more typical.)

The file description entry is the same as in Example 8.2. The desired key will be passed from the main program in the linkage section and must be moved into the data record for the indexed file. Again, the flag RECORD-FLAG will be set by the READ-MASTER paragraph. The open and close statements shown in Example 7.5 are suitable. We need only the following paragraphs to complete the program:

```
*   TO READ A RECORD
    MOVE PART-NO IN LINK-RECORD
        TO PART-NO IN MASTER-RECORD.
    MOVE TRUE TO RECORD-FLAG.
    READ MASTER-FILE INTO LINK-RECORD
        INVALID KEY MOVE FALSE TO RECORD-FLAG.

*   TO INSERT A RECORD
    WRITE MASTER-RECORD
        INVALID KEY DISPLAY "INVALID KEY ON WRITE".

*   TO REWRITE A RECORD
    REWRITE MASTER-RECORD
        INVALID KEY DISPLAY "INVALID KEY ON REWRITE".

*   TO DELETE A RECORD
    DELETE MASTER-FILE
        INVALID KEY DISPLAY "INVALID KEY ON DELETE".
```

Note that the program logic assures that an INVALID KEY condition
cannot occur on writing, rewriting, or deleting a record because the
presence or absence of a record is determined by a read statement, and
after that, only a permissible operation is done. However, standard
COBOL requires that the clause be present.

8.13. FILE STATEMENTS IN PL/I

The description here is based on the American National Standard Programming Language PL/I [I5] and on the American National Standard
Programming Language PL/I General Purpose Subset [I6], which we will
refer to as "Subset-G." The latter document states that "The subset can
be efficiently implemented on small and medium size computers including most minicomputers and some microprocessor-based systems." In fact,
Subset-G has been implemented almost completely at least on Intel 8080
and 8086 processors, and Digital Research, Inc., has announced versions
for the Motorola 68000 and National Semiconductor processors. Subset-
G includes most of the commonly used features of PL/I, but excludes
many of the error-prone features of full PL/I. For most programming,
whether for scientific, data-processing, or systems-programming applications, Subset-G is probably more satisfactory than full PL/I. In what
follows, when a feature not in Subset-G is discussed, it will be noted. Of
course, the discussion will not be comprehensive—rather, the most important features will be discussed to illustrate the basic concepts.

Files in PL/I are classified as STREAM files or RECORD files. Statements defined for one type of file cannot be used for the other. For example, it is not permissible to use the statements WRITE and PUT with

the same file, because WRITE is defined for use with RECORD files and PUT is defined for use with STREAM files.

The standard defines a stream file as containing symbols, *linemarks*, *pagemarks*, and *carriage returns*. The symbols will be characters defined in the character code being used, normally either ASCII or EBCDIC, as described in Appendix A. The file consists of a stream of these characters, and nothing is said about whether this stream is divided into physical blocks. In practice, it almost certainly would be divided into blocks for convenience in storing the data. Furthermore, the *linemark* might be the same as an end-of-block mark (such as a tape gap). In any event, the intent of stream files is to permit programs to read or write sequences of data-items without regard to any physical boundaries.

RECORD files are composed of zero or more records. The records may consist entirely of ASCII or EBCDIC characters, but they also may contain data in other codes, such as the internal machine-dependent codes used for arithmetic data. The standard is unclear about the organization of files. A file is called KEYED if it is capable of direct access by specifying a key. Thus, both relative files and indexed sequential files are KEYED. But the standard does not describe indexed sequential or relative files specifically—the same statements apply to all random-access files and any further differences between them are considered to be implementation-dependent details. Thus, a PL/I implementation will almost always include an implementation of relative files and frequently an implementation of indexed sequential files. These are the two types of KEYED files; the type and other details needed will be specified in the ENVIRONMENT attribute in the DECLARE statement or the OPEN statement. The ENVIRONMENT attribute is included specifically for specifying implementation-dependent information. The type is usually required so that the compiler knows which set of I-O procedures to utilize.

Subset-G requires explicit declaration of all variables. In particular, every internal logical file name must be declared, and the DECLARE statement may contain a number of attributes of the file. First, it may contain STREAM or RECORD. It may contain PRINT, meaning a file intended for printing and, hence, may contain endpage markers. PRINT implies STREAM. It may contain INPUT, OUTPUT, or UPDATE. UPDATE implies RECORD, because stream files can be used only for input or output. It may contain KEYED and/or SEQUENTIAL or DIRECT, all of which imply a RECORD file. KEYED means a file capable of direct access, and SEQUENTIAL or DIRECT refers to the mode of access actually used in the given program. The declaration may contain the word ENVIRONMENT followed by any required implementation-dependent information enclosed in parentheses.

Files must be opened before they are used and closed before the program is terminated. However, PL/I does not require explicit OPEN and

CLOSE statements. If explicit statements are not included, then the system is supposed to open each file before its first use and close it when the program is terminated. The OPEN statement consists of the word OPEN FILE followed by the internal logical file name enclosed in parentheses. That may be followed by any permissible combination of the attributes described above for the DECLARE statement for files. The title option, consisting of the word TITLE followed by an expression in parentheses, may be included to specify an external file name diferent from the internal one. The external file name, that is, the value of the title expression, may be used in an implementation-dependent way; for example, the system might take the external name as the physical file name. For STREAM files, the word LINESIZE followed by the desired number of characters per line enclosed in parentheses may be included. For PRINT files, the page size also may be specified by the word PAGESIZE and the number of lines per page enclosed in parentheses.

A file may be opened, closed, and then reopened. Closing and reopening a file may be done to position the file pointer back to the beginning of the file. One may open a file for output, write into it, close, open for input, and then read what was written. Also, one may open a KEYED file for SEQUENTIAL output, write data into it, close it, reopen it for DIRECT access, and then access the data by key. A file may be opened with a TITLE option designating that an internal logical file name be associated with a certain external file name, then closed, and then reopened with the TITLE option designating a different external file name.

8.14. STREAM AND SEQUENTIAL FILES IN PL/I

The input statements for STREAM files use the keyword GET. The statement may specify the internal logical file name—if not, a default name normally associated with a terminal or card reader is used. It may specify either LIST or EDIT. If LIST is specified, data-items are assumed to be separated by commas and/or spaces, and are read one by one from the file. If EDIT is specified, the statement also must contain a list of format specifications to guide the conversion of the input data. The output statement uses the keyword PUT. Again, the file may or may not be specified; if not, a default file name normally associated with a terminal or printer is assumed. It may specify either LIST or EDIT. If LIST is specified, the data-items are converted to characters by fixed rules and transmitted to the file. If EDIT is specified, then the PUT statement also must include a list of format items that specify the exact form of the conversion from internal representation to characters. PL/I STREAM I-O statements usually are explained well in introductory books on PL/I programming and will not be explained in detail here.

For sequential files (not keyed), instead of GET and PUT, the following I-O statements are provided:

```
WRITE FILE(logical file name) FROM(identifier);
READ FILE(logical file name) INTO(identifier);
REWRITE FILE(logical file name) FROM(identifier);
```

For WRITE, the file must be opened for output; for READ, for input or update; for REWRITE, for update. REWRITE must rewrite the last record read, which, of course, can be done only for disk files. An End-of-file is handled by the ENDFILE ON-condition, which is described in the next section.

Example 8.4

In Example 7.5, a sequential update program is given for a simple inventory system. The I-O statements required to complete the example in COBOL were given in Section 8.10. Here we furnish the equivalent statements in PL/I. First of all, file declarations are needed:

```
DECLARE OLDMAST FILE SEQUENTIAL INPUT,
        TRANS FILE SEQUENTIAL INPUT,
        NEWMAST FILE SEQUENTIAL OUTPUT;
```

These files will default to sequential access since they are not explicitly declared to be direct. INPUT or OUTPUT may be included either in the declaration or the OPEN statement. Next we need the ENDFILE ON-units for each file. These units should be placed at the beginning of the program, where they will be executed once, because they must be executed to take effect and it wastes time to execute them unnecessarily.

```
ON ENDFILE(OLDMAST) OLD_MASTER_RECORD.PART_NO =
   HIGH(6);
ONENDFILE(TRANS) TRANSACTION_RECORD.PART_NO =
   HIGH(6);
```

(HIGH(6) and LOW(6) are "built-in functions" whose values are the highest and lowest possible six-character strings, respectively.)

Finally, we need the read and write procedures:

```
READ_MASTER: PROCEDURE;
   READ FILE(OLDMAST) INTO(OLD_MASTER_RECORD);
END;

READ_TRANSACTION: PROCEDURE;
   READ FILE(TRANS) INTO(TRANSACTION_RECORD);
END;
```

```
WRITE_MASTER: PROCEDURE;
    WRITE FILE(NEWMAST) FROM (NEW_MASTER_RECORD);
END;
```

8.15. KEYED FILES IN PL/I

KEYED files may be opened for SEQUENTIAL access. The same statements as are used for sequential files can be used for KEYED files, except
that for WRITE the KEYFROM option, which consists of the keyword
KEYFROM followed by the name of the identifier containing the key in
parentheses, should be included to furnish the value of the key to be
stored with the record. For READ, the option KEYTO followed by the
name of an identifier where the key is to be stored when the record is
read should be included. Unlike COBOL indexed files, in PL/I the key
need not be part of the data record.

KEYED files also may be opened for DIRECT access. In this case, the
READ, WRITE, and REWRITE statements have the form:

```
WRITE FILE(logical file name) FROM(identifier)
    KEYFROM(identifier);
REWRITE FILE(logical file name) FROM(identifier)
    KEY(expression);
READ FILE(logical file name) INTO(identifier)
    KEY(expression);
```

For WRITE, the file must be opened for OUTPUT or UPDATE; for READ,
it must be INPUT or UPDATE; for REWRITE, it must be opened for
UPDATE. The WRITE statement is used to write a record into the file
with a key that did not exist previously. REWRITE is used to replace a
record already in the file that has the designated key. If READ or RE-
WRITE is given and no record with the designated key exists, or if WRITE
is given and the key does exist, then the KEY ON-condition is brought
up.

In addition to the KEY ON-condition just mentioned, there is the END-
FILE ON-condition which is turned on if a file is opened for sequential
access and a READ statement is given after the last record in the file
has been read (or on the first read, if there is no data in the file). There
is the ENDPAGE ON-condition that goes on when the end of a page is
met on a PRINT file. There also is an UNDEFINEDFILE condition that
comes up when an attempt is made to open a file that does not exist.
These conditions can cause some special action by using, for example,
the following ON-units.

```
ON KEY(MASTER) NO_RECORD = TRUE;
```

```
ON ENDFILE(OLDMAST) OLD_RECORD.ID = '999999';

ON ENDPAGE(MAIN_REPORT) BEGIN;
    /*  PRINT FOOTING ON THIS PAGE  */
    PUT SKIP(2);
    PUT EDIT('PAGE',PAGE_NO)(A,F(3));
    PAGE_NO = PAGE_NO+1;
    /*  SKIP TO NEXT PAGE AND PRINT HEADING ON IT  */
    PUT PAGE EDIT(HEADING)(A);
END;

ON UNDEFINEDFILE(TRANSACTION) CALL NOTRANS;
```

Example 8.5

In Example 7.6, there is an example of a complete on-line inventory system that only lacks the I-O procedures for a specific file organization. As with COBOL, there are several possible approaches possible;

(a) If the maximum key, k_{max}, is not too large and if most numbers between 0 and k_{max} actually are in use or will be used as keys, then it is practical to use a relative file. Most PL/I systems provide relative files, and relative file access, being simple, is fast.

(b) If an indexed sequential file system is available, then it could be used.

(c) It is possible to implement either an indexed sequential file system or a hashed file system using the built-in relative file system for the actual file I-O.

For alternative (c), an example of an implementation of a hashed file is included in Appendix C. For (a) or (b), the type of file system and necessary parameters are specified in the ENVIRONMENT statement and are implementation-dependent, because the PL/I standard does not specify any details about the way a random-access file system should be implemented. The standard also does not specify how a direct-access file is created. This must be found from the documentation of the particular system used. One can expect to have to at least open the file for output, probably sequential output, and then close it again to cause it to be created. It may be desirable to load the file initially sequentially before starting to use it for random access, or it may be more convenient to start with an empty direct-access file and to insert all the records by direct access.

For alternatives (a) and (b), other than the considerations in the preceding paragraph, for standard PL/I, the I-O procedures for a relative file system or an indexed sequential file system are identical.

(However, the examples given in Appendix C were run using the IBM PL/I Optimizing Compiler and differ from the standard in a number of details. For example, relative files are called REGIONAL files, of which there are three types.) The master file must be declared:

```
DECLARE MASTER FILE KEYED DIRECT UPDATE
   ENVIRONMENT(implementation-dependent information);
```

It should be opened

```
OPEN FILE(MASTER);
```

Note that the attributes could have been in either the declaration or the OPEN statement. Next we need the ON-unit for invalid keys:

```
ON KEY(MASTER) RECORD_FOUND = FALSE;
```

Finally we need the four actual I-O procedures. These procedures are written on the assumption that they are internal procedures, and, therefore, the identifiers declared in the main procedure are available.

```
READ_MASTER: PROCEDURE;
   RECORD_FOUND = TRUE;
   READ FILE(MASTER) INTO(MASTER_RECORD)
      KEY(TRANSACTION.ID);
END;

WRITE_MASTER: PROCEDURE;
   WRITE FILE(MASTER) FROM(MASTER_RECORD)
      KEYFROM(MASTER_RECORD.ID);
END;

REWRITE_MASTER: PROCEDURE;
   REWRITE FILE(MASTER) FROM(MASTER_RECORD)
      KEY(MASTER_RECORD.ID);
END;

DELETE_MASTER: PROCEDURE;
   DELETE FILE(MASTER) KEY(MASTER_RECORD.ID);
END;
```

The edit checking procedure includes something like this:

```
IF CODE = 'A' & RECORD_FOUND THEN DO;
   ERROR = TRUE;
   WRITE FILE(TERMINAL) FROM(DUPLICATE_RECORD_MSG);
END;
ELSE IF CODE ~= 'A' & ~RECORD_FOUND THEN DO;
   ERROR = TRUE;
```

```
    WRITE FILE(TERMINAL) FROM(NOT_FOUND_MSG);
END;
```

Note that RECORD_FOUND, being set true before reading and set false in the ON-unit if the record is not found, will be true if there is a record with a key matching the transaction key and false if not. With this error checking, it is easy to verify that there will never be an attempt to write if the record is already present or to rewrite or delete if it is not. Thus, we are guaranteed that we will not have an invalid key on WRITE, REWRITE, or DELETE.

8.16. FILE PROGRAMMING IN FORTRAN

The FORTRAN standard [I1] defines a full language and a "subset FORTRAN," the latter intended for smaller machines. Subset FORTRAN includes all of the most important features for I-O, and, with a few exceptions that will be noted, the discussion will be limited to subset FORTRAN. The previous standard [I2] did not include direct-access facilities, although many older implementations of FORTRAN did include it as an extension.

There are two distinct kinds of files in FORTRAN, formatted files and unformatted files. In formatted files, all data are represented in character code, that is, letters, digits, and special characters. In unformatted files, data are represented in the internal machine code. Formatted files are written or read using WRITE or READ statements that reference FORMAT statements that specify how the data are to be converted from internal code to the external character code or vice versa. Unformatted files use I-O statements that transfer data with no conversion whatsoever. In general, data written out on one computer and read on a different one must be formatted files; unformatted files are suitable only to be read on the same computer (or one of the same kind) as the computer that wrote them. Because there is no conversion, unformatted files require less computer time than formatted files for reading or writing. Also, the data usually require less storage space in unformatted files, because the internal codes are generally more concise than character codes for numerical data. Data intended for printing must be written as a formatted file, and similarly, data coming directly or indirectly from typing on a keyboard must be read using a READ statement that uses a FORMAT statement.

One READ or WRITE statement reads or writes one record with unformatted files. With formatted files, each READ or WRITE starts at the beginning of a record. It is possible to specify in the FORMAT statement that the data written or read with a formatted file is to be divided into more than one record, for example, by indicating the dividing points between records by slashes (/) in the FORMAT statement.

There are two methods of accessing files in FORTRAN: sequential and direct. A file that is accessed sequentially is called a sequential file, and one that is accessed randomly is called a direct file. The standard specifies that the method of accessing must be specified at the time that the file is created. A sequential file must not be read or written by direct-access I-O statements, and similarly, direct-access files must not be read or written by sequential-access I-O statements. The standard defines an *endfile record* that normally will be written as the last record of a sequential file.

Subset FORTRAN requires that direct-access files be unformatted, but the full FORTRAN allows formatted direct-access files. Subset FORTRAN also requires that a maximum record number be specified at the time a file is created for direct-access files, although full FORTRAN does not have that requirement. Although the standard does not specify it, presumably files with the maximum record number specified will be relative files. It is not clear what form direct-access files in which the maximum record number is not specified are to take. They might be relative files capable of expanding dynamically or hashed files. Clearly, there are some details that will be implementation-dependent. In any case, the conceptual model is a relative file.

Files are referred to by *unit names* that are zero or positive integers. Unit names or numbers play the role of internal logical file names in FORTRAN. They may be "connected to" physical file names. The actual connection is established by some implementation-dependent method. (In some systems, the external name is derived from the unit name—e.g., FT05F0001 is derived from unit number 5 in certain IBM implementations.) Full FORTRAN, but not the subset, permits an external file name to be specified in the OPEN statement. In turn, this external name can be connected to (or by default coincide with) a physical name in a job control statement.

In subset FORTRAN, the OPEN statement is used only for direct-access files; it is a requirement for them. There is no CLOSE statement. Sequential files are opened automatically when they are first used, and all files are closed automatically when a program terminates without error. Full FORTRAN allows the OPEN statement for sequential files and has a CLOSE statement as well as several options not included in subset FORTRAN.

8.17. SEQUENTIAL FILE PROGRAMMING IN FORTRAN

The input statements have the form

```
READ (u,f)list    or
READ (u,f,END=s)list
```

for formatted files, and

```
READ (u)list     or
READ (u,END=s)list
```

for unformatted files. Similarly, the output statements have the form

```
WRITE (u,f)list
```

for formatted files, or

```
WRITE (u)list
```

for unformatted files, where u is the unit number, f is the statement number of the appropriate FORMAT statement, "list" is a list of variable names into which values are to be read or written, and s is the statement number of the statement to jump to when an endfile record is read. The list may contain the names of variables or arrays and *implied-DO loops* (e. g., (X(I),I = 1,100,2)) that specify part of one or more arrays to be transferred. If the name of an array is included without a subscript or an implied-DO loop, all elements of the array will be read or written. Full FORTRAN allows the lists for output statements to contain expressions, but subset FORTRAN only allows variables. Details of the form of the variable lists and the FORMAT statements are covered well in ordinary FORTRAN textbooks and will not be covered here.

There are also three *file positioning* statements.

```
BACKSPACE (u)
```

moves the file pointer back to the beginning of the preceding record and is available only if it is possible on the designated I-O unit.

```
REWIND (u)
```

moves the file pointer to the beginning of the file, which requires actual rewinding for tape files. Finally,

```
ENDFILE (u)
```

writes an endfile record on the file.

Example 8.6

We will show the subroutines needed for I-O in a batch file update program, such as the one given in COBOL in Chapter 7. Assume that unit number 21 has been connected to the old master file, unit number 22 to the transaction file, and unit number 23 to the new master file. Then the following subroutine is suitable for reading the next transaction:

```
SUBROUTINE READTR
C
C      THIS PROCEDURE READS ONE TRANSACTION AND IF THE
C      READ OCCURS ON END OF FILE, THE TRANSACTION ID
C      IS SET TO ALL-9'S
C
       CHARACTER*6 TRID
       CHARACTER*4 TRQ
       CHARACTER*15 TRDESC
       CHARACTER*1 TCODE
       COMMON TRID,TRQ,TRDESC,TCODE
       READ(21,11,END=1)TRID,TCODE,TRQ,TRDESC
    11 FORMAT(A6,A1,A4,A15)
       RETURN
C
     1 TRID = '999999'
       RETURN
C
       END
```

The following subroutine reads an old master record:

```
SUBROUTINE READMA
C
C      THIS PROCEDURE READS THEN NEXT OLD MASTER RECORD,
C      SETTING OMID TO ALL-9'S IF THE READ OCCURS AT END
C      OF FILE
C
       CHARACTER*6 OMID
       INTEGER OMQ
       CHARACTER*15 OMDESC
       COMMON OMQ,OMID,OMDESC
       READ(22,END=1)OMID,OMQ,OMDESC
       RETURN
C
     1 OMID = '999999'
       RETURN
C
       END
```

Finally, writing a new master record requires one statement:

```
       WRITE(23)NMID,NMQ,NMDESC
```

8.18. DIRECT-ACCESS FILES IN FORTRAN

Standard FORTRAN provides direct-access facilities only for relative files. Direct-access files must be opened. The form of the OPEN statement is

```
OPEN (u,ACCESS = 'DIRECT',RECL = rl,MAXREC = maxr)
```

where u is the unit number, rl is the record length, and maxr is the maximum record number. (More options are available in full FORTRAN, including a FILE = fname clause, where fname is an external file name.)

The I-O statements are

```
READ (u,REC=rn)list, or READ (u,REC=rn,ERR=s)list
WRITE (u,REC = rn)list
```

where u is the unit number, rn is the record number of the desired record, s is the number of the statement to go to in the case of an invalid record number, and list is the list of variables whose values are to be read or written. No distinction is made between writing a new record and re-writing a record that previously existed. If a READ statement is given specifying a record that has not been written previously, then the standard states that the values of variables in the variable list in the READ statement will be "undefined." Thus, it is the responsibility of the programmer to see to it that no record is read unless it has been written previously.

Example 8.7

In Appendix D, there is a FORTRAN program that implements the inventory system used as an example in Chapter 7. In that program, just as with the COBOL and PL/I program examples for the on-line system, all the I-O statements are collected into one subroutine and the parameter of the subroutine is an integer that indicates which I-O operation is required. Because FORTRAN provides only relative files, if an indexed or hashed file system is required, it must be programmed using relative files. Two versions of the I-O subroutine, one for simple use of a relative file and one implementing a hashed file using a FORTRAN relative file, are included in Appendix D. Here we show the relative-file implementation, which includes examples of all the needed I-O statements.

It is not necessary to include the key in the record, but we will include it because we did in other examples. Because we must be able, given any key, to read and determine whether a record exists for that key, and because it is not permitted in FORTRAN to read a record that has not been written, all unused record positions should have dummy records written into them. One way to do this is to write a suitable dummy record into every position in the file when it is created, and then, to write in the real records, which will replace the original dummy records. Assume that the key value 000000 never occurs as a real key; then it will be suitable to make dummy records with spaces as the description and zeros as the ID and quantity. We will assume that this has been done. It also will be suitable to delete a record by replacing its key by 000000.

```
      SUBROUTINE FILEIO(OP)
C     THIS VERSION OF FILEIO IMPLEMENTS A SIMPLE RELATIVE
C     FILE.
C
C     FOR FILEIO, THE FOLLOWING VALUES ARE PASSED AS THE
C     PARAMETER, TO INDICATE WHICH OPERATION: 1--OPENOP,
C     2--READOP, 3--WRITOP, AND 4--DELEOP
C
      INTEGER OPENOP,READOP,WRITOP,DELEOP
      DATA OPENOP/1/READOP/2/WRITOP/3/DELEOP/4/
C
C     NOTE THAT FOUND IS SET TRUE OR FALSE ACCORDING TO
C     WHETHER OR NOT THE RECORD AT THE POSITION READ HAS
C     THE CORRECT KEY, OR A KEY OF ALL ZEROS, THE LATTER
C     INDICATING A DUMMY RECORD. NOTE ALSO THAT TO DELETE
C     A RECORD, WE SET ITS ID TO ALL ZEROS AND REWRITE IT.
C
      IF(OP.EQ.OPENOP)THEN
         OPEN(UNIT=22,ACCESS='DIRECT',RECL=6,STATUS='OLD')
      ELSE IF(OP.EQ.READOP)THEN
         READ(22,REC=RECORD)MID,MQ,MDESC
         FOUND = (MID.EQ.TRID)
      ELSE IF(OP.EQ.WRITOP)THEN
         WRITE(22,REC=RECORD)MID,MQ,MDESC
      ELSE IF(OP.EQ.DELEOP)THEN
         MID = '000000'
         WRITE(22,REC=RECORD)MID,MQ,MDESC
      ENDIF
         RETURN
      END
```

8.19. PROGRAMMING OF HASHED FILES

Most programming language implementations do not include built-in hashed file systems. Most do include relative file systems, however, and a hashed file system can be implemented fairly easily using the relative file system. This section shows how this can be done by implementing the master file for the inventory system (used as an example throughout this chapter) as a hashed file.

First of all, we must choose parameters for the file system, using the concepts and methods of Chapters 6 and 7. Assume that we want a total capacity of 10,000 records and that we want a bucket capacity of five records. Then we need 2000 buckets. We use a relative file with a capacity of 2000 relative records, each large enough to hold five of our inventory records. Thus, what we think of as a block or bucket is a record in the relative file system, and actually has the capacity to hold five inventory records.

Next, we need a hashing function. We will divide by N, for some chosen N, and use the remainder. The number of buckets, 2000, is not a good choice for N, because it is best to avoid numbers that have common factors with the number base, which is 10 in this case. If we take $N = 1999$, we should get satisfactory results. The remainder always will be less than 1999 and the last bucket will be used only for overflow, but that is certainly not a problem.

We have to know when a record is present in any given position in the file. This might be done by including a one-character flag with each record, but we will assume that the key 000000 is never used for real records and so it can be used to indicate an unused record position. Then to create the file, we must write it full of records that have 000000 in the key position, and, for lack of a better choice, spaces or zeros in the rest of the record.

Now all we need are subroutines to insert a record, read a record, rewrite a record, or delete a record. Suitable algorithms for these four subroutines follow. These are written assuming that in the case of reading a record, there is a flag that we will call the record flag, that is set true if the record being sought is found, and false otherwise. We also will assume that there is a record pointer (bucket number and position within the bucket) that points to the record, if it is found, or to the first unused record space, if no record with the specified key is found. In the case of rewrite and delete, we will assume that the record pointer points to the record to be rewritten or deleted. Finally, for insertion, we will assume that the record pointer points to the unused space in the file where the record is to be written. We intend to always read first and after reading, do a write, rewrite, or delete if such an operation is needed. Then the algorithms for these four operations are as follows:

```
Read a record
     calculate the hashed address;
     start at that bucket and search, continuing from the
     beginning after the last record, if necessary, until
     one of the three following conditions is met.

          (a) a record with the desired key is found,
```

(b) a key equal to □□□□□□ is found, in which case we
know the record is not present, or

(c) the search has continued to the last bucket, and
continued from the first bucket back to the starting
point, in which case, we know again that the record is
not in the file, and in addition, that the file is
full;

then set the record-flag true if the record is present,
false if not, and leave the record pointer set pointing
at the last record read.

Insert a record

store the record in the unused space in the
bucket that the record pointer points to;
rewrite that bucket into the relative file on the disk.

Rewrite a record

make the necessary changes to the record in the
bucket that is in the read area in memory;
rewrite that bucket to the disk unit.
{Note that it is not permissible to change the key of a
record and then rewrite it.}

Delete a record

set the key to □□□□□□;
    {indicating that the record is unused}
set P to point to that bucket;
set L equal to P;
while bucket L is full and not all buckets have been
    examined do begin
        make L point to the next bucket;
        for each record in bucket L do begin
            set H equal to hashed address of that record;
            if H≤P<L or L<H≤P or P<L<H then begin
                move that record to bucket P;
                set P equal to L
            end;
        end; {of for loop}
    end; {of while loop}

The deletion algorithm is based on Knuth's idea [H1, p. 526] of moving
records backwards, as mentioned in Section 6.7. Since bucket P has an
open space, we search for a record that would be closer to its hashed
address if it is moved to bucket P. H is the hashed address of the record
being considered and the bucket number of the bucket where it is located
is L. Then the condition that this record would be closer to its hashed
address if it were put into bucket P instead of where it is would be true
if starting from bucket H and searching to the end of the file, then continuing from the beginning back to bucket H again, we meet bucket P
before we meet bucket L. In terms of inequalities, this may occur three
ways:

1. If starting from H, we meet P and L before we get to the end of the file, that is, if H≤P<L.

2. If starting from H, we meet P, and then the end of the file. Continuing from the beginning, we meet L, that is, if L<H≤P.

3. If we start from H and meet the end of the file, go back to the beginning, find P, and then L, that is, if P<L<H.

Thus, in the algorithm we test for the condition

$$H \leq P < L \text{ or } L < H \leq P \text{ or } P < L < H \tag{8.1}$$

Example 8.8

To illustrate these ideas more concretely, we have implemented the on-line inventory update procedures in COBOL (Appendix B.5), PL/I (Appendix C.5), and Fortran (Appendix D.4). In each case, the hashing algorithms described in this section were utilized; see the programs called FILEIO in the appended sections. Note that, in the three respective programs, the condition given in Eq. 8.1 is checked starting at line 254 in Appendix B.5, line 226 in Appendix C.5, and line 165 in Appendix D.4.

NOTES

ANSI standards for COBOL, FORTRAN, and PL/I are given in [I1]–[I6]. Many of the numerous textbooks on these languages do not describe their file facilities in much detail. Among the textbooks that treat direct-access facilities are [I9] (COBOL), [I10] (FORTRAN), and [I11] (PL/I). See also [I12] (APL), [I13] (BASIC), and [I14] (RPG). Descriptions of numerous other programming languages appear in [I7]; more detailed descriptions of the major languages are given in [I8].

A brief discussion of job control languages is included in Appendix E. A general discussion of job control languages appears in [A5] and [K13]. IBM's JCL is described in [J8] and [J9]. Unix is described in [J11]. CP/M, database system dBaseII, and word-processing system Wordstar are described in [J10].

EXERCISES

8-1. (a) Find how a physical file name is associated with an internal file name in some actual compiler implementation(s). Does it use a third (external) name?

(b) Explain why direct association of a physical file name with an internal logical file name, instead of an indirect association via a third name, limits portability from one operating system to another.

8-2. From the discussion on *stream* files, we may conclude that it is possible, for example, to read two data-items from a physical block of tape via one read statement (e.g., "INPUT FILE(fname) A,B"), and then continue reading three more data items starting from the same block via a subsequent read statement (e.g., "INPUT FILE-(fname) C,D,E"). Assume that A, B, C, D, and E have identical lengths equal to (say) eight characters each. How is this consistent with the fact that a hardware read command always reads to the physical end of a block (to the gap) and if all of the data is not requested, the remainder of the block gets lost?

8-3. If an odd number of records are written into a sequential file with two records per block, some systems will write the last record into a short block (of half the block size) rather than padding the last block with filler.

(a) How does such a system know when to write this half-block (i.e., that it is not going to get another record to fill up the block)?

(b) What advantage does padding the last block, if necessary, with an extra dummy record have?

8-4. Assume an input file consists of 10 records, each record containing a single number, the first record having a 1, the second record having a 2, the third record having a 3, and so on. Also assume conventional system buffering (i.e., two buffers each for input and for output, where the input buffers are kept filled by reading ahead and the output buffers are emptied at the system's convenience). Consider the program segment:

```
GET-LOCATE (I)
GET-LOCATE (J)
MOVE (I) TO (X)
PUT-LOCATE (X)
MOVE (X) TO (Y)
PUT-LOCATE (Y)
MOVE (J) TO (Y)
PUT-MOVE (I,J,X,Y)
```

What will be printed out by the three PUT statements? (Your answer should include a "trace" of the program, where each statement is explained.)

8-5. What is done when a disk file is opened for sequential output that is not done when opened for random update?

8-6. What action is taken when a sequential file is opened for input (with buff-

ering) that is not taken when opened for output?

8-7. When a record is deleted from a hashed file, why should its flag not just be changed from "exists" to "absent"?

8-8. Some systems permit the use of the REWRITE statement for files opened for sequential access, but more restrictive systems treat this as a programming language error. Explain this discrepancy.

8-9. We have a sequential file of 20,000 records of 800 bytes each. We want a copy of these data on another sequential file with the same records written in reverse order. Using any language in which a relative file system is implemented, write a program to accomplish this. (Note that the file is much too large to read the whole file into memory at one time. A program of about 13 statements that will run in seconds or at most a few minutes on most machines is possible because of the special nature of the problem.)

8-10. We have a sequential file of 6000 records, each of which has a key that is a number between 1 and 6000 (with no duplicate keys, of course). Because of the special nature of this file, it is possible to sort it with a short, but efficient program (probably fewer than 20 statements) if a relative file system is available. Write such a program. The output file should be a sequential file. Do not use an internal sort.

Projects: *A most useful exercise is to implement a fairly realistic file system. We suggest implementing sequential batch update systems and on-line update systems using both indexed files and hashed files. In either case, insertions and deletions and one or more other kinds of transactions should be possible. Very much simplified versions of such systems as payroll (for sequential only), a phone directory, retail billing system, utility company billing, inventory, or airline reservations are some examples of suitable systems to implement. We also recommend using several different languages, compilers, and operating systems.*

Data Coding

A.1. INTRODUCTION

Computer memory fundamentally stores binary digits, or bits, each of which may have a value of either 0 or 1. Memory is made up of small groups of bits. For some computers, the fundamental group is a word, which generally consists of as few as 16 bits in most microcomputers to as many as 60 bits in some large scientific machines. For other computers, the fundamental unit is the byte, which consists of eight bits. Some kinds of processing need bytes and some need larger units, so in word-type computers some provision is made for considering a word to be made up of several bytes, whereas byte-type computers also handle words made up of several bytes. Disk and tape storage generally store bytes.

All the information processed by computers has to be represented internally by binary digits using some code. In choosing a code, there are three primary considerations:

1. Ease of doing the required processing.
2. Economy of storage.
3. Simplicity and ease of human use.

These requirements cannot be met by a single code; therefore, different coding is used for (a) character data, (b) decimal numbers, (c) binary numbers, and (d) floating point numbers.

A.2. CHARACTER DATA

For storing character data, the most widely used code is the ASCII (American Standard Code for Information Interchange) code adopted by ANSI in 1977[K4]. It uses seven bits per character. The 128 possible combinations are used to encode the 26 uppercase letters, 26 lowercase letters, 10 digits, 33 special characters, and 33 encodings for various control signals that are normally not printed, including line-feed, backspace, carriage return, and bell, as well as certain characters used in communication protocol. ASCII code is shown in Table A.1. Frequently, a parity bit chosen to make the number of 1's odd (or even) is added to the ASCII code during transmission.

ASCII code was preceded by several codes used with teletype machines and paper-tape machines, including a code created in the early 1950s by IBM called BCD code. BCD uses six bits per character. The 64 possible codes are used for uppercase letters, digits, and a number of special characters, but are insufficient for handling lowercase and control characters. Modern data processing requires a larger character set. When IBM developed the IBM 360, they adopted an eight-bit code called EBCDIC (Extended BCD Interchange Code), a part of which is shown in Table A.2. This code is used on all modern IBM equipment and, for compati-

Table A.1   ASCII CODE

Last 4 Bits	First 3 Bits							
	000	001	010	011	100	101	110	111
0000	nul	^P	Space	0	@	P	'	p
0001	^A	^Q	!	1	A	Q	a	q
0010	^B	^R	"	2	B	R	b	r
0011	^C	^S	#	3	C	S	c	s
0100	^D	^T	$	4	D	T	d	t
0101	^E	^U	%	5	E	U	e	u
0110	^F	^V	&	6	F	V	f	v
0111	^G	^W	'	7	G	W	g	w
1000	^H	^X	(	8	H	X	h	x
1001	^I	^Y	)	9	I	Y	i	y
1010	^J	^Z	*	:	J	Z	j	z
1011	^K	esc	+	;	K	[	k	{
1100	^L	fs	,	<	L	\	l	|
1101	^M	gs	-	=	M	]	m	}
1110	^N	ks	.	>	N	^	n	~
1111	^O	us	/	?	O	_	o	del

Note: The symbols indicated by ^ followed by a letter are normally obtained on keyboards by depressing the CTRL key and the key for that letter. They have the following alternate designations:

^A	soh	^F	ack	^K	vt	^P	dle	^U	nak	^Z	sub
^B	stx	^G	bel	^L	ff	^Q	dc1	^V	syn
^C	etx	^H	bs	^M	cr	^R	dc2	^W	etb
^D	edt	^I	ht	^N	so	^S	dc3	^X	can
^E	enq	^J	lf	^O	si	^T	dc4	^Y	em

(^G is bell, ^H is backspace, ^J is line-feed, ^L is form-feed, and ^M is carriage return.)

Table A.2   EBCDIC CODE FOR UPPERCASE LETTERS AND NUMBERS

						0	1111 0000
A	1100 0001	J	1101 0001	/	1110 0001	1	1111 0001
B	1100 0010	K	1101 0010	S	1110 0010	2	1111 0010
C	1100 0011	L	1101 0011	T	1110 0011	3	1111 0011
D	1100 0100	M	1101 0100	U	1110 0100	4	1111 0100
E	1100 0101	N	1101 0101	V	1110 0101	5	1111 0101
F	1100 0110	O	1101 0110	W	1110 0110	6	1111 0110
G	1100 0111	P	1101 0111	X	1110 0111	7	1111 0111
H	1100 1000	Q	1101 1000	Y	1110 1000	8	1111 1000
I	1100 1001	R	1101 1001	Z	1110 1001	9	1111 1001

bility, on certain equipment manufactured by other corporations. EBCDIC, with its 256 possible encodings, encodes upper and lowercase letters, digits, defined control character codes, and still leaves many encodings undefined.

The EBCDIC code and its predecessor BCD are closely related to the Hollerith code, which is used with IBM (punched) cards. In fact, the BCD code was derived from the Hollerith code, and the EBCDIC code from BCD. There is now a card code defined for every EBCDIC character. The codes for uppercase letters and digits are shown in Table A.3. IBM cards are organized into 80 columns with 12 punch positions in each column. The positions are designated, from top to bottom, 12 (or +), 11 (or −), 0, 1, 2, 3, 4, 5, 6, 7, 8, and 9. In Hollerith code, as shown in Table A.3, digits are coded by a single punched hole. Uppercase letters are coded by a combination of two punches: the first punch is either 12, 11, or 0, and is called the zone punch; the other is chosen from 1 through 9, and is called the digit punch. Comparing Tables A.2 and A.3 shows that the first four bits in the EBCDIC code designate the zone, with 1100 for a 12 zone punch, 1101 for an 11 zone, 1110 for a 0 zone, and 1111 for no zone punch. The last four bits designate the digit punch. The full EBCDIC

Table A.3   HOLLERITH CODE FOR UPPERCASE LETTERS AND NUMBERS

						0	0
A	12-1	J	11-1	/	0-1	1	1
B	12-2	K	11-2	S	0-2	2	2
C	12-3	L	11-3	T	0-3	3	3
D	12-4	M	11-4	U	0-4	4	4
E	12-5	N	11-5	V	0-5	5	5
F	12-6	O	11-6	W	0-6	6	6
G	12-7	P	11-7	X	0-7	7	7
H	12-8	Q	11-8	Y	0-8	8	8
I	12-9	R	11-9	Z	0-9	9	9

and Hollerith codes also correspond in this general way. IBM's preference for EBCDIC results from their long history of working with cards and their desire for simple conversion between cards and computer equipment.

There is one difference between ASCII code and EBCDIC code that affects the user in an important way. In ASCII code, the binary code for a digit is less than the binary code for a letter. When a digit is compared to a letter, the digit is indicated to be smaller. In EBCDIC code, the opposite is true. This affects the outcome of the comparison of character strings in programs.

A.3. BINARY DATA

Because the computer stores binary digits, the binary representation of a number can be stored in the obvious way. Numbers usually are stored in words of fixed size, and the hardware is capable of processing words of one or more sizes. For example, in the "8-bit" microcomputers, binary numbers of 8 or 16 bits can be processed directly by machine instructions; in the "16-bit" microcomputers, words of 16 and possibly 32 bits can be processed. The IBM 370 and its successors process "half-words" of 16 bits and "full words" of 32 bits.

Representation of negative numbers brings in some complications. The simplest coding, from the viewpoint of a human, is to reserve the first bit for the sign, using 0 to represent $+$ and 1 to represent $-$. The rest of the bits represent the number in binary code. This is called true or *sign-magnitude* representation. For example, the 16-bit representations of $+1$ and -1 in this system are

$$+1 = 0000\ \ 0000\ \ 0000\ \ 0001$$
$$-1 = 1000\ \ 0000\ \ 0000\ \ 0001$$

In this system, there are 15 bits to represent the value of the number, assuming 16 bit words, which means that the value can range from 0 to $2^{15} - 1$. There are, unfortunately, two representations of zero, $+0$ and -0.

The most commonly used representation of negative numbers in modern computers is the so-called *2's complement* representation. For an n-bit word, a positive number is represented as before and a negative number $-x$ is represented by $2^n - x$. Numbers must be in the range from -2^{n-1} to $+2^{n-1} - 1$; the first bit will be zero for all positive numbers and one for all negative numbers. Zero has a unique representation, namely, a word of all zeros. For example, for $n = 16$,

$$+1 = 0000\ \ 0000\ \ 0000\ \ 0001$$
$$-1 = 1111\ \ 1111\ \ 1111\ \ 1111$$

It turns out that this system results in simpler and slightly faster hardware, and outside of the fact that it looks a little strange to humans, it has no disadvantage. Persons using higher level languages do not see the internal representation, anyway.

A.4. PACKED DECIMAL CODE

Sometimes it is convenient to represent decimal numbers in the computer and sometimes decimal computations also are done, either with built-in hardware for decimal arithmetic or by software. One motivation is to get answers that are precisely the same as what a person would get using a decimal calculator or pencil and paper. This is important especially for accounting, where a discrepancy of one penny is not tolerated, and it takes some considerable care to achieve that using binary arithmetic.

To represent one digit with a fixed number of bits requires four bits because three bits allow only eight patterns, although ten are needed. Almost invariably, the binary representation of a decimal digit using four bits is adopted.

0	0000	5	0101
1	0001	6	0110
2	0010	7	0111
3	0011	8	1000
4	0100	9	1001

Two digits then can be put in one byte; this representation is called *packed decimal*. (Representation of numerical data using one byte per digit, for example using ASCII or EBCDIC code, is called *unpacked* or *zoned decimal*. This form is used for I-O, but not generally for computation.) When a sign is used, one of the six unused codes is used for each $+$ and $-$, and the sign is stored at the right end of the number. Thus, the lowest-order byte will contain one digit and the sign. IBM chooses either 1100 or 1111 to represent $+$ and any of the other four codes to represent $-$. Thus, for example,

$$+100 = 0001\ 0000\ 0000\ 1100$$
$$-100 = 0001\ 0000\ 0000\ 1101$$

A.5. FLOATING POINT REPRESENTATION

In written text, floating point numbers are expressed in the following form:

$$x = f * b^e$$

where the fraction f is a number that is of order of magnitude near 1, if it is not exactly zero, b is the number base or radix, and e is the exponent. For example,

$$x = 1.6 * 10^{-19}$$
$$y = 3.0 * 10^{8}$$

Inside the computer, we have to be a little more precise. The base b usually is chosen to be 2, although ten is used occasionally, and IBM uses 16. Usually, if f is not exactly zero, f must be less than 1 but not less than $1/b$, so that the left of the radix point is all zeros and the first digit on the right is not zero; then the number is said to be normalized. There is a limit on e determined by the number of bits m allocated to it, and furthermore e is stored in excess notation, i.e., as the number $e' = e + 2^{m-1}$. Suppose, for example, that e is represented by a byte. Then, for example,

$$e = 0 \text{ is represented by } 10000000$$
$$e = 1 \text{ is represented by } 10000001$$
$$e = -1 \text{ is represented by } 01111111$$
$$e = 127 \text{ is represented by } 11111111$$
$$e = -127 \text{ is represented by } 00000001$$

The complete representation of a floating point number is a combination of three parts. First is the sign of the number, which is usually represented by a single bit: zero for plus, one for minus. Next is the representation of the exponent, usually in excess notation. Finally comes the fraction part f. The number of digits allocated to f determines the precision and may be anywhere from 24 binary digits to more than 100.

For example, in the DEC-10 and 20 series, single-precision floating point numbers are represented in 36-bit words: the first bit is the sign, the next eight bits represent the exponent in excess notation, and the last 27 bits are used for the fraction. If the number is normalized, the first of those 27 bits is a one, unless the value is zero, in which case all 27 bits are zero. In the IBM 370 series of machines, floating hexadecimal is used. The first bit is used as the sign and the next seven bits represent the exponent; a zero exponent is represented by 64. The fraction is 6 hexadecimal digits for single precision, 14 hexadecimal digits for double precision, and 30 hexadecimal digits for "extended" precision. If the number is normalized, the first hexadecimal digit must be nonzero, but its first bit may not be zero.

The IEEE recently has adopted a standard for floating point numbers for use in microcomputers[K5]. They defined standards for 32-bit words and 64-bit words. For the 32-bit format, the first bit is the sign, the next eight bits are the exponent, and the remaining 23 bits are used for the fraction. The fraction part is considered to be 24 bits, and a one to the left of the binary point is assumed but not stored. The stored value for the exponent is $e' = e + 127$, where e is the exponent value. Zero is represented by a stored exponent e' of all zeros and a zero fraction. An exponent of all ones with a fraction of all zeros is used to represent infinity and an exponent of all ones with a nonzero fraction is considered to be "not a number." The 64-bit format is similar, but it uses an 11-bit exponent and 48 bits to store the fraction.

A.6. CONCLUSION

Different codes are used in different situations, because a single code cannot meet the needs for efficiency and convenience in all circumstances. Thus, for example, the number $+100$ can be represented in at least four different ways:

ASCII Character Code

$$+ \qquad 1 \qquad 0 \qquad 0$$
$$0101011 \quad 0110001 \quad 0110000 \quad 0110000$$

Packed-Decimal Code

$$1 \quad 0 \quad 0 \quad +$$
$$00010000 \quad 00001100$$

Table A.4   DATA REPRESENTATION IN IBM COMPUTERS

Data Type	Length (bytes)	COBOL	FORTRAN	PL/I
integer binary	—	COMP	—	—
(half word)	2	PIC(1-4)	INTEGER*2	FIXED BINARY(15)
(full word)	4	PIC(5-9)	INTEGER*4	FIXED BINARY(31)
(double word)	8	PIC(10-18)	—	—
floating point				DECIMAL
(single precision)	4	COMP-1	REAL	FLOAT(6)
(double precision)	8	COMP-2	DOUBLE	FLOAT(16)
(extended precision)	16	—	—	FLOAT(33)
packed decimal	—	COMP-3	—	—
(n digits + sign)	(n+1)/2	PIC S9(n)	—	FIXED DECIMAL(n)
character code	n	DISPLAY	CHARACTER*n	CHARACTER(n)
(n digits—no sign)		PIC 9(n)		or PICTURE '(n)9'
logical				
(byte)	1	—	LOGICAL*1	BIT(8)
(word)	4	—	LOGICAL*4	BIT(32)

Fixed-Binary Code

0000 0000 0110 0100

Floating Binary (IEEE Standard)

0 10000101 10010000000000000000000

Knowledge of how data are coded is necessary to determine record lengths for files, and the details depend upon the computer and implementation used. As an example, we provide the relevant information for some large typical computers in Table A.4.

COBOL Program Examples

This appendix contains example programs written in COBOL to illustrate sequential processing and on-line processing with relative files, indexed files, and hashed files. All programs are written for the examples in Chapters 7 and 8 and provide more detailed illustrations of file programming. The first program is a sequential update program. Next is a main program for the on-line inventory system described in the examples in Chapter 7. The main program contains no file instructions, only calls to a subprogram that will do the file operations. Following that are three subprograms using a relative file, an indexed file, and a hashed file, respectively. With the relative file subprogram is a short program that uses sequential reading of the relative file to list its contents. There is also a short program with the indexed file subprogram to read that file sequentially and list its contents. Finally, with the hashed file subprogram there are short programs to create and initialize the hashed file and to dump its contents.

These programs are included to give examples of I-O programming. In other respects, the programs are very much simplified. All of these programs have been tested on a DEC TOPS-20 system. We have made a serious effort to make these programs conform to 1974 Standard COBOL. Parts of them are used as examples in Chapters 7 and 8.

B.1. BATCH UPDATE PROGRAM

This is a sequential update program using the single-loop approach. For this program, the original master file was created as a null file, that is, a file with no records. On the first run of the update program, a number of records were inserted.

```
1.  IDENTIFICATION DIVISION.
2.  PROGRAM-ID. SEQUP.
3.  ENVIRONMENT DIVISION.
4.  CONFIGURATION SECTION.
5.  SOURCE-COMPUTER. DECSYSTEM-20.
6.  OBJECT-COMPUTER. DECSYSTEM-20.

7.  INPUT-OUTPUT SECTION.
8.  FILE-CONTROL.
9.      SELECT OLD-MASTER ASSIGN TO DSK.
10.     SELECT NEW-MASTER ASSIGN TO DSK.
11.     SELECT TRANSACTIONS ASSIGN TO DSK.

12. DATA DIVISION.
13. FILE SECTION.
14. FD  OLD-MASTER
15.     VALUE OF ID IS "OLDMAS   "
16.     RECORDING MODE IS ASCII.
17. 01  OLD-MASTER-RECORD.
18.     02 PART-NO PICTURE XXXXXX.
19.     02 QUANTITY PICTURE 9999.
20.     02 DESCRIPTION PICTURE X(15).

21. FD  NEW-MASTER
22.     VALUE OF ID IS "NEWMAS   "
23.     RECORDING MODE IS ASCII.
24. 01  NEW-MASTER-RECORD.
25.     02 PART-NO PICTURE XXXXXX.
26.     02 QUANTITY PICTURE 9999.
27.     02 DESCRIPTION PICTURE X(15).

28. FD  TRANSACTIONS
29.     VALUE OF ID IS "TRANS    "
30.     RECORDING MODE IS ASCII.
31. 01  TRANSACTION-RECORD.
32.     02 PART-NO PICTURE XXXXXX.
33.     02 T-CODE PICTURE X.
34.         88 INSERT-RECORD VALUE IS "A".
35.         88 RECEIVE-GOODS VALUE IS "B".
36.         88 DISBURSE-GOODS VALUE IS "C".
37.         88 DELETE-RECORD VALUE IS "D".
38.         88 VALID-CODE VALUE IS "A" THRU "D".
39.         88 NEED-QUANTITY VALUE IS "A" THRU "C".
40.     02 QUANTITY PICTURE 9999.
41.     02 DESCRIPTION PICTURE X(15).

42. WORKING-STORAGE SECTION.
43. 77  OLD-QUANTITY PICTURE 9999.
44. 77  RECEIVE-COUNT PICTURE 9999.
45. 77  DISBURSE-COUNT PICTURE 9999.
46. 77  ERROR-FLAG PICTURE 9.
47.     88 OK VALUE IS 0.
48. 77  TRUE PICTURE 9 VALUE IS 1.
49. 77  FALSE PICTURE 9 VALUE IS 0.
```

```
50.* OLD-QUANTITY IS THE QUANTITY BEFORE THE BEGINNING
51.* OF THIS PERIOD, AND RECEIVE-COUNT AND DISBURSE-
52.* COUNT ARE THE QUANTITIES RECEIVED AND DISBURSED
53.* DURING THIS PERIOD. THE ERROR-FLAG IS SET TRUE
54.* WHEN AN ERRONEOUS TRANSACTION IS MET.

55. PROCEDURE DIVISION.
56. MAIN-PROGRAM.
57.    OPEN INPUT OLD-MASTER TRANSACTIONS.
58.    OPEN OUTPUT NEW-MASTER.
59.    MOVE LOW-VALUES TO PART-NO IN NEW-MASTER.
60.    PERFORM READ-TRANSACTION.
61.    PERFORM READ-MASTER.
62.    DISPLAY "PART-NO  DESCRIPTION   QUANTITY"
63.    DISPLAY
64.     "                    OLD  IN   OUT  NEW".
65.    PERFORM MAIN-LOOP UNTIL PART-NO IN NEW-MASTER-RECORD
66.        IS EQUAL TO HIGH-VALUES.
67.    CLOSE OLD-MASTER NEW-MASTER TRANSACTIONS.
68.    DISPLAY "PROCESSING FINISHED".
69.    STOP RUN.

70. MAIN-LOOP.

71.* EACH  TIME  THROUGH  THE MAIN LOOP,  ONE  RECORD
72.* IS  PROCESSED,  EITHER A TRANSACTION OR A  MASTER
73.* RECORD,  AND  THE NEXT RECORD IS READ.  THE FILES
74.* ARE   ASSUMED SORTED IN SEQUENCE BY  PART-NO,  AND
75.* ALL PROCESSING FOR ONE PART-NO IS DONE BEFORE  THE
76.* NEXT  HIGHER PART-NO IS STARTED.  ALL TRANSACTIONS
77.* FOR A GIVEN PART-NO ARE DONE,  AND AFTER THAT  THE
78.* MASTER  FILE RECORD IS PROCESSED.  ON END OF FILE,
79.* THE   COBOL  BUILT-IN  CONSTANT  "HIGH   VALUES"
80.* IS  INSERTED  INTO  THE  PART-NO  FIELD.  SUCH  A
81.* "RECORD" WON'T BE PROCESSED,  AND  ALL PROCESSING
82.* IS FINISHED WHEN  NO OTHER RECORDS REMAIN.
83.* SIMILARLY,  WHEN WE START,  THERE IS NO RECORD IN
84.* THE  NEW-MASTER-RECORD  STRUCTURE,  AND THE  FIRST
85.* RECORD TO GO  THERE MAY BE AN OLD MASTER RECORD OR
86.* AN INSERTED NEW RECORD.  WE START BY SETTING  ITS
87.* PART-NO TO THE COBOL CONSTANT "LOW-VALUES", AND WE
88.* NEVER  PROCESS  A  RECORD WHOSE PART-NO  IS  "LOW-
89.* VALUES".  ALSO,  THEN,  WHEN WE HAVE  COMPLETELY
90.* PROCESSED A MASTER RECORD,  WE INSERT "LOW VALUES"
91.* INTO ITS PART-NO FIELD TO MAKE CLEAR THAT FACT.

92.* IF   THERE  ARE  NO  MORE  TRANSACTIONS  FOR  THE
93.* CURRENT  NEW-MASTER-RECORD,  FINISH PROCESSING  IT
94.* AND WRITE IT OUT.

95.    IF PART-NO IN NEW-MASTER-RECORD IS LESS THAN PART-NO
96.        IN TRANSACTION-RECORD AND NOT EQUAL TO
97.        LOW-VALUES PERFORM FINAL-PROCESSING
```

```
 98.        PERFORM WRITE-MASTER
 99.        MOVE LOW-VALUES TO PART-NO IN NEW-MASTER-RECORD.

100.* IF THE NEXT PROCESSING IS TO APPLY TO THE RECORD
101.* IN OLD-MASTER-RECORD, MOVE IT TO NEW-MASTER-RECORD.

102.    IF PART-NO IN OLD-MASTER-RECORD IS NOT GREATER THAN
103.        PART-NO IN TRANSACTION-RECORD
104.        MOVE OLD-MASTER-RECORD TO NEW-MASTER-RECORD
105.        PERFORM READ-MASTER
106.        PERFORM INITIAL-PROCESSING

107.* OTHERWISE WE ARE READY TO PROCESS THE NEXT
108.* TRANSACTION.

109.    ELSE PERFORM EDIT-CHECK
110.        PERFORM PROCESS-TRANSACTION
111.        PERFORM READ-TRANSACTION.

112.* INITIAL DOES WHATEVER MUST BE DONE WHEN WE START
113.* PROCESSING A NEW MASTER RECORD.

114. INITIAL-PROCESSING.
115.    IF PART-NO IN NEW-MASTER-RECORD IS NOT EQUAL
116.          TO HIGH-VALUES
117.        MOVE QUANTITY IN NEW-MASTER-RECORD
118.          TO OLD-QUANTITY.
119.        MOVE ZERO TO RECEIVE-COUNT DISBURSE-COUNT.

120.* FINAL DOES WHATEVER MUST BE DONE AFTER ALL
121.* TRANSACTIONS HAVE BEEN PROCESSED FOR THE CURRENT
122.* MASTER RECORD TO COMPLETE ITS PROCESSING

123. FINAL-PROCESSING.
124.    DISPLAY PART-NO IN NEW-MASTER-RECORD " "
125.          DESCRIPTION IN NEW-MASTER-RECORD
126.          OLD-QUANTITY " "
127.          RECEIVE-COUNT " "
128.          DISBURSE-COUNT " "
129.          QUANTITY IN NEW-MASTER-RECORD.

130.* EDIT-CHECK CHECKS THE INFORMATION IN THE
131.* TRANSACTION FOR VALIDITY AND CONSISTENCY
132.* WITH THE MASTER FILE.

133. EDIT-CHECK.
134.    MOVE FALSE TO ERROR-FLAG.
135.    IF PART-NO IN TRANSACTION-RECORD IS NOT NUMERIC
136.        MOVE TRUE TO ERROR-FLAG
137.        DISPLAY  "--PART-NO NOT NUMERIC".

138.* NOTE THAT THE FOLLOWING TWO CHECKS CAN BE MADE
139.* BECAUSE IF THERE EXISTS A MASTER RECORD THAT
140.* MATCHES THIS TRANSACTION, THEN IT MUST NOW BE IN
141.* THE NEW-MASTER-RECORD STRUCTURE.
```

```
142.     IF OK AND INSERT-RECORD AND PART-NO IN
143.         TRANSACTION-RECORD IS EQUAL TO PART-NO IN
144.         NEW-MASTER-RECORD
145.         MOVE TRUE TO ERROR-FLAG
146.         DISPLAY "--DUPLICATE PART-NO"
147.     ELSE IF OK AND NOT INSERT-RECORD AND PART-NO IN
148.         TRANSACTION-RECORD IS NOT EQUAL TO PART-NO IN
149.         NEW-MASTER-RECORD
150.         MOVE TRUE TO ERROR-FLAG
151.         DISPLAY "--MASTER RECORD NOT FOUND".

152.     IF NOT VALID-CODE
153.         MOVE TRUE TO ERROR-FLAG
154.         DISPLAY "--INVALID CODE".
155.     IF NEED-QUANTITY AND QUANTITY IN
156.         TRANSACTION-RECORD IS NOT NUMERIC
157.         MOVE TRUE TO ERROR-FLAG
158.         DISPLAY "--QUANTITY NOT NUMERIC"
159.     ELSE IF DISBURSE-GOODS AND OK AND QUANTITY IN
160.         TRANSACTION-RECORD IS GREATER THAN QUANTITY
161.         IN NEW-MASTER-RECORD
162.         MOVE TRUE TO ERROR-FLAG
163.         DISPLAY "--NOT ENOUGH IN STOCK".
164.     IF INSERT-RECORD AND DESCRIPTION IN
165.         TRANSACTION-RECORD IS EQUAL TO SPACES
166.         MOVE TRUE TO ERROR-FLAG
167.         DISPLAY "--DESCRIPTION MISSING".
168.     IF DELETE-RECORD AND OK AND QUANTITY IN
169.         NEW-MASTER-RECORD IS NOT EQUAL TO ZERO
170.         MOVE TRUE TO ERROR-FLAG
171.         DISPLAY "QUANTITY NOT ZERO ON DELETE".

172.     IF NOT OK DISPLAY TRANSACTION-RECORD.

173. PROCESS-TRANSACTION.
174.     IF NOT OK DISPLAY "TRANSACTION NOT PROCESSED"
175.     ELSE IF INSERT-RECORD PERFORM INSERTION
176.     ELSE IF RECEIVE-GOODS PERFORM RECEPTION
177.     ELSE IF DISBURSE-GOODS PERFORM DISBURSAL
178.     ELSE PERFORM DELETION.

179. INSERTION.
180.     MOVE PART-NO IN TRANSACTION-RECORD TO PART-NO IN
181.         NEW-MASTER-RECORD.
182.     MOVE ZEROS TO QUANTITY IN NEW-MASTER-RECORD.
183.     MOVE DESCRIPTION IN TRANSACTION-RECORD TO
184.         DESCRIPTION IN NEW-MASTER-RECORD.
185.     PERFORM INITIAL-PROCESSING.
186.     PERFORM RECEPTION.

187. RECEPTION.
188.     ADD QUANTITY IN TRANSACTION-RECORD TO
189.         QUANTITY IN NEW-MASTER-RECORD.
```

```
190.      ADD QUANTITY IN TRANSACTION-RECORD TO RECEIVE-COUNT.

191. DISBURSAL.
192.      SUBTRACT QUANTITY IN TRANSACTION-RECORD FROM
193.          QUANTITY IN NEW-MASTER-RECORD.
194.      ADD QUANTITY IN TRANSACTION-RECORD TO DISBURSE-COUNT.

195. DELETION.
196.      DISPLAY PART-NO IN TRANSACTION-RECORD " DELETED".
197.      PERFORM FINAL-PROCESSING.
198.      MOVE LOW-VALUES TO PART-NO IN NEW-MASTER-RECORD.
199.* WITH LOW-VALUES IN THE PART-NO, IT WILL NOT BE WRITTEN
200.* ONTO THE NEW MASTER FILE.

201. READ-MASTER.
202.      IF PART-NO IN NEW-MASTER-RECORD IS NOT EQUAL TO
203.              HIGH-VALUES
204.          READ OLD-MASTER AT END MOVE HIGH-VALUES
205.              TO PART-NO IN OLD-MASTER-RECORD.

206. READ-TRANSACTION.
207.      READ TRANSACTIONS AT END MOVE HIGH-VALUES
208.          TO PART-NO IN TRANSACTION-RECORD.

209. WRITE-MASTER.
210.      WRITE NEW-MASTER-RECORD.
```

B.2. MAIN PROGRAM FOR ON-LINE UPDATE

This program calls a subprogram for all file operations. Subprograms using a relative file, an indexed file, and a hashed file follow. These subroutines have multiple entry points, one each for open, close, read, write, rewrite, and delete. The subroutine could equally well have been written with one entry point and a parameter that designates which function to perform. The corresponding PL/I program examples are so written.

```
1. IDENTIFICATION DIVISION.
2. PROGRAM-ID. ONLINE.

3.* THIS IS THE MAIN PROGRAM FOR AN IMPLEMENTATION OF THE
4.* ON-LINE INVENTORY SYSTEM. THE PART-NO'S ARE ASSUMED
5.* TO BE SIX-DIGIT NUMBERS, BUT 000000 IS NOT ALLOWED AS
6.* A KEY.

7.* THIS SYSTEM IS VERY MUCH OVERSIMPLIFIED. THE USUAL
8.* PRACTICAL SYSTEM WOULD HAVE TO KEEP A RECORD OF
9.* EVERY TRANSACTION AND PROVIDE FOR COMPLETE REPORTS.
10.* THE PURPOSE OF THIS EXAMPLE IS TO ILLUSTRATE THE
11.* PROGRAMMING OF INPUT-OUTPUT OPERATIONS IN COBOL.
```

```
12.* THIS PROGRAM CALLS A SUBPROGRAM TO DO ALL FILE
13.* OPERATIONS. FOLLOWING THIS PROGRAM, THERE ARE THREE
14.* VERSIONS OF THE FILE I-O SUBPROGRAM, ONE USING A
15.* RELATIVE FILE, ONE USING AN INDEXED FILE, AND ONE
16.* USING A HASHED FILE. ANY OF THEM WILL RUN WITH THIS
17.* MAIN PROGRAM WITH NO CHANGES IN THE MAIN PROGRAM.

18. ENVIRONMENT DIVISION.
19. CONFIGURATION SECTION.
20. SOURCE-COMPUTER. DECSYSTEM-20.
21. OBJECT-COMPUTER. DECSYSTEM-20.

22. DATA DIVISION.
23. WORKING-STORAGE SECTION.
24. 77  INPUT-PART-NO PICTURE 999999.
25. 77  INPUT-QUANTITY PICTURE 9999.
26. 77  INPUT-DESCRIPTION PICTURE X(15).
27.*     ABOVE ARE VALUES READ FROM TERMINAL
28. 77  RECORD-FLAG PICTURE 9.
29.      88 RECORD-FOUND VALUE IS 1.
30.*     RECORD FLAG IS SET TO SHOW WHETHER A RECORD IS
31.*     FOUND WHEN AN ATTEMPT TO READ IS MADE.
32. 77  ERROR-FLAG PICTURE 9.
33.      88 OK VALUE IS 0.
34.*     ERROR-FLAG IS SET TRUE WHEN AN ERROR IS
35.*     FOUND IN DATA READ FROM THE TERMINAL.
36. 77  TRUE PICTURE 9 VALUE IS 1.
37. 77  FALSE PICTURE 9 VALUE IS ZERO.
38. 77  COMMAND PICTURE X.
39.*     THIS IS THE ONE-LETTER COMMAND READ FROM
40.*     THE TERMINAL.
41.      88 INSERT-RECORD VALUE IS "A".
42.      88 RECEIVE-GOODS VALUE IS "B".
43.      88 DISBURSE-GOODS VALUE IS "C".
44.      88 DELETE-RECORD VALUE IS "D".
45.      88 INQUIRE VALUE IS "Q".
46.      88 STOP-RUN VALUE IS "S".
47.      88 HELP VALUE IS "H".
48.      88 VALID-COMMAND VALUE IS "A" THRU "D",
49.         "Q", "S", "H".
50.      88 NEED-QUANTITY VALUE IS "A" THRU "C".
51.      88 NEED-TO-READ VALUE IS "A" THRU "D", "Q".

52. 01  MASTER-RECORD.
53.      02 PART-NO PICTURE 999999.
54.      02 QUANTITY PICTURE 9999.
55.      02 DESCRIPTION PICTURE X(15).

56. PROCEDURE DIVISION.

57.*THERE ARE SIX ENTRIES TO THE FILE-HANDLING SUBPROGRAM:
58.*     OPENM     OPEN THE MASTER FILE
59.*     CLOSEM    CLOSE THE MASTER FILE
```

```
60.*    READM     IF THE RECORD WITH THE KEY IN THE MASTER
61.*              RECORD IS FOUND, SET THE RECORD FLAG TRUE
62.*              AND READ THE MASTER FILE INTO MASTER-RECORD
63.*    WRITEM    WRITE A NEW RECORD FROM MASTER-RECORD
64.*    REWRM     REWRITE FROM THE MASTER-RECORD
65.*    DELM      DELETE THE RECORD LAST READ.
66. MAIN-PROGRAM.
67.     DISPLAY "INVENTORY SYSTEM--COMMAND H FOR HELP".
68.     CALL OPENM.
69.     PERFORM MAIN-LOOP UNTIL STOP-RUN.
70.     CALL CLOSEM.
71.     DISPLAY "INVENTORY SYSTEM--END OF RUN".
72.     STOP RUN.
73. MAIN-LOOP.
74.*    THIS LOOP IS PERFORMED ONCE FOR EACH
75.*    TRANSACTION READ FROM THE TERMINAL.
76.     MOVE FALSE TO ERROR-FLAG.
77.     PERFORM GET-COMMAND.
78.     IF NEED-TO-READ PERFORM GET-PART-NO.
79.     IF OK AND NEED-TO-READ CALL READM
80.         USING MASTER-RECORD RECORD-FLAG
81.         PERFORM CHECKING.
82.     IF OK AND NEED-QUANTITY PERFORM GET-QUANTITY.
83.     IF OK AND INSERT-RECORD PERFORM GET-DESCRIPTION.
84.     IF NOT OK DISPLAY "NOT DONE BECAUSE OF ERROR"
85.     ELSE IF INSERT-RECORD PERFORM INSERTION
86.     ELSE IF RECEIVE-GOODS PERFORM RECEPTION
87.     ELSE IF DISBURSE-GOODS PERFORM DISBURSAL
88.     ELSE IF DELETE-RECORD PERFORM DELETION
89.     ELSE IF HELP PERFORM HELP-LISTING.
90.     IF OK AND DELETE-RECORD DISPLAY "RECORD DELETED"
91.     ELSE IF OK AND NEED-TO-READ
92.         DISPLAY PART-NO IN MASTER-RECORD " "
93.                 DESCRIPTION IN MASTER-RECORD
94.                 " QUANTITY ON HAND "
95.                 QUANTITY IN MASTER-RECORD.
96. GET-COMMAND.
97.     DISPLAY "ENTER COMMAND".
98.     ACCEPT COMMAND.
99.     IF NOT VALID-COMMAND MOVE TRUE TO ERROR-FLAG
100.        DISPLAY "INVALID COMMAND".
101. GET-PART-NO.
102.     DISPLAY "ENTER PART-NO (SIX DIGITS)".
103.     ACCEPT INPUT-PART-NO.
104.     IF INPUT-PART-NO IS NOT NUMERIC
105.         MOVE TRUE TO ERROR-FLAG
106.         DISPLAY "PART-NO NOT ALL DIGITS"
```

```
107.     ELSE IF INPUT-PART-NO IS EQUAL TO 000000
108.         MOVE TRUE TO ERROR-FLAG
109.         DISPLAY "NOT ALLOWED AS PART-NO"
110.     ELSE MOVE INPUT-PART-NO TO PART-NO IN MASTER-RECORD.
111.*    TO SEND TO THE SUB-PROGRAM TO USE AS KEY IN READING.

112. CHECKING.
113.     IF INSERT-RECORD AND RECORD-FOUND
114.         MOVE TRUE TO ERROR-FLAG
115.         DISPLAY "DUPLICATE PART-NO FOUND"
116.     ELSE IF NOT INSERT-RECORD AND NOT RECORD-FOUND
117.         MOVE TRUE TO ERROR-FLAG
118.         DISPLAY "RECORD NOT FOUND".

119. GET-DESCRIPTION.
120.     DISPLAY "ENTER DESCRIPTION--MAX 15 CHAR".
121.     ACCEPT INPUT-DESCRIPTION.
122.     IF INPUT-DESCRIPTION IS EQUAL TO SPACES
123.         MOVE TRUE TO ERROR-FLAG
124.         DISPLAY "NOT ENTERED".

125. GET-QUANTITY.
126.     DISPLAY "ENTER QUANTITY (FOUR DIGITS)".
127.     ACCEPT INPUT-QUANTITY.
128.     IF INPUT-QUANTITY IS NOT NUMERIC
129.         MOVE TRUE TO ERROR-FLAG
130.         DISPLAY "NOT NUMERIC"
131.     ELSE IF DISBURSE-GOODS AND INPUT-QUANTITY
132.         IS GREATER THAN QUANTITY IN MASTER-RECORD
133.         MOVE TRUE TO ERROR-FLAG
134.         DISPLAY "NOT ENOUGH IN STOCK".

135. INSERTION.
136.*    NOTE THAT WE HAVE PREVIOUSLY SEARCHED FOR A
137.*    RECORD WITH THIS PART-NO IN THE MASTER FILE, AND
138.*    HAVE FOUND NO RECORD WITH THIS PART-NO IN THE FILE.
139.     MOVE INPUT-QUANTITY TO QUANTITY IN MASTER-RECORD.
140.     MOVE INPUT-DESCRIPTION TO DESCRIPTION IN MASTER-RECORD.
141.     CALL WRITEM USING MASTER-RECORD.

142. RECEPTION.
143.     ADD INPUT-QUANTITY TO QUANTITY IN MASTER-RECORD.
144.     CALL REWRM USING MASTER-RECORD.

145. DISBURSAL.
146.     SUBTRACT INPUT-QUANTITY FROM
147.         QUANTITY IN MASTER-RECORD.
148.     CALL REWRM USING MASTER-RECORD.

149. HELP-LISTING.
150.     DISPLAY "COMMANDS:".
151.     DISPLAY "A  INSERT RECORD".
152.     DISPLAY "B  RECEIVE GOODS".
```

```
153,       DISPLAY "C  DISBURSE GOODS",
154,       DISPLAY "D  DELETE RECORD",
155,       DISPLAY "Q  INQUIRY",
156,       DISPLAY "H  HELP--LIST COMMANDS",
157,       DISPLAY "S  STOP RUN",

158, DELETION,
159,       CALL DELM,
```

B.3. RELATIVE FILE I-O PROCEDURES

The following program is a subprogram with six entry points (open, close, read, write, rewrite, and delete) that can be used with the main program in Section B.2, and uses a relative file with the part numbers as relative keys. Note that unless most possible keys are actually in use, this system will be quite wasteful of disk space.

The relative file is created by simply opening the file for output, inserting some records if desired, and then closing it.

```
1, IDENTIFICATION DIVISION,
2, PROGRAM-ID, FILEIO,

3,*THIS FILE-IO SUBPROGRAM USES A RELATIVE FILE AND THE
4,*PART-NO IS USED AS THE RELATIVE KEY, NOTE THAT THIS
5,*MEANS THAT IF ONLY A SMALL FRACTION OF ALL POSSIBLE
6,*PART NUMBERS ARE USED, THEN DISK SPACE WILL NOT BE
7,*USED EFFICIENTLY,

8,*THERE ARE SIX ENTRY POINTS:
9,*       OPENM    OPEN THE MASTER FILE
10,*      CLOSEM   CLOSE THE MASTER FILE
11,*      READM    READ THE MASTER FILE RECORD WHOSE KEY IS
12,*               THE PART-NO IN THE LINK-RECORD, INTO
13,*               THE LINK-RECORD AND SET THE RECORD-FLAG
14,*               TRUE IF THE RECORD IS FOUND, FALSE IF NOT,
15,*      WRITEM   WRITE A NEW RECORD FROM THE LINK-RECORD
16,*      REWRM    REWRITE FROM THE LINK-RECORD
17,*      DELM     DELETE THE LAST RECORD READ,

18, ENVIRONMENT DIVISION,
19, CONFIGURATION SECTION,
20, SOURCE-COMPUTER, DECSYSTEM-20,
21, OBJECT-COMPUTER, DECSYSTEM-20,

22, INPUT-OUTPUT SECTION,
23, FILE-CONTROL,
24,      SELECT MASTER-FILE ASSIGN TO DSK
25,          ORGANIZATION IS RELATIVE
26,          ACCESS IS RANDOM
27,          RELATIVE KEY IS PART-NO-KEY,
```

```
28. DATA DIVISION.
29. FILE SECTION.
30. FD  MASTER-FILE
31.     VALUE OF ID IS "MASTER    "
32.     BLOCK CONTAINS 1 RECORD
33.     RECORDING MODE IS ASCII.
34. 01  MASTER-RECORD.
35.     02 PART-NO PICTURE 999999.
36.     02 QUANTITY PICTURE 9999.
37.     02 DESCRIPTION PICTURE X(15).

38. WORKING-STORAGE SECTION.
39. 77 PART-NO-KEY PICTURE 999999.
40. 77 TRUE PICTURE 9 VALUE 1.
41. 77 FALSE PICTURE 9 VALUE 0.

42. LINKAGE SECTION.
43. 77 RECORD-FLAG PICTURE 9.
44. 01 LINK-RECORD.
45.     02 PART-NO PICTURE 999999.
46.     02 QUANTITY PICTURE 9999.
47.     02 DESCRIPTION PICTURE X(15).

48. PROCEDURE DIVISION.
49.     ENTRY OPENM.
50.     OPEN I-O MASTER-FILE.
51.     EXIT PROGRAM.

52.     ENTRY CLOSEM.
53.     CLOSE MASTER-FILE.
54.     EXIT PROGRAM.

55.     ENTRY READM USING LINK-RECORD RECORD-FLAG.
56.     MOVE PART-NO IN LINK-RECORD TO PART-NO-KEY.
57.     MOVE TRUE TO RECORD-FLAG.
58.     READ MASTER-FILE INTO LINK-RECORD
59.         INVALID KEY MOVE FALSE TO RECORD-FLAG.
60.     EXIT PROGRAM.

61.     ENTRY WRITEM USING LINK-RECORD.
62.     WRITE MASTER-RECORD FROM LINK-RECORD
63.         INVALID KEY DISPLAY "INVALID KEY ON WRITE".
64.     EXIT PROGRAM.
65.*    NOTE THAT INVALID KEY WON'T OCCUR BECAUSE
66.*    AN ATTEMPT TO READ THE RECORD HAS BEEN
67.*    MADE, AND NO ATTEMPT TO WRITE WILL BE
68.*    MADE IF THE RECORD EXISTS. HOWEVER COBOL
69.*    REQUIRES THAT THIS STATEMENT BE PRESENT.

70.     ENTRY REWRM USING LINK-RECORD.
71.     REWRITE MASTER-RECORD FROM LINK-RECORD
72.         INVALID KEY DISPLAY "INVALID KEY ON REWRITE".
73.     EXIT PROGRAM.
74.*    NOTE THAT INVALID KEY WON'T OCCUR BECAUSE
```

```
75.*     AN ATTEMPT TO READ THE RECORD HAS BEEN MADE,
76.*     AND NO ATTEMPT TO REWRITE WILL BE MADE IF
77.*     THE RECORD DOES NOT EXIST. HOWEVER COBOL
78.*     REQUIRES THAT THIS STATEMENT BE PRESENT.

79.      ENTRY DELM.
80.      DELETE MASTER-FILE INVALID KEY
81.          DISPLAY "INVALID KEY ON DELETE".
82.      EXIT PROGRAM.
83.*     NOTE THAT INVALID KEY WON'T OCCUR BECAUSE
84.*     AN ATTEMPT TO READ THE RECORD HAS BEEN MADE,
85.*     AND NO ATTEMPT TO DELETE WILL BE MADE IF
86.*     THE RECORD DOES NOT EXIST. HOWEVER COBOL
87.*     REQUIRES THAT THIS STATEMENT BE PRESENT.
```

The following is a program that will read the relative file from the preceding program and list its contents in the order in which they are stored in the file, that is, in sequence by part number.

```
1.  IDENTIFICATION DIVISION.
2.  PROGRAM-ID. RELREP.
3.* THIS PROGRAM PRINTS A VERY SIMPLE REPORT CONSISTING
4.* OF ONE LINE PER MASTER RECORD FOR THE RELATIVE-FILE
5.* IMPLEMENTATION OF THE ON-LINE INVENTORY SYSTEM,
6.* SHOWING THE PART-NO, DESCRIPTION, AND QUANTITY. IT
7.* ILLUSTRATES THE USE OF SEQUENTIAL READING OF A
8.* RELATIVE FILE.

9.  ENVIRONMENT DIVISION.
10. CONFIGURATION SECTION.
11. SOURCE-COMPUTER. DECSYSTEM-20.
12. OBJECT-COMPUTER. DECSYSTEM-20.

13. INPUT-OUTPUT SECTION.
14. FILE-CONTROL.
15.     SELECT MASTER-FILE ASSIGN TO DSK
16.         ORGANIZATION IS RELATIVE
17.         ACCESS IS SEQUENTIAL.

18. DATA DIVISION.
19. FILE SECTION.
20. FD  MASTER-FILE
21.     VALUE OF ID IS "MASTER    "
22.     BLOCK CONTAINS 1 RECORD
23.     RECORDING MODE IS ASCII.
24. 01  MASTER-RECORD.
25.     02 PART-NO PICTURE 999999.
26.     02 QUANTITY PICTURE 9999.
27.     02 DESCRIPTION PICTURE X(15).

28. WORKING-STORAGE SECTION.
29. 77  END-FLAG PICTURE 9.
30.     88 END-OF-FILE VALUE IS 1.
```

```
31.  77  TRUE PICTURE 9 VALUE IS 1.
32.  77  FALSE PICTURE 9 VALUE IS ZERO.

33.  PROCEDURE DIVISION.
34.  MAIN-PROGRAM.
35.      DISPLAY "INVENTORY REPORT".
36.      DISPLAY "PART-NO    DESCRIPTION     QUANTITY".
37.      OPEN INPUT MASTER-FILE.
38.      MOVE FALSE TO END-FLAG.
39.      READ MASTER-FILE AT END MOVE TRUE TO END-FLAG.
40.      PERFORM MAIN-LOOP UNTIL END-OF-FILE.
41.      CLOSE MASTER-FILE.
42.      DISPLAY "INVENTORY SYSTEM--END OF RUN".
43.      STOP RUN.

44.  MAIN-LOOP.
45.      DISPLAY PART-NO "     " DESCRIPTION QUANTITY.
46.      READ MASTER-FILE AT END MOVE TRUE TO END-FLAG.
47.*     NOTE THAT THIS WILL SKIP OVER UNUSED PART-NO'S,
48.*     READING ONLY ACTIVE RECORDS.
```

B.4. INDEXED SEQUENTIAL FILE I-O PROCEDURES

This subprogram, when used with the main program in Section B.2, implements the on-line inventory system using a COBOL indexed file. With this implementation of COBOL, an indexed file is created using utility programs that are provided by the computer manufacturer. The amount of space for data and indices must be specified at that time. An empty file may be created and afterwards loaded in any sequence. Alternatively, the file may be initially loaded in key order sequence when it is created.

```
1.  IDENTIFICATION DIVISION.
2.  PROGRAM-ID. FILEIO.

3.*THIS FILE-IO SUBPROGRAM USES AN INDEXED FILE AND THE
4.*PART-NO IS USED AS THE RECORD  KEY.

5.*THERE ARE SIX ENTRY POINTS:
6.*      OPENM   OPEN THE MASTER FILE
7.*      CLOSEM  CLOSE THE MASTER FILE
8.*      READM   READ THE MASTER FILE RECORD WHOSE KEY IS
9.*              THE PART-NO IN LINK-RECORD, INTO LINK-RECORD,
10.*             AND SET THE RECORD-FLAG TRUE IF FOUND.
11.*     WRITEM  WRITE A NEW RECORD FROM THE LINK-RECORD
12.*     REWRM   REWRITE FROM THE LINK-RECORD
13.*     DELM    DELETE THE LAST RECORD READ.

14.  ENVIRONMENT DIVISION.
15.  CONFIGURATION SECTION.
```

```
16. SOURCE-COMPUTER. DECSYSTEM-20.
17. OBJECT-COMPUTER. DECSYSTEM-20.

18. INPUT-OUTPUT SECTION.
19. FILE-CONTROL.
20.     SELECT MASTER-FILE ASSIGN TO DSK
21.         ORGANIZATION IS INDEXED
22.         ACCESS IS RANDOM
23.         RECORD KEY IS PART-NO IN MASTER-RECORD.

24. DATA DIVISION.
25. FILE SECTION.
26. FD  MASTER-FILE
27.     VALUE OF ID IS "MASTERIDX"
28.     BLOCK CONTAINS 1 RECORD
29.     RECORDING MODE IS ASCII.
30. 01  MASTER-RECORD.
31.     02 PART-NO PICTURE XXXXXX.
32.     02 QUANTITY PICTURE 9999.
33.     02 DESCRIPTION PICTURE X(15).

34. WORKING-STORAGE SECTION.
35. 77  TRUE PICTURE 9 VALUE 1.
36. 77  FALSE PICTURE 9 VALUE 0.

37. LINKAGE SECTION.
38. 77  RECORD-FLAG PICTURE 9.
39.*    SET TRUE (FOUND) OR FALSE (NOT FOUND) BY READM.
40. 01  LINK-RECORD.
41.     02 PART-NO PICTURE 999999.
42.     02 QUANTITY PICTURE 9999.
43.     02 DESCRIPTION PICTURE X(15).

44. PROCEDURE DIVISION.
45.     ENTRY OPENM.
46.     OPEN I-O MASTER-FILE.
47.     EXIT PROGRAM.

48.     ENTRY CLOSEM.
49.     CLOSE MASTER-FILE.
50.     EXIT PROGRAM.

51.     ENTRY READM USING LINK-RECORD RECORD-FLAG.
52.     MOVE PART-NO IN LINK-RECORD
53.         TO PART-NO IN MASTER-RECORD.
54.     MOVE TRUE TO RECORD-FLAG.
55.     READ MASTER-FILE INTO LINK-RECORD
56.         INVALID KEY MOVE FALSE TO RECORD-FLAG.
57.     EXIT PROGRAM.
58.     ENTRY WRITEM USING LINK-RECORD.
59.     WRITE MASTER-RECORD FROM LINK-RECORD
60.         INVALID KEY DISPLAY "INVALID KEY ON WRITE".
61.     EXIT PROGRAM.
```

```
62.*    NOTE THAT INVALID KEY WON'T OCCUR BECAUSE
63.*    AN ATTEMPT TO READ THE RECORD HAS BEEN
64.*    MADE, AND NO ATTEMPT TO WRITE WILL BE
65.*    MADE IF THE RECORD EXISTS. HOWEVER COBOL
66.*    REQUIRES THAT THIS STATEMENT BE PRESENT.

67.     ENTRY REWRM USING LINK-RECORD.
68.     REWRITE MASTER-RECORD FROM LINK-RECORD
69.         INVALID KEY DISPLAY "INVALID KEY ON REWRITE".
70.     EXIT PROGRAM.
71.*    NOTE THAT INVALID KEY WON'T OCCUR BECAUSE
72.*    AN ATTEMPT TO READ THE RECORD HAS BEEN MADE,
73.*    AND NO ATTEMPT TO REWRITE WILL BE MADE IF
74.*    THE RECORD DOES NOT EXIST. HOWEVER COBOL
75.*    REQUIRES THAT THIS STATEMENT BE PRESENT.

76.     ENTRY DELM.
77.     DELETE MASTER-FILE INVALID KEY
78.         DISPLAY "INVALID KEY ON DELETE".
79.     EXIT PROGRAM.
80.*    NOTE THAT INVALID KEY WON'T OCCUR BECAUSE
81.*    AN ATTEMPT TO READ THE RECORD HAS BEEN MADE,
82.*    AND NO ATTEMPT TO DELETE WILL BE MADE IF
83.*    THE RECORD DOES NOT EXIST. HOWEVER COBOL
84.*    REQUIRES THAT THIS STATEMENT BE PRESENT.
```

The following program will list the contents of the indexed sequential file of the previous program in sequence by part number using a sequential read statement.

```
1.  IDENTIFICATION DIVISION.
2.  PROGRAM-ID. INDREP.

3.* THIS PROGRAM PRINTS A VERY SIMPLE REPORT CONSISTING
4.* OF ONE LINE PER MASTER RECORD FOR THE INDEXED-FILE
5.* IMPLEMENTATION OF THE ON-LINE INVENTORY SYSTEM,
6.* SHOWING THE PART-NO, DESCRIPTION, AND QUANTITY. IT
7.* ILLUSTRATES THE USE OF SEQUENTIAL READING OF AN
8.* INDEXED FILE.

9.  ENVIRONMENT DIVISION.
10. CONFIGURATION SECTION.
11. SOURCE-COMPUTER. DECSYSTEM-20.
12. OBJECT-COMPUTER. DECSYSTEM-20.

13. INPUT-OUTPUT SECTION.
14. FILE-CONTROL.
15.     SELECT MASTER-FILE ASSIGN TO DSK
16.         ORGANIZATION IS INDEXED
17.         ACCESS IS SEQUENTIAL
18.         RECORD KEY IS PART-NO.

19. DATA DIVISION.
```

```
20. FILE SECTION.
21. FD  MASTER-FILE
22.     VALUE OF ID IS "MASTERIDX"
23.     BLOCK CONTAINS 1 RECORD
24.     RECORDING MODE IS ASCII.
25. 01  MASTER-RECORD.
26.     02 PART-NO PICTURE 999999.
27.     02 QUANTITY PICTURE 9999.
28.     02 DESCRIPTION PICTURE X(15).

29. WORKING-STORAGE SECTION.
30. 77  END-FLAG PICTURE 9.
31.     88 END-OF-FILE VALUE IS 1.
32. 77  TRUE PICTURE 9 VALUE IS 1.
33. 77  FALSE PICTURE 9 VALUE IS ZERO.

34. PROCEDURE DIVISION.
35. MAIN-PROGRAM.
36.     DISPLAY "INVENTORY REPORT".
37.     DISPLAY "PART-NO   DESCRIPTION    QUANTITY".
38.     OPEN INPUT MASTER-FILE.
39.     MOVE FALSE TO END-FLAG.
40.     READ MASTER-FILE AT END MOVE TRUE TO END-FLAG.
41.     PERFORM MAIN-LOOP UNTIL END-OF-FILE.
42.     CLOSE MASTER-FILE.
43.     DISPLAY "INVENTORY SYSTEM--END OF RUN".
44.     STOP RUN.

45. MAIN-LOOP.
46.     DISPLAY PART-NO "    " DESCRIPTION QUANTITY.
47.     READ MASTER-FILE AT END MOVE TRUE TO END-FLAG.
```

B.5. HASHED FILE I-O PROCEDURES

The following subprogram, again usable with the main program in Section B.2, implements a hashed file system. Following this program is a program that will create and suitably initialize a hashed file for use with this system.

```
 1. IDENTIFICATION DIVISION.
 2. PROGRAM-ID. FILEIO.

 3.*THIS FILE-IO SUBPROGRAM USES A HASHED FILE AND THE
 4.*PART-NO IS USED AS THE KEY. THE FILE HAS 5 RECORDS
 5.*PER BLOCK, ONE BLOCK BEING USED AS ONE BUCKET, AND
 6.*HAS 23 BUCKETS. THE HASHED ADDRESS IS CALCULATED BY
 7.*DIVIDING THE PART-NO BY 23 AND USING THE REMAINDER.

 8.*THERE ARE SIX ENTRY POINTS:
 9.*    OPENM    OPEN THE MASTER FILE
10.*    CLOSEM   CLOSE THE MASTER FILE
```

```
11.*     READM    READ THE MASTER FILE RECORD WHOSE KEY IS
12.*              THE PART-NO IN THE LINK-RECORD, INTO
13.*              THE LINK-RECORD AND SET THE RECORD-FLAG
14.*              TRUE IF THE RECORD IS FOUND, FALSE IF NOT.
15.*     WRITEM   WRITE A NEW RECORD FROM THE LINK-RECORD
16.*     REWRM    REWRITE FROM THE LINK-RECORD
17.*     DELM     DELETE THE LAST RECORD READ.

18. ENVIRONMENT DIVISION.
19. INPUT-OUTPUT SECTION.
20. FILE-CONTROL.
21.     SELECT MASTER-FILE ASSIGN TO DSK
22.         ORGANIZATION IS RELATIVE
23.         ACCESS IS RANDOM
24.         RELATIVE KEY IS BUCKET-NO.

25. DATA DIVISION.
26. FILE SECTION.
27. FD  MASTER-FILE
28.     VALUE OF ID IS "MASTER    "
29.     BLOCK CONTAINS 1 RECORDS
30.     RECORD CONTAINS 125 CHARACTERS
31.     RECORDING MODE IS ASCII
32.     DATA RECORD IS MASTER-BLOCK.

33. 01  MASTER-BLOCK.
34.     02 MASTER-RECORD OCCURS 5 TIMES.
35.         03 PART-NO PICTURE 999999.
36.         03 QUANTITY PICTURE 9999.
37.         03 DESCRIPTION PICTURE X(15).

38. WORKING-STORAGE SECTION.
39. 77  BUCKET-NO PICTURE 9999.
40. 77  N PICTURE 9999.
41.*    N IS RECORD NUMBER WITHIN BUCKET
42. 77  J PICTURE 9999.
43. 77  K PICTURE 9999.
44.*    J AND K ARE TEMPORARIES.
45. 77  BUCKET-COUNT PICTURE 9999.
46.*    COUNTS BUCKETS READ TO CHECK FOR FULL FILE
47. 77  Q PICTURE 999999.
48.*    Q STORES UNUSED QUOTIENT ON DIVIDE
49.*    WHEN THE HASHED ADDRESS IS CALCULATED.
50. 77  H PICTURE 9999.
51.*    HASHED ADDRESS OF A RECORD THAT MAY BE MOVED
52.*    WHILE DELETING A RECORD
53. 77  SEARCH-FLAG PICTURE 9.
54.     88 END-OF-SEARCH VALUE IS 1.
55. 77  RECORD-CHECK-FLAG PICTURE 9.
56.     88 CHECK-FINISHED VALUE IS 1.
57. 77  MOVE-FLAG PICTURE 9.
58.     88 MOVE-RECORD VALUE IS 1.
```

```
59. 77  TRUE PICTURE 9 VALUE IS 1.
60. 77  FALSE PICTURE 9 VALUE IS ZERO.
61. 77  MAX-BUCKET PICTURE 9999 VALUE IS 23.
62.*    THIS IS THE NUMBER OF BUCKETS IMPLEMENTED
63. 77  BUCKET-SIZE PICTURE 99 VALUE IS 5.
64.*    THIS IS THE NUMBER OF RECORDS PER BUCKET.
65. 77  HASH-CONSTANT PICTURE 9999 VALUE IS 23.
66.*    WE DIVIDE BY THIS AND USE THE REMAINDER AS
67.*    THE HASHED ADDRESS.
68. 77  LAST-BUCKET PICTURE 9999.
69.*    THIS IS THE LAST BUCKET TO BE EXAMINED WHEN
70.*    DELETING, IF THE FILE IS FULL.
71. 77  OPEN-BUCKET PICTURE 9999.
72. 77  OPEN-RECORD PICTURE 9999.
73.*    THESE ARE USED TO SAVE THE LOCATION OF AN OPEN
74.*    PLACE LEFT BY A DELETED RECORD WHILE WE SEARCH
75.*    TO SEE WHETHER SOME OTHER RECORD SHOULD BE
76.*    MOVED INTO THAT PLACE TO REDUCE THE LENGTH OF
77.*    SEARCH.
78. 01  TEMP-RECORD.
79.     02 PART-NO PICTURE 999999.
80.     02 QUANTITY PICTURE 9999.
81.     02 DESCRIPTION PICTURE X(15).
82.*    THIS IS USED ALSO ON DELETING, TO STORE A RECORD
83.*    TEMPORARILY WHILE READING THE BLOCK IT WILL BE
84.*    MOVED INTO.

85. LINKAGE SECTION.
86. 77  RECORD-FLAG PICTURE 9.
87.     88 RECORD-FOUND VALUE IS 1.
88.*    RECORD FLAG IS TRUE WHEN A RECORD IS FOUND,
89.*    FALSE WHEN NOT FOUND, ON READING A RECORD.
90. 01  LINK-RECORD.
91.     02 PART-NO PICTURE 999999.
92.     02 QUANTITY PICTURE 9999.
93.     02 DESCRIPTION PICTURE X(15).

94. PROCEDURE DIVISION.
95.     ENTRY OPENM.
96.     OPEN I-O MASTER-FILE.
97.     EXIT PROGRAM.

98.     ENTRY CLOSEM.
99.     CLOSE MASTER-FILE.
100.    EXIT PROGRAM.

101. READ-MASTER-ENTRY.
102.    ENTRY READM USING LINK-RECORD RECORD-FLAG.
103.*   THIS CALCULATES THE HASHED ADDRESS AND CARRIES
104.*   OUT THE SEARCH FOR THE DESIRED RECORD.

105.    DIVIDE PART-NO IN LINK-RECORD BY HASH-CONSTANT
106.        GIVING Q REMAINDER BUCKET-NO.
```

```
107.        ADD 1 TO BUCKET-NO.
108.*       ASSUMING FIRST RELATIVE RECORD IS NUMBERED 1
109.        MOVE ZERO TO BUCKET-COUNT.
110.        MOVE FALSE TO RECORD-FLAG.
111.        MOVE FALSE TO SEARCH-FLAG.
112.        PERFORM READ-LOOP UNTIL END-OF-SEARCH.
113.        IF RECORD-FOUND MOVE MASTER-RECORD (N) TO LINK-RECORD.
114.        EXIT PROGRAM.

115. READ-LOOP.
116.        IF BUCKET-COUNT IS GREATER THAN MAX-BUCKET
117.*           DISPLAY "FILE FULL"
118.            MOVE TRUE TO SEARCH-FLAG
119.        ELSE MOVE 1 TO N
120.            PERFORM READ-BLOCK
121.            PERFORM SEARCH-LOOP UNTIL END-OF-SEARCH
122.                OR N IS GREATER THAN BUCKET-SIZE
123.            IF NOT END-OF-SEARCH PERFORM INCREMENT-BUCKET.

124. SEARCH-LOOP.
125.        IF PART-NO IN MASTER-RECORD (N) IS EQUAL
126.            TO PART-NO IN LINK-RECORD
127.            MOVE TRUE TO RECORD-FLAG SEARCH-FLAG
128.        ELSE IF PART-NO IN MASTER-RECORD (N) IS EQUAL TO ZEROS
129.            MOVE TRUE TO SEARCH-FLAG
130.        ELSE ADD 1 TO N.

131. INCREMENT-BUCKET.
132.        ADD 1 TO BUCKET-COUNT.
133.        ADD 1 TO BUCKET-NO.
134.        IF BUCKET-NO IS GREATER THAN MAX-BUCKET
135.            MOVE 1 TO BUCKET-NO.
136.*               TO CONTINUE SEARCH AT BEGINNING
137.*               AFTER HITTING END.

138. READ-BLOCK.
139.        READ MASTER-FILE INVALID KEY
140.            DISPLAY "INVALID KEY ON READ".
141.*       NOTE THAT INVALID KEY WILL NEVER ACTUALLY
142.*       OCCUR IF FILE IS PROPERLY MADE BECAUSE ALL
143.*       RECORD SPACES HAVE EITHER REAL OR DUMMY
144.*       RECORDS IN THEM AT ALL TIMES. HOWEVER,
145.*       COBOL REQUIRES THAT THIS STATEMENT BE PRESENT.

146. WRITE-MASTER-ENTRY.
147.        ENTRY WRITEM USING LINK-RECORD.
148.        MOVE LINK-RECORD TO MASTER-RECORD (N).
149.        PERFORM REWRITE-MASTER.
150.        EXIT PROGRAM.

151. REWRITE-MASTER-ENTRY.
152.        ENTRY REWRM USING LINK-RECORD.
153.        MOVE LINK-RECORD TO MASTER-RECORD (N).
154.        PERFORM REWRITE-MASTER.
```

```
155.      EXIT PROGRAM.

156. REWRITE-MASTER.
157.      REWRITE MASTER-BLOCK INVALID KEY
158.          DISPLAY "INVALID KEY ON REWRITE".
159.*     NOTE THAT INVALID KEY WILL NEVER ACTUALLY
160.*     OCCUR IF FILE IS PROPERLY MADE BECAUSE ALL
161.*     RECORD SPACES HAVE RECORDS IN THEM. HOWEVER,
162.*     COBOL REQUIRES THAT THIS STATEMENT BE PRESENT.

163. DELETE-MASTER-ENTRY.
164.      ENTRY DELM.

165.*     THIS IMPLEMENTS KNUTH'S ALGORITHM FOR MOVING
166.*     RECORDS BACK INTO A VACATED POSITION IF THERE
167.*     IS A RECORD WHOSE LENGTH OF SEARCH WOULD BE
168.*     SHORTENED BY THE MOVE. THIS MAINTAINS THE FILE
169.*     AT THE SAME AVERAGE LENGTH OF SEARCH AS WOULD
170.*     OCCUR IF THE PRESENT RECORDS HAD BEEN INSERTED,
171.*     AND NO DELETIONS HAD TAKEN PLACE.

172.      MOVE BUCKET-NO TO OPEN-BUCKET.
173.      MOVE N TO OPEN-RECORD.
174.*     TO REMEMBER WHERE THE OPEN PLACE IS.
175.      SUBTRACT 1 FROM BUCKET-NO GIVING LAST-BUCKET.
176.      IF LAST-BUCKET IS EQUAL TO ZERO
177.          MOVE MAX-BUCKET TO LAST-BUCKET.
178.*     THIS IS WHERE WE STOP.

179.*     NOW WE SEARCH BUCKETS FOLLOWING THIS ONE TO
180.*     FIND A RECORD THAT SHOULD BE MOVED BACK TO THIS
181.*     OPEN SPACE. THIS STOPS WHEN WE GET TO "LAST-BUCKET",
182.*     WHICH IS WHERE WE STARTED, OR WHEN WE FIND AN EMPTY
183.*     RECORD SPACE. IN FACT, IF THERE IS AN EMPTY SPACE
184.*     IN THE SAME BUCKET WHERE THE RECORD WAS DELETED,
185.*     WE STOP RIGHT THERE.

186.      MOVE FALSE TO SEARCH-FLAG.
187.      IF PART-NO IN MASTER-RECORD (BUCKET-SIZE) IS
188.          EQUAL TO ZERO MOVE TRUE TO SEARCH-FLAG.
189.      PERFORM CHECK-BUCKETS UNTIL END-OF-SEARCH.

190.*     AFTER NO MORE MOVING IS INDICATED, WE MOVE
191.*     THE RECORDS UP IN THE BUCKET, LEAVING THE OPEN
192.*     SPACE AT THE END OF THE BUCKET, AND THEN WE SET
193.*     THE PART-NO IN THE OPEN SPACE TO 000000 TO
194.*     INDICATE THAT NO RECORD IS THERE.

195.      IF OPEN-BUCKET IS NOT EQUAL TO BUCKET-NO
196.          MOVE OPEN-BUCKET TO BUCKET-NO
197.          PERFORM READ-BLOCK.
198.      PERFORM MOVE-RECORD-BACK VARYING N FROM
199.          OPEN-RECORD BY 1 UNTIL N IS EQUAL TO
200.          BUCKET-SIZE.
```

```
201.      MOVE ZERO TO PART-NO IN MASTER-RECORD (BUCKET-SIZE).
202.      PERFORM REWRITE-MASTER.
203.      EXIT PROGRAM.

204. CHECK-BUCKETS.

205.*     HERE EACH TIME WE CHECK ONE BUCKET TO SEE WHETHER IT
206.*     CONTAINS A RECORD THAT SHOULD BE MOVED BACK TO THE
207.*     OPEN RECORD POSITION.

208.      ADD 1 TO BUCKET-NO.
209.      IF BUCKET-NO IS GREATER THAN MAX-BUCKET
210.          MOVE 1 TO BUCKET-NO.
211.      PERFORM READ-BLOCK.
212.      MOVE FALSE TO MOVE-FLAG RECORD-CHECK-FLAG.
213.*     MOVE-FLAG WILL BE SET TRUE IF A RECORD THAT SHOULD BE
214.*     MOVED IS FOUND. RECORD-CHECK-FLAG WILL BE SET TRUE
215.*     WHEN WE ARE FINISHED CHECKING THE RECORDS IN THIS BUCKET.
216.      MOVE 1 TO N.
217.      PERFORM CHECK-RECORDS UNTIL CHECK-FINISHED.
218.      IF MOVE-RECORD
219.          MOVE BUCKET-NO TO K
220.*         FIRST MOVE THIS RECORD TO OPEN PLACE
221.          MOVE MASTER-RECORD (N) TO TEMP-RECORD
222.          MOVE OPEN-BUCKET TO BUCKET-NO
223.          PERFORM READ-BLOCK
224.          MOVE TEMP-RECORD TO
225.              MASTER-RECORD (OPEN-RECORD)
226.          PERFORM REWRITE-MASTER
227.*         NOW REMEMBER WHERE THE NEW OPEN RECORD IS
228.          MOVE K TO OPEN-BUCKET BUCKET-NO
229.          MOVE N TO OPEN-RECORD
230.          PERFORM READ-BLOCK.
231.*     NOW DECIDE WHETHER TO CONTINUE SEARCH FOR ANOTHER
232.*     RECORD TO MOVE IN THE NEXT BUCKET.
233.      IF PART-NO IN MASTER-RECORD (BUCKET-SIZE)
234.          IS EQUAL TO ZERO OR
235.          BUCKET-NO IS EQUAL TO LAST-BUCKET
236.          MOVE TRUE TO SEARCH-FLAG.

237. CHECK-RECORDS.
238.*     HERE WE CHECK ONE RECORD. IF A NONEMPTY RECORD
239.*     IS FOUND HERE.
240.      IF PART-NO IN MASTER-RECORD(N) IS EQUAL TO ZERO
241.          MOVE TRUE TO RECORD-CHECK-FLAG
242.      ELSE
243.          DIVIDE PART-NO IN MASTER-RECORD (N) BY
244.              HASH-CONSTANT GIVING Q REMAINDER H
245.          ADD 1 TO H

246.*         IF THE CONDITION IS MET IN THE FOLLOWING
247.*         STATEMENT, THEN MOVING THAT RECORD INTO
248.*         THE OPEN PLACE REDUCES ITS LENGTH OF SEARCH.
```

```
249.*         THE HASHED ADDRESS OF THE RECORD BEING
250.*         CONSIDERED IS H, ITS LOCATION, CALLED L IN THE
251.*         EXPLANATION IN CHAPTER 8, IS BUCKET-NO, AND
252.*         "OPEN-BUCKET" HERE CORRESPONDS TO P IN THE
253.*         EXPLANATION.

254.          IF H IS NOT GREATER THAN OPEN-BUCKET AND
255.                 OPEN-BUCKET IS LESS THAN BUCKET-NO OR
256.              BUCKET-NO IS LESS THAN H AND
257.                 H IS NOT GREATER THAN OPEN-BUCKET OR
258.              OPEN-BUCKET IS LESS THAN BUCKET-NO AND
259.                 BUCKET-NO IS LESS THAN H
260.              MOVE TRUE TO MOVE-FLAG RECORD-CHECK-FLAG
261.*         OTHERWISE GO ON TO THE NEXT RECORD, IF THERE IS ONE
262.          ELSE ADD 1 TO N
263.              IF N IS GREATER THAN BUCKET-SIZE
264.                 MOVE TRUE TO RECORD-CHECK-FLAG.
265. MOVE-RECORD-BACK.
266.     ADD N 1 GIVING J.
267.     MOVE MASTER-RECORD (J) TO MASTER-RECORD (N).
```

The following program creates a relative file and suitably initializes it for use as a hashed file with the preceding program.

```
1. IDENTIFICATION DIVISION.
2. PROGRAM-ID. MKHASH.

3.* THIS PROGRAM GENERATES THE HASH FILE REQUIRED
4.* FOR THE ON-LINE INVENTORY SYSTEM BY INITIALIZING
5.* ALL THE RECORDS WITH ZEROS AS KEYS AND SPACES
6.* IN THE REST OF THE RECORD.

7. ENVIRONMENT DIVISION.
8. CONFIGURATION SECTION.
9. SOURCE-COMPUTER. DECSYSTEM-20.
10. OBJECT-COMPUTER. DECSYSTEM-20.

11. INPUT-OUTPUT SECTION.
12. FILE-CONTROL.
13.     SELECT MASTER-FILE ASSIGN TO DSK
14.         ORGANIZATION IS RELATIVE
15.         ACCESS IS SEQUENTIAL
16.         RELATIVE KEY IS BUCKET-NO.

17. DATA DIVISION.
18. FILE SECTION.
19. FD  MASTER-FILE
20.     VALUE OF ID IS "MASTER    "
21.     BLOCK CONTAINS 1 RECORDS
22.     RECORD CONTAINS 125 CHARACTERS
23.     RECORDING MODE IS ASCII
24.     DATA RECORD IS MASTER-BLOCK.
25. 01  MASTER-BLOCK PICTURE X(125).
```

```
26. WORKING-STORAGE SECTION.
27. 77  BUCKET-NO PICTURE 9999.
28. 77  MAX-BUCKET PICTURE 9999 VALUE IS 23.
29.*    THIS IS THE NUMBER OF BUCKETS IMPLEMENTED
30. 01  DUMMY-BLOCK.
31.     02 MASTER-RECORD OCCURS 5 TIMES.
32.        03 PART-NO PICTURE 999999.
33.        03 OTHER-DATA PICTURE X(19).

34. PROCEDURE DIVISION.
35. MAIN-PROGRAM.
36.     DISPLAY "GENERATING HASH FILE".
37.     MOVE SPACES TO MASTER-BLOCK.
38.     MOVE ZEROS TO PART-NO (1) PART-NO (2)
39.        PART-NO (3) PART-NO (4) PART-NO (5).
40.     OPEN OUTPUT MASTER-FILE.
41.     PERFORM LOOP VARYING BUCKET-NO FROM 1 BY 1
42.        UNTIL BUCKET-NO IS GREATER THAN MAX-BUCKET.

43.     CLOSE MASTER-FILE.
44.     DISPLAY "FINISHED".
45.     STOP RUN.

46. LOOP.
47.     WRITE MASTER-BLOCK FROM DUMMY-BLOCK
48.        INVALID KEY DISPLAY "INVALID KEY".
49.*    NOTE THAT INVALID KEY WON'T OCCUR IF THE
50.*    FILE REALLY IS A NEW FILE.
```

The following program will list the contents of the hashed file, showing the part number in each bucket, and thus showing how the file is structured internally.

```
1. IDENTIFICATION DIVISION.
2. PROGRAM-ID. LISTHASH.

3.* THIS PROGRAM LISTS THE HASH FILE USED IN THE
4.* HASHED FILE EXAMPLE, BUCKET BY BUCKET, SO WE
5.* CAN SEE EXACTLY HOW THE FILE IS SET UP. THE
6.* PART-NO AND ITS HASHED ADDRESS IS PRINTED FOR ALL
7.* THE RECORDS IN EACH BUCKET, ONE BUCKET PER LINE.

8. ENVIRONMENT DIVISION.
9. CONFIGURATION SECTION.
10. SOURCE-COMPUTER. DECSYSTEM-20.
11. OBJECT-COMPUTER. DECSYSTEM-20.

12. INPUT-OUTPUT SECTION.
13. FILE-CONTROL.
14.     SELECT MASTER-FILE ASSIGN TO DSK
15.        ORGANIZATION IS RELATIVE
16.        ACCESS IS SEQUENTIAL
17.        RELATIVE KEY IS BUCKET-NO.
```

```
18. DATA DIVISION.
19. FILE SECTION.
20. FD  MASTER-FILE
21.     VALUE OF ID IS "MASTER    "
22.     BLOCK CONTAINS 1 RECORDS
23.     RECORD CONTAINS 125 CHARACTERS
24.     RECORDING MODE IS ASCII
25.     DATA RECORD IS MASTER-BLOCK.
26. 01  MASTER-BLOCK.
27.     02 PART-NO1 PICTURE 999999.
28.     02 FILLER PICTURE X(19).
29.     02 PART-NO2 PICTURE 999999.
30.     02 FILLER PICTURE X(19).
31.     02 PART-NO3 PICTURE 999999.
32.     02 FILLER PICTURE X(19).
33.     02 PART-NO4 PICTURE 999999.
34.     02 FILLER PICTURE X(19).
35.     02 PART-NO5 PICTURE 999999.
36.     02 FILLER PICTURE X(19).
37. WORKING-STORAGE SECTION.
38. 77  N PICTURE 9999.
39. 77  BUCKET-NO PICTURE 9999.
40. 77  FILE-SIZE PICTURE 9999 VALUE IS 23.
41. 77  HASH-CONSTANT PICTURE 9999 VALUE IS 23.
42.*     THIS IS THE NUMBER OF BUCKETS IMPLEMENTED
43. 77  BUCKET-SIZE PICTURE 9999 VALUE IS 5.
44. 77  FALSE PICTURE 9 VALUE 0.
45. 77  Q PICTURE 999999.
46. 77  H1 PICTURE 99.
47. 77  H2 PICTURE 99.
48. 77  H3 PICTURE 99.
49. 77  H4 PICTURE 99.
50. 77  H5 PICTURE 99.

51. PROCEDURE DIVISION.
52. MAIN-PROGRAM.
53.     DISPLAY "LISTING HASH FILE".
54.     OPEN INPUT MASTER-FILE.
55.     PERFORM LOOP VARYING BUCKET-NO FROM 1 BY 1
56.         UNTIL BUCKET-NO IS GREATER THAN FILE-SIZE.
57.     CLOSE MASTER-FILE.
58.     DISPLAY "FINISHED".
59.     STOP RUN.

60. LOOP.
61.* THIS PARAGRAPH PRINTS THE CONTENTS OF ONE BUCKET
62.* ON ONE LINE. IT ASSUMES FIVE RECORDS PER BUCKET.

63.     READ MASTER-FILE AT END DISPLAY "AT END".
64.     DIVIDE PART-NO1 BY HASH-CONSTANT GIVING Q
65.         REMAINDER H1.
```

```
66.     ADD 1 TO H1.
67.     DIVIDE PART-NO2 BY HASH-CONSTANT GIVING Q
68.         REMAINDER H2.
69.     ADD 1 TO H2.
70.     DIVIDE PART-NO3 BY HASH-CONSTANT GIVING Q
71.         REMAINDER H3.
72.     ADD 1 TO H3.
73.     DIVIDE PART-NO4 BY HASH-CONSTANT GIVING Q
74.         REMAINDER H4.
75.     ADD 1 TO H4.
76.     DIVIDE PART-NO5 BY HASH-CONSTANT GIVING Q
77.         REMAINDER H5.
78.     ADD 1 TO H5.

79.     DISPLAY "BUCKET NO. " BUCKET-NO ":" PART-NO1 " "
80.         H1 "  " PART-NO2 " " H2  "   " PART-NO3 " "
81.         H3 "  " PART-NO4 " " H4  "   " PART-NO5 " "
82.         H5.
```

PL/I Program Examples

This appendix contains example programs written in PL/I to illustrate sequential processing and on-line processing with relative files, indexed files, and hashed files. All programs are written for the examples in Chapters 7 and 8 and provide more detailed illustrations of file programming. The first program is a sequential update program. Next is a main program for the on-line inventory system described in the examples in Chapter 7. The main program contains no file instructions, only calls to a subprogram that will do the file operations. Following that are three subprograms using a relative file, an indexed file, and a hashed file, respectively. With the relative file subprogram is a short program that uses sequential reading of the relative file to list its contents. There also are short programs with the indexed file subprogram to create the file, to read it sequentially, and to list its contents. Finally, with the hashed file subprogram there are short programs to create and initialize the hashed file and dump its contents.

These programs are included to give examples of I-O programming. In other respects, the programs are very much simplified. All of these programs have been tested on an IBM system running OS/VS. There are a number of details that come up in a practical program that are implementation dependent and not spelled out in the PL/I Standard, and there are some details of the standard to which the IBM implementation does not conform.

C.1. BATCH UPDATE PROGRAM

For this program, the master file is created initially as an empty file. The following program can be used to initially load the file, by inserting records in key order, as well as for routine updating afterwards.

```
1.  UPDATE: PROCEDURE OPTIONS(MAIN);
2.  /******************************************************/
3.  /*                                                    */
4.  /*          THIS PROGRAM IMPLEMENTS THE BATCH-TYPE    */
5.  /*     INVENTORY SYSTEM DISCUSSED IN CHAPTER 7. THE   */
6.  /*     OLD MASTER FILE IS CALLED OLDMAST, THE NEW ONE */
7.  /*     IS NEWMAST, AND THE TRANSACTIONS ARE ON A FILE */
8.  /*     NAMED TRANS.                                   */
9.  /*                                                    */
10. /*          THE TRANSACTION CODES ARE:               */
11. /*                                                    */
12. /*          A    INSERT RECORD                        */
13. /*          B    RECEIVE GOODS                        */
14. /*          C    DISBURSE GOODS                       */
15. /*          D    DELETE RECORD                        */
16. /*                                                    */
17. /******************************************************/
18.     DECLARE OLDMAST FILE,
19.             NEWMAST FILE,
20.             TRANS FILE;
21.     DECLARE 1 OLD_MASTER_RECORD,
22.               2 PART_NO CHARACTER(6),
23.               2 QUANTITY PICTURE '9999',
24.               2 DESCRIPTION CHARACTER(15),
25.               2 FILLER CHARACTER(55);
26.     DECLARE 1 NEW_MASTER_RECORD,
27.               2 PART_NO CHARACTER(6),
28.               2 QUANTITY PICTURE '9999',
29.               2 DESCRIPTION CHARACTER(15),
30.               2 FILLER CHARACTER(55);
31.     DECLARE 1 TRANSACTION_RECORD,
32.               2 PART_NO CHARACTER(6),
33.               2 CODE CHARACTER(1),
34.               2 QUANTITY PICTURE '9999',
35.               2 DESCRIPTION CHARACTER(15),
36.               2 FILLER CHARACTER(54);
37. /******************************************************/
38. /*                                                    */
39. /*          IN THE ABOVE, THE VARIABLES FILLER ARE    */
40. /*     INSERTED TO MAKE THE RECORDS 80 CHARACTERS,    */
41. /*     FOR CONVENIENCE.                               */
42. /*                                                    */
43. /*          THE VARIABLES OLD_QUANTITY, RECEIVE_COUNT,*/
44. /*     AND DISBURSE_COUNT SAVE QUANTITIES NEEDED FOR  */
45. /*     THE REPORT. ERROR IS SET TRUE WHEN AN ERROR IS */
46. /*     FOUND IN ANY TRANSACTION, AND TRUE AND FALSE   */
47. /*     ARE USED AS CONSTANTS.                         */
48. /*                                                    */
49. /******************************************************/
```

```
50.    DECLARE OLD_QUANTITY BINARY FIXED(15),
51.            RECEIVE_COUNT BINARY FIXED(15),
52.            DISBURSE_COUNT BINARY FIXED(15),
53.            ERROR BIT(1),
54.            TRUE BIT(1) STATIC INITIAL('1'B),
55.            FALSE BIT(1) STATIC INITIAL('0'B);

56. /*********************************************************/
57. /*                                                     */
58. /*        NOTE THAT WHEN "LOW(6)" IS IN THE NEW        */
59. /*   MASTER RECORD PART_NO, IT IS CONSIDERED THAT      */
60. /*   NO RECORD IS THERE. THUS, "LOW(6)" IS PUT THERE   */
61. /*   INITIALLY, WHENEVER A RECORD IS DELETED, AND      */
62. /*   AFTER A RECORD HAS BEEN COMPLETELY PROCESSED      */
63. /*   AND WRITTEN TO THE NEW MASTER FILE.               */
64. /*                                                     */
65. /*********************************************************/

66.    ON ENDFILE(OLDMAST)
67.       OLD_MASTER_RECORD.PART_NO = HIGH(6);
68.    ON ENDFILE(TRANS)
69.       TRANSACTION_RECORD.PART_NO = HIGH(6);

70.    OPEN FILE(OLDMAST) RECORD INPUT;
71.    OPEN FILE(TRANS) RECORD INPUT;
72.    OPEN FILE(NEWMAST) RECORD OUTPUT;
73.    NEW_MASTER_RECORD.PART_NO = LOW(6);
74.    READ FILE(TRANS) INTO (TRANSACTION_RECORD);
75.    READ FILE(OLDMAST) INTO (OLD_MASTER_RECORD);
76.    PUT SKIP EDIT('PART_NO   DESCRIPTION      QUANTITY')
77.        (A);
78.    PUT SKIP EDIT('OLD   IN    OUT   NEW')(COL(25),A);

79.    DO WHILE(NEW_MASTER_RECORD.PART_NO<HIGH(6));

80. /*********************************************************/
81. /*                                                     */
82. /*        FIRST, IF THERE IS A RECORD IN THE           */
83. /*   NEW_MASTER_RECORD AND IF THERE ARE NO MORE        */
84. /*   TRANSACTIONS THAT APPLY TO IT, THEN WE FINISH     */
85. /*   ITS PROCESSING AND WRITE IT OUT.                  */
86. /*                                                     */
87. /*********************************************************/

88.       IF NEW_MASTER_RECORD.PART_NO~=LOW(6)   &
89.          NEW_MASTER_RECORD.PART_NO<
90.          TRANSACTION_RECORD.PART_NO
91.          THEN DO;
92.          CALL FINAL_PROCESSING;
93.          WRITE FILE(NEWMAST) FROM(NEW_MASTER_RECORD);
94.          NEW_MASTER_RECORD.PART_NO = LOW(6);
95.       END;  /*  OF FINISHING UP A MASTER RECORD  */
```

```
 96. /*********************************************************/
 97. /*                                                       */
 98. /*          NEXT, IF THE TIME HAS COME TO MOVE THE       */
 99. /*    NEXT MASTER RECORD TO THE NEW_MASTER_RECORD        */
100. /*    POSITION, WE DO THAT AND THE INITIAL PROCESSING    */
101. /*    FOR THAT RECORD.                                   */
102. /*                                                       */
103. /*********************************************************/
104.      IF OLD_MASTER_RECORD.PART_NO<=
105.          TRANSACTION_RECORD.PART_NO THEN DO;
106.          NEW_MASTER_RECORD = OLD_MASTER_RECORD;
107.          IF NEW_MASTER_RECORD.PART_NO~=HIGH(6) THEN DO;
108.              READ FILE(OLDMAST) INTO(OLD_MASTER_RECORD);
109.              CALL INITIAL_PROCESSING;
110.          END;
111.      END;  /*  OF MOVING IN NEXT MASTER RECORD  */
112. /*********************************************************/
113. /*                                                       */
114. /*          OTHERWISE IT IS TIME TO CHECK THE NEXT       */
115. /*    TRANSACTION AND, IF IT IS OK, PROCESS IT.          */
116. /*                                                       */
117. /*********************************************************/
118.      ELSE DO;
119.          CALL EDIT_CHECK;
120.          CALL PROCESS_TRANSACTION;
121.          READ FILE(TRANS) INTO(TRANSACTION_RECORD);
122.      END;  /*  OF HANDLING ONE TRANSACTION  */
123.   END;  /*  OF MAIN LOOP  */
124.   CLOSE FILE(OLDMAST);
125.   CLOSE FILE(NEWMAST);
126.   CLOSE FILE(TRANS);
127. /*********************************************************/
128. /*                                                       */
129. /*          THIS IS WHAT MUST BE DONE AT THE START OF    */
130. /*    PROCESSING EACH RECORD.                            */
131. /*                                                       */
132. /*********************************************************/
133. INITIAL_PROCESSING: PROCEDURE;
134.    OLD_QUANTITY = NEW_MASTER_RECORD.QUANTITY;
135.    RECEIVE_COUNT = 0;
136.    DISBURSE_COUNT = 0;
137. END;
138. /*********************************************************/
139. /*                                                       */
140. /*          THIS IS WHAT MUST BE DONE AT THE END OF      */
141. /*    PROCESSING OF EACH RECORD.                         */
142. /*                                                       */
143. /*********************************************************/
```

```
144. FINAL_PROCESSING: PROCEDURE;
145.    PUT SKIP EDIT(NEW_MASTER_RECORD.PART_NO,' ',
146.             NEW_MASTER_RECORD.DESCRIPTION,
147.             OLD_QUANTITY,' ',
148.             RECEIVE_COUNT,' ',
149.             DISBURSE_COUNT,' ',
150.             NEW_MASTER_RECORD.QUANTITY)
151.       (3 A,F(4),A,F(4),A,F(4),A,F(4));
152. END;
153. /*********************************************************/
154. /*                                                       */
155. /*         THIS PROCEDURE SIMPLY SETS THE ERROR FLAG     */
156. /*      AND PRINTS THE ERROR MESSAGE THAT IT RECEIVES    */
157. /*      AS THE VALUE OF X. IT PRINTS THE TRANSACTION     */
158. /*      BEFORE PRINTING THE FIRST ERROR MESSAGE.         */
159. /*                                                       */
160. /*********************************************************/

161. PUT_ERROR: PROCEDURE(X);
162.    DECLARE X CHARACTER(30) VARYING;
163.    IF ~ERROR THEN PUT SKIP EDIT
164.       (TRANSACTION_RECORD.PART_NO,' ',CODE,' ',
165.        TRANSACTION_RECORD.QUANTITY,' ',
166.        TRANSACTION_RECORD.DESCRIPTION,'--',X)(9 A);
167.    ERROR = TRUE;
168. END; /*  OF PUT_ERROR PROCEDURE  */

169. EDIT_CHECK: PROCEDURE;
170.    ERROR = FALSE;
171.    IF VERIFY(TRANSACTION_RECORD.PART_NO,'0123456789')
172.       ~=0 THEN CALL PUT_ERROR('PART_NO NOT NUMERIC');
173.    ELSE IF CODE='A' & NEW_MASTER_RECORD.PART_NO=
174.       TRANSACTION_RECORD.PART_NO THEN
175.       CALL PUT_ERROR('DUPLICATE PART_NO');
176.    ELSE IF CODE~='A' & NEW_MASTER_RECORD.PART_NO~=
177.       TRANSACTION_RECORD.PART_NO THEN
178.          CALL PUT_ERROR('RECORD NOT FOUND');
179.    IF ~(CODE='A' | CODE='B' | CODE='C' | CODE='D') THEN
180.       CALL PUT_ERROR('INVALID CODE');

181.    IF CODE='A' | CODE='B' | CODE='C' THEN DO;
182.       IF VERIFY(TRANSACTION_RECORD.QUANTITY,'0123456789')
183.          ~=0 THEN CALL PUT_ERROR('QUANTITY NOT NUMERIC');
184.       ELSE DO;
185.          IF CODE='C' & ~ERROR &
186.             TRANSACTION_RECORD.QUANTITY>
187.                NEW_MASTER_RECORD.QUANTITY
188.             THEN CALL PUT_ERROR('NOT ENOUGH IN STOCK');
189.       END; /*  OF ELSE DO  */
190.    END; /*  OF IF CODE IS A OR B OR C  */

191.    IF CODE='A' & TRANSACTION_RECORD.DESCRIPTION=' '
192.       THEN CALL PUT_ERROR('DESCRIPTION MISSING');
```

```
193.    IF ~ERROR & CODE='D' & NEW_MASTER_RECORD.QUANTITY~=0
194.       THEN CALL PUT_ERROR('QUANTITY NOT ZERO ON DELETE');
195. END;  /*  OF EDIT_CHECK PROCEDURE  */

196. PROCESS_TRANSACTION: PROCEDURE;
197.    IF ERROR THEN DO;
198.       PUT SKIP EDIT('TRANSACTION NOT PROCESSED')(A);
199.       RETURN;
200.    END;

201.    IF CODE='A' THEN DO;  /*  INSERTION  */
202.       NEW_MASTER_RECORD.PART_NO =
203.          TRANSACTION_RECORD.PART_NO;
204.       NEW_MASTER_RECORD.QUANTITY = 0;
205.       NEW_MASTER_RECORD.DESCRIPTION =
206.          TRANSACTION_RECORD.DESCRIPTION;
207.       CALL INITIAL_PROCESSING;
208.    END;  /*  OF INSERT RECORD  */

209.    IF CODE='A' | CODE='B' THEN DO;
210.       /*  RECEIVE GOODS  */
211.       NEW_MASTER_RECORD.QUANTITY =
212.          TRANSACTION_RECORD.QUANTITY +
213.          NEW_MASTER_RECORD.QUANTITY;
214.       RECEIVE_COUNT = RECEIVE_COUNT+
215.          TRANSACTION_RECORD.QUANTITY;
216.    END;  /* OF RECEIVE GOODS  */

217.    ELSE IF CODE='C' THEN DO;  /*  DISBURSE GOODS  */
218.       NEW_MASTER_RECORD.QUANTITY =
219.          NEW_MASTER_RECORD.QUANTITY-
220.          TRANSACTION_RECORD.QUANTITY;
221.       DISBURSE_COUNT = DISBURSE_COUNT+
222.          TRANSACTION_RECORD.QUANTITY;
223.    END;  /*  OF DISBURSE GOODS  */

224.    ELSE IF CODE='D' THEN  /*  DELETE RECORD  */
225.       NEW_MASTER_RECORD.PART_NO = LOW(6);
226. END;  /*  OF PROCESS_TRANSACTION PROCEDURE  */
227. END;  /*  OF UPDATE MAIN PROCEDURE  */
```

C.2. MAIN PROGRAM FOR ON-LINE UPDATE

This program calls a subprogram for all file operations. Subprograms using a relative file, an indexed file, and a hashed file follow.

```
1.  ONLINE: PROCEDURE OPTIONS(MAIN);
```

```
 2.  /**************************************************************/
 3.  /*                                                          */
 4.  /*        THIS PROGRAM IMPLEMENTS THE ON-LINE INVENTORY     */
 5.  /*    SYSTEM DISCUSSED IN CHAPTER 7.                        */
 6.  /*                                                          */
 7.  /*        THE COMMAND CODES ARE:                            */
 8.  /*                                                          */
 9.  /*        A    INSERT RECORD                                */
10.  /*        B    RECEIVE GOODS                                */
11.  /*        C    DISBURSE GOODS                               */
12.  /*        D    DELETE RECORD                                */
13.  /*        Q    QUERY                                        */
14.  /*        S    STOP RUN                                     */
15.  /*        H    HELP                                         */
16.  /*                                                          */
17.  /*    THIS MAIN PROGRAM IMPLEMENTS THE LOGIC OF THE ONLINE  */
18.  /*    FILE SYSTEM, BUT CALLS ANOTHER PROCEDURE TO DO ALL    */
19.  /*    THE FILE OPERATIONS. THAT PROCEDURE, CALLED FILEIO,   */
20.  /*    COMMUNICATES WITH ONLINE USING A PARAMETER THAT       */
21   /*    INDICATES WHICH OF THE FOLLOWING OPERATIONS IS TO BE  */
22.  /*    DONE, AND TWO EXTERNAL VARIABLES, THE RECORD AND A    */
23.  /*    FLAG SET DURING READING TO SHOW WHETHER THE RECORD    */
24.  /*    WAS FOUND OR NOT. THESE ARE THE OPERATIONS:           */
25.  /*                                                          */
26.  /*        1. OPEN        OPEN THE MASTER FILE               */
27.  /*        2. CLOSE       CLOSE THE MASTER FILE              */
28.  /*        3. READ        IF A RECORD WITH THE SAME KEY      */
29.  /*                       IS FOUND, SET THE FLAG TRUE        */
30.  /*                       AND READ THE RECORD. OTHERWISE     */
31.  /*                       SET THE FLAG FALSE.                */
32.  /*        4. WRITE       WRITE A NEW MASTER RECORD          */
33.  /*        5. REWRITE     REWRITE FROM THE MASTER RECORD     */
34.  /*        6. DELETE      DELETE THE RECORD LAST READ        */
35.  /*                                                          */
36.  /*    FOLLOWING THIS PROGRAM THERE ARE THREE DIFFERENT      */
37.  /*    VERSIONS OF THE PROCEDURE FILEIO, ONE USING A         */
38.  /*    RELATIVE FILE, ONE USING AN INDEXED SEQUENTIAL FILE,  */
39.  /*    AND ONE USING A HASHED FILE. ALL OF THEM WORK WITH    */
40.  /*    THIS PROGRAM, ALTHOUGH THE FILES THEMSELVES ARE       */
41.  /*    QUITE DIFFERENT AND INCOMPATIBLE. MRECORD IS THE      */
42.  /*    RECORD PASSED TO THE I-O PROCEDURE, AND RFOUND IS     */
43.  /*    THE FLAG.                                             */
44.  /*                                                          */
45.  /**************************************************************/
46.      DECLARE 1 MRECORD EXTERNAL,
47.                2 PART_NO CHARACTER(6),
48.                2 QUANTITY BINARY FIXED(15),
49.                2 DESCRIPTION CHARACTER(15);

50.      DECLARE RFOUND BIT(1) EXTERNAL;
```

```
 51.    DECLARE FILEIO ENTRY(BINARY FIXED(15)) EXTERNAL;
 52. /****************************************************************/
 53. /*                                                            */
 54. /*    THE FOLLOWING ARE USED AS CONSTANTS FOR THE             */
 55. /*    PARAMETER THAT INDICATES WHICH OPERATION IS TO BE       */
 56. /*    DONE BY THE FILEIO PROCEDURE.                           */
 57. /*                                                            */
 58. /****************************************************************/
 59.    DECLARE OPEN BINARY FIXED(15) INITIAL(1),
 60.            CLOSE BINARY FIXED(15) INITIAL(2),
 61.            READ BINARY FIXED(15) INITIAL(3),
 62.            WRITE BINARY FIXED(15) INITIAL(4),
 63.            REWRITE BINARY FIXED(15) INITIAL(5),
 64.            DELETE BINARY FIXED(15) INITIAL(6);
 65. /****************************************************************/
 66. /*                                                            */
 67. /*    OTHER VARIABLES:                                        */
 68. /*        COMMAND             OPERATOR-ENTERED COMMAND        */
 69. /*        INPUT_PART_NO       OPERATOR-ENTERED DATA           */
 70. /*        INPUT_DESCRIPTION                                   */
 71. /*        INPUT_QUANTITY                                      */
 72. /*        NUM_QUANTITY        OPERATOR-ENTERED QUANTITY       */
 73. /*                               AFTER CONVERSION TO          */
 74. /*                               NUMERIC                      */
 75. /*        OK                  FLAG SET FALSE IF BAD           */
 76. /*                            DATA IS ENTERED                 */
 77. /*        NEED_TO_READ        FLAG SET TRUE FOR               */
 78. /*                            COMMANDS THAT NEED A            */
 79. /*                            MASTER-RECORD READ              */
 80. /*        TRUE, FALSE         CONSTANTS                       */
 81. /*                                                            */
 82. /****************************************************************/
 83.    DECLARE COMMAND CHARACTER(1),
 84.            INPUT_PART_NO CHARACTER(6),
 85.            INPUT_DESCRIPTION CHARACTER(15),
 86.            INPUT_QUANTITY CHARACTER(4),
 87.            NUM_QUANTITY BINARY FIXED(15),
 88.            OK BIT(1),
 89.            NEED_TO_READ BIT(1),
 90.            TRUE BIT(1) STATIC INITIAL('1'B),
 91.            FALSE BIT(1) STATIC INITIAL('0'B);
 92. /****************************************************************/
 93. /*                                                            */
 94. /*        THIS IS THE MAIN PROGRAM. THE MAIN LOOP IS          */
 95. /*    EXECUTED ONCE FOR EACH COMMAND ENTERED BY THE           */
 96. /*    OPERATOR. OTHERWISE THE LOGIC IS QUITE STRAIGHT-        */
 97. /*    FORWARD. WHEN AN ERROR IS FOUND, THE ENTIRE LOOP IS     */
 98. /*    REPEATED FROM THE BEGINNING.                            */
 99. /*                                                            */
100. /****************************************************************/
```

```
101.     PUT SKIP EDIT
102.        ('INVENTORY SYSTEM--COMMAND H FOR HELP')(A);
103.     COMMAND = ' ';
104.     CALL FILEIO(OPEN);
105.     DO WHILE(COMMAND~='S');
106.        OK = TRUE;
107.        CALL GET_COMMAND;
108.        NEED_TO_READ = ((COMMAND>='A' & COMMAND<='D') |
109.           COMMAND='Q');
110.        IF NEED_TO_READ THEN CALL GET_PART_NO;
111.        IF OK & NEED_TO_READ THEN DO;
112.           CALL FILEIO(READ);
113.           CALL CHECKING;
114.        END;

115.        IF OK & (COMMAND='A' | COMMAND='B' |
116.           COMMAND='C') THEN CALL GET_QUANTITY;
117.        IF OK & COMMAND='A' THEN CALL GET_DESCRIPTION;

118.        IF ~OK THEN
119.           PUT SKIP EDIT('NOT DONE BECAUSE OF ERROR')(A);
120.        ELSE IF NEED_TO_READ THEN CALL PROCESS_TRANSACTION;
121.        ELSE IF COMMAND='H' THEN CALL HELP;

122.        IF OK & COMMAND='D' THEN
123.           PUT SKIP EDIT('RECORD DELETED')(A);
124.        ELSE IF OK & NEED_TO_READ THEN PUT SKIP EDIT
125.           (PART_NO,' ',DESCRIPTION,
126.           'QUANTITY ON HAND ',QUANTITY)(4 A,F(4));
127.     END;  /* OF MAIN LOOP  */
128.     CALL FILEIO(CLOSE);
129.     PUT SKIP EDIT('INVENTORY SYSTEM--END OF RUN')(A);

130. GET_COMMAND: PROCEDURE;
131.     PUT SKIP EDIT('ENTER COMMAND:')(A);
132.     GET EDIT(COMMAND)(A(1));
133.     IF ~(COMMAND='A' | COMMAND;'B' | COMMAND='C' |
134.        COMMAND='D' | COMMAND='Q' | COMMAND='S' |
135.        COMMAND='H') THEN DO;
136.        OK = FALSE;
137.        PUT EDIT('INVALID COMMAND')(A);
138.     END;
139. END GET_COMMAND;

140. GET_PART_NO: PROCEDURE;
141.     PUT EDIT('ENTER PART NO(6 DIGITS):')(A);
142.     GET EDIT(INPUT_PART_NO)(A(6));
143.     IF VERIFY(INPUT_PART_NO,'0123456789')~=0 THEN DO;
144.        PUT EDIT('PART NO NOT NUMERIC')(A);
145.        OK = FALSE;
146.     END;
147.     MRECORD.PART_NO = INPUT_PART_NO;
148.     /*  TO SEND PART NO TO FILEIO PROCEDURE  */
149. END GET_PART_NO;
```

```
150.  CHECKING: PROCEDURE;
151.     IF COMMAND='A' & RFOUND THEN DO;
152.        OK = FALSE;
153.        PUT EDIT('DUPLICATE PART NO FOUND')(A);
154.     END;
155.     ELSE IF COMMAND~='A' & ~RFOUND THEN DO;
156.        OK = FALSE;
157.        PUT EDIT('RECORD NOT FOUND')(A);
158.     END;
159.  END CHECKING;

160.  GET_DESCRIPTION: PROCEDURE;
161.     PUT EDIT('ENTER DESCRIPTION(MAX 15 CHAR):')(A);
162.     GET EDIT(INPUT_DESCRIPTION)(A(15));
163.     IF INPUT_DESCRIPTION=' ' THEN DO;
164.        OK = FALSE;
165.        PUT EDIT('NOT ENTERED')(A);
166.     END;
167.  END GET_DESCRIPTION;

168.  GET_QUANTITY: PROCEDURE;
169.     PUT EDIT('ENTER QUANTITY(4 DIGITS):')(A);
170.     GET EDIT(INPUT_QUANTITY)(A(4));
171.     IF VERIFY(INPUT_QUANTITY,'0123456789')~=0 THEN DO;
172.        OK = FALSE;
173.        PUT EDIT('QUANTITY NOT NUMERIC')(A);
174.     END;
175.     ELSE DO;
176.        NUM_QUANTITY = INPUT_QUANTITY;
177.        IF COMMAND='C' & OK &
178.        NUM_QUANTITY>QUANTITY THEN DO;
179.           OK = FALSE;
180.           PUT EDIT('NOT ENOUGH IN STOCK')(A);
181.        END;
182.     END;  /*  OF ELSE DO  */
183.  END GET_QUANTITY;

184.  PROCESS_TRANSACTION: PROCEDURE;
185.     IF COMMAND='A' THEN DO;  /* INSERT RECORD  */
186.        PART_NO = INPUT_PART_NO;
187.        QUANTITY = NUM_QUANTITY;
188.        DESCRIPTION = INPUT_DESCRIPTION;
189.        CALL FILEIO(WRITE);
190.     END;  /*  OF INSERT RECORD  */

191.     ELSE IF COMMAND='B' THEN DO;  /*  RECEIVE GOODS  */
192.        QUANTITY = QUANTITY+NUM_QUANTITY;
193.        CALL FILEIO(REWRITE);
194.     END;  /*  OF RECEIVE GOODS  */

195.     ELSE IF COMMAND='C' THEN DO;  /*  DISBURSE GOODS  */
196.        QUANTITY = QUANTITY-NUM_QUANTITY;
197.        CALL FILEIO(REWRITE);
```

```
198.    END;  /*  OF DISBURSE GOODS  */
199.
200.    ELSE IF COMMAND='D' THEN
201.        CALL FILEIO(DELETE);

202. END PROCESS_TRANSACTION;

203. HELP: PROCEDURE;
204.    PUT SKIP EDIT('COMMANDS:')(A);
205.    PUT SKIP EDIT('A   INSERT RECORD')(A);
206.    PUT SKIP EDIT('B   RECEIVE GOODS')(A);
207.    PUT SKIP EDIT('C   DISBURSE GOODS')(A);
208.    PUT SKIP EDIT('D   DELETE RECORD')(A);
209.    PUT SKIP EDIT('Q   INQUIRY')(A);
210.    PUT SKIP EDIT('S   STOP RUN')(A);
211.    PUT SKIP EDIT('H   HELP')(A);
212. END HELP;

213. END ONLINE;
```

C.3. RELATIVE FILE I-O PROCEDURES

The following is a subprogram that can be used with the main program
in Section C.2. It uses a relative file in which the part numbers are the
relative keys. Note that unless most possible keys actually are in use,
this system will be quite wasteful of disk space. This procedure does one
of the six I-O operations: open, close, read, write, rewrite, delete, depending on the value of the parameter OP.

```
1.  FILEIO: PROCEDURE(OP);

2.  /***********************************************************/
3.  /*                                                         */
4.  /*         THIS IS A VERSION OF "FILEIO", THE PROCEDURE     */
5.  /*      THAT DOES ALL THE I-O OPERATIONS FOR THE ONLINE     */
6.  /*      INVENTORY SYSTEM. THIS VERSION USES A RELATIVE FILE,*/
7.  /*      AND ASSUMES THAT ALL PART NUMBERS ARE ACTUALLY FOUR */
8.  /*      DIGITS, SO THAT THE FILE CAN BE SET UP WITH 10000   */
9.  /*      RECORDS AND THE PART NUMBER USED AS THE RELATIVE    */
10. /*      RECORD NUMBER IN THE FILE. FOR THAT TO BE EFFICIENT,*/
11. /*      MOST OF THOSE NUMBERS SHOULD ACTUALLY BE IN USE.    */
12. /*      NOTE THAT EACH RECORD "PHYSICALLY" EXISTS, SO THAT  */
13. /*      A FLAG OF SOME SORT MUST BE SET IN THE RECORD TO    */
14. /*      DISTINGUISH RECORDS HAVING ACTUAL DATA FROM "DUMMY" */
15. /*      RECORDS.                                            */
16. /*                                                         */
17. /*         FILEIO COMMUNICATES WITH ONLINE USING TWO        */
18. /*      EXTERNAL VARIABLES, THE RECORD MRECORD AND A FLAG   */
19. /*      RFOUND WHICH IS SET DURING READING TO SHOW WHETHER  */
20. /*      THE RECORD WAS FOUND OR NOT, AND A PARAMETER THAT    */
```

```
21.  /*      INDICATES WHICH OF THE FOLLOWING OPERATIONS IS TO     */
22.  /*      BE DONE:                                              */
23.  /*                                                            */
24.  /*          1. OPEN          OPEN THE MASTER FILE             */
25.  /*          2. CLOSE         CLOSE THE MASTER FILE            */
26.  /*          3. READ          IF A RECORD WITH THE SAME KEY    */
27.  /*                           IS FOUND, SET THE FLAG TRUE      */
28.  /*                           AND READ THE RECORD. OTHERWISE   */
29.  /*                           SET THE FLAG FALSE.              */
30.  /*          4. WRITE         WRITE A NEW MASTER RECORD        */
31.  /*          5. REWRITE       REWRITE FROM THE MASTER RECORD   */
32.  /*          6. DELETE        DELETE THE RECORD LAST READ      */
33.  /*                                                            */
34.  /*          IN THE FILE DECLARATION, THE ENVIRONMENT          */
35.  /*      PARAMETER IS IMPLEMENTATION DEPENDENT. IN THE IBM     */
36.  /*      SYSTEMS, REGIONAL(1) IS ONE FORM OF RELATIVE FILE.    */
37.  /*                                                            */
38.  /*          A RELATIVE FILE IS CREATED IN THE IBM SYSTEM BY   */
39.  /*      OPENING THE FILE FOR DIRECT OUTPUT AND THEN CLOSING   */
40.  /*      IT. THE SYSTEM THEN WRITES THE FILE FULL OF "DUMMY    */
41.  /*      RECORDS" IN WHICH THE FIRST BYTE IS USED AS A FLAG    */
42.  /*      WHICH IS SET TO HIGH(1) (I. E., A BYTE WHOSE BITS     */
43.  /*      ARE ALL ONES) IN EVERY RECORD. WITH OUR RECORD        */
44.  /*      LAYOUT, THIS FLAG IS THE FIRST BYTE OF THE KEY,       */
45.  /*      HENCE THE KEY IN A DUMMY RECORD WILL BE GREATER THAN  */
46.  /*      ANY VALID KEY. WE USE THIS FACT IN OUR PROGRAM TO     */
47.  /*      DETERMINE WHETHER THE RECORD JUST READ IS A VALID     */
48.  /*      RECORD OR A DUMMY RECORD.                             */
49.  /*                                                            */
50.  /**************************************************************/

51.      DECLARE MFILE FILE RECORD ENVIRONMENT(REGIONAL(1));

52.      DECLARE 1 MRECORD EXTERNAL,
53.                 2 PART_NO CHARACTER(6),
54.                 2 QUANTITY BINARY FIXED(15),
55.                 2 DESCRIPTION CHARACTER(15);
56.
57.      DECLARE RFOUND BIT(1) EXTERNAL;

58.  /**************************************************************/
59.  /*                                                            */
60.  /*          OP IS THE PARAMETER THAT INDICATES WHICH          */
61.  /*      OPERATION IS TO BE DONE FOR FILEIO, AND THE           */
62.  /*      FOLLOWING ARE USED AS CONSTANTS FOR THE PARAMETER     */
63.  /*      BY THE FILEIO PROCEDURE.                              */
64.  /*                                                            */
65.  /**************************************************************/

66.      DECLARE OP BINARY FIXED(15),
67.              OPEN BINARY FIXED(15) INITIAL(1),
```

```
68.              CLOSE BINARY FIXED(15) INITIAL(2),
69.              READ BINARY FIXED(15) INITIAL(3),
70.              WRITE BINARY FIXED(15) INITIAL(4),
71.              REWRITE BINARY FIXED(15) INITIAL(5),
72.              DELETE BINARY FIXED(15) INITIAL(6);

73. /**************************************************************/
74. /*                                                          */
75. /*       RELATIVE_KEY IS THE RELATIVE RECORD NUMBER OF      */
76. /*    THE CURRENT MASTER RECORD. TRUE AND FALSE ARE USED    */
77. /*    AS CONSTANTS.                                         */
78. /*                                                          */
79. /**************************************************************/

80.    DECLARE RELATIVE_KEY BINARY FIXED(15),
81.            TRUE BIT(1) STATIC INITIAL('1'B),
82.            FALSE BIT(1) STATIC INITIAL('0'B);

83. /**************************************************************/
84. /*                                                          */
85. /*       THE FOLLOWING IS THE MAIN PROCEDURE OF FILEIO.     */
86. /*    IN THIS IBM IMPLEMENTATION, THE DELETE STATEMENT MAY  */
87. /*    BE USED, AND IT FLAGS DELETED RECORDS BY PLACING A    */
88. /*    BYTE OF HIGH VALUES (ALL ONES) AT THE BEGINNING OF    */
89. /*    THE RECORD. THAT RECORD IS CONSIDERED TO STILL EXIST  */
90. /*    IN SOME SENSE--A READ STATEMENT WILL RETRIEVE IT.     */
91. /*    WE CAN CHECK THAT FLAG, BECAUSE WITH THE ALL-ONES     */
92. /*    BYTE AT THE BEGINNING OF THE RECORD, AND THEREFORE    */
93. /*    AT THE BEGINNING OF THE KEY, THE KEY IN THE RECORD    */
94. /*    READ WILL BE GREATER THAN THE LARGEST VALID KEY.      */
95. /*    A KEY CONDITION ARISES ONLY IF THE RELATIVE RECORD    */
96. /*    NUMBER SPECIFIED FOR THE KEY IS NEGATIVE OR IS TOO    */
97. /*    LARGE (I. E. GREATER THAN THE SIZE OF THE ALLOCATED   */
98. /*    FILE).                                                */
99. /*                                                          */
100. /**************************************************************/

101.    ON KEY(MFILE) BEGIN;
102.      PUT SKIP EDIT('OUT-OF-RANGE KEY USED')(A);
103.      STOP;
104.    END;
105.    IF OP=OPEN THEN DO;
106.      OPEN FILE(MFILE) DIRECT UPDATE;
107.    END;

108.    ELSE IF OP=CLOSE THEN CLOSE FILE(MFILE);

109.    ELSE IF OP=READ THEN DO;
110.      RELATIVE_KEY = PART_NO;   /*  CONVERT KEY TO BINARY  */
111.      READ FILE(MFILE) INTO(MRECORD)
112.          KEY(RELATIVE_KEY);
113.      RFOUND = (MRECORD.PART_NO <= '999999');
114.    END;
```

```
115,     ELSE IF OP=WRITE THEN DO;
116,        RELATIVE_KEY = PART_NO;  /*  CONVERT KEY TO BINARY  */
117,        WRITE FILE(MFILE) FROM(MRECORD)
118,           KEYFROM(RELATIVE_KEY);
119,     END;

120,     ELSE IF OP=REWRITE THEN DO;
121,        RELATIVE_KEY = PART_NO;  /*  CONVERT KEY TO BINARY  */
122,         REWRITE FILE(MFILE) FROM(MRECORD) KEY(RELATIVE_KEY);
123,     END;

124,     ELSE IF OP=DELETE THEN DO;
125,        RELATIVE_KEY = PART_NO;  /*  CONVERT KEY TO BINARY  */
126,         DELETE FILE(MFILE) KEY(RELATIVE_KEY);
127,     END;

128, END FILEIO;
```

The following is a program that will read the relative file from the preceding program and list its contents in the order in which they are stored in the file, that is, in sequence by part number.

```
 1, RELREPT: PROCEDURE OPTIONS(MAIN);

 2, /***************************************************************/
 3, /*                                                           */
 4, /*        THIS PROGRAM LISTS THE CONTENTS OF THE FILE        */
 5, /*     PRODUCED BY THE RELATIVE-FILE VERSION OF FILEIO.      */
 6, /*     IT ILLUSTRATES SEQUENTIAL READING OF A RELATIVE       */
 7, /*     FILE. NOTE THAT IN THE IBM IMPLEMENTATION, RECORDS    */
 8, /*     FLAGGED DELETED ARE RETRIEVED BY THE READ STATEMENT,  */
 9, /*     BUT CAN BE DETECTED BECAUSE, WITH THE FIRST BYTE SET  */
10, /*     TO ALL ONES, THE KEY FOR A DELETED RECORD WILL BE     */
11, /*     GREATER THAN THE LARGEST VALID KEY.                   */
12, /*                                                           */
13, /***************************************************************/

14,     DECLARE MASTER FILE RECORD ENVIRONMENT(REGIONAL(1));

15,     DECLARE 1 MASTER_RECORD,
16,                 2 PART_NO CHARACTER(6),
17,                 2 QUANTITY BINARY FIXED(15),
18,                 2 DESCRIPTION CHARACTER(15);

19,     DECLARE END_OF_FILE BIT(1),
20,             TRUE BIT(1) INITIAL('1'B),
21,             FALSE BIT(1) INITIAL('0'B);

22,     ON ENDFILE(MASTER) END_OF_FILE = TRUE;

23,     PUT SKIP LIST('INVENTORY REPORT');
24,     PUT SKIP LIST('ID      DESCRIPTION      IN STOCK');
25,     OPEN FILE(MASTER) SEQUENTIAL INPUT;
26,     END_OF_FILE = FALSE;
27,     READ FILE(MASTER) INTO(MASTER_RECORD);
```

```
28,    DO WHILE(~END_OF_FILE);
29,       IF PART_NO<='999999' THEN DO;
30,          PUT SKIP EDIT(PART_NO,DESCRIPTION,QUANTITY)
31,             (A(6),COL(8),A(15),COL(25),P'BZZZ9');
32,       END; /*  OF HANDLING AN EXISTING RECORD  */
33,       READ FILE(MASTER) INTO(MASTER_RECORD);
34,    END; /*  OF LOOP  */
35,    CLOSE FILE(MASTER);
36,    PUT SKIP LIST('INVENTORY REPORT--END OF RUN');
37, END RELREPT;
```

C.4. INDEXED SEQUENTIAL FILE I-O PROCEDURES

This subprogram, when used with the main program in Section C.2, implements the on-line inventory system using an IBM PL/I indexed file. With this implementation of PL/I, an indexed file is created using a separate program, MAKEISF, which is shown following FILEIO.

```
1, FILEIO: PROCEDURE(OP);
2, /***************************************************************/
3, /*                                                           */
4, /*         THIS IS A VERSION OF "FILEIO", THE PROCEDURE       */
5, /*    THAT DOES ALL THE I-O OPERATIONS FOR THE ONLINE         */
6, /*    INVENTORY SYSTEM, THIS VERSION USES AN INDEXED FILE,    */
7, /*                                                           */
8, /*         FILEIO COMMUNICATES WITH ONLINE USING TWO          */
9, /*    EXTERNAL VARIABLES, THE RECORD MRECORD AND A FLAG       */
10, /*   RFOUND SET DURING READING TO SHOW WHETHER THE RECORD    */
11, /*   WAS FOUND OR NOT, AND A PARAMETER THAT INDICATES        */
12, /*   WHICH OF THE FOLLOWING OPERATIONS IS TO BE DONE:        */
13, /*                                                           */
14, /*        1, OPEN        OPEN THE MASTER FILE                */
15, /*        2, CLOSE       CLOSE THE MASTER FILE               */
16, /*        3, READ        IF A RECORD WITH THE SAME KEY       */
17, /*                       IS FOUND, SET THE FLAG TRUE         */
18, /*                       AND READ THE RECORD, OTHERWISE      */
19, /*                       SET THE FLAG FALSE,                 */
20, /*        4, WRITE       WRITE A NEW MASTER RECORD           */
21, /*        5, REWRITE     REWRITE FROM THE MASTER RECORD      */
22, /*        6, DELETE      DELETE THE RECORD LAST READ         */
23, /*                                                           */
24, /*         IN THE IBM SYSTEM, AN INDEXED FILE IS CREATED     */
25, /*    BY OPENING THE FILE FOR SEQUENTIAL OUTPUT AND          */
26, /*    WRITING SOME RECORDS INTO IT IN SEQUENCE BY KEY, IT    */
27, /*    DOES NOT SEEM TO BE ACCEPTABLE TO SIMPLY OPEN THE      */
28, /*    FILE FOR SEQUENTIAL OUTPUT AND CLOSE IT AGAIN          */
29, /*    WITHOUT WRITING ANY RECORDS, (THE RATIONALE PROBABLY   */
30, /*    IS THAT LOADING AN INDEXED FILE BY INSERTION IS        */
```

```
31. /*    INEFFICIENT.) ALSO, WHEN THE FILE IS CREATED, IT IS    */
32. /*    NECESSARY TO SPECIFY A NUMBER OF "DCB" PARAMETERS,      */
33. /*    AMONG THEM "OPTCD=LY" TO INDICATE THAT RECORDS MAY      */
34. /*    BE INSERTED AND DELETED, SINCE THE DEFAULT IS NOT       */
35. /*    TO PROVIDE FOR INSERTION AND DELETION OF RECORDS.       */
36. /*                                                            */
37. /*         RECORDS ARE DELETED BY SETTING THE FIRST BYTE      */
38. /*    IN THE RECORD TO HIGH(1) (ALL ONES), AND IN THE         */
39. /*    IBM SYSTEM, IT IS NOT PERMITTED TO ALTER THE KEY        */
40. /*    OF A DELETED RECORD. THEREFORE, IT IS NOT PERMITTED     */
41. /*    FOR THE KEY IN THE RECORD TO BE AT THE BEGINNING        */
42. /*    OF THE RECORD, AS WE HAVE CHOSEN TO PLACE IT IN OUR     */
43. /*    APPLICATION. FOR THAT REASON, IN THIS PROCEDURE, WE     */
44. /*    HAVE INSERTED AN ADDITIONAL BYTE TO ACCOMMODATE THE     */
45. /*    RECORD-DELETED FLAG IN THE RECORD WHICH WE ACTUALLY     */
46. /*    WRITE INTO THE FILE. WE SET THAT FLAG TO A SPACE IN     */
47. /*    VALID RECORDS. MRECORD IS THE RECORD PASSED FROM THE    */
48. /*    MAIN PROGRAM TO THIS PROCEDURE, AND MFILE_RECORD IS     */
49. /*    THE RECORD ACTUALLY WRITTEN INTO THE INDEXED FILE.      */
50. /*    THE INDEXED-FILE SYSTEM, UNLIKE THE RELATIVE FILE       */
51. /*    SYSTEM, TURNS ON THE ON KEY CONDITION CODE ON AN        */
52. /*    ATTEMPT TO READ A DELETED AS WELL AS A NEVER-           */
53. /*    INSERTED RECORD.                                        */
54. /*                                                            */
55. /**************************************************************/

56.     DECLARE MFILE FILE RECORD
57.        ENVIRONMENT(INDEXED,KEYLENGTH(6),KEYLOC(2));

58.     DECLARE 1 MRECORD EXTERNAL,
59.              2 PART_NO CHARACTER(6),
60.              2 QUANTITY BINARY FIXED(15),
61.              2 DESCRIPTION CHARACTER(15);

62.     DECLARE 1 MFILE_RECORD,
63.              2 FLAG CHARACTER(1),
64.              2 RECORD,
65.                3 PART_NO CHARACTER(6),
66.                3 QUANTITY BINARY FIXED(15),
67.                3 DESCRIPTION CHARACTER(15);

68.     DECLARE RFOUND BIT(1) EXTERNAL,
69.            TRUE BIT(1) INITIAL('1'B),
70.            FALSE BIT(1) INITIAL('0'B);

71. /**************************************************************/
72. /*                                                            */
73. /*         OP IS THE PARAMETER THAT INDICATES WHICH           */
74. /*    OPERATION IS TO BE DONE FOR FILEIO, AND THE             */
75. /*    FOLLOWING ARE USED AS CONSTANTS FOR THE PARAMETER       */
76. /*    BY THE FILEIO PROCEDURE.                                */
77. /*                                                            */
78. /**************************************************************/
```

```
79.     DECLARE OP BINARY FIXED(15),
80.             OPEN BINARY FIXED(15) INITIAL(1),
81.             CLOSE BINARY FIXED(15) INITIAL(2),
82.             READ BINARY FIXED(15) INITIAL(3),
83.             WRITE BINARY FIXED(15) INITIAL(4),
84.             REWRITE BINARY FIXED(15) INITIAL(5),
85.             DELETE BINARY FIXED(15) INITIAL(6);


86. /*************************************************************/
87. /*                                                         */
88. /*          A KEY CONDITION ARISES ON READING IF A RECORD  */
89. /*    WITH THE SPECIFIED KEY IS NOT FOUND IN THE FILE, AND  */
90. /*    WE USE THIS FACT TO DETERMINE WHETHER A RECORD WITH   */
91. /*    THE KEY SPECIFIED BY THE USER EXISTS OR NOT. A KEY    */
92. /*    CONDITION OCCURS ON WRITE IF A RECORD WITH THAT KEY   */
93. /*    ALREADY EXISTS, AND ON REWRITE AND DELETE IF THE      */
94. /*    RECORD DOES NOT EXIST. WITH THIS PROGRAM, WE ALWAYS   */
95. /*    READ FIRST TO DETERMINE WHETHER THE RECORD EXISTS,    */
96. /*    AND THEREBY ASSURE THAT A KEY CONDITION WILL NEVER    */
97. /*    ARISE ON WRITE, REWRITE, OR DELETE.                   */
98. /*                                                         */
99. /*************************************************************/


100.    ON KEY(MFILE) RFOUND = FALSE;

101.    RECORD = MRECORD;

102.    IF OP=OPEN THEN OPEN FILE(MFILE) DIRECT UPDATE;

103.    ELSE IF OP=CLOSE THEN CLOSE FILE(MFILE);

104.    ELSE IF OP=READ THEN DO;
105.       RFOUND = TRUE;
106.       READ FILE(MFILE) INTO(MFILE_RECORD)
107.          KEY(RECORD.PART_NO);
108.       /*  NOTE THAT RFOUND WILL BE SET FALSE BY THE     */
109.       /*   ON KEY STATEMENT IF THE RECORD IS NOT FOUND  */
110.    END;

111.    ELSE IF OP=WRITE THEN
112.       WRITE FILE(MFILE) FROM(MFILE_RECORD)
113.          KEYFROM(RECORD.PART_NO);

114.    ELSE IF OP=REWRITE THEN
115.       REWRITE FILE(MFILE) FROM(MFILE_RECORD)
116.          KEY(RECORD.PART_NO);

117.    ELSE IF OP=DELETE THEN
118.       DELETE FILE(MFILE) KEY(RECORD.PART_NO);

119.    MRECORD = RECORD;

120. END FILEIO;  /*  INDEXED VERSION  */
```

The following program was used to create the indexed file.

```
1. MAKEISF: PROCEDURE OPTIONS(MAIN);

2. /*************************************************************/
3. /*                                                           */
4. /*          THIS PROGRAM CREATES AN INDEXED FILE. THESE      */
5. /*     PL/I ON-LINE PROGRAMS WERE RUN ON THE TSO SYSTEM,     */
6. /*     BUT INDEXED FILES CANNOT BE CREATED USING THE TSO     */
7. /*     ALLOCATE COMMAND. THEREFORE, THIS BATCH PROGRAM WAS   */
8. /*     USED TO CREATE THE FILE. IT INSERTS DATA RECORDS      */
9. /*     READ FROM "SYSIN" INTO THE INDEXED FILE.              */
10./*                                                           */
11./*          AN INDEXED FILE IN THE IBM SYSTEM IS CREATED     */
12./*     BY OPENING THE FILE FOR SEQUENTIAL OUTPUT, WRITING    */
13./*     SOME RECORDS INTO IT, AND THEN CLOSING IT. IT SEEMS   */
14./*     THAT SOME RECORDS MUST BE WRITTEN, AND IT DOES NOT    */
15./*     SUFFICE TO SIMPLY OPEN THE FILE AND CLOSE IT. A       */
16./*     MINIMUM SPACE ALLOCATION OF ONE FULL (CONTIGUOUS)     */
17./*     CYLINDER IS REQUIRED. ALSO THE DCB PARAMETER          */
18./*     "OPTCD=LY" IS NEEDED TO SPECIFY THAT RECORDS WILL     */
19./*     BE INSERTED AND DELETED--THE DEFAULT SEEMS TO BE NOT  */
20./*     TO PROVIDE FOR INSERTIONS AND DELETIONS. THE          */
21./*     COMPLETE CODING FOR THE DD CARD IN THE JCL WAS AS     */
22./*     FOLLOWS:                                              */
23./*                                                           */
24./*     //GO.MFILE DD DSN=W433610.IMAIN.DATA,UNIT=TSODA,      */
25./*     //          SPACE=(CYL,1),DCB=(DSORG=IS,RECFM=FB,     */
26./*     //          BLKSIZE=240,LRECL=24,KEYLEN=6,OPTCD=LY,   */
27./*     //          CYLOFL=5),DISP=(NEW,CATLG)                */
28./*                                                           */
29./*************************************************************/

30.    DECLARE MFILE FILE RECORD
31.       ENVIRONMENT(INDEXED,KEYLENGTH(6),KEYLOC(2));

32.    DECLARE 1 MRECORD,
33.                 2 FLAG CHARACTER(1) INITIAL(' '),
34.                 2 PART_NO CHARACTER(6),
35.                 2 QUANTITY BINARY FIXED(15),
36.                 2 DESCRIPTION CHARACTER(15),
37.            ENDDATA BIT(1);

38.    ON ENDFILE(SYSIN) ENDDATA = '1'B;

39.    OPEN FILE(MFILE) KEYED SEQUENTIAL OUTPUT;
40.    GET SKIP EDIT(PART_NO,QUANTITY,DESCRIPTION)
41.                 (A(6),F(4),A(15));
42.    DO WHILE(~ENDDATA);
43.       WRITE FILE(MFILE) FROM(MRECORD) KEYFROM(PART_NO);
44.       GET SKIP EDIT(PART_NO,QUANTITY,DESCRIPTION)
45.                 (A(6),F(4),A(15));
46.    END;
47.    CLOSE FILE(MFILE);
48. END MAKEISF;
```

The following program will list the contents of the indexed sequential file of the previous program in sequence by part number using a sequential read statement.

```
1.  INDXREP: PROCEDURE OPTIONS(MAIN);

2.  /*******************************************************************/
3.  /*                                                               */
4.  /*        THIS PROGRAM LISTS THE CONTENTS OF THE INDEXED         */
5.  /*     FILE PRODUCED BY THE INDEXED VERSION OF FILEIO. IT        */
6.  /*     ILLUSTRATES THE USE OF SEQUENTIAL ACCESS TO INDEXED       */
7.  /*     FILES. ALL RECORDS WILL BE RETRIEVED IN SEQUENCE BY       */
8.  /*     KEY REGARDLESS OF THE ORDER IN WHICH THEY WERE            */
9.  /*     INSERTED. DELETED AND DUMMY RECORDS ARE NOT               */
10. /*     RETRIEVED AT ALL                                         */.
11. /*                                                               */
12. /*******************************************************************/

13.     DECLARE MFILE FILE RECORD
14.         ENVIRONMENT(INDEXED,KEYLENGTH(6),KEYLOC(2));

15.     DECLARE 1 MRECORD ,
16.                2 FLAG CHARACTER(1) ,
17.                2 PART_NO CHARACTER(6) ,
18.                2 QUANTITY BINARY FIXED(15) ,
19.                2 DESCRIPTION CHARACTER(15);

20.     DECLARE END_OF_FILE BIT(1) ,
21.             TRUE BIT(1) INITIAL('1'B) ,
22.             FALSE BIT(1) INITIAL('0'B);

23.     ON ENDFILE(MFILE) END_OF_FILE = TRUE;

24.     OPEN FILE(MFILE) SEQUENTIAL INPUT;

25.     PUT SKIP EDIT('PART-NO','QUANTITY','DESCRIPTION')
26.                     (A,          COL(10),A, COL(20),A);
27.     END_OF_FILE = FALSE;
28.     READ FILE(MFILE) INTO(MRECORD);
29.     DO WHILE(~END_OF_FILE);
30.        PUT SKIP EDIT(PART_NO,QUANTITY,DESCRIPTION)
31.                     (A,COL(10),F(4),COL(20),A);
32.        READ FILE(MFILE) INTO(MRECORD);
33.     END;

34.     PUT SKIP EDIT('END OF DATA')(A);

35. END INDXREP;
```

C.5. HASHED FILE I-O PROCEDURES

The following subprogram, again usable with the main program in Section C.2, implements a hashed file system.

```
1.  FILEIO: PROCEDURE(OP);

2.  /*********************************************************/
3.  /*                                                       */
4.  /*          THIS IS A VERSION OF "FILEIO", THE PROCEDURE */
5.  /*      THAT DOES ALL THE I-O OPERATIONS FOR THE ONLINE  */
6.  /*      INVENTORY SYSTEM. THIS VERSION USES A HASHED FILE.*/
7.  /*                                                       */
8.  /*          FILEIO COMMUNICATES WITH ONLINE USING TWO    */
9.  /*      EXTERNAL VARIABLES, THE RECORD AND A FLAG SET DURING */
10. /*      READING TO SHOW WHETHER THE RECORD WAS FOUND OR NOT, */
11. /*      AND A PARAMETER THAT INDICATES WHICH OF THE      */
12. /*      FOLLOWING OPERATIONS IS TO BE DONE:              */
13. /*                                                       */
14. /*          1. OPEN        OPEN THE MASTER FILE          */
15. /*          2. CLOSE       CLOSE THE MASTER FILE         */
16. /*          3. READ        IF A RECORD WITH THE SAME KEY */
17. /*                         IS FOUND, SET THE FLAG TRUE   */
18. /*                         AND READ THE RECORD. OTHERWISE*/
19. /*                         SET THE FLAG FALSE.           */
20. /*          4. WRITE       WRITE A NEW MASTER RECORD     */
21. /*          5. REWRITE     REWRITE FROM THE MASTER RECORD*/
22. /*          6. DELETE      DELETE THE RECORD LAST READ   */
23. /*                                                       */
24. /*          FOR THIS HASHED FILE, WE ARE USING 23 BUCKETS,*/
25. /*      EACH BUCKET A BLOCK, WITH 5 RECORDS PER BLOCK. WE */
26. /*      MUST DO THE BLOCKING AND UNBLOCKING IN THIS PROGRAM,*/
27. /*      AND THEREFORE WHAT IS A LOGICAL BLOCK FOR THIS   */
28. /*      PROGRAM IS A RECORD TO THE SYSTEM--WE USE A RELATIVE*/
29. /*      FILE IN WHICH EACH RECORD OF THE RELATIVE FILE IS */
30. /*      A BUCKET FOR THE HASHED FILE. MFILE IS THE MASTER */
31. /*      FILE AND MASTER_BUCKET IS THE AREA INTO WHICH WE  */
32. /*      READ A BLOCK. IT MUST BE DECLARED STATIC, SO THAT */
33. /*      WE CAN READ A BLOCK, PASS ONE RECORD BACK TO THE  */
34. /*      MAIN PROGRAM, HAVE THE MAIN PROGRAM SEND BACK A   */
35. /*      MODIFIED RECORD, AND STILL HAVE THE REST OF THE   */
36. /*      BLOCK THERE TO REWRITE. MRECORD AND RFOUND ARE THE*/
37. /*      EXTERNAL VARIABLES USED TO PASS A RECORD EITHER TO*/
38. /*      OR FROM THE MAIN PROGRAM, AND THE FLAG TO THE MAIN*/
39. /*      PROGRAM.                                         */
40. /*                                                       */
41. /*          THE IBM SYSTEM REQUIRES TWO-BYTE VARIABLES   */
42. /*      (DECLARED BINARY FIXED(15)) TO BE ON EVEN ADDRESSES.*/
43. /*      WE HAVE CHOSEN AN ODD-LENGTH RECORD. IN ORDER TO  */
44. /*      SATISFY THE EVEN-ADDRESS REQUIREMENT, WE HAVE ADDED*/
45. /*      THE ONE "FILLER" BYTE INTO THE BLOCK AT THE END OF*/
46. /*      EACH RECORD. REGIONAL(1) IS IBM'S DESIGNATION FOR */
47. /*      A SIMPLE RELATIVE FILE. NOTE THAT THE FIRST RECORD*/
48. /*      IS NUMBERED ZERO.                                */
49. /*                                                       */
50. /*********************************************************/
```

```
51.     DECLARE MFILE FILE RECORD ENVIRONMENT(REGIONAL(1));

52.     DECLARE 1 MASTER_BUCKET STATIC,
53.               2 RECORD_AREA(5),
54.                 3 MASTER_RECORD,
55.                   4 PART_NO CHARACTER(6),
56.                   4 QUANTITY BINARY FIXED(15),
57.                   4 DESCRIPTION CHARACTER(15),
58.                 3 FILLER CHARACTER(1);

59.     DECLARE 1 MRECORD EXTERNAL,
60.               2 PART_NO CHARACTER(6),
61.               2 QUANTITY BINARY FIXED(15),
62.               2 DESCRIPTION CHARACTER(15);

63.     DECLARE RFOUND BIT(1) EXTERNAL;

64. /************************************************************/
65. /*                                                        */
66. /*       OP IS THE PARAMETER THAT INDICATES WHICH         */
67. /*   OPERATION IS TO BE DONE FOR FILEIO, AND THE          */
68. /*   FOLLOWING ARE USED AS CONSTANTS FOR THE PARAMETER    */
69. /*   BY THE FILEIO PROCEDURE.                             */
70. /*                                                        */
71. /************************************************************/

72.     DECLARE OP BINARY FIXED(15),
73.             OPEN BINARY FIXED(15) INITIAL(1),
74.             CLOSE BINARY FIXED(15) INITIAL(2),
75.             READ BINARY FIXED(15) INITIAL(3),
76.             WRITE BINARY FIXED(15) INITIAL(4),
77.             REWRITE BINARY FIXED(15) INITIAL(5),
78.             DELETE BINARY FIXED(15) INITIAL(6);

79. /************************************************************/
80. /*                                                        */
81. /*       BUCKET_NUMBER AND RECORD_NUMBER REFER TO THE     */
82. /*   PLACE WE ARE LOOKING IN THE FILE. BUCKET_COUNT IS    */
83. /*   USED TO DETERMINE WHEN WE HAVE SEARCHED THE WHOLE    */
84. /*   FILE, AND SHOULD SEARCH NO MORE. OPEN_BUCKET AND     */
85. /*   OPEN_RECORD ARE USED DURING DELETION TO RECORD WHERE */
86. /*   A RECORD WAS REMOVED WHILE WE SEARCH FOR ONE THAT    */
87. /*   MIGHT BE PUT BACK IN ITS PLACE. HASH_CONSTANT IS     */
88. /*   USED IN THE HASH FUNCTION--HERE WE USE THE NUMBER OF */
89. /*   BUCKETS, WHICH WE HAVE CHOSEN TO BE A PRIME NUMBER.  */
90. /*   SEARCHING IS SET TRUE WHILE WE ARE SEARCHING FOR A   */
91. /*   RECORD WHILE READING. TRUE AND FALSE ARE CONSTANTS.  */
92. /*   I AND J ARE TEMPORARIES. NOTE THAT BUCKET_NUMBER AND */
93. /*   RECORD_NUMBER MUST BE REMEMBERED BY THE PROGRAM FROM */
94. /*   THE TIME A RECORD IS READ UNTIL IT IS REWRITTEN OR   */
95. /*   DELETED, AND HENCE MUST BE DECLARED STATIC.          */
96. /*                                                        */
```

```
97. /*          TEMP_RECORD IS USED TO HOLD THE RECORD BEING    */
98. /*    MOVED FROM ONE BUCKET TO ANOTHER IN THE DELETION      */
99. /*    PROCESS.                                              */
100. /*                                                         */
101. /***************************************************************/

102.    DECLARE BUCKET_NUMBER BINARY FIXED(15) STATIC,
103.            BUCKET_COUNT BINARY FIXED(15),
104.            OPEN_BUCKET BINARY FIXED(15),
105.            RECORD_NUMBER BINARY FIXED(15) STATIC,
106.            OPEN_RECORD BINARY FIXED(15),
107.            HASH_CONSTANT BINARY FIXED(15) INITIAL(23),
108.            FILE_SIZE BINARY FIXED(15) INITIAL(23),
109.            BUCKET_SIZE BINARY FIXED(15) INITIAL(5),
110.            (I,J) BINARY FIXED(15),
111.            SEARCHING BIT(1),
112.            TRUE BIT(1) STATIC INITIAL('1'B),
113.            FALSE BIT(1) STATIC INITIAL('0'B);

114.    DECLARE 1 TEMP_RECORD,
115.              3 TPART_NO CHARACTER(6),
116.              3 TQUANTITY BINARY FIXED(15),
117.              3 TDESCRIPTION CHARACTER(15);

118. /***************************************************************/
119. /*                                                           */
120. /*          SINCE THE FILE IS A RELATIVE FILE, A KEY ERROR    */
121. /*    WILL OCCUR ONLY IF THE KEY IS OUT OF RANGE, I. E.,      */
122. /*    LESS THAN ZERO OR GREATER THAN THE FILE SIZE. THE       */
123. /*    LOGIC OF THIS PROGRAM WILL PREVENT THIS. THEREFORE,     */
124. /*    IF A KEY ERROR OCCURS, THEN EITHER THERE IS SOMETHING   */
125. /*    WRONG WITH THE PROGRAM, OR ELSE THERE IS SOMETHING      */
126. /*    WRONG WITH THE FILE.                                    */
127. /*                                                           */
128. /***************************************************************/

129.    ON KEY(MFILE) BEGIN;
130.       PUT SKIP LIST('SOMETHING HORRIBLE HAPPENED!');
131.       STOP;
132.    END;

133. /***************************************************************/
134. /*                                                           */
135. /*          HASHING IS DONE BY THE MOST COMMON ALGORITHM,     */
136. /*    DIVIDING THE NUMERIC KEY BY THE NUMBER OF BUCKETS       */
137. /*    AND KEEPING THE REMAINDER.                             */
138. /*                                                           */
139. /***************************************************************/

140.    HASH: PROCEDURE(ID) RETURNS(BINARY FIXED(15));
141.       DECLARE I BINARY FIXED(15),
142.               ID CHARACTER(6);
```

```
143.        I = ID;
144.        RETURN(MOD(I,HASH_CONSTANT));
145.    END HASH;


146. /************************************************************/
147. /*                                                          */
148. /*          THIS IS THE MAIN PART OF THE FILEIO PROCEDURE.  */
149. /*                                                          */
150. /************************************************************/


151.    IF OP=OPEN THEN OPEN FILE(MFILE) DIRECT UPDATE;

152.    ELSE IF OP=CLOSE THEN CLOSE FILE(MFILE);

153.    ELSE IF OP=READ THEN DO;
154.       BUCKET_NUMBER = HASH(MRECORD.PART_NO);
155.       SEARCHING = TRUE;
156.       RFOUND = FALSE;
157.       DO BUCKET_COUNT = 1 TO FILE_SIZE WHILE(SEARCHING);
158.          READ FILE(MFILE) INTO(MASTER_BUCKET)
159.             KEY(BUCKET_NUMBER);
160.          RECORD_NUMBER = 1;
161.          DO WHILE(RECORD_NUMBER<=BUCKET_SIZE & SEARCHING);
162.             IF MASTER_RECORD.PART_NO(RECORD_NUMBER)=
163.                MRECORD.PART_NO THEN DO;
164.                SEARCHING = FALSE;
165.                RFOUND = TRUE;
166.                MRECORD = MASTER_RECORD(RECORD_NUMBER);
167.             END;
168.             ELSE IF MASTER_RECORD.PART_NO(RECORD_NUMBER)=
169.                '000000' THEN SEARCHING = FALSE;
170.             ELSE RECORD_NUMBER = RECORD_NUMBER+1;
171.          END;  /* OF DO RECORD_NUMBER  */
172.          IF SEARCHING THEN BUCKET_NUMBER = BUCKET_NUMBER+1;
173.          IF BUCKET_NUMBER=FILE_SIZE THEN BUCKET_NUMBER = 0;
174.       END;  /* OF DO BUCKET_COUNT  */
175.       IF SEARCHING THEN DO;
176.          PUT SKIP EDIT(
177.             'FILE FULL--NO MORE RECORDS CAN BE INSERTED')
178.             (A);
179.          STOP;
180.       END;
181.    END;  /* OF READ CASE  */

182.    ELSE IF OP=WRITE | OP=REWRITE THEN DO;
183.       MASTER_RECORD(RECORD_NUMBER) = MRECORD;
184.       REWRITE FILE(MFILE) FROM(MASTER_BUCKET)
185.          KEY(BUCKET_NUMBER);
186.    END;  /* OF WRITE AND REWRITE CASES  */
```

```
187.  /******************************************************************/
188.  /*                                                                */
189.  /*        THIS IMPLEMENTS KNUTH'S ALGORITHM FOR MOVING            */
190.  /*    RECORDS BACK INTO A VACATED POSITION IF THERE IS A          */
191.  /*    RECORD WHOSE LENGTH OF SEARCH WOULD BE SHORTENED BY         */
192.  /*    THE MOVE. THIS MAINTAINS THE FILE AT THE SAME               */
193.  /*    AVERAGE LENGTH OF SEARCH AS WOULD OCCUR IF THE              */
194.  /*    PRESENT RECORDS HAD BEEN INSERTED, AND NO DELETIONS         */
195.  /*    HAD TAKEN PLACE.                                            */
196.  /*                                                                */
197.  /******************************************************************/

198.      ELSE IF OP=DELETE THEN DO;
199.        OPEN_BUCKET = BUCKET_NUMBER;
200.        OPEN_RECORD = RECORD_NUMBER;
201.        /*  TO REMEMBER WHERE THE OPEN PLACE IS.            */
202.        /*  NOW WE SEARCH BUCKETS FOLLOWING THIS ONE TO     */
203.        /*  FIND A RECORD THAT SHOULD BE MOVED BACK TO THIS */
204.        /*  OPEN SPACE. THIS STOPS WHEN WE HAVE EXAMINED    */
205.        /*  ALL BUCKETS, OR WHEN WE FIND AN EMPTY RECORD    */
206.        /*  SPACE.IN FACT, IF THERE IS AN EMPTY SPACE IN    */
207.        /*  THE SAME BUCKET WHERE THE RECORD WAS DELETED,   */
208.        /*  WE STOP RIGHT THERE.                            */
209.        DO BUCKET_COUNT = 1 TO FILE_SIZE
210.           WHILE(MASTER_RECORD.PART_NO(BUCKET_SIZE)~='000000');
211.           BUCKET_NUMBER = BUCKET_NUMBER+1;
212.           IF BUCKET_NUMBER>=FILE_SIZE THEN BUCKET_NUMBER = 0;
213.           READ FILE(MFILE) INTO(MASTER_BUCKET)
214.               KEY(BUCKET_NUMBER);
215.           DO RECORD_NUMBER = 1 TO BUCKET_SIZE WHILE
216.              (MASTER_RECORD.PART_NO(RECORD_NUMBER)~='000000');
217.              J = HASH(MASTER_RECORD.PART_NO(RECORD_NUMBER));
218.              /*  IF THE CONDITION IS MET IN THE FOLLOWING    */
219.              /*  STATEMENT, THEN MOVING THAT RECORD INTO     */
220.              /*  THE OPEN PLACE REDUCES ITS LENGTH OF        */
221.              /*  SEARCH. THE HASHED ADDRESS OF THE RECORD    */
222.              /*  BEING CONSIDERED IS J; ITS LOCATION,        */
223.              /*  CALLED L IN THE EXPLANATION IN CHAPTER 8,   */
224.              /*  IS BUCKET-NO; AND "OPEN-BUCKET" HERE        */
225.              /*  CORRESPONDS TO P IN THE EXPLANATION.        */
226.              IF J<=OPEN_BUCKET & OPEN_BUCKET<BUCKET_NUMBER |
227.                 OPEN_BUCKET<BUCKET_NUMBER & BUCKET_NUMBER<J |
228.                 BUCKET_NUMBER<J & J<=OPEN_BUCKET THEN DO;
229.                 TEMP_RECORD = MASTER_RECORD(RECORD_NUMBER);
230.                 READ FILE(MFILE) INTO(MASTER_BUCKET)
231.                     KEY(OPEN_BUCKET);
232.                 MASTER_RECORD(OPEN_RECORD) = TEMP_RECORD;
233.                 REWRITE FILE(MFILE) FROM(MASTER_BUCKET)
234.                     KEY(OPEN_BUCKET);
235.                 OPEN_BUCKET = BUCKET_NUMBER;
236.                 OPEN_RECORD = RECORD_NUMBER;
```

```
237,                     MASTER_RECORD.PART_NO(OPEN_RECORD) = '000000';
238,              END;  /*  OF IF RECORD SHOULD BE MOVED  */
239,           END;  /*  OF DO RECORD_NUMBER  */
240,        END;  /*  OF LOOP ONCE PER BUCKET  */
241, /**************************************************************/
242, /*                                                          */
243, /*        AFTER NO MORE MOVING IS INDICATED, WE MOVE THE    */
244, /*     RECORDS UP IN THE BUCKET, LEAVING THE OPEN SPACE AT  */
245, /*     THE END OF THE BUCKET, AND THEN WE SET THE PART-NO   */
246, /*     IN THE OPEN SPACE TO 000000 TO INDICATE THAT NO      */
247, /*     RECORD IS THERE.                                     */
248, /*                                                          */
249, /**************************************************************/
250,        READ FILE(MFILE) INTO(MASTER_BUCKET) KEY(OPEN_BUCKET);
251,        DO I = OPEN_RECORD TO BUCKET_SIZE-1;
252,           /*  MOVE RECORDS DOWN--LEAVE OPEN SPACE AT END  */
253,           MASTER_RECORD(I) = MASTER_RECORD(I+1);
254,        END;
255,        MASTER_RECORD.PART_NO(BUCKET_SIZE) = '000000';
256,        REWRITE FILE(MFILE) FROM(MASTER_BUCKET)
257,           KEY(OPEN_BUCKET);
258,     END;  /*  OF DELETE CASE  */
259, END FILEIO;  /*  FOR HASHED CASE  */
```

The following program creates a relative file and suitably initializes it for use as a hashed file with the preceding program.

```
 1, MKEHASH: PROCEDURE OPTIONS(MAIN);
 2, /**************************************************************/
 3, /*                                                          */
 4, /*        THIS PROGRAM GENERATES A HASHED FILE BY WRITING   */
 5, /*     IT FULL OF DUMMY RECORDS SEQUENTIALLY. IN THE IBM    */
 6, /*     SYSTEM, IT IS NECESSARY TO DECLARE THE FILE "KEYED"  */
 7, /*     WHEN WRITING OR READING SEQUENTIALLY TO SHOW CLEARLY */
 8, /*     THAT IT IS NOT AN ORDINARY SEQUENTIAL FILE. WE HAVE  */
 9, /*     INSERTED A SINGLE "FILLER" CHARACTER AFTER EACH      */
10, /*     RECORD TO MAKE EACH RECORD FALL ON AN EVEN BOUNDARY, */
11, /*     BECAUSE THE IBM SYSTEM REQUIRES THAT TWO-BYTE BINARY */
12, /*     NUMBERS FALL ON EVEN ADDRESSES.                      */
13, /*                                                          */
14, /**************************************************************/
15,    DECLARE MFILE FILE RECORD KEYED
16,       ENVIRONMENT(REGIONAL(1));
17,    DECLARE 1 MASTER_BLOCK,
18,            2 MASTER_RECORD(5),
19,               3 PART_NO CHARACTER(6),
20,               3 QUANTITY BINARY FIXED(15),
21,               3 DESCRIPTION CHARACTER(15),
22,               3 FILLER CHARACTER(1);
```

```
23,    DECLARE BLOCK_SIZE BINARY FIXED(15) INITIAL(5),
24,            FILE_SIZE BINARY FIXED(15) INITIAL(23),
25,            I BINARY FIXED(15);

26,    OPEN FILE(MFILE) SEQUENTIAL OUTPUT;
27,    PUT SKIP EDIT('CREATE AND LOAD HASH FILE')(A);
28,    /*  INITIALIZE THE BLOCK TO DUMMY RECORDS  */
29,    DO I = 1 TO BLOCK_SIZE;
30,        PART_NO(I) = '000000';
31,        QUANTITY(I) = 0;
32,        DESCRIPTION(I) = ' ';
33,        FILLER(I) = ' ';
34,    END;

35,    DO I = 0 TO FILE_SIZE-1;
36,        WRITE FILE(MFILE) FROM(MASTER_BLOCK) KEYFROM(I);
37,    END;

38,    CLOSE FILE(MFILE);

39, END MKEHASH;
```

The following program will list the contents of the hashed file, showing the part number in each bucket, and thus showing how the file is structured internally.

```
 1, LSTHASH: PROCEDURE OPTIONS(MAIN);

 2, /*****************************************************************/
 3, /*                                                             */
 4, /*         THIS PROGRAM READS THE HASHED FILE SEQUENTIALLY */
 5, /*     AND SHOWS WHICH RECORDS ARE IN WHICH BLOCKS. THIS      */
 6, /*     LISTING WILL SHOW THE STRUCTURE OF THE HASHED FILE.    */
 7, /*     IT ALSO ILLUSTRATES SEQUENTIAL READING OF A RELATIVE   */
 8, /*     FILE.                                                  */
 9, /*                                                            */
10, /*****************************************************************/

11,    DECLARE MFILE FILE RECORD KEYED ENVIRONMENT(REGIONAL(1));

12,    DECLARE 1 MASTER_BLOCK,
13,            2 MASTER_RECORD(5),
14,             3 PART_NO CHARACTER(6),
15,             3 QUANTITY BINARY FIXED(15),
16,             3 DESCRIPTION CHARACTER(15),
17,             3 FILLER CHARACTER(1);

18, /*****************************************************************/
19, /*                                                             */
20, /*         FILE_SIZE, BUCKET_SIZE, TRUE, AND FALSE, AND        */
21, /*     HASH_CONSTANT ARE CONSTANTS OF THE INDICATED           */
22, /*     MEANING. BUCKET_NUMBER AND RECORD_NUMBER ARE WHERE     */
23, /*     A RECORD IS FOUND, AND J IS ITS HASHED ADDRESS.        */
24, /*     TOTAL_COUNT COUNTS THE RECORDS, AND TOTAL_SEARCH       */
```

```
25.  /*    IS THE NUMBER OF BUCKETS THAT WOULD HAVE TO BE        */
26.  /*    EXAMINED TO ACCESS EVERY RECORD ONCE. THEIR RATIO     */
27.  /*    IS AVE_SEARCH, THE AVERAGE LENGTH OF SEARCH.          */
28.  /*                                                          */
29.  /************************************************************/

30.     DECLARE FILE_SIZE BINARY FIXED(15) INITIAL(23),
31.             BUCKET_SIZE BINARY FIXED(15) INITIAL(5),
32.             BUCKET_NUMBER BINARY FIXED(15),
33.             HASH_CONSTANT BINARY FIXED(15) INITIAL(23),
34.             RECORD_NUMBER BINARY FIXED(15),
35.             J BINARY FIXED(15),
36.             TOTAL_COUNT BINARY FIXED(15),
37.             TOTAL_SEARCH BINARY FIXED(15),
38.             AVE_SEARCH DECIMAL FLOAT(6),
39.             TRUE BIT(1) INITIAL('1'B),
40.             FALSE BIT(1) STATIC INITIAL('0'B);

41.  /************************************************************/
42.  /*                                                          */
43.  /*        THIS IS THE SAME HASH FUNCTION AS IS USED IN      */
44.  /*    THE FILEIO PROCEDURE.                                 */
45.  /*                                                          */
46.  /************************************************************/
47.     HASH: PROCEDURE(ID) RETURNS(BINARY FIXED(15));
48.        DECLARE I BINARY FIXED(15),
49.                ID CHARACTER(6);
50.        I = ID;
51.        RETURN(MOD(I,HASH_CONSTANT));
52.     END HASH;

53.     OPEN FILE(MFILE) SEQUENTIAL INPUT;
54.     PUT SKIP EDIT
55.        ('LISTING OF CONTENTS OF HASH FILE')(A);

56.     TOTAL_SEARCH = 0;
57.     TOTAL_COUNT = 0;
58.     DO BUCKET_NUMBER = 0 TO FILE_SIZE-1;
59.        PUT SKIP EDIT(BUCKET_NUMBER)(F(3));
60.        READ FILE(MFILE) INTO(MASTER_BLOCK);
61.        DO RECORD_NUMBER = 1 TO BUCKET_SIZE;
62.           J = HASH(PART_NO(RECORD_NUMBER));
63.           IF PART_NO(RECORD_NUMBER)~='000000' THEN DO;
64.              TOTAL_COUNT = TOTAL_COUNT+1;
65.              IF J<=BUCKET_NUMBER THEN TOTAL_SEARCH =
66.                 TOTAL_SEARCH + BUCKET_NUMBER - J + 1;
67.              ELSE TOTAL_SEARCH = TOTAL_SEARCH +
68.                 FILE_SIZE + BUCKET_NUMBER - J + 1;
69.           END;
70.           PUT EDIT('--',PART_NO(RECORD_NUMBER,J)(A,A,F(4));
```

```
71.         END;  /*  OF RECORD LOOP  */
72.     END;  /*  OF BUCKET LOOP  */

73.     CLOSE FILE(MFILE);
74.     IF TOTAL_COUNT>0 THEN
75.         AVE_SEARCH = TOTAL_SEARCH/TOTAL_COUNT;
76.     ELSE AVE_SEARCH = 0;
77.     PUT SKIP EDIT('TOTAL LENGTH OF SEARCH =',TOTAL_SEARCH)
78.         (A,F(6));
79.     PUT SKIP EDIT('TOTAL COUNT =',TOTAL_COUNT)(A,F(6));
80.     PUT SKIP EDIT('AVERAGE LENGTH OF SEARCH =',AVE_SEARCH)
81.         (A,F(6,2));

82. END LSTHASH;
```

APPENDIX

FORTRAN Program Examples

This appendix contains example programs written in FORTRAN to illustrate sequential processing and on-line processing with relative files and hashed files. All programs are written for the examples in Chapters 7 and 8 and provide more detailed illustrations of file programming. The first program is a sequential update program. Next is a main program for the on-line inventory system described in the examples in Chapter 7. The main program contains no file instructions, only calls to a subprogram that does the file operations. Following that are two subprograms— one using a relative file and another using a hashed file. With the relative file subprogram is a short program to create that file and one that uses sequential reading of the relative file to list its contents. With the hashed file subprogram there are short programs to create and initialize the hashed file and to dump its contents.

These programs are included to give examples of I-O programming. In other respects, the programs are very much simplified. All of these programs have been tested on a DEC-20 system using TOPS20. We have made a serious effort to make them conform to the FORTRAN77 Standard.

D.1. BATCH UPDATE PROGRAM

For this program, the master file is created initially as an empty file. Then an update run is made to insert records into it. Thus, the following program can be used to initialize the file, as well as for routine updating afterwards.

```
1.C      THIS IS A SIMPLE BATCH UPDATE PROGRAM
2.C      FOR THE INVENTORY APPLICATION USED AS
```

```
 3.C      AN EXAMPLE IN CHAPTER 7.
 4.C
 5.C      THIS IS THE MAIN PROGRAM. OTHER PROCEDURES ARE:
 6.C
 7.C      READTR    READ ONE TRANSACTION
 8.C      READMA    READ ONE OLD MASTER RECORD
 9.C      INITAL    DO INITIAL PROCESSING ON A NEW MASTER RECORD
10.C      FINAL     DO FINAL PROCESSING ON A NEW MASTER RECORD
11.C      EDITCK    EDIT CHECK ONE TRANSACTION
12.C      PROCTR    PROCESS ONE TRANSACTION
13.C
14.C      THE FOLLOWING IS THE COMMON STORAGE DECLARATION:
15.C      (NOTE THAT THESE TOGETHER WITH THE READ STATEMENTS
16.C      DEFINE THE FORMATS OF TRANSACTION AND MASTER RECORDS.)
17.C
.18.     CHARACTER*6 OMID,NMID,TRID
19.      CHARACTER*4 TRQ
20.      INTEGER OMQ,NMQ,TQ,OLDQ,RCOUNT,DCOUNT
21.      CHARACTER*15 OMDESC,NMDESC,TRDESC
22.      CHARACTER*1 TCODE
23.      LOGICAL OK
24.      COMMON OMQ,NMQ,TQ,OLDQ,RCOUNT,DCOUNT,OK,OMID,NMID,TRID,
25.     XTRQ,OMDESC,NMDESC,TRDESC,TCODE
26.C
27.C      OMID      ID IN OLD MASTER
28.C      OMQ       QUANTITY IN OLD MASTER
29.C      OMDESC    DESCRIPTION OLD MASTER
30.C      NMID      ID IN NEW MASTER
31.C      NMQ       QUANTITY IN NEW MASTER
32.C      NMDESC    DESCRIPTION IN NEW MASTER
33.C      TRID      ID IN TRANSACTION
34.C      TRQ       QUANTITY IN TRANSACTION
35.C      TQ        TRQ, AFTER CONVERSION TO BINARY
36.C      TRDESC    DESCRIPTION IN TRANSACTION
37.C      TCODE     TRANSACTION CODE
38.C      OLDQ      OLD QUANTITY
39.C      RCOUNT    RECEIVED-GOODS COUNT
40.C      DCOUNT    DISBURSED-GOODS COUNT
41.C      OK        SET FALSE WHEN ERROR FOUND IN TRANSACTION
42.C
43.      CHARACTER*60 HEADER
44.C
45.C      HEADER IS USED ONLY FOR PRINTING REPORT HEADINGS
46.C
47.C      INITIALIZATION
48.C
49.      NMID = '000000'
50.      CALL READTR 51.
51.      CALL READMA
52.      HEADER = 'ID       DESCRIPTION     QUANTITY'
53.      WRITE(20,11)HEADER
```

```
54.         HEADER =
55.     X'                           OLD    IN    OUT    NEW'
56.         WRITE(20,11)HEADER
57.   11 FORMAT(1X,A60)
58.C
59.C     MAIN LOOP
60.C
61.    1 IF (NMID.LT.'999999') THEN
62.C
63.C         IF THERE ARE NO MORE TRANSACTIONS FOR THE CURRENT
64.C         NEW MASTER RECORD, FINISH PROCESSING IT AND WRITE
65.C         IT OUT.
66.C
67.         IF(NMID.LT.TRID.AND.NMID.NE.'000000') THEN
68.            CALL FINAL
69.            WRITE(23)NMID,NMQ,NMDESC
70.            NMID = '000000'
71.         END IF
72.C
73.C         IF THE NEXT RECORD TO BE PROCESSED WILL BE THE
74.C         OLD MASTER RECORD LAST READ, MOVE IT TO THE NEW
75.C         MASTER RECORD VARIABLES
76.C
77.         IF(OMID.LE.TRID) THEN
78.            NMID = OMID
79.            NMQ = OMQ
80.            NMDESC = OMDESC
81.            IF(NMID.NE.'999999')THEN
82.               CALL READMA
83.               CALL INITAL
84.            ENDIF
85.C
86.C         OTHERWISE WE ARE READY TO PROCESS THE NEXT
87.C         TRANSACTION
88.C
89.         ELSE
90.            CALL EDITCK
91.            IF(OK) CALL PROCTR
92.            CALL READTR
93.         END IF
94.C
95.         GO TO 1
96.      END IF
97.C     END OF MAIN LOOP
98.C
99.      STOP
100.     END
101.C
102.     SUBROUTINE READTR
103.C
104.C     THIS PROCEDURE READS ONE TRANSACTION AND IF THE
```

```
105.C      READ OCCURS ON END OF FILE, THE TRANSACTION ID
106.C      IS SET TO ALL-9'S
107.C
108.C      ID'S LESS THAN ONE OR GREATER THAN 999998 ARE
109.C      NOT ALLOWED--A CHECK IS MADE HERE FOR SUCH ID'S
110.C      AND THEY ARE REJECTED HERE.
111.C
112.       CHARACTER*6 OMID,NMID,TRID
113.       CHARACTER*4 TRQ
114.       INTEGER OMQ,NMQ,TQ,OLDQ,RCOUNT,DCOUNT
115.       CHARACTER*15 OMDESC,NMDESC,TRDESC
116.       CHARACTER*1 TCODE
117.       LOGICAL OK
118.       COMMON OMQ,NMQ,TQ,OLDQ,RCOUNT,DCOUNT,OK,OMID,NMID,TRID,
119.      XTRQ,OMDESC,NMDESC,TRDESC,TCODE
120.    2     READ(21,11,END=1)TRID,TCODE,TRQ,TRDESC
121.   11     FORMAT(A6,A1,A4,A15)
122.          IF(TRID.LE.'000000'.OR.TRID.GE.'999999') THEN
123.          MESSAG = '--ID OUT OF RANGE'
124.          WRITE(20,12)TRID,TCODE,TRQ,TRDESC,MESSAG
125.   12     FORMAT(1X,A6,1X,A1,1X,A4,1X,A15,1X,A25)
126.          GO TO 2
127.       ENDIF
128.       RETURN
129.C
130.    1 TRID = '999999'
131.       RETURN
132.C
133.       END
134.C
135.       SUBROUTINE READMA
136.C
137.C      THIS PROCEDURE READS THE NEXT OLD MASTER RECORD,
138.C      SETTING OMID TO ALL-9'S IF THE READ OCCURS AT END
139.C      OF FILE
140.C
141.       CHARACTER*6 OMID,NMID,TRID
142.       CHARACTER*4 TRQ
143.       INTEGER OMQ,NMQ,TQ,OLDQ,RCOUNT,DCOUNT
144.       CHARACTER*15 OMDESC,NMDESC,TRDESC
145.       CHARACTER*1 TCODE
146.       LOGICAL OK
147.       COMMON OMQ,NMQ,TQ,OLDQ,RCOUNT,DCOUNT,OK,OMID,NMID,TRID,
148.      XTRQ,OMDESC,NMDESC,TRDESC,TCODE
149.       READ(22,END=1)OMID,OMQ,OMDESC
150.       RETURN
151.C
152.    1 OMID = '999999'
153.       RETURN
154.C
```

```
155,      END
156,C
157,      SUBROUTINE INITAL
158,C
159,C     THIS PROCEDURE DOES WHATEVER PROCESSING IS NEEDED
160,C     AT THE START OF A NEW MASTER RECORD,
161,C
162,      CHARACTER*6 OMID,NMID,TRID
163,      CHARACTER*4 TRQ
164,      INTEGER OMQ,NMQ,TQ,OLDQ,RCOUNT,DCOUNT
165,      CHARACTER*15 OMDESC,NMDESC,TRDESC
166,      CHARACTER*1 TCODE
167,      LOGICAL OK
168,      COMMON OMQ,NMQ,TQ,OLDQ,RCOUNT,DCOUNT,OK,OMID,NMID,TRID,
169,     XTRQ,OMDESC,NMDESC,TRDESC,TCODE
170,      OLDQ = NMQ
171,      RCOUNT = 0
172,      DCOUNT = 0
173,      END
174,C
175,      SUBROUTINE FINAL
176,C
177,C     FINAL DOES WHAT MUST BE DONE AFTER ALL THE
178,C     TRANSACTIONS HAVE BEEN PROCESSED FOR A NEW MASTER
179,C     RECORD TO COMPLETE ITS PROCESSING,
180,C
181,      CHARACTER*6 OMID,NMID,TRID
182,      CHARACTER*4 TRQ
183,      INTEGER OMQ,NMQ,TQ,OLDQ,RCOUNT,DCOUNT
184,      CHARACTER*15 OMDESC,NMDESC,TRDESC
185,      CHARACTER*1 TCODE
186,      LOGICAL OK
187,      COMMON OMQ,NMQ,TQ,OLDQ,RCOUNT,DCOUNT,OK,OMID,NMID,TRID,
188,     XTRQ,OMDESC,NMDESC,TRDESC,TCODE
189,      WRITE(20,11)NMID,NMDESC,OLDQ,RCOUNT,DCOUNT,NMQ
190,   11 FORMAT(1X,A6,1X,A15,4I5)
191,      END
192,C
193,      SUBROUTINE EDITCK
194,C     THIS PROCEDURE DOES ALL THE EDIT CHECKING OF THE
195,C     TRANSACTION LAST READ
196,      CHARACTER*6 OMID,NMID,TRID
197,      CHARACTER*4 TRQ
198,      INTEGER OMQ,NMQ,TQ,OLDQ,RCOUNT,DCOUNT
199,      CHARACTER*15 OMDESC,NMDESC,TRDESC
200,      CHARACTER*1 TCODE
201,      LOGICAL OK
202,      COMMON OMQ,NMQ,TQ,OLDQ,RCOUNT,DCOUNT,OK,OMID,NMID,TRID,
203,     XTRQ,OMDESC,NMDESC,TRDESC,TCODE
204,      LOGICAL E
```

```
205.       INTEGER I,J
206.       CHARACTER*25 MESSAG
207.C
208.C     E, I, AND J ARE USED AS TEMPORARIES.
209.C     MESSAG IS THE ERROR MESSAGE TO BE PRINTED
210.C
211.C     FIRST WE CHECK WHETHER THE ID IS ALL DIGITS
212.       E = .FALSE.
213.       DO 1 I = 1,6
214.           E = E.OR.(TRID(I:I).LT.'0'.OR.TRID(I:I).GT.'9')
215.    1 CONTINUE
216.       IF(E) THEN
217.           MESSAG = '--ID NOT ALL NUMERIC'
218.           WRITE(20,11)TRID,TCODE,TRQ,TRDESC,MESSAG
219.    11     FORMAT(1X,A6,1X,A1,1X,A4,1X,A15,1X,A25)
220.       END IF
221.       OK = .NOT.E
222.C
223.C     NOTE THAT THE FOLLOWING TWO CHECKS CAN BE MADE
224.C     BECAUSE THE MATCHING MASTER RECORD DATA ARE THE
225.C     NEW MASTER RECORD DATA, IF A MATCHING RECORD EXISTS
226.C
227.       IF(OK.AND.TCODE.EQ.'A'.AND.TRID.EQ.NMID) THEN
228.           OK = .FALSE.
229.           MESSAG = '--DUPLICATE ID'
230.           WRITE(20,11)TRID,TCODE,TRQ,TRDESC,MESSAG
231.C
232.       ELSE IF(OK.AND..NOT.(TCODE.EQ.'A')
233.     X     .AND.TRID.NE.NMID) THEN
234.           OK = .FALSE.
235.           MESSAG = '--MASTER RECORD NOT FOUND'
236.           WRITE(20,11)TRID,TCODE,TRQ,TRDESC,MESSAG
237.       END IF
238.C
239.       IF(TCODE.NE.'A'.AND.TCODE.NE.'B'.AND.TCODE.NE.'C'
240.     X     .AND.TCODE.NE.'D') THEN
241.           OK = .FALSE.
242.           MESSAG = '--INVALID CODE'
243.           WRITE(20,11)TRID,TCODE,TRQ,TRDESC,MESSAG
244.       END IF
245.C
246.       IF(TCODE.EQ.'A'.OR.TCODE.EQ.'B'.OR.TCODE.EQ.'C') THEN
247.C          QUANTITY IS NEEDED--CHECK WHETHER NUMERIC
248.C          IF NUMERIC CONVERT TO BINARY AND STORE IN TQ
249.           E = .FALSE.
250.           DO 2 I = 1,4
251.               E = E.OR.(TRQ(I:I).LT.'0'.OR.TRQ(I:I).GT.'9')
252.    2      CONTINUE
253.           IF(E) THEN
254.               OK = .FALSE.
```

```
255.              MESSAG = '--QUANTITY NOT NUMERIC'
256.              WRITE(20,11)TRID,TCODE,TRQ,TRDESC,MESSAG
257.           ELSE
258.              TQ = 0
259.              DO 3 I=1,4
260.                 J = 0
261.                 IF(TRQ(I:I).EQ.'1') J = 1
262.                 IF(TRQ(I:I).EQ.'2') J = 2
263.                 IF(TRQ(I:I).EQ.'3') J = 3
264.                 IF(TRQ(I:I).EQ.'4') J = 4
265.                 IF(TRQ(I:I).EQ.'5') J = 5
266.                 IF(TRQ(I:I).EQ.'6') J = 6
267.                 IF(TRQ(I:I).EQ.'7') J = 7
268.                 IF(TRQ(I:I).EQ.'8') J = 8
269.                 IF(TRQ(I:I).EQ.'9') J = 9
270.                 TQ = TQ*10 + J
271.     3        CONTINUE
272.           END IF
273.        END IF
274.C
275.        IF(OK.AND.TCODE.EQ.'C'.AND.TQ.GT.NMQ) THEN
276.           OK = .FALSE.
277.           MESSAG = '--NOT ENOUGH IN STOCK'
278.           WRITE(20,11)TRID,TCODE,TRQ,TRDESC,MESSAG
279.        END IF
280.C
281.        IF(TCODE.EQ.'A'.AND.TRDESC.EQ.' ') THEN
282.           OK = .FALSE.
283.           MESSAG = '--DESCRIPTION MISSING'
284.           WRITE(20,11)TRID,TCODE,TRQ,TRDESC,MESSAG
285.        END IF
286.C
287.        IF(TCODE.EQ.'D'.AND.NMQ.NE.0) THEN
288.           OK = .FALSE.
289.           MESSAG = 'QUANTITY NOT 0 ON DELETE'
290.           WRITE(20,11)TRID,TCODE,TRQ,TRDESC,MESSAG
291.        END IF
292.        RETURN
293.        END
294.C
295.        SUBROUTINE PROCTR
296.C
297.C     THIS PROCEDURE CARRIES OUT THE ACTUAL TRANSACTION
298.C     PROCESSING
299.C
300.        CHARACTER*6 OMID,NMID,TRID
301.        CHARACTER*4 TRQ
302.        INTEGER OMQ,NMQ,TQ,OLDQ,RCOUNT,DCOUNT
303.        CHARACTER*15 OMDESC,NMDESC,TRDESC
304.        CHARACTER*1 TCODE
```

```
305.  ,      LOGICAL OK
306.         COMMON OMQ,NMQ,TQ,OLDQ,RCOUNT,DCOUNT,OK,OMID,NMID,TRID,
307.        XTRQ,OMDESC,NMDESC,TRDESC,TCODE
308.C    INSERT NEW RECORD
309.       IF(TCODE.EQ.'A') THEN
310.          NMID = TRID
311.          NMQ = 0
312.          NMDESC = TRDESC
313.          CALL INITAL
314.       END IF
315.C
316.C    RECEIVE GOODS, INCLUDING WHEN NEW RECORD INSERTED
317.       IF(TCODE.EQ.'A'.OR.TCODE.EQ.'B') THEN
318.          NMQ = NMQ+TQ
319.          RCOUNT = RCOUNT+TQ
320.C
321.C    DISBURSE GOODS
322.       ELSE IF(TCODE.EQ.'C') THEN
323.          NMQ = NMQ-TQ
324.          DCOUNT = DCOUNT+TQ
325.C
326.C    DELETE RECORD
327.       ELSE
328.          NMID = '000000'
329.       END IF
330.       RETURN
331.       END
```

D.2. MAIN PROGRAM FOR ON-LINE UPDATE

This program calls a subprogram for all file operations. A FILEIO subroutine using a relative file and one using a hashed file follow.

```
 1.C      THIS PROGRAM DOES THE INVENTORY SYSTEM ON LINE.
 2.C      LOGICAL I-O UNIT 5 IS THE TERMINAL. COMMAND CODES
 3.C      ARE:
 4.C
 5.C      A     INSERT NEW RECORD
 6.C      B     DISBURSE GOODS
 7.C      C     RECEIVE GOODS
 8.C      D     DELETE RECORD
 9.C      Q     INQUIRY
10.C      H     HELP
11.C      S     STOP RUN
12.C
13.C      THIS PROGRAM ASSUMES THAT THE MASTER FILE HAS HAD
14.C      DUMMY RECORDS WRITTEN INTO ALL POSSIBLE RECORD
15.C      POSITIONS INITIALLY, WITH ZEROS WRITTEN IN AS ID'S
```

```
16.C
17.C      THE FOLLOWING IS THE COMMON STORAGE DECLARATION:
18.C      (NOTE THAT THESE TOGETHER WITH THE READ STATEMENTS
19.C      DEFINE THE FORMATS OF TRANSACTION AND MASTER RECORDS.)
20.C
21.       CHARACTER*6 MID,TRID
22.       CHARACTER*4 TRQ
23.       INTEGER MQ,TQ,RECORD
24.       CHARACTER*15 MDESC,TRDESC
25.       CHARACTER*1 TCODE
26.       LOGICAL OK,FOUND
27.       COMMON RECORD,MQ,TQ,OK,FOUND,MID,TRID,
28.      XTRQ,MDESC,TRDESC,TCODE
29.C
30.C      MID      ID IN MASTER
31.C      MQ       QUANTITY IN MASTER
32.C      MDESC    DESCRIPTION MASTER
33.C      TRID     ID IN TRANSACTION
34.C      TRQ      QUANTITY IN TRANSACTION
35.C      TQ       TRQ, AFTER CONVERSION TO BINARY
36.C      TRDESC   DESCRIPTION IN TRANSACTION
37.C      TCODE    TRANSACTION CODE
38.C      RECORD   RECORD NUMBER (= ID CONVERTED TO BINARY)
39.C      OK       SET FALSE WHEN ERROR FOUND IN TRANSACTION
40.C
41.C      THE FOLLOWING SUBROUTINES ARE USED:
42.C      GETCOM   GET COMMAND FROM TERMINAL
43.C      GETID    GET ID FROM TERMINAL
44.C      GETQ     GET QUANTITY FROM TERMINAL
45.C      GETDES   GET DESCRIPTION FROM TERMINAL
46.C      PROCES   PROCESS TRANSACTION
47.C      FILEIO   ALL FILE OPERATIONS
48.C
49.C      FOLLOWING THIS MAIN PROGRAM AND THE OTHER SUBROUTINES,
50.C      THERE ARE TWO VERSIONS OF THE FILEIO SUBROUTINE, ONE
51.C      USES A SIMPLE RELATIVE FILE, AND THE OTHER A HASHED
52.C      FILE. FOR FILEIO, THE FOLLOWING VALUES ARE PASSED AS
53.C      THE PARAMETER, TO INDICATE WHICH OPERATION: OPEN:
54.C      OPENOP=1, READ: READOP=2, WRITE: WRITOP=3, AND
55.C      DELETE: DELEOP=4.
56.C
57.       INTEGER OPENOP,READOP,WRITOP,DELEOP
58.       DATA OPENOP/1/READOP/2/WRITOP/3/DELEOP/4/
59.C
60.       LOGICAL NEEDRD
61.C      NEEDRD IS SET TRUE IF A MASTER RECORD MUST BE READ
62.C
63.C      THIS IS THE BEGINNING OF THE MAIN PROGRAM
64.C
65.       WRITE(5,*)' INVENTORY SYSTEM--COMMAND H FOR HELP'
```

```
66.        CALL FILEIO(OPENOP)
67.        TCODE = ' '
68.C
69.C      THIS IS THE MAIN LOOP, REPEATED FOR EACH COMMAND,
70.C      REPEATED UNTIL A COMMAND S (STOP) IS ENTERED.
71.C      FIRST IT GETS THE COMMAND, THEN IT GETS THE ID,
72.C      THEN IF OK, IT TRIES TO READ. THEN, IF NEEDED, IT
73.C      GETS THE QUANTITY AND DESCRIPTION AND TAKES THE
74.C      INDICATED ACTION. FINALLY, IT PRINTS THE CONTENT
75.C      OF THE RECORD JUST PROCESSED.
76.C
77.     1 IF(TCODE.NE.'S') THEN
78.          OK = .TRUE.
79.          CALL GETCOM
80.          NEEDRD = (TCODE.NE.'S'.AND.TCODE.NE.'H')
81.          IF(OK.AND.NEEDRD) CALL GETID
82.          IF(OK.AND.NEEDRD) THEN
83.             CALL FILEIO(READOP)
84.             IF(TCODE.EQ.'A'.AND.FOUND) THEN
85.                WRITE(5,*)' DUPLICATE RECORD'
86.                OK = .FALSE.
87.             ELSE IF(TCODE.NE.'A'.AND..NOT.FOUND)THEN
88.                WRITE(5,*)' RECORD NOT FOUND'
89.                OK = .FALSE.
90.             ELSE IF(TCODE.EQ.'D'.AND.MQ.NE.0)THEN
91.                WRITE(5,*)'QUANTITY NOT ZERO ON DELETE'
92.                OK = .FALSE.
93.             END IF
94.          END IF
95.C
96.          IF(OK.AND.(TCODE.EQ.'A'.OR.TCODE.EQ.'B'.OR.
97.     X      TCODE.EQ.'C')) CALL GETQ
98.C
99.          IF(OK.AND.TCODE.EQ.'A') CALL GETDES
100.C
101.         IF(TCODE.EQ.'H')THEN
102.            WRITE(5,*)'ENTER ONE-LETTER COMMAND NAME:'
103.            WRITE(5,*)'A      INSERT NEW RECORD'
104.            WRITE(5,*)'B      RECEIVE GOODS     '
105.            WRITE(5,*)'C      DISBURSE GOODS    '
106.            WRITE(5,*)'D      DELETE RECORD     '
107.            WRITE(5,*)'Q      INQUIRY          '
108.            WRITE(5,*)'H      HELP             '
109.            WRITE(5,*)'S      STOP RUN         '
110.         ELSE IF(OK) THEN
111.            CALL PROCTR
112.         ELSE
113.            WRITE(5,*)' NOT DONE BECAUSE OF ERROR'
114.         END IF
115.C
```

```
116.            IF(OK.AND.NEEDRD) THEN
117.               WRITE(5,11)MID,MDESC,MQ
118.    11        FORMAT(1X,A6,1X,A15,' QUANTITY ON HAND ',I4)
119.            END IF
120.        GO TO 1
121.C
122.C    END OF MAIN LOOP
123.C
124.        END IF
125.C
126.        WRITE(21,*)'RUN FINISHED'
127.        STOP
128.        END
129.C               •
130.C-------------------------------------------------------------
131.C
132.        SUBROUTINE GETCOM
133.C    GET A COMMAND FROM THE TERMINAL AND CHECK IT
134.C
135.C    THE FOLLOWING IS THE COMMON STORAGE DECLARATION:
136.C    (SEE MAIN PROGRAM FOR DEFINITIONS)
137.C
138.        CHARACTER*6 MID,TRID
139.        CHARACTER*4 TRQ
140.        INTEGER MQ,TQ,RECORD
141.        CHARACTER*15 MDESC,TRDESC
142.        CHARACTER*1 TCODE
143.        LOGICAL OK,FOUND
144.        COMMON RECORD,MQ,TQ,OK,FOUND,MID,TRID,
145.       XTRQ,MDESC,TRDESC,TCODE
146.C
147.        WRITE(5,*)' ENTER COMMAND'
148.        READ(5,11)TCODE
149.    11 FORMAT(A1)
150.        IF(TCODE.NE.'A'.AND.TCODE.NE.'B'.AND.TCODE.NE.'C'
151.       X   .AND.TCODE.NE.'D'.AND.TCODE.NE.'Q'.AND.TCODE.NE.'S'
152.       X   .AND.TCODE.NE.'H') THEN
153.        WRITE(5,*)' INVALID COMMAND'
154.        OK = .FALSE.
155.        END IF
156.C
157.        RETURN
158.        END
159.C
160.C-------------------------------------------------------------
161.C
162.        SUBROUTINE GETID
163.C    GET THE ID FROM THE TERMINAL
164.C
165.C    THE FOLLOWING IS THE COMMON STORAGE DECLARATION:
```

```
166.C      (SEE MAIN PROGRAM FOR DEFINITIONS)
167.C
168.       CHARACTER*6 MID,TRID
169.       CHARACTER*4 TRQ
170.       INTEGER MQ,TQ,RECORD
171.       CHARACTER*15 MDESC,TRDESC
172.       CHARACTER*1 TCODE
173.       LOGICAL OK,FOUND
174.       COMMON RECORD,MQ,TQ,OK,FOUND,MID,TRID,
175.      XTRQ,MDESC,TRDESC,TCODE
176.C
177.       LOGICAL E
178.       INTEGER J
179.C      E AND J ARE USED AS TEMPORARIES
180.C
181.       WRITE(5,*)' ENTER ID(6 DIGITS)'
182.       READ(5,11)TRID
183.    11 FORMAT(A6)
184.C      NEXT WE CHECK WHETHER THE ID IS ALL DIGITS
185.       E = .FALSE.
186.       DO 1 I = 1,6
187.          E = E.OR.(TRID(I:I).LT.'0'.OR.TRID(I:I).GT.'9')
188.     1 CONTINUE
189.       OK = .NOT.E
190.       IF(E) THEN
191.          WRITE(5,*)' --ID NOT ALL NUMERIC'
192.       ELSE IF(TRID.EQ.'000000'.OR.TRID.EQ.'999999') THEN
193.          WRITE(5,*)' NOT ALLOWED AS ID'
194.          OK = .FALSE.
195.       END IF
196.C      CONVERT ID TO BINARY
197.       IF(OK) THEN
198.          RECORD = 0
199.          DO 2 I = 3,6
200.             J = 0
201.             IF(TRID(I:I).EQ.'1') J = 1
202.             IF(TRID(I:I).EQ.'2') J = 2
203.             IF(TRID(I:I).EQ.'3') J = 3
204.             IF(TRID(I:I).EQ.'4') J = 4
205.             IF(TRID(I:I).EQ.'5') J = 5
206.             IF(TRID(I:I).EQ.'6') J = 6
207.             IF(TRID(I:I).EQ.'7') J = 7
208.             IF(TRID(I:I).EQ.'8') J = 8
209.             IF(TRID(I:I).EQ.'9') J = 9
210.             RECORD = RECORD*10 + J
211.     2     CONTINUE
212.       END IF
213.       RETURN
214.       END
215.C
216.C-------------------------------------------------------------
```

```
217.C
218.      SUBROUTINE GETDES
219.C     GET DESCRIPTION FROM TERMINAL
220.C
221.C     THE FOLLOWING IS THE COMMON STORAGE DECLARATION:
222.C     (SEE MAIN PROGRAM FOR DEFINITIONS)
223.C
224.      CHARACTER*6 MID,TRID
225.      CHARACTER*4 TRQ
226.      INTEGER MQ,TQ,RECORD
227.      CHARACTER*15 MDESC,TRDESC
228.      CHARACTER*1 TCODE
229.      LOGICAL OK,FOUND
230.      COMMON RECORD,MQ,TQ,OK,FOUND,MID,TRID,
231.     XTRQ,MDESC,TRDESC,TCODE
232.C
233.      WRITE(5,*)' ENTER DESCRIPTION -- MAX 15 CHARACTERS'
234.      READ(5,11)TRDESC
235.   11 FORMAT(A11)
236.      IF(TRDESC.EQ.'                ') THEN
237.         WRITE(5,*)' NOT ENTERED'
238.         OK = .FALSE.
239.      END IF
240.      END
241.C
242.C------------------------------------------------------------
243.C
244.      SUBROUTINE GETQ
245.C     GET QUANTITY FROM TERMINAL
246.C
247.C     THE FOLLOWING IS THE COMMON STORAGE DECLARATION:
248.C     (SEE MAIN PROGRAM FOR DEFINITIONS)
249.C
250.      CHARACTER*6 MID,TRID
251.      CHARACTER*4 TRQ
252.      INTEGER MQ,TQ,RECORD
253.      CHARACTER*15 MDESC,TRDESC
254.      CHARACTER*1 TCODE
255.      LOGICAL OK,FOUND
256.      COMMON RECORD,MQ,TQ,OK,FOUND,MID,TRID,
257.     XTRQ,MDESC,TRDESC,TCODE
258.C
259.      LOGICAL E
260.      INTEGER J
261.C     E AND J ARE USED AS TEMPORARIES
262.C
263.      WRITE(5,*)' ENTER QUANTITY (4 DIGITS)'
264.      READ(5,11)TRQ
265.   11 FORMAT(A4)
266.C     CHECK WHETHER QUANTITY IS NUMERIC
267.      E = .FALSE.
```

```
268.      DO 2 I = 1,4
269.         E = E.OR.(TRQ(I:I).LT.'0'.OR.TRQ(I:I).GT.'9')
270.    2 CONTINUE
271.      IF(E) THEN
272.         OK = .FALSE.
273.         WRITE(5,*)' QUANTITY NOT NUMERIC'
274.      ELSE
275.C      CONVERT QUANTITY TO BINARY
276.         TQ = 0
277.         DO 1 I = 1,4
278.            J = 0
279.            IF(TRQ(I:I).EQ.'1') J = 1
280.            IF(TRQ(I:I).EQ.'2') J = 2
281.            IF(TRQ(I:I).EQ.'3') J = 3
282.            IF(TRQ(I:I).EQ.'4') J = 4
283.            IF(TRQ(I:I).EQ.'5') J = 5
284.            IF(TRQ(I:I).EQ.'6') J = 6
285.            IF(TRQ(I:I).EQ.'7') J = 7
286.            IF(TRQ(I:I).EQ.'8') J = 8
287.            IF(TRQ(I:I).EQ.'9') J = 9
288.            TQ = TQ*10 + J
289.    1    CONTINUE
290.         IF(TCODE.EQ.'C'.AND.TQ.GT.MQ) THEN
291.            OK = .FALSE.
292.            WRITE(5,*)'--NOT ENOUGH IN STOCK'
293.         END IF
294.C
295.      END IF
296.      RETURN
297.      END
298.C
299.C------------------------------------------------------------
300.C
301.      SUBROUTINE PROCTR
302.C      THIS PROCEDURE CARRIES OUT THE ACTUAL TRANSACTION
303.C      PROCESSING
304.C
305.C      THE FOLLOWING IS THE COMMON STORAGE DECLARATION:
306.C      (SEE MAIN PROGRAM FOR DEFINITIONS)
307.C
308.      CHARACTER*6 MID,TRID
309.      CHARACTER*4 TRQ
310.      INTEGER MQ,TQ,RECORD
311.      CHARACTER*15 MDESC,TRDESC
312.      CHARACTER*1 TCODE
313.      LOGICAL OK,FOUND
314.      COMMON RECORD,MQ,TQ,OK,FOUND,MID,TRID,
315.     XTRQ,MDESC,TRDESC,TCODE
316.C
317.C      FOR FILEIO, THE FOLLOWING VALUES ARE PASSED AS THE
```

```
318.C       PARAMETER, TO INDICATE WHICH OPERATION: 1--OPENOP,
319.C       2--READOP, 3--WRITOP, AND 4--DELEOP
320.C
321.        INTEGER OPENOP,READOP,WRITOP,DELEOP
322.        DATA OPENOP/1/READOP/2/WRITOP/3/DELEOP/4/
323.C
324.C       INSERT NEW RECORD
325.        IF(TCODE.EQ.'A') THEN
326.           MID = TRID
327.           MQ = 0
328.           MDESC = TRDESC
329.        END IF
330.C
331.C       RECEIVE GOODS, INCLUDING WHEN NEW RECORD INSERTED
332.        IF(TCODE.EQ.'A'.OR.TCODE.EQ.'B') THEN
333.           MQ = MQ+TQ
334.           CALL FILEIO(WRITOP)
335.C
336.C       DISBURSE GOODS
337.        ELSE IF(TCODE.EQ.'C') THEN
338.           MQ = MQ-TQ
339.           CALL FILEIO(WRITOP)
340.C
341.C       DELETE RECORD
342.        ELSE IF(TCODE.EQ.'D')THEN
343.           CALL FILEIO(DELEOP)
344.        END IF
345.        RETURN
346.        END
```

D.3. RELATIVE FILE I-O PROCEDURES

The following program is a subprogram using a relative file that does one of the four operations: open, read, write, delete, according to the value of the parameter. Note that unless most possible keys are actually in use, this system will be quite wasteful of disk space.

```
1.        SUBROUTINE FILEIO(OP)
2.C       THIS VERSION OF FILEIO IMPLEMENTS A SIMPLE RELATIVE
3.C       FILE. THIS VERSION ASSUMES THAT THE ID IS AN INTEGER
4.C       LESS THAN 10000, AND THERE IS A FILE OF 10000 RECORDS.
5.C       THUS, IT IS EFFICIENT ONLY IF MOST OF THOSE POSSIBLE
6.C       ID'S ARE ACTUALLY USED.
7.C
8.C       THE FOLLOWING IS THE COMMON STORAGE DECLARATION:
9.C       (SEE MAIN PROGRAM FOR DEFINITIONS)
10.C
11.        CHARACTER*6 MID,TRID
```

```
12.         CHARACTER*4 TRQ
13.         INTEGER MQ,TQ,RECORD,OP
14.         CHARACTER*15 MDESC,TRDESC
15.         CHARACTER*1 TCODE
16.         LOGICAL OK,FOUND
17.         COMMON RECORD,MQ,TQ,OK,FOUND,MID,TRID,
18.        XTRQ,MDESC,TRDESC,TCODE
19.C
20.C        FOR FILEIO, THE FOLLOWING VALUES ARE PASSED AS THE
21.C        PARAMETER, TO INDICATE WHICH OPERATION: 1--OPENOP,
22.C        2--READOP, 3--WRITOP, AND 4--DELEOP
23.C
24.         INTEGER OPENOP,READOP,WRITOP,DELEOP
25.         DATA OPENOP/1/READOP/2/WRITOP/3/DELEOP/4/
26.C
27.C        NOTE THAT FOUND IS SET TRUE OR FALSE ACCORDING TO
28.C        WHETHER OR NOT THE RECORD AT THE POSITION READ HAS
29.C        THE CORRECT KEY, OR A KEY OF ALL ZEROS, THE LATTER
30.C        INDICATING A DUMMY RECORD. NOTE ALSO THAT TO DELETE
31.C        A RECORD, WE SET ITS ID TO ALL ZEROS AND REWRITE IT.
32.C
33.         IF(OP.EQ.OPENOP)THEN
34.            OPEN(UNIT=22,ACCESS='DIRECT',RECL=6,STATUS='OLD')
35.         ELSE IF(OP.EQ.READOP)THEN
36.            READ(22,REC=RECORD)MID,MQ,MDESC
37.            FOUND = (MID.EQ.TRID)
38.         ELSE IF(OP.EQ.WRITOP)THEN
39.            WRITE(22,REC=RECORD)MID,MQ,MDESC
40.         ELSE IF(OP.EQ.DELEOP)THEN
41.            MID = '000000'
42.            WRITE(22,REC=RECORD)MID,MQ,MDESC
43.         ENDIF
44.         RETURN
45.         END
```

The following is a program that will create a relative file and initialize its contents to all null records.

```
1.C        THIS PROGRAM CREATES A RELATIVE FILE FOR THE
2.C        INVENTORY SYSTEM EXAMPLE. INITIALLY ALL RECORDS
3.C        ARE UNUSED RECORDS AND HAVE ALL ZEROS INSERTED
4.C        AS THEIR ID. FORTRAN DOES NOT INITIALIZE THE
5.C        RECORDS, SO WE MUST DO IT WITH THIS PROGRAM.
6.C        WITH THE DEC-20 SYSTEM, SIMPLY OPENING THE FILE
7.C        FOR DIRECT ACCESS CREATES THE FILE. THE STANDARD
8.C        SPECIFIES THAT FOR THE SUBSET FORTRAN, THE
9.C        PARAMETER MAXREC MUST BE INCLUDED IN THE OPEN
10.C       STATEMENT, BUT THE MAXREC PARAMETER IS NOT
11.C       IMPLEMENTED IN THE DEC SYSTEM.
12.C
13.        CHARACTER*6 MID
```

```
14,        INTEGER MQ,N
15,        CHARACTER*15 MDESC
16,        LOGICAL OK,FOUND
17,C
18,C       MID       ID IN MASTER
19,C       MQ        QUANTITY IN MASTER
20,C       MDESC     DESCRIPTION IN MASTER
21,C       N         RECORD NUMBER
22,C
23,        CHARACTER*60 MESSAG
24,C
25,        MESSAG = ' CREATE RELATIVE FILE FOR INVENTORY'
26,        WRITE(5,10)MESSAG
27,    10 FORMAT(A60)
28,        OPEN(22,ACCESS='DIRECT',RECL=6,STATUS='NEW')
29,C
30,        MID = '000000'
31,        MQ = 0
32,        MDESC = '              '
33,        DO 1 N = 1,10000
34,            WRITE(22,RECN=N)MID,MQ,MDESC
35,     1 CONTINUE
36,C
37,        MESSAG = ' FINISHED'
38,        WRITE(5,10)MESSAG
39,        CLOSE 22
40,        STOP
41,        END
```

The following program will read the relative file from the preceding programs and list its contents in the order in which they are stored in the file, that is, in sequence by part number.

```
1,C    THIS PROGRAM PRINTS A LIST OF THE RECORDS IN THE
2,C    RELATIVE FILE FOR THE INVENTORY SYSTEM EXAMPLE,
3,C    UNUSED RECORDS IN THE FILE HAVE ALL ZEROS AS THEIR
4,C    ID, THOSE RECORDS ARE NOT PRINTED,
5,C
6,     CHARACTER*6 MID
7,     INTEGER MQ,N
8,     CHARACTER*15 MDESC
9,     LOGICAL OK,FOUND
10,C
11,C    MID       ID IN MASTER
12,C    MQ        QUANTITY IN MASTER
13,C    MDESC     DESCRIPTION IN MASTER
14,C    N         RECORD NUMBER (= ID CONVERTED TO BINARY)
15,C
16,    WRITE(5,*)' INVENTORY REPORT'
17,    WRITE(5,*)' ID     DESCRIPTION     NUMBER IN STOCK'
```

```
18,        OPEN(22,ACCESS='DIRECT',RECL=6,
19,     X    STATUS='OLD')
20,C
21,        DO 1 N = 1,10000
22,            READ(22,REC=N)MID,MQ,MDESC
23,            IF(MID,NE,'000000')THEN
24,                WRITE(5,11)MID,MDESC,MQ
25,     11        FORMAT(X,A6,X,A15,I5)
26,            ENDIF
27,      1 CONTINUE
28,C
29,        WRITE(5,*)' END OF REPORT'
30,        STOP
31,        END
```

D.4. HASHED FILE I-O PROCEDURES

The following subprogram, in conjunction with the main program in Section D.2, implements a hashed file system.

```
1,         SUBROUTINE FILEIO(OP)
2,C
3,C        THIS VERSION OF FILEIO IMPLEMENTS A HASHED FILE, FOR
4,C        THIS HASHED FILE, WE ARE USING 23 BUCKETS, EACH BUCKET
5,C        A BLOCK, WITH 5 RECORDS PER BLOCK, WE MUST DO THE
6,C        BLOCKING AND UNBLOCKING IN THIS PROGRAM, AND THEREFORE
7,C        WHAT IS A LOGICAL BLOCK FOR THIS PROGRAM IS A RECORD
8,C        TO THE SYSTEM--WE USE A RELATIVE FILE IN WHICH EACH
9,C        RECORD OF THE RELATIVE FILE IS A BUCKET FOR THE HASHED
10,C       FILE, FORTRAN UNIT 23 IS THE MASTER FILE, THE DATA FOR
11,C       THE FIVE RECORDS IN ONE BUCKET ARE READ INTO THE
12,C       ARRAYS BID, BQ, AND BDESC WHICH CONTAIN FIVE ID'S,
13,C       5 QUANTITIES, AND 5 DESCRIPTIONS RESPECTIVELY, ONE
14,C       RECORD IS PASSED BACK AND FORTH TO THE MAIN PROGRAM
15,C       USING MID, MQ, AND MDESC RESPECTIVELY,
16,C
17,C       FOR FILEIO, THE FOLLOWING VALUES ARE PASSED AS THE
18,C       PARAMETER, TO INDICATE WHICH OPERATION: 1--OPENOP,
19,C       2--READOP, 3--WRITOP, AND 4--DELEOP
20,C
21,        INTEGER OPENOP,READOP,WRITOP,DELEOP
22,        DATA OPENOP/1/READOP/2/WRITOP/3/DELEOP/4/
23,C
24,C       THE FOLLOWING IS THE COMMON STORAGE DECLARATION, MOST
25,C       OF WHICH ARE NOT USED HERE: (SEE MAIN PROGRAM FOR
26,C       DEFINITIONS,) TRID IS THE ID OF THE DESIRED RECORD,
27,C       AND RECORD IS THE NUMERIC VALUE OF TRID, FOUND IS SET
28,C       TRUE OR FALSE ON READING ACCORDING TO WHETHER THE
29,C       DESIRED RECORD IS FOUND OR NOT,
```

```
30.C
31.       CHARACTER*6 MID,TRID
32.       CHARACTER*4 TRQ
33.       INTEGER MQ,TNQ,RECORD,OP
34.       CHARACTER*15 MDESC,TRDESC
35.       CHARACTER*1 TCODE
36.       LOGICAL OK,FOUND
37.       COMMON RECORD,MQ,TNQ,OK,FOUND,MID,TRID,
38.      XTRQ,MDESC,TRDESC,TCODE
39.C
40.C      THE FOLLOWING VARIABLES ARE USED HERE:
41.C
42.C      BN      CURRENT BUCKET NUMBER
43.C      RN      CURRENT RECORD POSITION IN CURRENT BUCKET
44.C      BC      BUCKET COUNT, USED TO DETERMINE WHEN WE HAVE
45.C              SEARCHED THE WHOLE FILE AND SHOULD QUIT
46.C      OPENB   OPEN BUCKET, AND
47.C      OPENR   OPEN RECORD, USED DURING DELETION TO RECORD
48.C              WHERE A RECORD WAS REMOVED WHILE WE SEARCH
49.C              FOR ONE TO PUT BACK IN ITS PLACE.
50.C      SEARCH  SET TRUE DURING THE SEARCH FOR A RECORD ON
51.C              READ
52.C      I, J    TEMPORARIES.
53.C      TID     THESE ARE USED DURING DELETE TO STORE A
54.C      TQ      RECORD TEMPORARILY THAT IS BEING MOVED BACK
55.C      TDESC   TO AN OPEN PLACE LEFT BY THE DELETION
56.C      FSIZE   THE NUMBER OF BUCKETS IN THE FILE
57.C      BSIZE   THE NUMBER OF RECORDS IN A BUCKET
58.C      HASH    THE HASH FUNCTION
59.C
60.       INTEGER RN,BN,BC,OPENB,OPENR,I,J,FSIZE,BSIZE
61.       INTEGER BQ(5),TQ,HASH
62.       CHARACTER*6 BID(5),TID
63.       CHARACTER*15 BDESC(5),TDESC
64.       LOGICAL SEARCH
65.       DATA FSIZE/23/BSIZE/5/
66.C
67.C          THIS IS THE MAIN PART OF THE FILEIO PROCEDURE.
68.C
69.       IF(OP.EQ.OPENOP)THEN
70.          OPEN(UNIT=23,ACCESS='DIRECT',RECL=30,STATUS='OLD')
71.C
72.       ELSE IF(OP.EQ.READOP)THEN
73.          BN = HASH(TRID)
74.          SEARCH = .TRUE.
75.          FOUND = .FALSE.
76.          BC = 1
77.C
78.C          LOOP ONCE PER BUCKET, SEARCHING FOR DESIRED RECORD
79.C
```

```
 80.    1      IF(BC.LE.FSIZE.AND.SEARCH)THEN
 81.              READ(23,REC=BN)(BID(I),BQ(I),BDESC(I),I=1,BSIZE)
 82.              RN = 1
 83.C
 84.C              LOOP ONCE PER RECORD, SEARCHING ONE BUCKET
 85.C
 86.    2          IF(RN.LE.BSIZE.AND.SEARCH)THEN
 87.                 IF(BID(RN).EQ.TRID)THEN
 88.                    SEARCH = .FALSE.
 89.                    FOUND = .TRUE.
 90.                    MID = BID(RN)
 91.                    MQ = BQ(RN)
 92.                    MDESC = BDESC(RN)
 93.                 ELSE IF(BID(RN).EQ.'000000')THEN
 94.                    SEARCH = .FALSE.
 95.                 ELSE
 96.                    RN = RN+1
 97.                 ENDIF
 98.                 GO TO 2
 99.              ENDIF
100.C            END OF LOOP FOR SEARCHING ONE BUCKET
101.C
102.              IF(SEARCH)BN = BN+1
103.              IF(BN.GT.FSIZE)BN = 1
104.              BC = BC+1
105.              GO TO 1
106.           ENDIF
107.C        END OF LOOP FOR SEARCHING FOR DESIRED RECORD
108.C
109.           IF(SEARCH)THEN
110.              WRITE(5,*)
111.    X            'FILE FULL--NO MORE RECORDS CAN BE INSERTED'
112.              STOP
113.           ENDIF
114.C      END OF READ CASE
115.C
116.        ELSE IF(OP.EQ.WRITOP)THEN
117.C        MOVE RECORD FROM MAIN PROGRAM INTO BUCKET
118.           BID(RN) = MID
119.           BQ(RN) = MQ
120.           BDESC(RN) = MDESC
121.           WRITE(23,REC=BN)(BID(I),BQ(I),BDESC(I),I=1,BSIZE)
122.C
123.C      DELETION OF RECORDS IS IMPLEMENTED USING KNUTH'S
124.C      ALGORITHM FOR MOVING RECORDS BACK INTO A VACATED
125.C      POSITION IF THERE IS A RECORD WHOSE LENGTH OF SEARCH
126.C      WOULD BE SHORTENED BY THE MOVE. THIS MAINTAINS THE
127.C      FILE AT THE SAME AVERAGE LENGTH OF SEARCH AS WOULD
128.C      OCCUR IF THE PRESENT RECORDS HAD BEEN INSERTED, AND
129.C      NO DELETIONS HAD TAKEN PLACE.
```

```
130.C
131.      ELSE IF(OP.EQ.DELEOP)THEN
132.          OPENB = BN
133.          OPENR = RN
134.C
135.C    NOW WE SEARCH BUCKETS FOLLOWING THIS ONE TO FIND A
136.C    RECORD THAT SHOULD BE MOVED BACK TO THIS OPEN SPACE.
137.C    THIS STOPS WHEN WE HAVE EXAMINED ALL BUCKETS, OR WHEN
138.C    WE FIND AN EMPTY RECORD SPACE. IN FACT, IF THERE IS
139.C    AN EMPTY SPACE IN THE SAME BUCKET WHERE THE RECORD
140.C    WAS DELETED, WE STOP RIGHT THERE. NOTE THAT WE ALWAYS
141.C    MOVE RECORDS DOWN SO THAT ALL EMPTY SPACES ARE AT THE
142.C    END OF THE BUCKET, AND THEREFORE THE LAST PLACE IN
143.C    THE BUCKET WILL BE OPEN IF AND ONLY IF THE BUCKET IS
144.C    NOT FULL.
145.C
146.          BC = 1
147.   3     IF(BC.LE.FSIZE.AND.BID(BSIZE).NE.'000000')THEN
148.              BN = BN+1
149.              IF(BN.GT.FSIZE)BN = 1
150.              READ(23,REC=BN)(BID(I),BQ(I),BDESC(I),I=1,BSIZE)
151.C
152.C    LOOP TO SEARCH ONE BUCKET FOR A RECORD TO MOVE BACK
153.C
154.              DO 4 RN = 1,BSIZE
155.                  IF(BID(RN).NE.'000000')THEN
156.                      J = HASH(BID(RN))
157.C
158.C    IF THE CONDITION IS MET IN THE FOLLOWING STATEMENT,
159.C    THEN MOVING THAT RECORD INTO THE OPEN PLACE REDUCES
160.C    ITS LENGTH OF SEARCH. THE HASHED ADDRESS OF THE
161.C    RECORD BEING CONSIDERED IS J; ITS LOCATION, CALLED L
162.C    IN THE EXPLANATION IN CHAPTER 8, IS BN HERE; AND
163.C    OPENB HERE CORRESPONDS TO P IN THE EXPLANATION.
164.C
165.                      IF(J.LE.OPENB.AND.OPENB.LT.BN.OR.
166.   X                    OPENB.LT.BN.AND.BN.LT.J.OR.
167.   X                    BN.LT.J.AND.J.LE.OPENB)THEN
168.C                        MOVE THE RECORD
169.                          TID = BID(RN)
170.                          TQ = BQ(RN)
171.                          TDESC = BDESC(RN)
172.                          READ(23,REC=OPENB)
173.   X                        (BID(I),BQ(I),BDESC(I),I=1,BSIZE)
174.                          BID(OPENR) = TID
175.                          BQ(OPENR) = TQ
176.                          BDESC(OPENR) = TDESC
177.                          WRITE(23,REC=OPENB)
178.   X                        (BID(I),BQ(I),BDESC(I),I=1,BSIZE)
179.                          OPENB = BN
```

```
180,                        OPENR = RN
181,                        BID(OPENR) = '000000'
182,                    ENDIF
183,                ENDIF
184,    4       CONTINUE
185,C           END OF LOOP TO SEARCH ONE BUCKET
186,C
187,            GO TO 3
188,        ENDIF
189,C       END OF LOOP TO SEARCH FROM BUCKET TO BUCKET
190,C
191,C     AFTER NO MORE MOVING IS INDICATED, WE MOVE THE
192,C     RECORDS UP IN THE BUCKET, LEAVING THE OPEN SPACE AT
193,C     THE END OF THE BUCKET, AND THEN WE SET THE PART-NO
194,C     IN THE OPEN SPACE TO 000000 TO INDICATE THAT NO
195,C     RECORD IS THERE,
196,C
197,        READ(23,REC=OPENB)BID(I),BQ(I),BDESC(I),I=1,BSIZE)
198,        DO 5 I = OPENR,BSIZE-1
199,            BID(I) = BID(I+1)
200,            BQ(I) = BQ(I+1)
201,            BDESC(I) = BDESC(I+1)
202,    5       CONTINUE
203,        BID(BSIZE) = '000000'
204,        WRITE(23,REC=OPENB)(BID(I),BQ(I),BDESC(I),I=1,BSIZE)
205,    ENDIF
206,C   END OF DELETE CASE
207,C
208,    RETURN
209,    END
210,C
211,C     HASHING IS DONE BY THE MOST COMMON ALGORITHM,
212,C     DIVIDING THE NUMERIC KEY BY THE NUMBER OF BUCKETS
213,C     AND KEEPING THE REMAINDER, HSHCON IS THE HASH
214,C     CONSTANT, SET EQUAL TO THE NUMBER OF BUCKETS, HERE
215,C     CHOSEN TO BE 23, A PRIME NUMBER, HERE WE ADD ONE TO
216,C     THE REMAINDER TO GET A HASHED ADDRESS BETWEEN 1 AND
217,C     23,
218,C
219,    FUNCTION HASH(ID)
220,    INTEGER HASH,I,J,K,HSHCON
221,    CHARACTER*6 ID
222,        HSHCON = 23
223,        K = 0
224,        DO 2 I = 3,6
225,            J = 0
226,            IF(ID(I:I),EQ,'1') J = 1
227,            IF(ID(I:I),EQ,'2') J = 2
228,            IF(ID(I:I),EQ,'3') J = 3
229,            IF(ID(I:I),EQ,'4') J = 4
```

```
230.              IF(ID(I:I).EQ.'5') J = 5
231.              IF(ID(I:I).EQ.'6') J = 6
232.              IF(ID(I:I).EQ.'7') J = 7
233.              IF(ID(I:I).EQ.'8') J = 8
234.              IF(ID(I:I).EQ.'9') J = 9
235.              K= K*10 + J
236.     2     CONTINUE
237.           HASH = MOD(K,HSHCON)+1
238.        RETURN
239.        END
```

The following program creates a relative file and suitably initializes it for use as a hashed file with the preceding program.

```
1.C      MKHASH INITIALIZES A HASH FILE FOR THE ON-LINE
2.C      INVENTORY SYSTEM THAT USES A HASHED FILE. THE FILE
3.C      IS CREATED AND THEN FILLED WITH DUMMY RECORDS,
4.C      WHICH HAVE ZEROS AS THEIR ID'S.
5.C
6.       CHARACTER*6 BID(5)
7.       INTEGER BQ(5),BSIZE,FSIZE,N
8.       CHARACTER*15 BDESC(5)
9.C
10.C      BID       ID IN MASTER FILE
11.C      BQ        QUANTITY IN MASTER FILE
12.C      BDESC     DESCRIPTION MASTER FILE
13.C      FSIZE     NUMBER OF BUCKETS IN FILE
14.C      BSIZE     NUMBER OF RECORDS IN BUCKET
15.C      N,I       LOOP INDEX
16.C
17.       FSIZE = 23
18.       BSIZE = 5
19.       WRITE(5,*)' INITIALIZE HASHED FILE'
20.C
21.C      INITIALIZE DATA TO DUMMY RECORDS
22.C
23.       DO 1 N=1,BSIZE
24.          BID(N) = '000000'
25.          BDESC(N) ='                   '
26.          BQ(N) = 0
27.        1 CONTINUE
28.C
29.C         CREATE FILE
30.C
31.       OPEN(UNIT=23,ACCESS='DIRECT',RECL=30,STATUS='NEW')
32.C
33.C      NOW WRITE FILE FULL OF DUMMY RECORDS
34.C
35.       DO 2 N = 1,FSIZE
36.          WRITE(23,REC=N)(BID(I),BQ(I),BDESC(I),I=1,BSIZE)
37.     2 CONTINUE
```

```
38.C
39.         WRITE(5,*)' FINISHED'
40.C
41.         STOP
42.         END
```

The following program lists the contents of the hashed file, showing the part numbers in each bucket and thus showing how the file is structured internally.

```
1.C    THIS PROGRAM LISTS THE CONTENTS OF THE HASHED FILE
2.C    USED FOR THE INVENTORY SYSTEM OF OUR EXAMPLES
3.C    SO THAT WE CAN OBSERVE HOW THE RECORDS ARE BEING
4.C    STORED. IT ALSO CALCULATES THE AVERAGE LENGTH OF
5.C    SEARCH.
6.C
7.     CHARACTER*6 BID(5)
8.     INTEGER BQ(5),BSIZE,FSIZE,N,HASH,HA
9.     CHARACTER*15 BDESC(5)
10.    REAL TOTAL,COUNT,AVELEN
11.C
12.C    BID       ID IN MASTER FILE
13.C    BQ        QUANTITY IN MASTER FILE
14.C    BDESC     DESCRIPTION MASTER FILE
15.C    FSIZE     NUMBER OF BUCKETS IN FILE
16.C    BSIZE     NUMBER OF RECORDS IN BUCKET
17.C    N,I       LOOP INDEX
18.C    TOTAL     TOTAL NUMBER OF BUCKETS WHICH WOULD HAVE
19.C              TO BE SEARCHED TO ACCESS ALL RECORDS STORED
20.C    COUNT     NUMBER OF RECORDS STORED
21.C    AVELEN    AVERAGE LENGTH OF SEARCH
22.C    HASH      THE HASH FUNCTION SUBROUTINE
23.C    HA        THE HASHED ADDRESS OF THE CURRENT RECORD
24.C
25.    FSIZE = 23
26.    BSIZE = 5
27.    TOTAL = 0
28.    COUNT = 0
29.    OPEN(UNIT=23,ACCESS='DIRECT',RECL=30,STATUS='OLD')
30.    WRITE(5,*)' LISTING OF HASHED FILE CONTENTS'
31.C
32.    DO 1 N = 1,FSIZE
33.        READ(23,REC=N)(BID(I),BQ(I),BDESC(I),I=1,BSIZE)
34.        WRITE(5,11)N,(BID(I),HASH(BID(I)),I=1,BSIZE)
35.  11    FORMAT(I5,'--',5(A6,I3,'   '))
36.        DO 2 I=1,BSIZE
37.            IF(BID(I).NE.'000000')THEN
38.                HA = HASH(BID(I))
39.                COUNT = COUNT+1
40.                IF(HA.LE.N)THEN
```

```
41.                         TOTAL = TOTAL + N - HA + 1
42.                    ELSE
43.                         TOTAL = TOTAL + FSIZE + N - HA + 1
44.                    ENDIF
45.                ENDIF
46.    2      CONTINUE
47.    1 CONTINUE
48.C
49.        IF(COUNT.GT.0)THEN
50.            AVELEN = TOTAL/COUNT
51.        ELSE
52.            AVELEN = 0
53.        ENDIF
54.        WRITE(5,12)TOTAL,COUNT,AVELEN
55.    12 FORMAT(' TOTAL SEARCH=',F7.0,'  COUNT=',F5.0,
56.      X'AVERAGE LENGTH OF SEARCH=',F6.2)
57.        STOP
58.        END
59.C
60.C     THIS FUNCTION CALCULATES THE HASHED ADDRESS FOR THE
61.C     ID RECEIVED AS ITS PARAMETER BY CALCULATING THE
62.C     REMAINDER AFTER DIVIDING BY THE HASH CONSTANT.
63.C
64.        FUNCTION HASH(ID)
65.        CHARACTER*6 ID
66.        INTEGER HASH,J,N,HSHCON
67.        HSHCON = 23
68.        N = 0
69.        DO 2 I = 3,6
70.           J = 0
71.           IF(ID(I:I).EQ.'1') J = 1
72.           IF(ID(I:I).EQ.'2') J = 2
73.           IF(ID(I:I).EQ.'3') J = 3
74.           IF(ID(I:I).EQ.'4') J = 4
75.           IF(ID(I:I).EQ.'5') J = 5
76.           IF(ID(I:I).EQ.'6') J = 6
77.           IF(ID(I:I).EQ.'7') J = 7
78.           IF(ID(I:I).EQ.'8') J = 8
79.           IF(ID(I:I).EQ.'9') J = 9
80.           N = N*10 + J
81.    2 CONTINUE
82.        HASH = MOD(N,HSHCON)+1
83.        RETURN
84.        END
```

APPENDIX

Command and Job Control Languages

E.1. INTRODUCTION

Most computers are used with an *operating system*, a collection of programs that help the user(s) use the computer. A good operating system makes the computer resources readily available to the user, but prevents errors to as great an extent as possible. This latter function is crucial in systems with multiple users or multiple tasks—the system must prevent one user from interfering with another and prevent two users from using the same resource—such as a printer—at the same time. The operating system allocates and controls the use of resources.

An essential and central part of the operating system is the file system. The file system allocates disk space and maintains a catalog to facilitate and control access to files. Using the file system, the user must be able to create, locate, delete, rename, read from, and write to files.

The other essential function of an operating system is to control execution of programs. Most commonly, programs are stored in disk files. The operating system must read the desired program from a disk file into the main memory, prepare it for execution, allocate to it the resources it needs, and start it executing.

In addition, the operating system provides communication to and/or from the user's terminal, printer, and other I-O devices. It may provide other services such as clock and calendar, interval timer, accounting, and communication between users or tasks.

There must be some direct interface between the user and the operating system. This is provided by a command language and a command-language processor.

One of the most famous command languages is IBM Job Control Language (JCL), which is used for batch jobs for the larger IBM computer systems. TSO (Time-Sharing Option) was the first general-purpose time-sharing interface to large IBM systems and is still widely used. Many of the same things must be done both by JCL and by TSO, but since JCL was not suitable, TSO was created as a new command language for time sharing.

In the UNIX operating system, the command-language processor is called the *shell* and the command language is called the *shell language*. CP/M is a widely used operating system for microcomputers. Its command-language processor is called the "Console Control Program"; there is no special name for its command language, which is very simple.

JCL, TSO, UNIX, and CP/M will be used as examples of command languages throughout this appendix. JCL and TSO are representative of large systems, and UNIX and CP/M are representative of small systems.

A set of IBM JCL commands is assembled as a deck of cards or a disk file of cardlike records. Each JCL command card or record starts with //. Data cards may be interspersed; source program statements are data to the system. The first card is the command JOB, which identifies the user and his account number. The last card is supposed to contain only //. JCL statements may have a label, which immediately follows the //. The command name is the first word following the first space in the statement, as it is in most assembler languages. In fact, JCL resembles typical macro assembly languages, especially in the way keyword and positional parameters are handled.

A TSO session must start with the user typing the command LOGIN, followed by an account number and password. When the computer completes this or any other command, it usually types READY signifying that it is ready to receive another command. The user then may type any command name followed by any other required or optional information for that command and return carriage to cause that command to be executed.

At the start of a terminal session, the UNIX system types "login:". After the user types a "login-name," UNIX requests the password, and the user types it. When UNIX satisfactorily completes processing this login or any shell command, it types a cue (or prompt) character, usually $ or %, indicating that it is ready for a shell command. The user then may type any shell command name, followed by other required or optional information for that command, and carriage return to cause that command to be executed.

When the CP/M system is started, usually simply upon turning on the microcomputer, it prints a short start message and then "A>", indicating that the logged-in disk drive is A and the system is ready for a console command. The user then types any command followed by any required or optional information for that command and carriage return. In general, after completing any console command, CP/M types the name of the logged-in disk drive followed by a ">" as a cue that it is awaiting a console command.

There is another way for users to interface with the operating system. Users may call operating system subroutines from programs that they write. Some of the required operating system functions and services may be done only through the command language, some only by subroutine calls, and some may be done either way. Exactly which are available in each mode differs from system to system. However, there must be some way for the user to tell the system to start executing a program, so such a statement is a part of every command language. Furthermore, any function that can be done by an operating system subroutine call can be made available in the command language. If one writes a program to perform a function using the operating system subroutine call, then this function can be performed any time by using a command language statement that causes this program to be executed.

It is not inherently true that anything that can be done by a command language command also can be done by a subroutine call; even if it can be done, it may not easy. In early versions of the operating system for the IBM 360, creating and deleting files could be done only by JCL statements. In later versions, these functions were made available as system calls, but use of these system calls is typically difficult and complicated. Similarly, in CP/M in principle anything that can be done by a command also can be done by statements in a program but not necessarily easily. For example, it is not practical to try to call the text editor from a user program. In contrast, UNIX has a system call that will execute any shell command; therefore, there is complete symmetry.

E.2. EXECUTING PROGRAMS

A command language must have a statement that causes the system to execute a specified program. For JCL the statement that causes a program to execute is EXEC. Its syntax is as follows:

```
//statement-label   EXEC   PGM=filename,PARM=string
```

where *statement-label* is an optional label given to this JCL statement, *file-name* is the name of a file containing an executable program, and *string* is a character string that is available to the program and may be used to furnish some information to the program. The "PARM = *string*" is optional. There are several other optional items that may be included to indicate the memory size required, a time limit, and so on. Here is an example of an EXEC statement:

```
//GO EXEC PGM=W533610,UPDATE,LOAD
```

TSO, working with the same computer system, must furnish the same information. The syntax is:

```
CALL file-name PARM=string
```

Although JCL requires the full file name, which normally includes a prefix indicating the user number of the owner of the file, TSO allows you to omit the user number if you are logged on with that number. When the full file name is included, it is quoted. Thus, the equivalent in TSO of the above example is

```
CALL 'W533610.UPDATE.LOAD'
```

or assuming you are logged on with ID W533610

```
CALL UPDATE.LOAD
```

In UNIX, to execute a program in a file, you simply type the file name immediately following the cue character $ or %. Unless you specify otherwise, UNIX assumes that the file is in the current directory. In CP/M, a program must be in a file of type CMD (for CP/M 86), for example, UP-DATE.CMD. To execute it, you simply type its name (e. g., UPDATE) following the cue character ">". CP/M assumes that the file is on the logged-in disk drive, unless you specify otherwise. In either UNIX or CP/M, you may type additional information on the same line following the program name and that string of characters is available to the program, like the PARM parameter in JCL and TSO.

Note that TSO makes a clear distinction between built-in system commands and user program names, the latter requiring a CALL statement. Both UNIX and CP/M treat user program names as commands syntactically indistinguishable from system commands.

E.3. FILE HANDLING

Many programs use, make, and/or operate on files. When you command the system to execute the program, you must tell it on which files to operate. There are two ways in which this can be done: (1) through the command language, and (2) by a system subroutine call within the program. In the latter case, the program may always use the same file name or it may read that information from the console or from another file. (If a program uses many files, a file containing a list of file names would be convenient. For example, one might furnish a list of files containing programs to be link edited to the link editor.)

In the large IBM systems, the second method is at best very inconvenient; files are specified through JCL or TSO commands. Furthermore, although in principle you could furnish file names in the parameter strings, in practice this is also very inconvenient. There are separate statements for specifying file assignments. In general, there are logical file names in the program, and for each logical file name, the name of the actual file must be specified. At the same time, one specifies whether the file is to be created and whether it is to be kept or deleted afterwards. If it is to be created, the amount of space must be specified. In addition, the type of organization, block size, and record size must be specified. There are a number of other details that may be specified.

In JCL, the statement that serves this function is called DD (for data definition). The DD statements follow the EXEC statement to which they apply. The precise syntax and details can be found in manuals or books on the subject[J9]. The following examples should adequately illustrate the concept. Assume that a program needs two files with logical (external) names INFILE and OUTFILE. (See Section 8.3 for a discussion of file name terminology.) Then two DD statements are needed and the logical file names must be used as labels:

```
//OUTFILE DD DSN=W533610.OUT.DATA,
           DISP=(NEW,CATLG),SPACE=(5000,(100,10)),
           DCB=(DSORG=PS,RECFM=FB,BLKSIZE=5000,
           LRECL=500),UNIT=USERDA
//INFILE DD DSN=W533610.IN.DATA,DISP=(OLD,KEEP)
```

Here OUTFILE is to be associated with a new file that is to be catalogued using the physical name W533610.OUT.DATA. It is to be allocated 100 5000-byte blocks initially, with additional blocks to be added 10 at a time if needed. DCB (Data Control Block) parameters specify that the "Data Set Organization" is physically sequential, the record format is fixed-length and blocked, the block size is 5000, and the record length is 500. The file is to be placed on a disk unit in the class designated USERDA. The DD statement associates the logical file INFILE with the physical file W533610.IN.DATA, which is presumably catalogued, in which case the unit and DCB parameters may be found in the catalog. The file being old, space need not be specified.

We now illustrate a complete set of command statements to do a task in each of the four operating systems used as an example in this appendix. We will show the commands needed to execute a program called "update" that requires an input file called "in.data," assumed to exist, and an output file called "out.data" that must be created. After the program is executed, the file "out.data" is to be printed and kept for future reference.

To print a file using JCL, it is necessary to execute a program that can print a file. A suitable program is the IBM-furnished utility program IEBGENER, which requires the logical files named SYSUT1, SYSUT2, SYSIN, and SYSPRINT to be defined. SYSUT1 is the input file, SYSUT2 is the output file, SYSIN is for input of parameters but will not be needed here, and SYSPRINT is for printed output such as error messages. The complete JCL statements follow. The lines starting //* are comments.

```
//*   EXECUTE UPDATE PROGRAM
//GO EXEC PGM=W533610.UPDATE.LOAD
//OUTFILE DD DSN=W533610.OUT.DATA,
           DISP=(NEW,CATLG),SPACE=(5000,(100,10)),
           DCB=(DSORG=PS,RECFM=FB,BLKSIZE=5000,
           LRECL=500),UNIT=USERDA
//INFILE DD DSN=W533610.IN.DATA,DISP=(OLD,KEEP)
//*   PRINT OUT.DATA
//    EXEC PGM=IEBGENER
//SYSUT1   DD   DSN=W533610.OUT.DATA,DISP=(OLD,KEEP)
//SYSUT2   DD   SYSOUT=A
//SYSIN    DD   DUMMY
//SYSPRINT DD SYSOUT=A
//
```

"DD DUMMY" designates a null file. "DD SYSOUT = A" directs an output file to the system printer.

Using TSO, you must furnish exactly the same information, because it is the same operating system, but you furnish it with a different syntax. The greatest difference is that you assign or *allocate* a logical file name to a physical file name before you call for a program's execution. This assignment continues in effect until cancelled (by a command "free" or a command reallocating the logical name) or the terminal session ends. If DCB parameters are needed, they are first specified in an attribute statement

```
ATTRIBUTE XXX DSORG(PS) RECFM(F B) BLKSIZE(5000) LRECL(500)
```

XXX is the name of the attribute specification. The rest has the same meaning as with JCL. Then the actual association of logical names with physical names used in the catalog is done by the allocate statement:

```
ALLOCATE   FILE(OUTFILE) DATASET(OUT.DATA)
           NEW SPACE(100,10) BLOCK(5000) USING(XXX)
ALLOCATE   FILE(INFILE)  DATASET(IN.DATA)
```

The meanings are the same as in the JCL statement examples. As in the CALL statement, the user-number qualifier on the physical file name may be omitted if it is the same as the number used to log onto the system. Thus, to run program UPDATE, which needs logical files INFILE and OUTFILE, you first need to enter the ATTRIBUTE statement, then the two ALLOCATE statements, and finally the CALL statement. To run it again with the same files, you only need to repeat the CALL statement—the others still will be in effect.

In TSO, there is a command LIST that prints the contents of a file. The complete set of statements to run the program "update" and then print "out.data" is as follows:

```
ATTRIBUTE XXX DSORG(PS) RECFM(F B) BLKSIZE(5000) LRECL(500)
ALLOCATE   FILE(OUTFILE) DATASET(OUT.DATA)
           NEW SPACE(100,10) BLOCK(5000) USING(XXX)
ALLOCATE   FILE(INFILE)  DATASET(IN.DATA)
CALL UPDATE.LOAD
LIST OUT.DATA
```

For UNIX or CP/M, file names may be and are passed to the executing program in any way that any data can be passed to an executing program. The most common method is to include the file names in the string that follows the command name and is passed to the program as a parameter string. Alternatively, file names may be typed on the terminal in response to a request by the program, or read from a file, or a constant name may be used. The necessary operations—including creating and deleting files—are done conveniently by system calls in the program.

For example, to execute the C compiler (which is named CC) using a file called update.C as input, you enter

```
$cc update.c
```

The compiler will extract the file name from the parameter string, read and compile the program in that file, and create a new file with the special name a.out (or replace the file that has that name, if one exists) and put the executable program into that file.

As another example, to use the CP/M 86 assembler to assemble a program called UPDATE.A86, you type

```
A>ASM86 UPDATE
```

The assembler extracts the file name UPDATE from the parameter string and reads and assembles the program from the file UPDATE.A86. It creates two new files: UPDATE.H86, which contains the assembled program, and UPDATE.LST, which contains the assembly listing.

The complete set of UNIX statements needed to execute the "update" program, using the existing file "in.data" as input and creating and writing a file "out.data" and then printing the file, is as follows (the command "pr" is used to print files):

```
$update in.data out.data
$pr out.data
```

To do the same in CP/M, the following commands may be used:

```
A>update in.data out.data
A>type out.data
```

The functions of creating, deleting, and renaming files are so commonly used that easy ways to do them using the command language must be provided. With JCL, files are created by specifying NEW and deleted by specifying DELETE in the DISP clause of the DD statement. A utility program is provided that can rename a file. In TSO, files are created by specifying NEW in the allocate statement. Specific TSO statements are provided to rename or delete files.

```
RENAME GEORGE.DATA ALICE.DATA
    (the first is the old name)
DELETE IN.DATA
```

Both UNIX and CP/M expect files to be created generally by programs as needed without requiring any specific command language statement. Files can be created, for example, using a text editor program. With WORDSTAR, a popular word-processing system used with CP/M, file names are entered in response to prompt messages displayed by the system. Specific command language statements are provided to rename and delete files. In UNIX, the commands are mv (move) and rm (remove), respectively.

```
$mv george.data alice.data
    (the first is the old name)
$rm in.data
```

In CP/M, the commands are called REN (rename) and ERA (erase).

```
A>REN ALICE.DAT=GEORGE.DAT
    (the first is the new name)
A>ERA IN.DAT
```

E.4. COMMAND PROCEDURES

There is another important facility commonly provided with command languages. Provision is made for writing a list of commands, storing it in a disk file, and causing them to be executed at any time. We will refer to such a list as a command procedure.

A list of JCL statements may be put in a library-type file (a *partitioned data set*) and executed using the EXEC command. For example,

```
// EXEC PLICG
```

causes the JCL statements in a file PLICG to be executed. The system distinguishes this from the command to execute a program by the fact that the keyword PGM = appears in the statement for executing a program. As it is, the system will expect PLICG to be in a special library of *cataloged procedures.* If it is in a different library, the name of the library must be given, usually in the following statement.

Similarly, in TSO the command EXEC GEORGE causes the system to look for a file called GEORGE.CLIST and to execute the commands it finds in that file. Note that EXEC refers to a command list, and CALL to a program.

In UNIX a list of commands is called a *shell program,* and the command to execute a shell program is simply the name of the file containing it, just as for an ordinary program. (The UNIX system can tell by examining a file whether it contains a shell program or an ordinary program.) Thus, to execute a shell program in a file called george, one simply types "george" and a carriage return after the cue character.

In CP/M one may write a list of console commands, store them in a file, and cause them to be executed by giving the command SUBMIT followed by the name of the file. If the file GEORGE.SUB contains a list of console commands, then the command SUBMIT GEORGE causes those commands to be executed.

Some way usually is provided to pass parameters to a command procedure at the time the procedure is called. We will show command procedures for the four systems we have used as examples for the task of calling the "update" program and printing the "out.data" file. We will name the procedure "up" and send the names of the input and output files to it as parameters.

For JCL, the procedure might look like this:

```
//UP   PROC   IN=A,OUT=B
//*   EXECUTE UPDATE PROGRAM
//GO EXEC PGM=W533610.UPDATE.LOAD
//OUTFILE DD DSN=W533610.&OUT
         DISP=(NEW,CATLG),SPACE=(5000,(100,10)),
         DCB=(DSORG=PS,RECFM=FB,BLKSIZE=5000,
         LRECL=500),UNIT-USERDA
//INFILE DD DSN=W533610.&IN,DISP=(OLD,KEEP)
//*   PRINT OUT.DATA
//    EXEC PGM=IEBGENER
//SYSUT1  DD   DSN=&OUT,DISP=(OLD,KEEP)
//SYSUT2  DD   SYSOUT=A
//SYSIN   DD   DUMMY
//SYSPRINT DD SYSOUT=A
//
```

The first statement indicates that this is a procedure, states that the name of the procedure is UP, and that it has two parameters named IN and OUT. "IN = A,OUT = B" indicates that if the parameters are omitted in the statement that calls the procedure, the values A and B should be used as default values for the parameters. Within the procedure, parameters are identified by being preceded by an ampersand, that is, &IN and &OUT. To call this procedure, one needs only the statement

```
//     EXEC    UP,IN=IN.DATA,OUT=OUT.DATA
```

IN.DATA and OUT.DATA will be substituted for &IN and &OUT, respectively, when the procedure is executed.

For TSO, the command procedure is called a "CLIST". For our example, the following statements would be placed in a file called UP.CLIST:

```
PROC 2 IN OUT
ATTRIBUTE XXX DSORG(PS) RECFM(F B) BLKSIZE(5000) LRECL(500)
ALLOCATE   FILE(OUTFILE) DATASET(&OUT)
           NEW SPACE(100,10) BLOCK(5000) USING(XXX)
ALLOCATE   FILE(INFILE)   DATASET(&IN)
CALL UPDATE.LOAD
LIST &OUT
```

In the PROC statement, the "2" means that there are two positional parameters, that is, parameters that must be in that relative position. (Keyword parameters like those used with JCL also may be used, with default values specified the same way as with JCL.) Within the procedure, the parameters appear with an ampersand in front of them. Entering the statement

```
EXEC UP IN.DATA OUT.DATA
```

will cause this procedure to be executed, with IN.DATA substituted for each occurrence of &IN and OUT.DATA substituted for each occurrence of &OUT. (There is one problem with this procedure. It cannot be executed twice in the same TSO session because executing an attribute statement with an already existing attribute name is not allowed.)

The corresponding UNIX command procedure, called a shell procedure, would look like this:

```
update $1 $2
pr $2
```

and would be placed in a file called "up." For the UNIX shell programs, $1 represents the first parameter, $2 the second parameter, and so on. In calling the shell program, the parameters follow the function name, so the statement to call this procedure would be

```
$up in.data out.data
```

The parameters "in.data" and "out.data" will be substituted for the parameters $1 and $2, respectively, as the procedure is executed.

CP/M handles command procedure parameters in an identical way. The procedure might look like this:

```
update $1 $2
type $1
```

and these statements would be put in a file called "up.sub." To cause this *submit file* to be executed, one only needs to enter the following statement:

```
A>submit up in.data out.data
```

Finally, most command languages make provisions for some control of execution sequence. The earliest version of IBM JCL provided for omitting execution of a step depending on a *completion code* from a previous step. Command procedures in the current versions of JCL, TSO, and UNIX shell language may contain statements that are the equivalent of IF-THEN-ELSE and loop control statements that are similar in function to Pascal's FOR and WHILE statements. UNIX shell language even includes a CASE statement. These structures in JCL and TSO are very awkward. UNIX shell language is more like a conventional programming language than JCL or TSO, but it is still rather strange. It is easier to use and is more widely used than earlier command procedure languages, and is considered a significant step forward. The trend seems to be in the direction of including more powerful and flexible commands and of using the natural syntax of a programming language rather than the awkward macro assembler-type syntax for the command language procedures. For example, it has been suggested that in the programming environment for language Ada, a subset of Ada might be used as the command language.

NOTES

General descriptions of job control and command languages appear in their associated operating system literature ([J1]–[J11]). For specific details, the manuals provided by manufacturers or suppliers should be consulted. See also [K13].

Cache Memory and Virtual Memory

F.1. INTRODUCTION

In very broad terms, the essence of the subject of files is to develop techniques for making the most effective use of the combination of economical, slower storage devices with a processor and limited fast storage. There are two techniques—cache memory and virtual storage—the purpose of which is to combine storage devices in a manner transparent to the user. Neither is considered a file system, nor normally used as such, although a virtual storage system with a large address space could be used as a file system. A virtual storage system must have a good random-access file system as an integral part of its implementation. Because of these relationships with file systems, we include here a brief description of cache memory and virtual storage.

Large computers often use two kinds of fast memory. The arrangements shown in Figures 1.1(b) and 1.1(c) are both common. For example, "mass" storage which is somewhat slower than main memory can be connected directly to a central processor. Typically, the lower memory addresses refer to the main memory and higher addresses to the mass storage. Programming is the same for both, but execution is slower when mass storage is used, so relatively seldom-used data and instructions are placed there. Other computers have mass storage arranged as in Figure 1.1(c), and data or instructions must be copied into the fast storage before they can be used. This can be done at very high speed. Which of the two arrangements is faster depends very much on the nature of the problem and the program.

F.2. CACHE MEMORY

A system that has recently become widely used is *cache memory*. It is shown in Figure F.1. [It uses the Type II arrangement shown in Figure 1.1(c).] The cache memory is small but very fast, and all data and instructions used by the processor must be copied into the cache memory before they can be used by the processor. (If they are changed while in cache memory, they also must be copied back to the main storage.) Thus, at any given time, a small part of the main storage data is also in the cache memory, which also keeps the main memory addresses of the data it holds.

The program is written using main-storage addresses. The programmer has no control over which data go into cache memory; this is decided by algorithms built into the hardware. One can predict to some extent what data will be needed. For example, current data very likely will be used again soon. The data physically (in main storage) following the current data is likely to be used soon, and to a lesser extent, the preceding data may be referenced soon. The computer designers build prediction algorithms based on these facts and perhaps others into the processor so that as often as possible when the processor requests data, it is already in the cache memory. When it is not, it must be fetched from the main storage, which will slow processing. The percentage of times the data are already in the cache memory when needed depends on the prediction algorithm, the size of the cache memory, and very much on the nature of the program. However, on the average, a substantial gain in processing speed compared with using main storage alone can be achieved at a cost much less than that of a main storage made entirely of very fast devices.

F.3. VIRTUAL STORAGE

Virtual storage is similar in concept to cache memory. There is an *address space* usually with a larger range of addresses than is ever used for data and instructions in one program. The physical arrangement, also basically the Type II arrangement shown in Figure 1.1(c), is shown in Figure F.2. Typically, the main storage is integrated circuits and the auxiliary storage is magnetic disk. The address space may be so large that if all

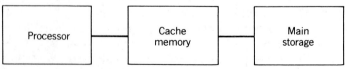

Figure F.1 Cache Memory System.

Figure F.2 Virtual Storage System.

addresses were used, even the auxiliary storage would not suffice. The program is written using the address space.

The data and instructions are stored in the auxiliary storage in blocks called *pages*, which typically contain a few thousand bits. Each address is transformed into a page number and a displacement within the page. Each page can be accessed in the auxiliary storage by an efficient indexing scheme, such as those described in Chapter 6. The main storage can hold, at any given time, a fairly large number of pages, but possibly only a portion of what a program may use. The main storage also contains the addresses of the pages it contains. A page must be in the main storage before it is used. When a program calls for a data item (or instruction) that is not in main storage, program execution is interrupted while the operating system fetches this page from the auxiliary storage. This is known as a *page fault*. (In multiprogramming systems, control may switch to another program when a page fault occurs.)

Because the main storage (or the portion of it allocated to the user) is limited, it soon fills, and whenever a new page is brought in or *paged in*, it must replace one that is in main storage. (If the page being replaced in main storage has been altered, it must be copied back or *paged out* to the auxiliary storage.) The choice of which page to replace is made by an algorithm built into the operating system. Replacement algorithms typically take into account how often and how recently each page has been used, how many pages this program is using, and sometimes other facts about the program.

With virtual storage, the programmer may use the whole address space and write programs as if the machine had a very large main storage. Yet the cost is modest, because the physical storage is a reasonable size. If the system worked ideally, we could have computers of modest cost that appear to the user to have very fast storage of very large capacity. Then this book would be very much shorter, because much of it is concerned with methods of efficiently processing large files of data stored in economical storage devices with medium or long access times.

The problem is that page faults take time because they require disk I-O operations. The time taken for a page fault is, within an order of magnitude or so, 10,000 times the time for a single processor instruction. Obviously, efficient execution requires that page faults do not occur too often. For faults to require not more than 10% of the time, the program must be such that roughly 100,000 instructions are executed per page fault. Some programs behave this way and run very well on a virtual-storage system. Some programs do not. For example, for a program that has several separate phases, each of which fits in the available main memory, one run of the program will require only a fairly small number of page faults at the beginning of each phase. On the other hand, for a program that does frequent table look-ups at random locations in a table much larger than the main storage, a page fault will occur almost every time a look-up occurs and the number of instructions executed per page fault may be quite small.

The number of page faults depends very much on the nature of the program and the total number of pages the program is allowed to have in main storage at one time. It also depends on the paging algorithm. Normally, any program at any given time will have a *working set* or *active set* of pages that consists of all pages recently or frequently used. The active set may change as the program proceeds. For example, many programs—most assemblers and many compilers—have two or more phases or passes. The active set for each pass will be different, although they may have common pages containing data or subroutines used in both passes. If the number of pages of main storage allocated to the program is greater than the size of the active set, then there will be few page faults, but if the allocated main storage is smaller than the active set, then the number of page faults will be large. Thus, the behavior expected of a "normal" program is roughly that shown in curve A of Figure F.3, assuming an active set of ten pages.

Not all programs are normal, of course. Let us consider two examples. First, assume a program of 10 pages that consists of a simple loop executing pages 1, 2,..., 9 in that order. After page 9, the program starts at page 1 again. Assume that all the data are in page 10. The program cannot run at all with less than two pages of main storage—one for part of the program and the other for the data. With two pages, there will a

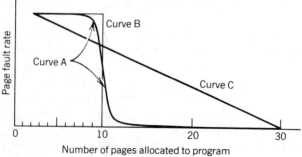

Figure F.3 Page Fault Curves.

page fault each time execution of all the instructions in one page is finished to get the next page of instructions. Assume that the paging algorithm replaces the least recently used page. If the number of pages allocated to the program is nine or fewer, then after once through the loop, every time the program starts on a new page, it must replace one page, the least recently used one; then just as with two pages, when execution of one page is finished, the next page of instructions is not in main memory and a page fault occurs. For example, if nine pages are allocated, then when page 8 is being executed, pages 1 through 8 are in memory. When page 8 finishes, the least recently used page, page 1, is replaced by page 9. When page 9 is finished, then the next needed page is page 1, which is not in memory. A page fault occurs, and page 1 replaces the least recently used page, page 2, and so on. Thus, the number of page faults is the same for 2, 3,..., 9 pages allocated. However, if 10 pages are allocated, the data and all instructions fit in memory and no page faults occur. Thus, curve B of Figure F.3 is appropriate for this program. Execution time with fewer than 10 pages could easily exceed 100 times that with 10 pages allocated.

Consider a program that fits in one page and randomly does table look-up in a large table of, say, 30 pages. Again, it cannot run with less than two pages. With two pages, one page contains the program and the other contains one page of the table. For each look-up, the probability is 1/30 that the required part of the table is in memory and, hence, no page fault occurs. The probability is 29/30 that the required data are not in the memory and a page fault will occur. If 31 pages are allocated, then no page faults occur once all pages are loaded into main memory. Suppose n pages are allocated, where n is less than 31. Then $n-1$ pages of table are in memory, $31-n$ pages are not, and the probability of a page fault is $(31-n)/30$. The average number of page faults is represented by curve C in Figure F.3.

In principle, one could have very large virtual address space and all data—files as well as programs—could be kept in virtual storage. Current systems generally do not use virtual storage to store data files. (One could, however, read an entire file into virtual storage and then portions of it would be paged in and paged out according to their levels of demand.)

Programs are normally kept as files. Programs that are too large to fit in the memory must be partitioned into segments, each small enough to fit in the memory, and some mechanism for swapping segments between main storage and auxiliary storage is necessary. Virtual storage is used principally for this purpose—a virtual storage system will bring the required segments into the main storage as they are needed without any special provisions made by the programmer. This is discussed in detail in the operating system literature. Without virtual storage, the programmer must design an *overlay structure* for the program, planning exactly which parts of the program will be in the memory at any one time and making sure that it will fit in the memory as planned. A good overlay system will load a segment automatically when the program references its contents.

It is clear that in writing programs that require a large amount of storage for a virtual-storage system, a programmer must be aware of how virtual storage works and the nature of the paging algorithm, and the way the number of pages per program is limited to avoid writing extremely inefficient programs. Furthermore, how programs and data are structured affects how they are distributed into pages, hence, their performance in a paging environment. The moral is that the virtual-storage system user cannot really ignore the fact that only a limited main storage is available.

NOTES

Cache memory is discussed in [E1]–[E3]. The basic concepts of virtual storage are presented in [E7]. Descriptions of specific virtual memory systems appear in [J1].

APPENDIX

G

An Example
of an I-O Processor

G.1. INTRODUCTION

In this appendix, how the processor, main memory, and I-O devices are connected and interact will be illustrated by a specific hypothetical simplified example. Actual machine language programs, simplified to the bare essentials, are included and explained. This requires an introduction to the machine language for the machine chosen for these example programs. The next section explains briefly those instructions and the features that are needed.

G.2. 8085 MACHINE LANGUAGE

A typical computer consists of a *bus* with various units connected to it. The units include a main processor, one or more memory units, and one or more I-O units. The bus is simply a collection of wires carrying all the signals that must be sent from one unit to another.

We will use the Intel 8085 for our examples, because it is quite simple and very widely used. The following explanation is somewhat simplified. The 8085 microprocessor itself is an integrated circuit (IC). One is shown in Figure G.1. It has a number of lines that send signals out or bring signals in, which connect to the pins that can be seen on the integrated circuit. There are 16 lines that send out a 16-bit address. There are eight lines used for a byte of data, either going out from the processor or coming in. There are lines that indicate (in coded form) when the processor is doing a memory read, a memory write, an I-O read, or an I-O write.

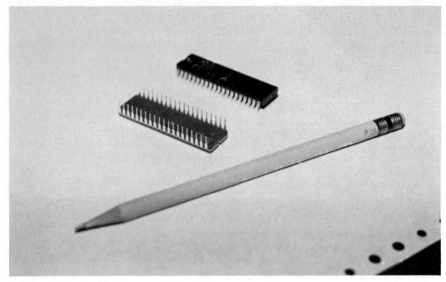

Figure G.1 An 8085 and an 8088 Microprocessor IC.

There is a line bringing a signal (called "hold") into the processor that causes the processor simply to wait—a one signal on the wait line causes the processor to stop at the end of the machine cycle that is in progress, and then when the wait line goes back to its normal value of zero, the processor continues where it left off. When the processor stops in response to the wait signal, it puts a signal (called "hold acknowledge") out on another line to indicate that it is waiting. There is also an interrupt line. When the interrupt line goes from its normal 0 to 1, the processor interrupts what it is doing, saves some information, and jumps to a fixed location. The above-named signals normally all will be carried on the bus and will be available to all other units connected to the bus.

Figure G.2 shows a processor circuit board for the S-100 bus. This board has both an 8085 processor and an 8088 processor and is capable of switching from one to the other. The two processors can be seen at the right edge of the board. Other integrated circuits provide clock signals, processor switching, and the interface to the bus.

A memory unit connected to the bus will serve a range of addresses. Circuits in the memory unit continuously examine the bus signals. When the memory unit finds an address on the bus that references its memory and other signals indicate a memory read, the memory unit reads the indicated byte from its memory and places the signal on the bus data lines. If the address is within range and the other signals indicate a memory write, the memory unit writes the data from the bus into the indicated cell in its memory.

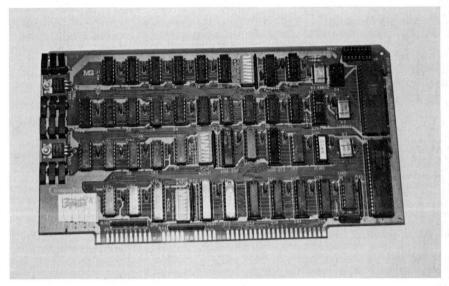

Figure G.2 A Microcomputer Processor Board for the S-100 Bus.

Inside the processor there are several registers that store data. We will use the A register and the C register, both of which can hold one byte, and the HL register, which can hold an address. In addition, there is a *program counter* (PC) which holds an address. The instructions must be coded in one, two, or three bytes and stored in the memory. The program counter must be set at the address of the first instruction. The processor reads one instruction from memory, adjusts the PC to point to the next instruction, and does what the instruction requires. Each instruction consists of a one-byte operation code (op code) that may be followed by one or two bytes of further information such as a number or memory address. We will use the following small subset of the 8085 instructions:

OP CODE   OPERAND DESCRIPTION

LHLD a Operation code followed by an address a. Two bytes are read from that memory address and placed in the HL register.

SHLD a Operation code followed by an address a. The contents of the HL register are stored at this address.

MOV   A,M   The contents of the memory location whose address is in the HL register are moved to the A register.

MOV	M,A	The contents of the A register are moved to the memory location whose address is in the HL register.
MVI	C,*n*	Operation code followed by a one-byte number *n*. That number is moved to register C. $0 \leq n \leq 255$.
STA	*a*	Operation code followed by an address *a*. The byte in register A is stored in memory at address *a*.
INX	H	Add 1 to the address in the HL register.
DCR	C	Subtract 1 from the number in the C register.
JMP	*a*	Operation code followed by an address *a*. PC register is set to this address, so that the next instruction will be taken from there, that is, go to *a*.
JNZ	*a*	Operation code followed by an address *a*. If the zero flag is not set, move the address to the PC register, so that the next instruction will be taken from that address. If the zero flag is set, do nothing. That is, if the zero flag is not set, go to *a*.
JZ	*a*	Operation code followed by an address *a*. If the zero flag is set, move the address to the PC register, so that the next instruction will be taken from that address. If the zero flag is not set, do nothing. That is, if the zero flag is set, go to *a*.
ANI	*n*	Operation code followed by one byte of data containing the number *n*. That byte is combined by a bit-by-bit *and* operation with the A register, the result being left in the A register. If the result is zero, the zero flag is set, and if not, it is reset.
CPI	*n*	Operation code followed by one byte of data containing the number *n*. That byte is compared with the A register. If they are equal, the zero flag is set, and otherwise it is reset.
PUSH H PUSH PSW PUSH D PUSH B		These instructions put the data from the designated PUSH registers on the stack. PSW means the program status word and includes the A register and some status data.

POP H		These instructions remove data from the
POP PSW		stack into the designated registers.
POP D		
POP B		
RET		Moves data from the stack into PC. Normally when RET is used, the return address from a program that called this subprogram is on the stack, and RET causes control to return to the calling program.
IN	n	Op code followed by a one-byte number n used as an I-O unit address. The processor signals an input operation, sets the bus address lines to the value n, and then moves the byte from the bus data lines into register A.
OUT	n	Op code followed by a one-byte number n used as an I-O unit address. The processor signals an output operation, sets the bus address lines to the value n, and the bus data lines to the value from the A register.
EI		Enable interrupts—interrupts will not occur unless the interrupt system is enabled.
DI		Disable interrupts.

On IN and OUT, what happens depends on the I-O devices connected to the bus. For example, if no I-O device with the given address is on the bus, nothing will happen (except that some undefined data will go into the A register on an IN instruction). We will consider some examples, in each case first defining a hypothetical I-O device.

If a signal occurs on the interrupt line, the processor immediately reads the byte on the bus data lines, saves the contents of the PC (that is, the address of the instruction being executed when the processor was interrupted) on the stack, and then puts 0, 8, 16, 24, 32, 40, 48, or 56 in the PC, depending on the byte found on the bus data lines.

G.3. DIRECT I-O

Typically, a simple I-O unit, such as a serial interface to a terminal, has an address built into the hardware. Switches are often provided on the unit for changing this hardware unit address. Each I-O unit also a status input address. For example, assume that the unit address for an I-O device is 4 and its status input address is 5. An IN 5 instruction will transfer a byte of data from this I-O unit to the A register in the processor, and within this byte, one bit (assume the lowest order bit) has the value 1 if there is data ready to read, zero otherwise. Assume that the next bit has the value 1 if the I-O unit is ready to accept a byte of output, zero otherwise. Then a simple, commonly used algorithm for reading reads and checks the status over and over until it shows that a byte is ready to read, it then reads that byte, and repeats. Here is a subroutine that will read characters and store them in memory in successive locations until a carriage return is read; it then returns to the calling program:

```
         LHLD    ADOR     ;ADDRESS WHERE DATA IS TO GO
LOOP     IN      5        ;READ STATUS
         ANI     1        ;SELECT READ STATUS
         JZ      LOOP     ;JUMP IF NOT READY
         IN      4        ;READ ONE DATA BYTE
         CPI     10       ;COMPARE TO CARRIAGE RETURN
         JZ      NEXT     ;JUMP IF EQUAL
         MOV     M,A      ;MOVE BYTE TO MEMORY
         INX     H        ;UPDATE MEMORY ADDRESS
         JMP     LOOP     ;REPEAT LOOP
NEXT     RET              ;RETURN TO CALLING PROGRAM
```

The analogous subroutine for writing is as follows (this program returns when it finds an all-zero byte in the data to be written):

```
         LHLD    ADDR     ;ADDRESS OF DATA TO WRITE
LOOP     IN      5        ;READ STATUS
         ANI     2        ;SELECT WRITE STATUS BIT
         JZ      LOOP     ;JUMP IF NOT READY
         MOV     A,M      ;GET DATA BYTE FROM MEMORY
         OUT     4        ;SEND BYTE TO I-O UNIT
         INX     H        ;UPDATE MEMORY ADDRESS
         MOV     A,M      ;GET DATA BYTE FROM MEMORY
         CPI     0        ;COMPARE TO ZERO
         JNZ     LOOP     ;REPEAT LOOP IF MORE DATA
NEXT     RET              ;OTHERWISE RETURN
```

This very simple approach to I-O does not address the problem of simultaneously reading, writing, and processing, but it is commonly used because it is the simplest and cheapest way to implement I-O. A variation is to have an interrupt system. For example, assuming the I-O device is a terminal, the I-O interface can be connected to cause an interrupt whenever a character comes from the terminal and is ready to be used by the processor. The program is written so that every time the interrupt occurs, the processor jumps to a special input procedure that gives the read command, moves the data to the desired place in storage, and then returns control to where it was when the interrupt occurred. On output, the program gives an output instruction to send one character to the terminal. The interrupt occurs when the terminal is ready to accept the next character. Between interrupts, the processor can do other processing.

Again assume the 8085 processor and that the input operation is finished when a carriage return is received. The main program will store the address where the data are to be placed in READADD, set a flag that we will call READFLAG to false, and enable the interrupts. Assume that the I-O unit puts a processor interrupt signal on the bus and causes the processor to jump to location 8 whenever a received character is ready to be sent to the processor. Since location 16 may be used for another interrupt, the read instructions must be somewhere else—assume location 1000. At location 8 we place two instructions. The first is an instruction disabling the interrupts to avoid the confusion of having another interrupt interrupt this interrupt service routine. This is followed by a jump instruction to the read routine.

```
        ORG     8
        DI                  ;DISABLE INTERRUPTS
        JMP     READ
        ORG     1000
READ    PUSH    PSW         ;SAVE PROCESSOR
        PUSH    H           ;STATUS AND ALL REGISTERS
        PUSH    D           ;ON STACK
        PUSH    B
        LHLD    READADD     ;GET MEMORY ADDRESS FOR NEXT BYTE
        IN      4           ;READ BYTE INTO A REGISTER
        MOV     M,A         ;MOVE IT INTO MEMORY
        INX     H           ;UPDATE MEMORY ADDRESS
        SHLD    READADD     ;SAVE MEMORY ADDRESS
        CPI     10          ;COMPARE TO CARRIAGE RETURN
        JNZ     EXIT
        MVI     A,1         ;SET FLAG TRUE IF END OF LINE
        STA     READFLAG
EXIT    POP     B           ;RESTORE PROCESSOR TO
        POP     D           ;ITS PRECISE CONDITION
        POP     H           ;BEFORE INTERRUPT
        POP     PSW
        EI                  ;ENABLE INTERRUPTS AGAIN
        RET                 ;GO BACK TO NEXT INSTRUCTION
                            ;IN MAIN PROGRAM
```

After setting READADD to the desired value, setting the READFLAG, and enabling interrupts, the main program can do other computations.

When it is ready it can simply check the flag, waiting if necessary until it indicates that the data are ready, and use the data that are read in by this routine.

G.4. I-O PROCESSORS

It is possible for two processors to share the same main storage, and in particular, to have a main processor executing a program while a separate processor devoted to I-O is reading data from an I-O device such as a disk or tape unit. In this section, we illustrate how that can be done, including assembly language programs simplified to include only the essentials.

Communication between the main processor and the I-O processor is typically accomplished as follows:

1. The first address and size of the data block in storage and perhaps other information typically are placed in a preassigned location in main memory by the program in the main processor to be used by the I-O processor.

2. The main processor sends a "start" signal to the I-O processor and the I-O processor sends a "finished" signal to the main processor at the appropriate times.

Typically, there is a "start I-O" machine instruction in the main processor to cause the start signal to be sent to the I-O processor. The "finished" signal from the I-O processor causes an interrupt in the main processor. To do an I-O operation, the programmer causes the data required by the I-O processor to be placed in memory and then issues the "start I-O" instruction. Then the program may do other things or just wait. When the I-O operation is finished, an interrupt indicating that the I-O operation is finished will occur. One way is to have the main processor interrupt routine set a flag when the interrupt occurs. Then the main program can check this flag when it wants to use the data; it proceeds if the flag indicates that the data are ready, or waits for the flag to be set if not.

As a final example, we describe how the main processor and an I-O processor for cassette tape I-O typically cooperate. Assume the same main 8085 processor as in the previous examples. The I-O processor might contain another 8085 microprocessor that interfaces to the bus in a very different way from the main processor. Assume the I-O processor contains 4096 bytes of read-only memory which contains the program for its 8085. If the address coming out of this 8085 is in the range 0–4095 and a memory read is indicated, this read-only memory is read and the data put on the data lines of the 8085 in the I-O processor. Otherwise, the address and memory read signals are put on the main bus, so that this processor can read and write to all of the main memory except bytes 0–4095. (When the I-O processor accesses the main memory, it puts the signal on the main processor "hold" line and waits until it receives the "hold acknowledgment" signal from the main processor before using the memory, because then it knows that the main processor is not using the memory.)

Assume that the circuitry in the I-O processor recognizes a main-processor instruction IN 8. When the main processor gives this instruction, it causes an interrupt in the I-O processor that causes its 8085 to jump to location 8. Also the I-O processor circuitry, in response to an OUT 9 instruction in the I-O processor, puts a signal on the bus to cause a main-processor interrupt and other signals on the bus data lines to cause that interrupt to result in the main processor's jumping to location 16. (Assume that the IN 8 instruction in the main-processor program starts the I-O processor and the OUT 9 instruction in the I-O processor program informs the main processor when it has finished.)

In addition, assume that the tape unit is connected directly to the I-O processor (not through the bus) in much the same way as the terminal was connected to the main processor in Example 4.1, so that we can use the type of program that appears in that example in the I-O processor. (Actually, with the 8085 and disk I-O, that type of program is too slow, and a slight modification is needed.) Finally, assume that when the system starts, the I-O processor starts by executing the instruction at location 0.

Now we have to write programs for both the main processor and the I-O processor. To make the problem simple and definite, assume that each tape record ends with a carriage-return character. Also assume that the main program stores in location 4096 the DMA address, that is, the address where the first character is to be placed. We will place a halt instruction at location zero in the I-O processor, so that the I-O processor is inactive initially.

When the main processor desires a record to be read, it gives an IN 8 instruction (and disregards the data returned in register A) to start the I-O processor. This causes the I-O processor to interrupt, jump to location 8, and do the input from the tape. At the end of the I-O processor program, it jumps to location 0 in the I-O processor and stops. Meanwhile, the main processor can do other things. When the main processor is finished with other things and wants to use this record, it checks the flag. If the flag indicates that the record is not ready, the main processor simply waits.

The I-O processor programs might look like this:

```
        ORG  0
        HLT
        ORG  8
READ    DI                      ;DISABLE INTERRUPT
        LHLD 4096               ;LOAD DMA ADDRESS
LOOP    IN   7                  ;READ STATUS OF TAPE DEVICE
        ANI  1                  ;SELECT READ STATUS BIT
        JZ   LOOP               ;JUMP IF NO BYTE READY
        IN   6                  ;READ BYTE IF READY
        CPI  10                 ;COMPARE TO CARRIAGE RETURN
        JZ   ENDED              ;IF EQUAL, THIS IS END OF RECORD
        MOV  M,A                ;PUT BYTE IN MEMORY
        INX  H                  ;UPDATE MEMORY ADDRESS
        JMP  LOOP               ;TO LOOK FOR NEXT BYTE
ENDED   OUT  9                  ;CAUSE MAIN PROCESSOR INTERRUPT
        EI                      ;ENABLE INTERRUPTS AGAIN
        JMP  0                  ;GO TO HALT INSTRUCTION AND WAIT
```

In the main program, the interrupt routine might look like this:

```
        ORG  16                 ;HANDLE INTERRUPT
        DI                      ;DISABLE INTERRUPTS
        JMP  INTR               ;JUMP TO INTERRUPT ROUTINE
        ORG  2000
INTR    PUSH PSW                ;SAVE REG A AND STATUS BITS ON STACK
        MVI  A,255
        STA  IOFLAG             ;SET FINISHED-FLAG TRUE
        POP  PSW                ;RESTORE REG A AND STATUS BITS
        EI                      ;ENABLE INTERRUPTS AGAIN
        RET                     ;GO BACK TO MAIN PROGRAM
```

Somewhere in the main program there would be a request to read, which would include instructions like this:

```
        LHLD BUFFADD            ;PUT DESIRED DMA ADDRESS
        SHLD 4096               ;AT 4096
        MVI  A,0                ;SET FINISHED-FLAG TO FALSE
        STA  IOFLAG
        IN   8                  ;START I-O PROCESSOR
         .
         .                      ;DO OTHER PROCESSING
         .
         .
WAIT    LDA  IOFLAG             ;CHECK WHETHER FINISHED
        ANI  255                ;THIS SETS PROCESSOR FLAGS
```

```
JZ      WAIT        ;REPEAT IF NOT READY
 .                  ;NOW DATA JUST READ MAY BE USED
 .                  ;CONTINUE PROGRAM
 .
```

After we find the flag to be nonzero, we know that the I-O processor is finished and it is safe to use the data.

This example is very much simplified. A practical I-O processor would check for errors. The main processor might have the capability of sending several different commands to the I-O processor for a single device, such as seek, read, and write for a disk unit or read, write, backspace, and rewind for a magnetic tape unit. It might even be possible for the main processor to put a list of commands in memory for the I-O processor to interpret and execute. A simple I-O processor might serve several different devices, possibly even "simultaneously," using the interrupt system of the I-O processor. Note that the additional required information can be passed between the main processor and the I-O processor using main-processor IN and OUT instructions that are recognized and carried out by the I-O processor, or by having one processor place data in the memory to be examined by the other.

NOTES

For additional information on I-O processor or channel programming, see the references at the end of Chapter 4. Greater detail may be found in Intel manuals.

References

A. GENERAL

[A1] P. Freeman, *Software Systems Principles*. Chicago: Science Research Associates, 1975.

[A2] E. Yourdon, *Design of On-line Computer Systems*. Englewood Cliffs, N.J.: Prentice-Hall, 1972.

[A3] H. Katzan, Jr., *Computer Systems Organization and Programming*. Chicago: Science Research Associates, 1976.

[A4] D. R. Judd, *Use of Files*. London: Macdonald, 1973.

[A5] D. E. Freeman and O. R. Perry, *I/O Design: Data Management in Operating Systems*. Rochelle Park, N.J.: Hayden, 1977.

[A6] O. Hanson, *Design of Computer Data Files*. Rockville, Md.: Computer Science Press, 1983.

[A7] B. G. Claybrook, *File Management Techniques*. New York: Wiley, 1983.

[A8] W. S. Boutell, *Computer-Oriented Business Systems*, 2nd Ed. Englewood Cliffs, N.J.: Prentice-Hall, 1973.

[A9] J. T. Murray, *Systems Analysis and Design: in an IBM Environment*. New York: McGraw-Hill, 1973.

[A10] C. T. Meadow, *The Analysis of Information Systems*, 2nd Ed. New York: Wiley, 1973.

[A11] H. S. Heaps, *Information Retrieval: Computational and Theoretical Aspects*. New York: Academic Press, 1978.

[A12] M. Blackman, *The Design of Real Time Applications*. London: Wiley, 1975.

[A13] J. D. Couger and R. W. Knapp (eds.), *System Analysis Techniques*. New York: Wiley, 1974.

B. MEMORY DEVICES

[B1] G. C. Feth, "Memories: Smaller, Faster, and Cheaper," *IEEE Spectrum*, Vol. 13, No. 6 (June 1976), pp. 36–43.

[B2] D. A. Hodges (ed.), *Semiconductor Memories*. New York: IEEE Press, 1972.

[B3] R. E. Matick, *Computer Storage Systems and Technology*. New York: Wiley, 1977.

[B4] A. S. Hoagland, "Storage Technology: Capabilities and Limitations," *Computer*, Vol. 12, No. 5 (May 1979), pp. 12–18.

[B5] D. Toombs, "CCD and Bubble Memories: System Implications," *IEEE pectrum*, Vol. 15, No. 5 (May 1978), pp. 36–39.

[B6] R. L. Sites, "Optimal Shift Strategy for a Block-Transfer CCD Memory," *Communications of the ACM*, Vol. 21, No. 5 (May 1978) pp. 423–425.

[B7] C. S. Chi, "Advances in Computer Mass Storage Technology," *Computer*, Vol. 15, No. 5 (May 1982), pp. 60–74.

C. MAGNETIC TAPE

[C1] *American National Standard Recorded Magnetic Tape for Information Interchange (200 CPI, NRZI)* (ANSI X3.14-1973). New York: American National Standards Institute, Inc., 1973.

[C2] *American National Standard Recorded Magnetic Tape for Information Interchange (800CPI, NRZI)* (ANSI X3.22-1973). New York: American National Standards Institute, Inc., 1973.

[C3] *American National Standard Recorded Magnetic Tape for Information Interchange (1600 CPI, PE)* (ANSI X3.39-1973). New York: American National Standards Institute, Inc., 1973.

[C4] *American National Standard Recorded Magnetic Tape for Information Interchange (6250CPI, Group Coded Recording)* (ANSI X3.54-1976). New York: American National Standards Institute, Inc., 1976.

[C5] *American National Standard Magnetic Tape Labels for Information Interchange* (ANSI X3.27-1969). New York: American National Standards Institute, Inc., 1970.

[C6] W. Sallet, "Magnetic Tape: A High Performer," *IEEE Spectrum*, Vol. 14, No. 7 (July 1977), pp. 26–31.

[C7] L. C. Hobbs, "Low-Cost Tape Devices," *Computer*, Vol. 9, No. 3 (March 1976) pp. 21–29.

[C8] S. W. Miller, "Guest Editor's Introduction: Mass Storage Systems and Evolution of Data Center Architectures," *Computer*, Vol. 15, No. 7 (July 1982), pp. 16–19.

[C9] P. D. Cernicica, "Evaluation of the Average Access Time for a Digital Cassette Memory System," *IEEE Trans. Soft. Engrg.*, Vol. SE-3, No. 4 (1977), pp. 310–324.

D. DISKS AND DRUMS

[D1] *Introduction to IBM Direct-Access Storage Devices and Organization Methods* (Form No. GC20-1649-8). White Plains, N.Y.: IBM Corp., 1974.

[D2] *File Design* (Order No. AL35). Honeywell Informations Systems, Inc., July 1973.

[D3] K. R. London, *Techniques for Direct Access: Hardware Systems Programming*. Philadelphia: Auerbach Publishers, 1973.

[D4] R. M. White, "Magnetic Disks: Storage Densities on the Rise," *IEEE Spectrum*, Vol. 20, No. 8 (August 1983), pp. 32–38.

[D5] A. J. Kolk, Jr., "Low-Cost Rotating Memories: Status and Future," *Computer*, Vol. 9, No. 3 (March 1976), pp. 30–34.

[D6] *ANS One-Sided Single-Density Unformatted 5.25 Inch Flexible Disk* (ANSI X3.82-1980). New York: American National Standards Institute, 1980.

[D7] S. J. Waters, "Estimating Magnetic Disc Seeks," *Computer J.*, Vol. 18, No. 1 (February 1975), pp. 12–17.

[D8] M. A. Pechura and J. D. Schoeffler, "Estimating File Access Time of Floppy Disks," *Communications of the ACM*, Vol. 26, No. 10 (Oct. 1983), pp. 754–763.

[D9] I. L. Wieselman and R. Stuart-Williams, "A Multiple-Access Disc File," AFIPS Conf. Proc. 1963 FJCC. Baltimore: Spartan, 1963.

E. DEVICE INTERFACING AND I-O ARCHITECTURE

[E1] H. S. Stone (ed.), *Introduction to Computer Architecture*. Chicago: Science Research Associates, 1975.

[E2] H. Lorin, *Parallelism in Hardware and Software: Real and Apparent Concurrency*. Englewood Cliffs, N.J.: Prentice-Hall, 1972.

[E3] C. C. Foster, *Computer Architecture*, 2nd Ed. New York: Van Nostrand Reinhold, 1976.

[E4] T. C. Bartee, *Digital Computer Fundamentals*, 4th Ed. New York: McGraw-Hill, 1977.

[E5] D. J. Kuck, *The Structure of Computers and Computations, Vol. I*. New York: Wiley, 1978.

[E6] G. A. Blaauw, *Digital Systems Implementation*. Englewood Cliffs: Prentice-Hall, 1976.

[E7] P. J. Denning, "Virtual Memory," *Computing Surveys*, Vol. 2, No. 3 (Sept. 1970), pp. 153–189.

[E8] C. G. Bell and A. Newell, *Computer Structures: Readings and Examples*. New York: McGraw-Hill, 1971.

[E9] J. F. Wakerly, *Microcomputer Architecture and Programming*. New York: Wiley, 1981.

[E10] G. W. Struble, *Assembler Language Programming: The IBM System 360/370*, 2nd Ed. Reading, Mass.: Addison-Wesley, 1975.

[E11] H. Hellerman, *Digital Computer System Principles*. New York: McGraw-Hill, 1967.

[E12] R. H. Eckhouse, Jr., *Minicomputer Systems: Organization and Programming (PDP-11)*. Englewood Cliffs, N.J.: Prentice-Hall, 1975.

[E13] H. M. Levy and R. H. Eckhouse, Jr., *Computer Programming and Architecture: The VAX-11*. Bedford, Mass.: Digital Press, 1980.

[E14] *The 8085 Family User's Manual*. Santa Clara, Calif.: Intel Corp., 1979.

F. DATA STRUCTURES

[F1] I. Flores, *Data Structure and Management*, 2nd Ed. Englewood Cliffs, N.J.: Prentice-Hall, 1977.

[F2] D. Lefkowitz, *File Structures for On-line Systems*. New York: Spartan Books, 1969.

[F3] J. Martin, *Computer Data-Base Organization*. Englewood Cliffs, N.J.: Prentice-Hall, 1975.

[F4] G. G. Dodd, "Elements of Data Management Systems," *Computing Surveys*, Vol. 1, No. 2 (June 1969), pp. 117–133.

[F5] D. E. Knuth, *The Art of Computer Programming, Vol 1: Fundamental Algorithms*. Reading, Mass.: Addison-Wesley, 1968.

[F6] J. Nievergelt, "Binary Search Trees and File Organization," *Computing Surveys*, Vol. 6, No. 3 (Sept 1974), pp. 195–207.

[F7] T. A. Standish, *Data Structure Techniques*. Reading, Mass.: Addison-Wesley, 1980.

[F8] E. Horowitz and S. Sahni, *Fundamental of Data Structures*. Woodland Hills, Calif.: Computer Science Press, 1976.

[F9] A. T. Berztiss, *Data Structures: Theory and Practice*, 2nd Ed. New York: Academic Press, 1975.

[F10] A. Lew, *Computer Science: A Mathematical Introduction*. London: Prentice-Hall International, 1985.

[F11] M. C. Harrison, *Data-Structures and Programming*. Glenview, Ill.: Scott, Foresman and Co., 1973.

G. DATABASE SYSTEMS

[G1] E. H. Sibley, "Guest Editor's Introduction: The Development of Data-Base Technology," *Computing Surveys*, Vol. 8, No. 1, (March 1976), pp. 1–5.

[G2] J. P. Fry and E. H. Sibley, "The Evolution of Data-Base Management Systems," *Computing Surveys*, Vol. 8, No. 1, (March 1976), pp. 7–42.

[G3] D. D. Chamberlin, "Relational Data-Base Management Systems," *Computing Surveys*, Vol. 8, No. 1, (March 1976), pp. 43–66.

[G4] R. W. Taylor and R. L. Frank, "CODASYL Data-Base Management Systems," *Computing Surveys*, Vol. 8, No. 1 (March 1976), pp. 67–104.

[G5] D. C. Tsichritzis and F. H. Lochovsky, "Hierarchical Data-Base Management," *Computing Surveys*, Vol. 8, No. 1, (March 1976), pp. 106–124.

[G6] A. S. Michaels, B. Mittman, and C. R. Carlson, "A Comparison of Relational and CODASYL Approaches to Data-Base Management," *Computing Surveys*, Vol. 8, No. 1, (March 1976), pp. 125–151.

[G7] C. J. Date, *An Introduction to Data-Base Systems*, 2nd Ed. Reading, Mass.: Addison-Wesley, 1977.

[G8] H. J. Katzan, *Computing Data Management and Data-Base Technology*. New York: Van Nostrand Reinhold, 1975.

[G9] D. Kroenke, *Data Base Processing*. Chicago: Science Research Associates, 1977.

[G10] J. D. Ullman, *Principles of Database Systems*. Potomac, Md.: Computer Science Press, 1980.

[G11] D. C. Tsichritzis and F. Lochovsky, *Data-Base Management Systems*. New York: Academic Press, 1977.

[G12] T. Haerder, "Implementing a Generalized Access Path Structure for a Relational Database System," *ACM Transactions on Database Systems*, Vol. 3, No. 3, (September 1978), pp. 285–298.

[G13] G. Wiederhold, *Database Design*. New York: McGraw-Hill, 1977.

[G14] J. Bradley, *File and Data Base Techniques*. New York: Holt, Rinehart and Winston, 1982.

[G15] T. J. Teorey and J. P. Fry, *Design of Database Structures*. Englewood Cliffs, N.J.: Prentice-Hall, 1982.

H. SORTING AND SEARCHING

[H1] D. E. Knuth, *The Art of Computer Programming, Vol. 3: Sorting and Searching*. Reading, Mass.: Addison-Wesley, 1973.

[H2] H. Lorin, *Sorting and Sort Systems*. Reading, Mass.: Addison-Wesley, 1975.

[H3] I. Flores, *Computer Sorting*. Englewood Cliffs, N.J.: Prentice-Hall, 1969.

[H4] W. A. Martin, "Sorting," *Computer Surveys*, Vol. 3, No. 4 (Dec. 1971), pp. 147–174.

[H5] C. E. Price, "Table Lookup Techniques," *Computing Surveys*, Vol. 3, No. 2 (June 1971), pp. 49–65.

[H6] W. W. Peterson, "Addressing for Random Access Storage," *IBM Journal*, Vol. 1, No. 2 (April 1957), pp. 130–146.

[H7] W. D. Maurer and T. G. Lewis, "Hash Table Methods," *Computing Surveys*, Vol. 7, No. 1 (March 1975), pp. 5–19.

[H8] R. L. Rivest and D. E. Knuth, "Computing Sorting," Bibliography 26, *Computing Reviews*, Vol. 13 (June 1972), pp. 283–289.

[H9] S. E. Goodman and S. T. Hedetniemi, *Introduction to the Design and Analysis of Algorithms*. New York: McGraw-Hill, 1977.

[H10] A. V. Aho, J. E. Hopcroft, and J. D. Ullman, *The Design and Analysis of Computer Algorithms*. Reading, Mass.: Addison-Wesley, 1974.

[H11] D. Comer, "The Ubiquitous B-Tree," *Computing Surveys*, Vol. 11, No. 2 (1979), pp. 121–137.

[H12] G. D. Knott, "Hashing Functions," *Computer J.*, Vol. 18, No. 3 (1975), pp. 265–278.

[H13] J. N. Bentley, "Programming Pearls: Cracking the Oyster," *Communications of the ACM*, Vol. 26, No. 8 (August 1983), pp. 550–552.

[H14] C. C. Gotlieb, "Sorting on Computers," *Communications of the ACM*, Vol. 6, No. 5 (May 1963), pp. 194–201.

[H15] W. J. Atkinson and P. A. DeSanctis, *Introduction to VSAM*. Rochelle Park, N.J.: Hayden, 1980.

I. PROGRAMMING LANGUAGES

[I1] *ANS Programming Language FORTRAN* (ANSI X3.9-1978). New York: American National Standards Institute, 1978.

[I2] *USA Standard FORTRAN* (USAS X3.9-1966). New York: American National Standards Institute, 1966.

[I3] *ANS Programming Language COBOL* (ANSI X3.23-1974). New York: American National Standards Institute, 1974.

[I4] *USA Standard COBOL* (USAS X3.23-1968). New York: American National Standards Institute, 1968.

[I5] *ANS Programming Language PL/I* (ANSI X3.53-1976). New York: American National Standards Institute, 1976.

[I6] *ANS Programming Language PL/I General Purpose Subset* (ANSI X3.74-1981). New York: American National Standards Institute, 1981.

[I7] J. E. Sammet, *Programming Languages: History and Fundamentals*. Englewood Cliffs, N.J.: Prentice-Hall, 1969.

[I8] W. W. Peterson, *An Introduction to Programming Languages*. Englewood Cliffs, N.J.: Prentice-Hall, 1974.

[I9] G. D. Brown, *Advanced ANS COBOL with Structured Programming*. New York: Wiley, 1977.

[I10] M. J. Merchant, *FORTRAN77: Language and Style*. Belmont, Calif.: Wadsworth, 1981.

[I11] S. V. Pollack and T. D. Sterling, *A Guide to PL/I*, 2nd Ed. New York: Holt, Rinehart and Winston, 1976.

[I12] R. P. Polivka and S. Pakin, *APL: The Language and its Usage*. Englewood Cliffs, N.J.: Prentice-Hall, 1975.

[I13] L. Finkel and J. R. Brown, *Data File Programming in BASIC*. New York: Wiley, 1981.

[I14] H. L. Seeds, *Programming RPG RPG II*. New York: Wiley, 1971.

[I15] J. G. P. Barnes, *Programming in Ada*. London: Addison-Wesley, 1984.

[I16] B. W. Kernighan and D. M. Ritchie, *The C Programming Language*. Englewood Cliffs, N.J.: Prentice-Hall, 1978.

J. OPERATING SYSTEMS

[J1] H. M. Deitel, *An Introduction to Operating Systems*. Reading, Mass.: Addison-Wesley, 1983.

[J2] A. C. Shaw, *The Logical Design of Operating Systems*. Englewood Cliffs, N.J.: Prentice-Hall, 1974.

[J3] H. Carroll, *OS Data Processing with Review of OS/VS*. New York: Wiley Interscience, 1974.

[J4] L. J. Cohen, *Operating Systems Analysis and Design*. New York: Spartan Books, 1970.

[J5] D. K. Hsiao, *Systems Programming: Concepts of Operating and Data Base Systems*. Reading, Mass.: Addison-Wesley, 1975.

[J6] E. G. Coffman, Jr. and P. J. Denning, *Operating System Theory*. Englewood Cliffs, N.J.: Prentice Hall, 1973.

[J7] E. I. Organick, *The Multics System: An Examination of its Structure*. Cambridge, Mass.: MIT Press, 1972.

[J8] R. Hannula, *System 360/370 Job Control Language and the Access Methods*. Reading, Mass.: Addison-Wesley, 1977.

[J9] G. D. Brown, *System/370 Job Control Language*. New York: Wiley, 1977.

[J10] T. A. Dwyer and M. Critchfield, *CP/M and the Personal Computer*. Reading, Mass.: Addison-Wesley, 1983.

[J11] S. R. Bourne, *The Unix System*. London: Addison-Wesley, 1983.

K. OTHER TOPICS

[K1] H. K. Reghbatti, "An Overview of Data Compression Techniques," *Computer*, Vol. 14, No. 4 (April 1981), pp. 71–75.

[K2] N. Abramson, *Information Theory and Coding*. New York: McGraw-Hill, 1963.

[K3] G. Held, *Data Compression: Techniques and Applications, Hardware and Software Considerations*. New York: Wiley, 1983.

[K4] *ANS Code for Information Interchange* (ANSI X3.4-1977). New York: American National Standards Institute, 1977.

[K5] IEEE Computer Society Microprocessor Standards Committee, "A Proposed Standard for Binary Floating-Point Arithmetic," *Computer*, Vol. 14, No.3 (March 1981), pp. 51–62.

[K6] *IBM J. R. and D.*, (special issue), Vol. 25, No. 5 (Sept. 1981).

[K7] C. A. R. Hoare, "Record Handling," in *Programming Languages*, ed. F. Genuys. London: Academic Press, 1968, pp. 291–347.

[K8] E.W. Dijkstra, *A Discipline of Programming*. Englewood Cliffs, N.J.: Prentice-Hall, 1976.

[K9] B. Dwyer, "One More Time—How to Update a Master File," *Communications of the ACM*, Vol. 24, No. 1 (Jan. 1981), pp. 3–8.

[K10] M. R. Levy, "Modularity and the Sequential File Update Problem," *Communications of the ACM*, Vol. 25, No. 6 (June 1982), pp. 362–367.

[K11] E. W. Dijkstra, "Co-operating Sequential Processes," in *Programming Languages*, ed. F. Genuys. London: Academic Press, 1968, pp. 43–112.

[K12] M. Ben-Ari, *Principles of Concurrent Programming*. Englewood Cliffs, N.J.: Prentice-Hall, 1983.

[K13] D. Simpson (ed.), *JCLs—Past, Present and Future*. London: NCC Publications, 1974.

Index